# Chinese Odyssey

Volumes 3 & 4

# Cheng & Tsui Publications of Related Interest

Chinese BuilderCards: The Lightning Path to Mastering Vocabulary
*Song Jiang and Haidan Wang*
Simplified Characters
      ISBN-13: 978-0-88727-434-3
      ISBN-10: 0-88727-434-X
Traditional Characters
      ISBN-13: 978-0-88727-426-8
      ISBN-10: 0-88727-426-9

The Enduring Legacy of Ancient China
*By the curriculum specialists at Primary Source, Inc.*
Paperback
      ISBN-13: 978-0-88727-508-1
      ISBN-10: 0-88727-508-7

Cheng & Tsui Chinese Character Dictionary
*Wang Huidi, Editor-in-Chief*
Paperback
      ISBN-13: 978-0-88727-314-8
      ISBN-10: 0-88727-314-9

Pop Chinese
A Cheng & Tsui Bilingual Handbook of Contemporary Colloquial Expressions, 2nd Edition
*Yu Feng, Yaohua Shi, Zhijie Jia, Judith M. Amory, and Jie Cai*
Paperback
      ISBN-13: 978-0-88727-563-0
      ISBN-10: 0-88272-563-X

Please visit www.cheng-tsui.com for more information on these and many other language-learning resources.

通向中国

# Chinese Odyssey

## Innovative Chinese Courseware

**SIMPLIFIED Character Edition**

## Vols. 3 & 4 • TEXTBOOK

Xueying Wang, Li-chuang Chi, and Liping Feng

王学英　　　祁立庄　　　冯力平

 CHENG & TSUI COMPANY Boston

Chinese Odyssey Volumes 3 & 4 Textbook

The contents of *Chinese Odyssey* were developed in part under a grant from the Fund for the Improvement of Postsecondary Education (FIPSE), U.S. Department of Education. However, these contents do not necessarily represent the policy of the Department of Education, and you should not assume endorsement by the Federal Government.

6th Printing, 2019

24 23 22 21 20 19          6 7 8 9 10 11

Published by
Cheng & Tsui Company, Inc.
25 West Street
Boston, MA 02111-1213 USA
Fax (617) 426-3669
www.cheng-tsui.com
"Bringing Asia to the World"™

Library of Congress Cataloging-in-Publication Data

Wang, Xueying.
Chinese odyssey : innovative Chinese courseware / Xueying Wang,
    Li-chuang Chi, and Liping Feng.
        p. cm.
    Includes an index.
    Chinese and English.
    ISBN 0-88727-495-1—ISBN 0-88727-496-X
    1. Chinese language—Textbooks for foreign speakers—English.
I. Chi, Li-chuang. II. Feng, Liping. III. Title.
PL1129.E5W385 2004
495.1'82421—dc22
                                        2004063504

Simplified Character Edition
ISBN-13: 978-0-88727-495-4
ISBN-10: 0-88727-495-1

Printed in the U.S.A.

*Chinese Odyssey* includes multimedia products, textbooks, workbooks, and audio products. Visit www.cheng-tsui.com for more information on the other components of *Chinese Odyssey*.

# Publisher's Note

Despite the increasing use of technology in foreign language education, there have been few multimedia courses in Chinese that focus on all four skills and span all levels of language instruction. At long last, we are pleased to present *Chinese Odyssey*, unique because it is the first stand-alone multimedia series designed for multi-year classroom instruction. *Chinese Odyssey*'s pace and oral/aural emphasis are geared to the American high school and college instructional environments, and its combination of multimedia, audio, and book products allows educators the flexibility to use it independently as a multimedia course, or to combine multimedia and paper formats.

The Cheng & Tsui Asian Language Series is designed to publish and widely distribute quality language learning materials created by leading instructors from around the world. We welcome readers' comments and suggestions concerning the publications in this series. Please send feedback to our Editorial Department (e-mail: editor@cheng-tsui.com), or contact the following members of our Editorial Board.

# Brief Table of Contents

# Contents

## 请吃饭
## Come Eat with Us!

In this lesson you will:

- Express hospitality to guests in your home.
- Show appreciation to a generous host/hostess.
- Talk about completed events or actions.
- Make a toast for a special occasion.

## 办签证
## How Do I Get a Visa?

In this lesson you will:

- Apply for a visa to study or travel in China.
- Speak to people at an embassy or consulate about visas.
- Fill out a Chinese visa application form.

## Lesson 23                                                                    33

送人

## Seeing Someone Off

In this lesson you will:

- Check in at the airport.

- Talk about departure and arrival times.

- Wish someone a safe and happy trip.

- Talk about events that will take place in the near future.

## Lesson 24                                                                    51

到达北京机场

## We Made It!

In this lesson you will:

- Talk about how long it takes you to complete certain tasks.

- Speak to someone you're picking up at the airport.

- Fill out the customs form for entering China.

## Lesson 25                                                                    69

体检

## Getting a Physical Examination

In this lesson you will:

- Speak to someone about getting a physical exam or seeing a doctor in China.

- Discuss your health with someone.
- Stay healthy in the same way that people in China typically try to stay healthy.
- Talk about experiences.

## Lesson 26    87

# 谈季节，谈天气

# Seasons and the Weather

In this lesson you will:

- Talk about the weather.
- Describe the four seasons.
- Understand the weather forecast over the radio or on TV.

## Lesson 27    103

# 去邮局

# Mail and the Post Office

In this lesson you will:

- Address an envelope in Chinese.
- Speak to people about mailing a letter and buying items in a post office.
- Describe where things are located in a room.

## Lesson 28     119

## 找路

## Knowing Where to Go

In this lesson you will:

- Ask for and give directions in Chinese.

- Discuss how to take a bus, subway, or taxi from one place to another.

- Work toward understanding the announcements made on a Chinese bus.

## Lesson 29     137

## 买礼物

## Choosing a Gift

In this lesson you will:

- Purchase things in China.

- Describe which items you would like to buy for an occasion and why.

- Compare things in Chinese.

## Lesson 30     155

## 逛夜市

## Browsing at the Night Market

In this lesson you will:

- Understand the proceedings at the Chinese night market.

- Use your bargaining skills to lower prices.
- Talk in detail about the similarities and differences between things.

## Lesson 31                                                           173

去银行

# Opening a Bank Account

In this lesson you will:

- Learn to open a bank account and conduct financial transactions in China.
- Read about the difference between Chinese debit and credit cards.
- Find out which methods of payment are accepted at stores in China.

## Lesson 32                                                           191

订火车票

# Taking the Train

In this lesson you will:

- Make a travel plan that includes places to visit and things to see.
- Learn to schedule a train trip.
- Learn how and where to buy train tickets.

## Lesson 33        211

# 风味小吃
# A Taste of China

**In this lesson you will:**

- Learn how to order dishes in a local specialty restaurant.
- Practice commenting on the food you ordered.
- Talk about Chinese snacks.

## Lesson 34        229

# 住旅馆
# Staying in a Hotel

**In this lesson you will:**

- Learn the dos and don'ts when staying in Chinese hotels.
- Learn the check in and check out procedures.
- Know what to watch out for when taking a taxi.

## Lesson 35        251

# 锻炼身体
# Keep Fit!

**In this lesson you will:**

- Talk about your favorite athlete.

- Talk about sports you are interested in.
- Talk about a sports meet/competition.

## Lesson 36                 271

### 我生病了

### I Don't Feel Well...

In this lesson you will:

- Learn how to describe your illness.
- Follow a doctor's instructions.
- Recognize different forms used by Chinese doctors.

## Lesson 37                 289

### 过春节

### Happy Chinese New Year!

In this lesson you will:

- Learn the vocabulary for the Spring Festival.
- Discuss Chinese Spring Festival traditions.
- Compare and contrast the Western and Chinese New Year traditions.

# Acknowledgments

I would like to thank Li-chuang Chi and Liping Feng, the other two authors of the *Chinese Odyssey* series, for their hard work in writing the manuscripts. Together, we have completed three years of Chinese language instructional materials for a total of six volumes. This project stimulated constant debate among the three of us, who miraculously still very much enjoy working with each other.

Special thanks also go to the following institutions and individuals whose contributions helped to push the project along and to make this multimedia courseware the best it could possibly be:

Thanks to the Fund for the Improvement of Post-Secondary Education (FIPSE) of the U.S. Department of Education for its generous funding. Thanks to the Dean's Office of the School of Arts and Science, whose support made this project possible; thanks also to the Johns Hopkins University students who beta-tested the book and provided valuable feedback.

Thanks to our publisher Cheng & Tsui Company for their kind editing and tireless reviewing of the manuscript. Thanks also to Blueshoe Technologies, Inc., our partner for developing the courseware, for adding additional features to the software in order to meet our needs and for providing technical support for the software.

Special thanks to Xi'an International Studies University and its School of Chinese Studies for their collaboration in filming the video clips for all six volumes. Their filming project started in the scorching summer heat of China, resulting in several project members falling ill because of heat stroke. Yet, under the superior leadership of Li Changxing, Director of the Center of Educational Technology, our university collaborators still completed a high quality project while maintaining a willing attitude. Thanks also to Jiang Xiaomin, Deputy Director of the School of Chinese Studies at Xi'an International Studies University, who always worked with the best interests of this project in mind.

Thanks especially to the following individuals who made significant contributions to the project:

- Chris Vee, Senior Technology Specialist at Johns Hopkins University, for his amazing talents in audio/video editing, shooting, and recording, and for his skills in troubleshooting all kinds of mysterious technical problems that we encountered during the course of the project. It seems like there is no problem he can't solve;

- Frank Keller, Language Lab IT Specialist, and Jesse Warford, Computer Support Specialist at the Johns Hopkins University Language Lab, for their technical support, advice, positive attitude, and encouragement;

- Graham Bouton, Manager of Desktop Computing Services at Johns Hopkins University, for providing us with technical support, manpower, and moral support;

- Luping Chen, for her involvement in writing during the early stages of the grant;

- Lillian Tian, for her involvement in writing some of the lessons in volumes three, four, five, and six during the early stages of the grant, for her constant constructive criticism of the content, and for her melodious voice, recorded in our audio and multimedia CDs;

- Project team members Jamie Tsui, Risa Lin, Zheng Wang, Huang Lu, Yow-Ning Wan, Huiping Liu, Ronghua Yang, past employees such as Dennis Chi, Jolene Porter, Ruyin Xue and many others, for their tireless efforts, attention to detail, ability to meet deadlines even if it meant working overtime, and constant suggestions on how to further improve the quality of the project;

- Sheng Xu, Ph.D. computer science student at Johns Hopkins University, for taking the time during his dissertation writing period to create an installer for our multimedia courseware;

- Cindy Simpson, the Language Laboratory Coordinator at Johns Hopkins University, and the lab student employees for their suggestions on the improvement of the project.

- Carol Young, the Language Teaching Center Administrator at Johns Hopkins University, for all her administrative assistance to the grant, including management of the grant budget, grant staff, and student payroll.

- Marina Koestler, a former Johns Hopkins University student, for her wonderful editing of the English portions of our manuscript.

Special thanks to my husband, Fanjiu Wang, for putting up with me over the last few years while I ignored him on weekends and evenings to work on this project. Special thanks also goes to my daughter, Jingya Wang, who took the time out of her busy college life to read and comment on the manuscript. Similarly, the other two authors would like to thank their family members for their moral support.

Due to limited space, we could not list everyone who made contributions. However, we extend thanks to everyone for anything s/he may have done for the project.

Xueying Wang, Ph.D.
Principal Investigator of the Grant Project

# Introduction

Welcome to *Chinese Odyssey*, an innovative multimedia language courseware for learning Chinese. *Chinese Odyssey* is designed to provide a comprehensive curriculum, laying the groundwork for building your Chinese language skills from beginning to advanced levels over a period of three years. Designed for high school, college, and adult learners, *Chinese Odyssey* teaches the full scope of language learning skills—listening, speaking, reading, and writing—in addition to grammar. And because it is completely multimedia-based, *Chinese Odyssey* provides unique access to video, audio, and interactive exercises, adding a new dimension of flexibility and richness to the language learning experience.

## Year-by-Year Learning Objectives

### First Year (Volumes 1 and 2)

The first year is designed to teach the basic survival skills you will need to communicate in Chinese. The exercises concentrate heavily on spoken language and pronunciation, with a special focus on pinyin and tones in Volume 1. In Volume 2, pronunciation exercises are gradually replaced by more communicative and grammar-based exercises.

### Second Year (Volumes 3 and 4)

In your second year of studying Chinese, you will complete the basic groundwork in Chinese, and you'll learn more about Chinese grammar. At this point, you should become more comfortable with Chinese customs and will be able to communicate about daily tasks with Chinese people. By the end of this year, you will have gained the necessary language skills for living in China.

### Third Year (Volumes 5 and 6)

At this level, you will be continuously honing your language skills and cultural understanding. You will develop the skills necessary to carry on a high-level discussion in Chinese, expressing your opinions as you talk about issues related to current events, Chinese society, politics, economics, the education system, and aspects of Chinese culture such as food, holidays, and Chinese medicine. You will also begin to learn the written form of Chinese (书面语), which is different from the modern spoken form of the language.

## *Chinese Odyssey*'s Pedagogical Approach

### Why Multimedia Is Best

In the past, most education took place in a classroom environment and was based primarily on interaction between the teacher and student. Today, people of all ages and backgrounds are seeking to enhance their language experience with multimedia tools. As a completely stand-alone multimedia courseware, Chinese Odyssey lets you effectively manage your own learning. Using the multimedia CD-ROMs, you can instantly see whether you've completed an exercise correctly, get explanations of answers, and record your exercise scores. You can participate in a variety of interactive situations that allow you to practice what you have learned. Thus, you can set your own pace and focus on your perceived areas of weakness.

The multimedia format easily accommodates students of varying backgrounds, skill levels, and aptitudes. For example, beginning students can spend more time learning to write Chinese characters by following animated stroke order, or focus on pronunciation drills. In the second and third years, students can take advantage of online resources—such as links to Internet pages related to lesson topics—which will enrich their learning experience. In short, for students, using the multimedia courseware is like having a private tutor.

Within the realm of traditional classroom-based instruction, the *Chinese Odyssey* courseware enables instructors to more effectively use their limited instructional hours for interaction with their students rather than for mechanical drills. For example, using the multimedia CD-ROM, students can do drills and exercises as well as review the lesson on their own time. This frees up class time for more meaningful interaction between teachers and students. Because the courseware contains a score-keeping function, language instructors don't have to spend lots of time grading students' homework. Instructors can simply ask students to print out their exercise score reports, which will automatically indicate the students' performance as well as the time taken to complete the exercise. Moreover, students absent from class can take their portable CDs with them in order to keep up with lessons, without having to use too much of the instructor's time to make up the class.

## A Note about the Exercises

*Chinese Odyssey* contains sophisticated multimedia exercises in grammar and the four basic language skills—listening, speaking, reading, and writing. In order to prepare you to take the *Hanyu Shuiping Kaoshi* (HSK), the Chinese Proficiency Test given by the Chinese government, some of the exercises are in HSK format (see "How *Chinese Odyssey* Provides Preparation for the HSK" on page xxv). Other multimedia exercises include matching games and pre-recorded dialogues that you can engage in with the computer; we hope that such activities are able to bring some fun and interaction to Chinese learning.

## Why We Introduce Conversational Chinese and Idiomatic Colloquial Speech

The dialogues in *Chinese Odyssey* are written in conversational Chinese, the language that people in mainland China use in their daily interactions. This differs from the standard textbook language found in most Chinese language learning materials. Some of the expressions may also differ from the language used in Taiwan.

We take this approach because we believe that the standard textbook language is heavily limited by vocabulary and grammar, and that it does not reflect natural spoken Mandarin Chinese. In the written passages, we use more formal language and less conversational language.

In addition to conversational Chinese, we also introduce authentic idiomatic colloquial speech to make learning more real and the everyday spoken language more accessible. These idiomatic expressions are explained in the notes that follow the dialogues. Heritage students and those who are highly motivated to learn can simply memorize the colloquial speech without a need to analyze the grammar. Those who have limited time do not have to memorize the idiomatic colloquial expressions.

## Topics in *Chinese Odyssey*

The course material contains practical topics such as greeting people, entertaining guests, opening a bank account, or going to the post office, as well as contemporary topics such as dating and opening a cell phone account. The grammar points and vocabulary are introduced based on the content of the topics. Before writing *Chinese Odyssey*, we held a series of discussions with our students in order to select topics that would be, from a learner's perspective, both interesting and practical. For example, dating is a topic that students love because it helps to bring Chinese learning from academia into their everyday world.

## Settings in *Chinese Odyssey*

The settings in *Chinese Odyssey* are designed to mirror the real experiences of students learning Chinese. In the first year, most students begin their language-learning journey in their home country. During the second and third years, however, students tend to travel abroad to enhance their language-learning experience in the target country of their chosen language. Thus, in parallel, our courseware begins in the home country of the novice Chinese learner, and then shifts to China, with increasingly sophisticated scenes as the students themselves advance in their language skills.

## Curriculum Planning

Each year of *Chinese Odyssey* covers two volumes of material, with 20 lessons for each of the first two years (approximately 5–6 instructional hours per lesson), and 10 lessons for the third year (approximately 9–10 instructional hours per lesson). To facilitate learning and teaching, we have tightly controlled the number of vocabulary words and the length of the text in each lesson. Grammar is graded in terms of level of difficulty, and difficult grammar points such as 的, 了, and verb complements usually appear more than once: first to introduce basic concepts, and later with increasingly detailed explanations and practice.

## How *Chinese Odyssey* Provides Preparation for the HSK

In addition to providing a rigorous Chinese language course, *Chinese Odyssey* is designed to prepare you for taking the *Hanyu Shuiping Kaoshi* (HSK), a proficiency-based, standardized aptitude test issued by the Chinese government. If you want to study abroad or work in China, you will eventually have to take this test. *Chinese Odyssey*'s testing software is modeled after the HSK, to give you a sense of what the actual exam is like and help you prepare for the exam.

## A Tour through *Chinese Odyssey*

### *Textbook*

#### Text

Each lesson is introduced with a dialogue, which we refer to as the lesson's "text." Based on the experiences of a group of friends studying Chinese, the dialogues reflect the daily life of a typical university student.

The situations in each of the lessons are real-life situations that you might encounter upon visiting or preparing to visit China, such as asking for directions, ordering food at a restaurant, or applying for a visa to study abroad. We have also incorporated a range of cultural material, including common idioms and slang, to enhance your working knowledge of Chinese culture and tradition.

## Vocabulary

Because Chinese is a non-alphabetic language, it is often fascinating but time-consuming for beginning students to learn the written form. To make it easier, we have divided the vocabulary in Volume 1 of the first year into the following two types:

- Basic: Basic vocabulary consists of common words that are used in everyday conversation. You will practice listening, speaking, and reading these words, but will not be responsible for writing them by hand.

- Core: From the pool of basic vocabulary words, there is a smaller set of core vocabulary, which you should learn to write. In the vocabulary lists, these core vocabulary words are starred.

Throughout *Chinese Odyssey*, you'll also find the following lists of words in the Vocabulary section.

- Notes: Explain special expressions or idioms that appear in the texts. These special expressions are not required learning, but because they are fun and convey something interesting about Chinese culture, most students enjoy learning them.

- Spoken Expressions (口头用语): Part of the required basic vocabulary, these are colloquial expressions that you will encounter frequently in everyday conversation.

- Featured Vocabulary (词汇注解): Contains further explanations and examples for the more difficult-to-use or commonly confused words and phrases.

- Supplementary Vocabulary (补充词汇): Additional words related to the lesson topic. Not required learning.

Starting in Volume 3 of the second year, as a preface to the opening dialogue we have included a background paragraph that provides additional information related to the topic. In the third year, the opening passages become more sophisticated as more written language is introduced, and the dialogues are shortened accordingly.

## Phonetics

This section (Lessons 1–8 in Volume 1) teaches you how to pronounce Chinese using pinyin, the standard romanization system. This section includes phonetic presentations along with exercises such as distinguishing tones, distinguishing sounds, pronunciation practice, and sight reading to help you master pinyin.

## Character Writing

This section (Lessons 2–8 in Volume 1) presents Chinese character composition, stroke types, stroke order, and radicals along with a Chinese character box for handwriting practice.

### Grammar

This section presents three to five grammar points related to the text in each lesson. The structures are introduced progressively from simple to complex and are displayed in chart form with plenty of supporting examples, making them accessible and easy to use for reference or self-study. You will start by learning parts of speech and the basic word order of a Chinese sentence. Gradually, you will begin to form more complex sentences using new grammatical structures, learn more function words (words with no substantial meaning, but specific grammatical roles), and more complex conjunctions unique to the Chinese language. Throughout the grammar sections, there are short "Practice" exercises that allow you to apply the grammar points you've just learned.

### Textbook Exercises

In each lesson of the textbook for volumes 1–4, we have added some classroom-based exercises to give you an opportunity to practice what you have learned with your teacher and your classmates. The textbook exercises focus on grammar and general understanding of the lessons. This allows the teacher to check whether you understand the materials presented in class and give you feedback as you develop your skills. In Volumes 5 & 6, the textbook exercises are expanded so that contextualized practice sections immediately follow each major section. After the vocabulary lists, there are related vocabulary exercises. And after grammar patterns are introduced, likewise there is a section of related grammar exercises. This structure accommodates more focused and contextualized language practice for students at the higher skill levels.

## Workbook

Volumes 1–4 of *Chinese Odyssey* each include a workbook that contains four sections: listening, speaking, reading, and writing. Each section has two to four tasks, starting at an easy level and gradually becoming more difficult as your skills progress. For example, in the listening section you first might be asked to listen to a set of Chinese phrases and select the corresponding English. Later on, you might hear a short conversation or monologue and be asked to respond to questions based on the text. Speaking exercises emphasize pronunciation, intonation, and conversational skills along with correct grammatical structure. Reading and writing exercises measure your ability to respond to authentic sections of Chinese text in real-life situations you might encounter (writing an e-mail, filling out a form, writing a summary based on Web research, etc.).

In Volumes 5 & 6 of *Chinese Odyssey*, the organization of exercises changes to allow for more integrated practice of all four skills. Instead of a separate workbook with exercises divided by skill type, the exercises in Volumes 5 & 6 combine at least two, and usually three, of the different language skills together. You will have the opportunity to listen and speak, or to read, speak, and write, for example, in a series of integrated tasks.

## Multimedia CD-ROM Set

The multimedia CD-ROM is a stand-alone courseware, and includes the same wide range of activities covering listening, speaking, reading, writing, and grammar that you'll find in the textbook and workbook. In addition, the multimedia CD-ROM includes interactive activities and detailed explanations for the practice material, and offers the following technological advantages to help you further improve your language skills:

- A variety of images, video, audio, and readings that incorporate all the basic language skills in a dynamic multimedia environment.

- An interactive platform that allows you to engage in pre-recorded dialogues with the computer.

- Voice-recording capability that allows you to compare your pronunciation with that of a native speaker.

- The flexibility to optimize activities to your own personal skill level, for example by choosing to hear audio clips at different speeds, and choosing to show or hide pinyin.

- Vocabulary lists that feature step-by-step demonstration of character creation and stroke order.

- Immediate feedback on exercise results, with relevant explanations.

- Video clips and authentic materials that help broaden your understanding of life in contemporary China.

- Easy-to-follow navigation and attractive layout.

For more information on the multimedia CD-ROM, please see "The *Chinese Odyssey* Multimedia CD-ROM" on page xxix.

## *Audio CD*

The audio CDs includes all lesson texts and vocabulary in the textbook, as well as all listening exercises and some speaking exercises in the workbook. The audio CDs are designed for those who either don't have access to a computer or who prefer not to use the multimedia CD-ROMs.

## Using the Materials in *Chinese Odyssey*

There are three major ways to utilize the materials in *Chinese Odyssey*.

### *Multimedia CD-ROM Set*

This is the primary element, and includes all lessons, grammar, vocabulary, and exercises in the program. It can be used as a stand-alone set, or in conjunction with other elements.

### *Textbook/Workbook + Multimedia CD-ROM Set*

The workbook allows you to do listening, reading, writing, and some speaking exercises without a computer. It includes all the workbook exercises on the CD-ROM, with the exception of some speaking exercises that require voice recording and playback.

### *Textbook/Workbook + Audio CD Set*

This combination works well for people who don't have access to a computer, and thus can't use the multimedia CD-ROMs. The audio CD set contains audio content for all lessons, plus listening exercises and some speaking exercises.

    *Chinese Odyssey* is an excellent courseware package, but like any teaching tool, it's only half of the equation. We've provided you with the materials, and now it's up to you to make the best use of them. Remember, the more you practice your Chinese, the better you will become. We wish you the best of luck and hope that you enjoy *Chinese Odyssey*.

# The Chinese Odyssey Multimedia CD-ROM

The Multimedia CD-ROM is the primary element in the *Chinese Odyssey* courseware, and may either be used as a stand-alone set or, for those who prefer to work with pen and paper, supplemented with the textbook and workbook. Directly correlated with the textbook and workbook, the multimedia CD-ROM allows you to practice listening, speaking, reading, and writing Chinese in an interactive format at your own pace.

## Texts

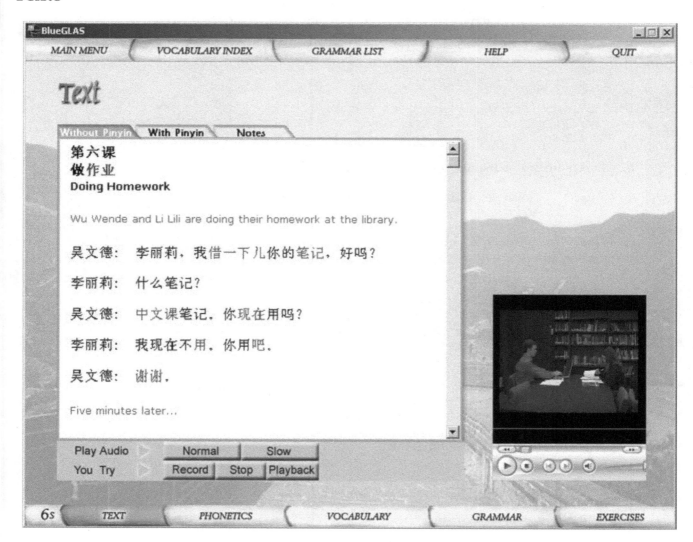

- Read and listen to each lesson's text.

- Show or hide pinyin.

- See a video in which speakers enact the dialogues.

# Phonetics

This section appears in Lessons 1–8 of Volume 1.

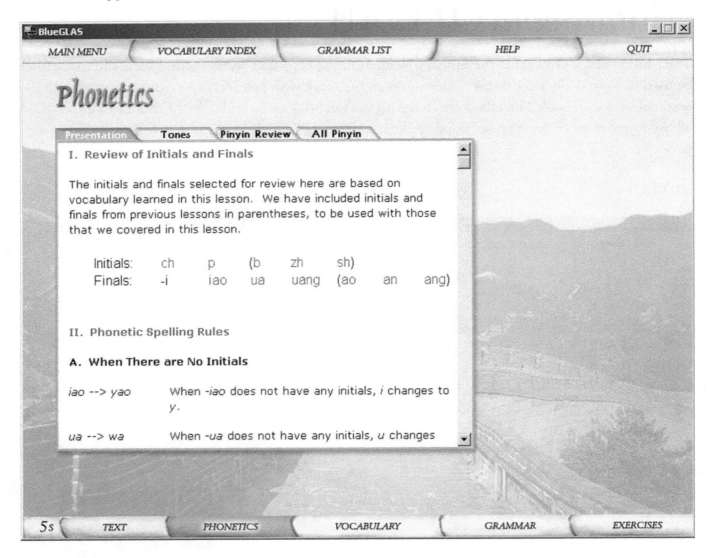

- Learn new sounds and tones.

- See a table containing all sounds in the Chinese language.

- Click on any word to hear its pronunciation.

# Vocabulary

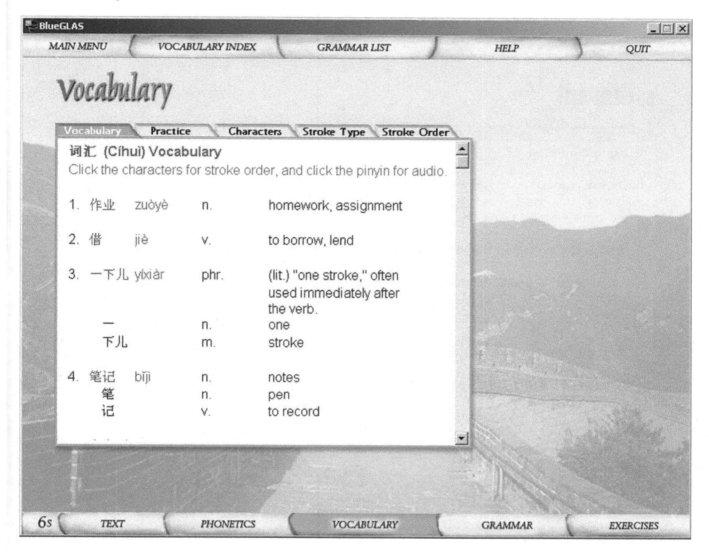

- View each lesson's vocabulary list.

- Click on any character to see how it's written.

- Click on any pinyin word to hear how it's pronounced.

- Record your voice and compare your pronunciation to that of a native speaker.

# Grammar

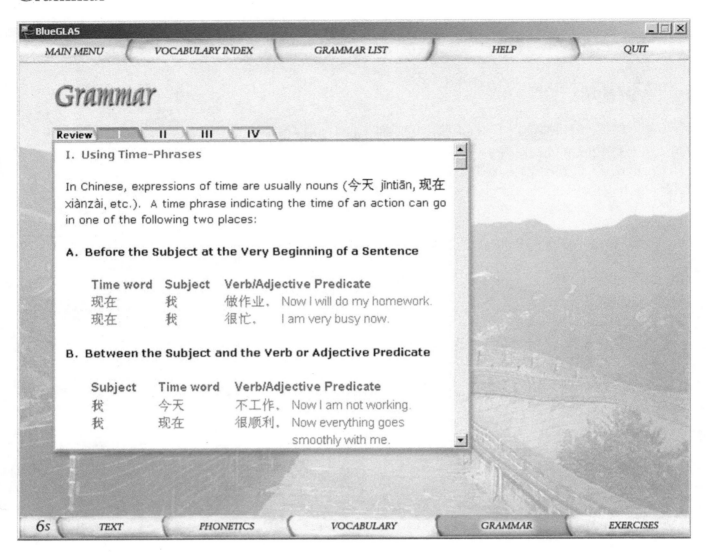

- Review each lesson's grammar points.

# Exercises

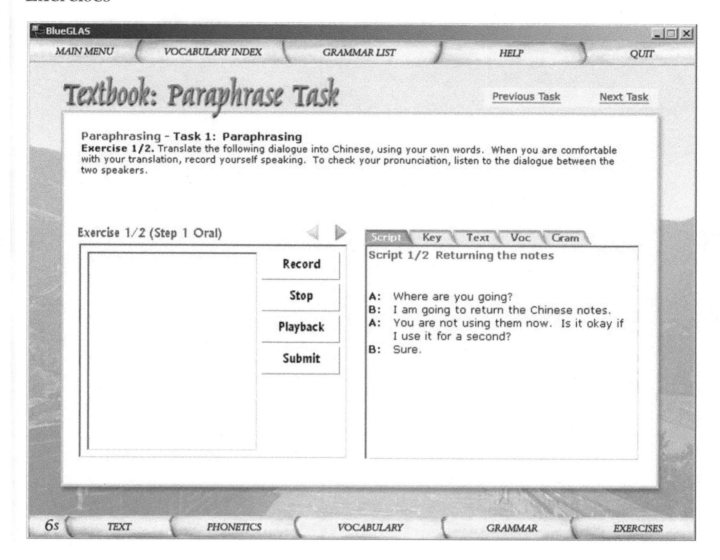

- Do exercises in the textbook and workbook.

- See a key with explanations of correct answers.

- Record your voice and compare your pronunciation to that of a native speaker.

- Easily reference the lesson's text, vocabulary list, and grammar notes.

- View your scores.

# List of Abbreviations

## General Abbreviations

| Abbreviation | Full Word |
| --- | --- |
| gram. | grammar |
| lit. | literally |
| sb. | somebody |
| sth. | something |
| voc. | vocabulary |
| vs. | versus |

## Part of Speech Abbreviations

| Abbreviation | Full Word |
| --- | --- |
| adj. | adjective |
| adj. phr. | adjective phrase |
| adv. | adverb |
| attr. | attributive |
| aux. | auxiliary |
| b.f. | bound form |
| conj. | conjunction |
| interj. | interjection |
| interrog. | interrogative |
| m.w. | measure word |
| n. | noun |
| n. phr. | noun phrase |
| num. | number |
| part. | particle |
| phr. | phrase |
| pref. | prefix |

| Abbreviation | Full Word |
| --- | --- |
| prep. | preposition |
| pron. | pronoun |
| p.w. | place word |
| s.e. | spoken expression |
| sent. | sentence |
| suff. | suffix |
| t.w. | time word |
| v. | verb |
| v. comp. | verb complement |
| v. obj. | verb object |
| v. phr. | verb phrase |

# 21

# 请吃饭

# Come Eat with Us!

> *In this lesson you will:*
> - Express hospitality to guests in your home.
> - Show appreciation to a generous host/hostess.
> - Talk about completed events or actions.
> - Make a toast for a special occasion.

很多中国人搬了家以后，都会请自己的朋友来家里吃饭。这叫庆祝"乔迁之喜[1]"。庆祝"乔迁之喜"也是一种中国文化。吴文德上个星期刚搬了家，林笛和李丽莉觉得这是一个大家能在一起说说话、吃吃饭、开开玩笑、放松放松的好机会！所以，一天下午林笛找了一个时间给吴文德打了一个电话。下面请看吴文德和他的室友高朋请林笛和李丽莉到家里庆祝"乔迁之喜"的一个小故事。

（一天下午林笛在她的宿舍给吴文德打电话。）

林笛：喂，吴文德，那天面试你去了吗？

吴文德：去了。一切顺利。我下个星期去签证。

林笛：太好了。我们应该庆祝庆祝。我请客。

吴文德：不敢当。不敢当。你帮我找了新住处[2]，还帮我找了一位好室友。我得好好谢谢你。我来请客。

林笛：对啊。乔迁之喜，你应该请我和李丽莉吃饭。

吴文德：乔迁之喜是什么意思啊？

林笛：乔迁之喜就是庆祝搬新家。你搬了家，应该请我们大家去你那儿吃饭。

吴文德：好吧。这个星期六晚上，你们来我们的新家吃饭，怎么样？高朋做的饭你们一定喜欢吃。

林笛：太好了，李丽莉听了一定非常高兴，谢谢你们。

（星期六晚上，大家都在吴文德和高朋的餐厅里。）

李丽莉：你们的餐厅真漂亮。

林笛：今天你们请我们吃什么好菜？这么香！我都快饿死了[3]。

吴文德：高师傅[4]今天做的都是他的拿手菜，有荤菜也有素菜。大家趁热吃吧。

高朋：对，大家别客气。这个鱼你们尝了没有？

李丽莉：尝了，真好吃。你也吃吧。我们自己来。

吴文德：高师傅做的鸡肉也非常好吃，但是，这个菜用筷子吃太费劲了。

林笛：以后你去中国学习，每天都要用筷子。你应该多练习用筷子吃饭。

吴文德：但是我现在这么瘦，再用筷子吃饭，半天吃一点儿，怎么能长胖呢？

高朋：吴文德，别开玩笑了。快吃饭吧。

吴文德：遵命。但是我想少吃一点饭，多吃一点儿甜点。咱们现在上甜点，好吗？

高朋：好。……甜点来了。大家慢慢吃。

……

*Friends and family wrapping dumplings together.*

李丽莉：我吃了这么多甜点。我现在太饱了。

高朋：今天是乔迁之喜，应该多吃一点儿。你们渴不渴？想不想喝茶？

林笛：我有一点儿渴。你帮我倒一杯吧。

吴文德：来，我们今天庆祝乔迁之喜，一人喝一杯酒，怎么样？

李丽莉：好，我来祝酒。为你们的新家干杯。

林笛：也为我们的友谊干杯。

大家：干杯！

## *Notes*

1. 乔迁之喜  (qiáoqiān zhī xǐ)

   A phrase to express congratulations to someone moving into a new house.

2. 住处  (zhùchù)

   A place to live. You will learn more about the word 处 in the next lesson.

3. 我都快饿死了。  (Wǒ dōu kuài è sǐ le.)

   I am almost dying of starvation.

4. 高师傅  (Gāo Shīfu)

   The term 师傅 was originally used to show respect for someone who had a certain expertise. It is now also used as a general form of polite address. Here, 高师傅 is used affectionately by Gao Peng's friends to compliment his cooking skills.

## *Cultural Note*

As a guest at a Chinese home, you might find the host repeatedly placing food on your plate and insisting that you eat more. This is the Chinese way of showing hospitality. If you want to please your host, don't be shy. Eat as much as you can! Sometimes even when you are full, your host will still want you to eat. To avoid both overeating and offending your host, you could make a joke by saying:

我实在吃不下了。再吃我肚子就要爆炸了。

(Wǒ shízài chībuxià le. Zài chī wǒ dúzi jiù yào bàozhà le.)

I really cannot eat anymore. If I do, my stomach will explode.

## 生词表 (Shēngcí Biǎo)
## Vocabulary

| Character | Pinyin | Part of Speech | English Definition |
|---|---|---|---|
| 1. 一切 | yīqiè | *n.* | the whole thing, the entire matter |

我在这儿一切都很好。

100 %

2. 签证　　　qiānzhèng　　　*n.*　　　visa

我还没有去中国的签证。

　　　　　　　　　　　*v. obj.*　　　to apply for a visa

我明天去大使馆办签证。

3. 餐厅　　　cāntīng　　　*n.*　　　dining hall, dining room

你们家的餐厅真大。

餐　　　　　　　　　　*b.f.*　　　meal

4. 饿　　　è　　　*adj.*　　　to be hungry (in contrast to full, 饱), to starve (especially animals)

我饿极了。

5. 香　　　xiāng　　　*adj.*　　　(of food) delicious, flavorful, fragrant

这儿的饭真香啊。

6. 师傅　　　shīfu　　　*n.*　　　skilled worker, master (often used as a form of polite address)

师傅，请问，您是哪儿人？

7. 拿手菜　　　náshǒucài　　　*phr.*　　　the cook's specialty dish

这是他的拿手菜。

拿手　　　　　　　*adj.*　　　especially good (at something)

菜　　　　　　　　*n.*　　　vegetables, dish

8. 荤菜　　　hūncài　　　*n.*　　　meat dish

你吃荤菜吗？

荤　　　　　　　　*n.*　　　meat, fish, or poultry

　　　　　　　　　*adj.*　　　(of food) containing meat, fish, or poultry

9. 素菜　　　sùcài　　　*n.*　　　vegetarian dish, vegetables

他只吃素菜。

素　　　　　　　　*n.*　　　vegetarian food

　　　　　　　　　*adj.*　　　simple, plain

10. 趁　　　chèn　　　*v.*　　　to take advantage of, to avail oneself of

你们趁热吃吧。

11. 热　　　rè　　　*adj.*　　　hot

今天太热了。

12. 鱼　　　yú　　　*n.*　　　fish

我们家的人都喜欢吃鱼。

13. 尝　　　cháng　　　*v.*　　　to taste (food)

你尝尝这个菜。

14. 鸡　　　　　jī　　　　　*n.*　　　　chicken
　　这是你家的鸡吗？

15. 肉　　　　　ròu　　　　*n.*　　　　(of animals) meat, flesh
　　这都是鸡肉。

16. 筷子　　　　kuàizi　　　*n.*　　　　chopsticks
　　你会用筷子吗？

17. 瘦　　　　　shòu　　　　*adj.*　　　thin
　　他太瘦了。

18. 长　　　　　zhǎng　　　*v.*　　　　to grow
　　这个孩子一定能长得很高。

19. 胖　　　　　pàng　　　　*adj.*　　　(of people or animals) plump, fat
　　他现在胖不胖？

20. 甜点　　　　tiándiǎn　　*n.*　　　　dessert, sweets
　　我爱吃甜点。

21. 饱　　　　　bǎo　　　　　*adj.*　　　(of stomach) full, filled up
　　我吃得太饱了。

22. 渴　　　　　kě　　　　　　*adj.*　　　thirsty
　　我渴了，你渴不渴？

23. 倒　　　　　dào　　　　　*v.*　　　　to invert, to turn upside down, to pour
　　我去给你倒点水。

24. 杯　　　　　bēi　　　　　*m.w.*　　　cup, glass
　　我想喝(一)杯咖啡。

25. 祝酒　　　　zhù jiǔ　　　*v. obj.*　　to make a toast
　　我给你们祝酒。

26. 为　　　　　wèi　　　　　*prep.*　　　for, for the sake of
　　他想为你们做几个中国菜。

27. 干杯　　　　gān bēi　　　*v. obj.*　　to make a toast; (lit.) to dry up the cup
　　来，为你的新工作干杯。

　　干　　　　　　　　　　　　*adj.*　　　dry

　　　　　　　　　　　　　　　*v.*　　　　to dry, to empty (a wine glass)

　　杯　　　　　　　　　　　　*m.w.*　　　glass, cup

28. 友谊            yǒuyì           *n.*         friendship

为我们的友谊干杯。

## 补充词汇 (Bǔchōng Cíhuì) Supplementary Vocabulary

1. 米饭            mǐfàn          *n.*         cooked rice
2. 炒饭            chǎofàn        *n.*         fried rice
                                  *v. obj.*    to fry rice
3. 面条            miàntiáo       *n.*         noodles
4. 饺子            jiǎozi         *n.*         dumplings
5. 青菜            qīngcài        *n.*         green vegetables
6. 烤鸭            kǎoyā          *n.*         roast duck
7. 甜酸苦辣         tián suān kǔ là  *phr.*     (lit.) sweet, sour, bitter, and spicy,
                                              a phrase used to describe the many
                                              varieties of food flavors
8. 肥             féi            *adj.*       (of food) fatty

# 口头用语 (Kǒutóu Yòngyǔ) Spoken Expressions

## 1. General Expressions

上（菜/甜点）
shàng (cài/tiándiǎn)
(lit.) to bring up (the food to be served)

费劲
fèijìng
requiring great effort (physical or mental)

半天
bàntiān
(lit.) half a day, a long while

遵命
zūnmìng
Yes, Sir., (lit.) respect/follow (your) orders

## 2. Expressions to Use as a Host

没什么菜。
Méi shénme cài.
There are not many dishes. (This phrase is frequently used by a host as a self-deprecating way to show hospitality.)

*A home-cooked dinner made by friends in Beijing.*

趁热吃，别客气。

Chèn rè chī, bié kèqi.

Eat while it is hot. Don't be too polite.

这个（菜/甜点）你尝了没有？

Zhè ge (cài/tiándiǎn) nǐ cháng le méiyǒu?

Have you tried this dish/dessert?

慢慢吃。一会儿还要上菜/甜点呢。

Mànmàn chī. Yīhuìr hái yào shàng cài/tiándiǎn ne.

Take your time. (We will) serve another dish/dessert in a few minutes.

请吧。你们自己来。

Qǐng ba. Nǐmen zìjǐ lái.

Please help yourself.

这是我的拿手菜。大家多吃一点儿。

Zhé shì wǒ de ná shǒu cài. Dàjiā duō chī yī diǎnr.

This is my specialty. Everybody, please eat a bit more!

再喝/干一杯。

Zài hē/gān yì bēi.

Let's have another toast.

## 3. Expressions to Use as a Guest

今天你做什么好吃的？这么香！

Jīntiān nǐ zuò shénme hǎochī de? Zhème xiāng!

What are you cooking today? It smells so delicious!

我昨天就没吃东西，现在快饿死了。
Wǒ zuótiān jiù méi chī dōngxi, xiànzài kuài è sǐ le.
I have not eaten anything since yesterday (in anticipation of this dinner). I am starving to death!
(This is a humorous way to tell your host that you are looking forward to this dinner.)

你做了这么多好吃的，太辛苦了。
Nǐ zuò le zhème duō hǎochī de, tài xīngkǔ le.
You've cooked so much delicious food. You must be tired.

你别客气。我们自己来。
Nǐ bié kèqi. Wǒmen zìjǐ lái.
You don't have to be so polite with us. We will help ourselves.

我吃了那么多菜，太好吃了。
Wǒ chī le nàme duō cài, tài hǎochī le.
I ate a lot of food. It was all so tasty!

我吃得太饱了。吃不下了。
Wǒ chī de tài bǎo le. Chī bú xià le.
I ate too much. I can't eat any more.

我得好好儿谢谢你。
Wǒ děi hǎohàor xièxie nǐ.
I must find a special way to thank you.

4. *Expressions to Use When Making a Toast*

为你们的新家干杯。
Wèi nǐmen de xīn jiā gānbēi.
Let's make a toast to your new home.

为我们的友谊干杯。
Wèi wǒmen de yǒuyì gānbēi.
Let's make a toast to our friendship.

我给大家祝（一杯）酒。祝大家身体好。
Wǒ gěi dàjiā zhù (yī bēi) jiǔ. Zhù dàjiā shēntǐ hǎo.
Let me make a toast to everyone. I wish everyone good health.

祝你们工作顺利。
Zhù nǐmen gōngzuò shùnlì.
I hope that everything goes smoothly with your work.

祝你生日快乐！
Zhù nǐ shēngrì kuàilè!
Happy birthday!

## 词汇注解 (Cíhuì Zhùjiě) Featured Vocabulary

| 最 | (Zuì) | superlative adv. | the most |
|---|---|---|---|

最 can only be followed by adjectives, certain verbs, or auxiliary verbs.

### 1. With Adjectives

最好   the best          最快   the fastest
最慢   the slowest       最胖   the fattest
最大   the biggest

### 2. With Certain Verbs

最喜欢           the things (I) like the most
最怕             the things (I) fear the most

### 3. With Auxiliary Verbs

最会 + Verb      to be most capable of doing
最爱 + Verb      to love doing something most

 ## 语法 (Yǔfǎ)

## Grammar

## I. The Perfect Aspect 了 (Le)

In Lesson 18, you began to learn how to express the aspect of an action, or whether an action is beginning, continuing, or complete. The first aspect you learned in that lesson indicated an action in progress, as expressed with the adverb 正在 and the sentence's final particle, 呢. In this lesson, you will learn how to use the Perfect Particle 了 to express the perfect or perfective aspect, which indicates completion of an action. In Lesson 16, we briefly introduced the Perfect Particle 了, which is also called "Verb 了" because the Perfect Particle 了 is always placed immediately after the verb.

As you learn the Chinese aspect system, bear in mind that while there are some areas where it overlaps with the English tense system, the two systems remain quite different. Pay close attention to the way the various example sentences translate into English. The structure is "Subject + Verb 了 (+ Object)." For example:

### A. Without an Object

|  | Subject | Verb | 了 |
|---|---|---|---|
| Positive: | 李丽莉 | 吃 | 了。 |

Li Lili ate/has eaten.
(The action of eating has already been completed.)

| Negative: | 李丽莉 | (还)没(有) | 吃(呢)。 |
|---|---|---|---|

Li Lili did not eat / has not eaten.

Question:　　　　李丽莉　　　吃了吗/没有？

Did Li Lili eat? / Has Li Lili eaten?

## *Notes*

1. The negative form is "没（有）Verb...," which is often combined with "还···（呢）." 了 is omitted in the negative form. DO NOT use 不 to negate the verb within the "Verb 了" pattern.

2. A question can be formed by adding either 吗 or 没有 to the end of the sentence.

## 🔲 PRACTICE

Try using verbs or verb phrases such as 来, 到, 开始, 休息, and 锻炼 to ask a question and then provide both positive and negative responses. For example:

问：老师来了吗？/老师来了没有？

答：老师来了。/老师没有来。

## B. With an Object

The object must be placed after "Verb 了." In addition, "Verb 了" plus a simple object usually does not make a complete sentence. To form a complete sentence, you may use one of the following options.

### *1. An Object Modifier*

A modifier can be a measure word, an adjective phrase, a clause, etc. For example:

我看了一本非常好看的书。
I read a very good book. (一本非常好看 functions as a modifier.)

他做了很多菜。
He made lots of dishes. (很多 functions as a modifier.)

## 🔲 PRACTICE

Use the above structure to make a two-line dialogue. Below are some suggested phrases, but feel free to use your own phrases.

Modifiers:　两个, 几本, 很大, 很多, 他做的那个.
Verb phrases:　尝拿手菜, 借杂志, 订做蛋糕, 背单词, 复习语法.

### *2. An Adverbial Adjunct*

A complicated adverbial adjunct is usually placed before the predicate to indicate time, location, etc. For example:

我在图书馆用那儿的中文软件给他回了信。
I used the Chinese software at the library to answer his letter. (The prepositional phrases 在图书馆 and 给他, as well as the verb phrase 用那儿的中文软件 function as adverbial adjuncts.)

你昨天跟他一起吃了饭没有？

Did you eat with him yesterday? (The time word 昨天 and the prepositional phrase "跟…一起" function as adverbial adjuncts.)

---

## ❧ PRACTICE

Try creating a sentence of your own with each of the suggested phrases.

Verb phrases:　做蛋糕, 买衣服, 造句子, 给笔友写信, 借书和杂志
Location:　在家, 在商店里
Time words:　上中文课的时候
Manner:　跟…一起, 从图书馆

### 3. A Follow-up Clause

If the object in a "Verb 了" clause does not have a modifier and the verb is not preceded by an adverbial adjunct, there is usually a follow-up clause. The "Verb 了" clause along with its follow-up clause usually indicates a sequence of actions. This kind of sentence can have two different subjects, or it can have one subject that is the agent of both actions. For example:

|  | 1st clause | 2nd clause |
|---|---|---|
| Two subjects: | 你吃了饭, | 我们再去看电影。 |
|  | After you finish eating, we will go and see a movie. | |
| One subject: | 我下了课, | （我）再去找他。 |
|  | After class, I am going to look for him again. | |

*Dumplings waiting to be boiled.*

## *Note*

The "Verb 了" structures can be used in multiple clauses indicating a series of events. For example:

我买了书，看了杂志，还喝了咖啡。
I bought a book, read a magazine, and had coffee.

---

## PRACTICE

Use verb phrases such as 回家, 吃饭, 停车, 唱歌, and 写信 to ask a question. When you're done, use the above "Verb 了" structure along with a follow-up clause to provide a response. For example:

问：下了课，你要做什么/去哪儿？
答：下了课，我去看朋友。

### 4. Modal 了

If none of the above three requirements are met, a Modal Particle 了 can be added at the end to complete the sentence. You will learn more about the Modal 了 in the next lesson.

我吃了饭了。        I finished eating.

我下了课了。        The class is over.

## C. Points for Consideration

1. Although "Verb 了" indicates the completion of an action, it is NOT equivalent to the English past tense, because it can be applied to actions that take place in the past, present, or future. The time when the action occurred, occurs, or will occur is indicated by time words (e.g., last week, yesterday, etc.) For example:

|          | Subject | Time | Verb | 了 |
|----------|---------|------|------|-----|
| Past:    | 李丽莉   | 昨天  | 走   | 了。|
|          | Li Lili left yesterday. | | | |
| Present: | 李丽莉   | 现在  | 来   | 了。|
|          | Li Lili has come now. | | | |
| Future:  | 李丽莉   | 明天就 | 走   | 了。|
|          | Li Lili is (scheduled to) leave tomorrow. | | | |

2. If the sentence has more than one verb, the last verb is usually the main verb. Make sure that 了 is placed after the main verb.

昨天我去看了一个电影。    I went to see a movie yesterday.
(In this sentence, the first verb is 去; the main verb, or the second verb, is 看. 了 is placed after the main verb.)
xxx INCORRECT: 我去了看一个电影。 xxx

3. If the object is a definite noun (that is, when both the speaker and listener know what the object refers to), then it can be placed before the subject. For example:

那些饭我都吃了。     I have eaten all the food.

## II. Summary of the Adverb 还

The adverb 还 has several different meanings.

### A. In Addition To

In this context, 还 can be translated as "in addition to," "also," "and," or "as well as." As an adverb, it always appears before the verb. For example:

我有一本英文词典，还有一本中文词典。
In addition to my English dictionary, I also have a Chinese dictionary.

我昨天借了一本书，还借了一本杂志。
I borrowed a book and a magazine yesterday.

### B. Still

The adverb 还 indicates the continuation of the current situation. It is usually placed before an auxiliary verb or used in the pattern "还在···呢."

| | |
|---|---|
| 你还想喝汤吗？ | Do you still want soup? |
| 我还要读一会儿书。 | I want to read a little longer. |
| 他还在看电视呢。 | He is still watching TV. |

It is also frequently used with the negative word 不. For example:

| | |
|---|---|
| 我还不懂。 | I still do not understand. |
| 你还不睡吗？ | You are still not going to sleep? |
| 你还不累吗？ | You are still not tired? |

### C. Not Bad

In colloquial Chinese, 还 is frequently used to indicate that something is neither too great nor too bad. For example:

| | |
|---|---|
| 我最近还好。 | I have been doing okay recently. |
| 这本书还不错。 | This book is so-so. |
| 他做的菜还可以。 | The dish he cooked is acceptable but not that great. |

### D. Not Yet with 没（有）

还 can also be used with the negative word 没 to say "not yet." The complete structure is "还没（有）···（呢）."

| | |
|---|---|
| 今天你还没有吃饭吗？ | Haven't you eaten yet today? |
| 我还没有吃呢。 | I have not eaten anything yet. |

## 🔳 PRACTICE

Use each of the above 还 patterns to make a sentence of your own. Be sure to demonstrate that you can differentiate between their meanings!

## III. 多 and 少 as Adverbs

When placed before a verb, 多 and 少 function as adverbs meaning "more" and "less," respectively. "多/少 + Verb" is usually followed by a phrase indicating a quantity or amount. For example:

| 多 + Verb + Quantity/Amount: |
| --- |

| 你应该多喝一点儿水。 | You should drink a little more water. |
| 我想多看几本书。 | I want to read a few more books. |

| 少 + Verb + Quantity/Amount: |
| --- |

| 你怕胖，就应该少吃一点儿饭。 | If you are afraid of gaining weight, you should eat less. |
| 他想少写几封信。 | He wants to write fewer letters. |

*Alaric Radosh*

*This Chinese student has prepared lunch for her friends.*

## 🔳 PRACTICE

Use the "多/少 + Verb + Quantity/Amount" structure to complete the following sentences. Follow the example given below:

Example: 我很累，想（少做一点儿工作，多休息一下儿）。

1. 我太瘦，我想 _____。

2. 明天有考试，我想 _____。

3. 你的房间这么乱，你应该 _____。

4. 你想家，就应该 _____。

## IV. Using the Preposition 为

The preposition 为 can be translated as "for," while the noun following it indicates the purpose or reason for the action. Therefore, the phrase "为 + Noun + Verb" can be translated as "for what purpose something is done." In this lesson, you are only going to learn how to use the preposition 为 to make a toast. See the examples below.

**Purpose**

| 为 | Noun | Verb |
|---|---|---|
| 为 | 你们的新家 | 干杯。 |

A toast to your new home.

| 为 | 我们的友谊 | 干杯。 |
|---|---|---|

A toast to our friendship.

 PRACTICE

Can you think of any other situations where you might use the "为 + Noun + Verb" pattern?

# Textbook Exercises

## 🎧💻 TASK 1. 课文问答 (KÈWÉN WÈNDÁ) QUESTIONS AND ANSWERS

How well did you understand the text? Check your comprehension by answering the following questions.

1. 林笛为什么要吴文德请她和李丽莉吃饭？

2. 吴文德请林笛和李丽莉吃饭的那一天，谁给大家做的饭？都做了什么吃的东西？

3. 林笛和李丽莉觉得饭好不好吃？为什么？

4. 你会不会做饭？如果你会做饭，你都会做什么？如果你不会做饭，为什么？

## 💻 TASK 2. 语法练习 (YǓFǍ LIÀNXÍ) GRAMMATICAL STRUCTURE PRACTICE

### A. Sentence Construction

Reconstruct the following into "Verb 了" sentences by adding 了 and any other necessary components. Then turn each sentence first into a question, and next into a negative form.

1. 我去买鱼。

2. 我吃拿手菜。

3. 素菜和荤菜我都尝。

4. 我昨天去签证。

5. 今天下午我尝鸡，吃鱼。

## B. Pick and Choose

In each of the following pairs there is a correct sentence and an incorrect one. Can you tell which one is correct and explain why the other one is incorrect?

1.

a) 他尝了我做的鸡。

b) 我没尝了那些鸡。

2.

a) 我昨天晚上买一些菜了。

b) 他上个星期看了很多电影。

3.

a) 昨天他下了课以后，跟朋友去商店买东西了。

b) 明天我吃了饭，要跟朋友去看了电影。

4.

a) 你怎么就喝这么一点儿，多喝一点儿吧。

b) 他做的拿手菜很好吃，你们应该吃多一点儿。

5.

a) 他来了我们家吃很多甜点。

b) 我去图书馆借了很多书。

---

## 📖 TASK 3. 翻译 (FĀNYÌ) PARAPHRASING

How well do you remember the grammar and vocabulary we've covered so far? Check yourself by translating the following sentences into Chinese.

1. At the party, we had Chinese food, drank some wine, and watched a Chinese movie. (Hint: Verb 了)

2. I just moved last week. (Hint: Verb 了) I would like to invite you to come over this Saturday to have dinner in my new home. We can go to a movie after dinner. What do you think? (Hint: 请, Verb 了 + Object)

*Pandas eating breakfast at the Chengdu Zoo.*

3. I made some meat dishes and vegetable dishes. (Hint: Verb 了) They are my specialties. (Hint: 拿手菜) I also made some desserts, and they will be served later. (Hint: 还 Verb 了) Go ahead and eat while the food is hot. (Hint: 趁) Don't be so polite!

4. I am also afraid of gaining weight, (Hint: 怕) but today is a house-warming party. Let's eat a little more today (Hint: 多 + Verb). Come, to our friendship! (Hint: 为) Cheers!

---

## 💻 TASK 4. 情景对话 (QÍNGJǏNG DUÌHUÀ) SITUATIONAL DIALOGUE

**Setting:**      A new home

**Cast:**        A host and a few guests (at least two)

**Situation:**   A host invites his/her friends to a house-warming party. If you are playing the role of the host, tell your guests what kind of food you have made. If you are one of the guests, tell your host how much you like the food. Don't forget to make toasts.

# 22

# 办签证

## How Do I Get a Visa?

In this lesson you will:
- Apply for a visa to study or travel in China.
- Speak to people at an embassy or consulate about visas.
- Fill out a Chinese visa application form.

很多学中文的学生都希望能有一次去中国的机会。但是，去中国一定要办签证，你知道怎么办去中国的签证吗？你知道办签证要带什么东西吗？你知道怎么填签证申请表吗？李丽莉的签证办得非常顺利。可是，吴文德的签证办得不太顺利，他去了好几次中国大使馆。你知道为什么吗？下面请看吴文德去中国大使馆办签证的小故事。

（刚上完了中文课，吴文德和李丽莉在教室聊天。）

吴文德：李丽莉，你去中国的签证办了吗？

李丽莉：办了。大使馆离我家很近。我上个月就办了签证了。现在离我们去中国还有一个月。你的签证办了没有？

吴文德：还没有办。我家离大使馆太远了。我得找个时间从学校去大使馆。办签证都需要带些什么东西？

李丽莉：学校的录取通知书、美国护照、照片，还要带美金。你得抓紧时间去办签证了。

吴文德：我知道。我这个星期就去办签证。办签证还要填表吧？

李丽莉：当然要填。你填表的时候一定要细心。字一定要写得很清楚。写得不清楚，大使馆说不定会拒签。

吴文德：你放心吧。我这个人办事儿，不会有错儿。

（在中国大使馆）

吴文德：请问，这是中国大使馆签证处吗？

工作人员：对。办签证请在那边排队。

……

吴文德：您好，麻烦您给我办一个去中国的签证。

工作人员：你办什么签证？旅游签证，学生签证，还是工作签证？

吴文德：学生签证。这是中国学校的录取通知书。这是我填的签证申请表。

工作人员：请稍等。你的国籍怎么没有填？这是一个错别字。请不要涂改。

吴文德：麻烦你再给我一张签证申请表吧。我重填一遍。这次一定是天衣无缝[1]。

（几分钟以后……）

吴文德：表填好了，您看看，这次我填的表怎么样？

工作人员：不错。但是你忘了签名了。请在这儿签名。……很好。您带护照了吗？

吴文德：带了。咦……我的护照上哪儿去了？请稍等，我再找一下儿。……对不起，我可能忘了带了。

工作人员：对不起，没有护照不能办签证。你明天再来吧。

（下午在学校图书馆）

李丽莉：今天上午你怎么没上课，你去哪儿了？

吴文德：我吃了早饭，就去中国大使馆了。

李丽莉：你办好签证了吗？

吴文德：没有。我忘带护照了。我明天再去。反正办签证总是要去大使馆两次。一次申请签证，一次取签证。

李丽莉：你明天办了签证，就不再去取签证了吗[2]？

## Notes

1. 天衣无缝　(tiān yī wú fèng)

seamless; (lit.) clothes made in heaven are seamless (and perfect). This is used to indicate that something is flawless. For more information, see Reading/Writing Exercises Task 1.

2. 你就不再去取签证了吗？　(Nǐ jiù bù zài qù qǔ qiānzhèng le ma?)

Won't you have to go back to pick up the visa? This is a rhetorical question chiding Wu Wende for his thoughtlessness in forgetting that he still must go back to pick up his visa.

*A man playing the* erhu.

 生词表 (Shēngcí Biǎo)
# Vocabulary

| Character | Pinyin | Part of Speech | English Definition |
|-----------|--------|----------------|--------------------|
| 1. 希望 | xīwàng | *v.* | to hope, to wish for |
| 他希望明年能去中国看看。 | | | |
| | | *n.* | hope, wish |
| 这只是我们的希望。 | | | |
| 2. 次 | cì | *m.w.* | measure word for actions |
| 这次我不想跟他们去看电影了。 | | | |
| 3. 大使馆 | dàshǐguǎn | *n.* | embassy |
| 你今天去大使馆了没有？ | | | |
| 大使 | | *n.* | ambassador |
| 4. 离 | lí | *prep.* | measuring from (one place or time to another, used to describe distance between places or times) |
| 我们学校离我家很近。 | | | |
| 5. 近 | jìn | *adj.* | close, near |
| 那儿离你们家近不近？ | | | |

6. 远　　　　　　　yuǎn　　　　　　　*adj.*　　　　distant, far away

那儿离我们家不远。

7. 录取通知书　　　lùqǔ tōngzhī shū　　*phr.*　　　letter of admission from a school

他的录取通知书已经来了。

录取　　　　　　　　　　　　　　　　　　*v.*　　　　to admit, to be accepted

通知　　　　　　　　　　　　　　　　　　*n.*　　　　announcement

　　　　　　　　　　　　　　　　　　　　*v.*　　　　to announce

书　　　　　　　　　　　　　　　　　　　*n.*　　　　book

　　　　　　　　　　　　　　　　　　　　*b.f.*　　　(classical Chinese) letter, correspondence

8. 护照　　　　　　hùzhào　　　　　　　*n.*　　　　passport

请给我看看你的护照。

9. 照片　　　　　　zhàopiàn　　　　　　*n.*　　　　photo

这是一张老照片。

照　　　　　　　　　　　　　　　　　　　*v.*　　　　to reflect, to take a photo

片　　　　　　　　　　　　　　　　　　　*n.*　　　　slice, piece

　　　　　　　　　　　　　　　　　　　　*m.w.*　　slice, piece

10. 美金　　　　　Měijīn　　　　　　　*n.*　　　　U.S. dollar

这要多少美金？

金　　　　　　　　　　　　　　　　　　　*n.*　　　　gold

11. 细心　　　　　xìxīn　　　　　　　　*adj.*　　　careful, attentive

他这个人做事很细心。

细　　　　　　　　　　　　　　　　　　　*adj.*　　　fine, thin (of texture)

12. 清楚　　　　　qīngchǔ　　　　　　　*adj.*　　　clear and distinct

今天老师说的你清楚不清楚？

13. 拒签　　　　　jù qiān　　　　　　　*v. obj.*　　to refuse to issue a visa

我怕大使馆会拒签我的签证。

拒　　　　　　　　　　　　　　　　　　　*b.f.*　　　to refuse, to reject, to resist

14. 放心　　　　　fàng xīn　　　　　　　*v. obj.*　　to rest at ease; (lit.) to release worry

我妈妈总是不放心我。

放　　　　　　　　　　　　　　　　　　　*v.*　　　　to let go, to release, to set free

15. 处　　　　　　chù　　　　　　　　　*b.f.*　　　office (of..), a division in an institution

这是中国大使馆签证处吗？

16. 人员　　　　　rényuán　　　　　　　*n.*　　　　personnel, staff members

我不是这儿的工作人员。

17. 排队　　　pái duì　　　v. obj.　　　to stand in line, to line up
　　请在那边排队。
　　排　　　　　　　　　　v.　　　　to arrange, to put in order, to line up
　　队　　　　　　　　　　n.　　　　line, team

18. 旅游　　　lǚyóu　　　n.　　　　travel, tourism
　　他以后想搞旅游。

　　　　　　　　　　　　v.　　　　to travel
　　你想去中国旅游，对不对？

19. 国籍　　　guójí　　　n.　　　　nationality
　　我的国籍是美国，但是我爸爸妈妈都是中国人。

20. 错别字　　cuòbiézì　　n.　　　　incorrectly written characters
　　我常常写错别字。

21. 涂改　　　túgǎi　　　v.　　　　to erase and change
　　请不要在这儿涂改。
　　涂　　　　　　　　　　v.　　　　to erase, to cross out.
　　改　　　　　　　　　　v.　　　　to make corrections, to revise, to edit

22. 重　　　　chóng　　　adv.　　　again
　　请重说一遍。

23. 遍　　　　biàn　　　m.w.　　　measure word for actions
　　这个电影我已经看了三遍了。

24. 忘　　　　wàng　　　v.　　　　to forget
　　我忘了他的电话号码了。

25. 签名　　　qiān míng　　v. obj.　　to sign one's name
　　请在这儿签名。

26. 反正　　　fǎnzhèng　　adv.　　　anyway, no matter what, in any case
　　今天晚上我反正不想去看电影。
　　反　　　　　　　　　　adj.　　　the opposite (side), the reverse (side)
　　正　　　　　　　　　　adj.　　　the right (side)

27. 取　　　　qǔ　　　　v.　　　　to pick up (sth. from sw.), to get (sth.) back (from sw.)
　　我们去大使馆取签证吧。

## 补充词汇 (Bǔchōng Cíhuì) Supplementary Vocabulary

| | | | |
|---|---|---|---|
| 1. 领事馆 | lǐngshìguǎn | *n.* | consulate |
| 2. 批准 | pīzhǔn | *v.* | to approve |
| 3. 询问 | xúnwèn | *v.* | (formal) to inquire |
| | | *n.* | inquiry |
| 4. 到期 | dào qī | *v. obj.* | to be due, (arrive at the) due date |
| 5. 过期 | guò qī | *v. obj.* | to be overdue, to pass the due date |
| 6. 粗心 | cūxīn | *adj.* | careless |
| 7. 修改 | xiūgǎi | *v.* | to edit, to make corrections |
| 8. 签字 | qiān zì | *v. obj.* | to sign (one's name) |
| | | *n.* | signature |
| 9. 入境日期 | rùjìng rìqī | *n. phr.* | entry date |
| 10. 工作单位 | gōngzuò dānwèi | *n. phr.* | workplace |

## 口头用语 (Kǒutóu Yòngyǔ) Spoken Expressions

| | | |
|---|---|---|
| 1. 说不定 | shuō bu dìng | maybe, perhaps |
| 2. 办事儿 | bàn shìr | to run an errand, to perform a task |
| 3. 有错儿 | yǒu cuòr | to have/make mistakes |
| 4. 上哪儿去了？ | Shàng nǎr qù le? | (Lit.) Where has it/something gone? |

## 词汇注解 (Cíhuì Zhùjiě) Featured Vocabulary

### 1. 旅游 (Lǚyóu) v. to travel

旅游 is an intransitive verb and thus CANNOT take an object. For example:
   CORRECT: 我去中国旅游。
   xxx INCORRECT: 我旅游中国。 xxx

### 2. 忘 (Wàng) v. to forget

忘 is commonly used in the following combinations: "忘了," "忘了 + Verb," and "忘记." For example:
   对不起，我忘了，你的书还在我那儿呢。
   Sorry, I have forgotten that your book is still at my place.
   他今天忘了吃饭了。
   He forgot to eat today.
   我忘记他的名字了。
   I forgot his name.

*A canal in Suzhou.*

 语法(Yǔfǎ)
# Grammar

## I. The Modal Particle 了 (Le)

In Lesson 15, we briefly introduced the Modal Particle 了, which indicates a changed state or new situation. Though the sentence with Modal Particle 了 may involve the completion of an action, its focus is not on completion of the action but on the new state resulting from the action having been carried out. The Modal Particle 了 usually appears at the end of a sentence and is therefore also called the Sentence-final 了. For example:

|  | Subject | Verb | （了） | Object | 了 |
|---|---|---|---|---|---|
| Positive: | 我 | 吃 | （了） | 饭 | 了。 |
|  | I have already eaten. | | | | |
| Negative: | 我 | （还）没（有）吃 | | 饭 | （呢）。 |
|  | I have not eaten yet. | | | | |
| Question: | 你 | 吃 | （了） | 饭 | 了没有？ |
|  | Have you had anything to eat? | | | | |
|  | 你 | 吃 | （了） | 饭 | 了吗？ |
|  | Did you eat? | | | | |
|  | 你 | 吃 | （了） | 什么 | 了？ |
|  | What did you eat? | | | | |

(The first 了 is Verb 了, which indicates the completion of the action 吃, while the second 了 is the Modal 了, which indicates that the speaker is no longer hungry.)

*The Summer Palace in Beijing.*

Lauren Brown

## *Note*

In the negative pattern, 没（有）is placed in front of the verb, and both the Modal Particle 了 and Verb 了 are taken out. The pattern "还···呢" or either 还 or 呢 separately can also be used in the negative sentence. The pattern "还···呢" places more emphasis on the negative continuation, i.e., that the action has not happened.

## 🔲 PRACTICE

Following the two examples below, use each suggested verb phrase to ask a question. Provide a positive and a negative response to each question.

问 1：他办了签证了没有？

(Suggested phrases: 锻炼身体, 收拾房间, 谈话, 留言, and 填表.)

问 2：昨天下了课，你做什么/去哪儿了？

(Suggested phrases: 回家, 吃晚饭, 停车, and 唱歌.)

## II. English Past Tense vs. Verb 了

There are many situations that would require the past tense in English but do NOT need "Verb 了" in Chinese. Unlike English verbs, Chinese verbs do not use tenses to indicate time. Instead, they use the aspect to indicate whether an action is beginning, continuing, or completed. Since in Chinese the time factor is indicated by time words (e.g., last week, yesterday, etc.), not all actions taking place in the past require "Verb 了." In the examples below, we summarize the situations in which "Verb 了" would normally not be used even though you are talking about the past.

1. ***With Non-Action Verbs (Including Auxiliary Verbs):*** 是, 有, 姓, 喜欢, 会, *etc.*

她以前姓张。          Her last name was Zhang.
我以前喜欢唱歌。      I used to like singing.

| | |
|---|---|
| 他以前不会开车。 | He did not know how to drive before. |
| 他以前是这儿的学生。 | He was a student here before. |
| 我以前有一本词典。 | I had a dictionary. |

## 2. To Describe a Habitual Past Action or Make a General Statement

| | |
|---|---|
| 我以前每天都唱歌儿。 | I used to sing every day. |
| 我以前常常唱中国歌儿。 | I used to sing Chinese songs. |

## 3. With Adjective Predicates

| | |
|---|---|
| 我们昨天很忙。 | We were very busy yesterday. |
| 他昨天很累。 | He was very tired yesterday. |

## 4. To Describe the Degree of Intensity of a Past Action

When the Complement of Degree (Verb + 得) is used to describe the extent/degree to which an action has been carried out, do NOT use 了. Since the emphasis is on the intensity of the action (how well, how much, how fast, how tall, etc.), the complement takes precedence even though you are describing a completed action.

| | |
|---|---|
| 我们昨天去他家玩儿得很高兴。 | We had a lot of fun at his house yesterday. |
| 我们昨天晚上吃得很饱。 | We were very full last night. |

## 5. In a Noun-modifying Clause (···的时候，···的人，···的地方, etc.)

Even though the noun-modifying clause deals with a completed action, the emphasis is NOT on the completed aspect, but on who, when, where, or what, as indicated by the noun-modifying clause.

你上个星期天给他打电话的时候，他还在中国。
When you called him last week, he was still in China.

昨天跟你跳舞的那个人是谁？
Who was the one that danced with you yesterday?

你们昨天去看电影的地方在哪儿？
Where did you go to see the movie yesterday?

## 6. In Narration

Even though narration generally describes a series of completed actions, you should avoid using 了 in storytelling. For example:

那天他来我家，跟我说他不想去中国。我告诉他，他可以去，也可以不去。

He came over yesterday and told me that he doesn't want to go to China. I told him that if he wants to go, he should go, but if he doesn't, then he should stay here.

# III. Using Measure Words 次 (Cì) and 遍 (Biàn)

In a typical sentence, "Number + 遍/次" functions as a verb complement. It should be placed after the verb. 遍 and 次 have similar meanings. Both of them can be translated as "once, twice…" and so on. For example:

一遍，两遍，…几遍？        once, twice, ...how many times?

一次，两次，…几次？        once, twice, ...how many times?

However, when used in a sentence, 遍 and 次 have different emphases. 遍 emphasizes that an action is carried out from beginning to end. In contrast, 次 indicates the frequency of an action. They are usually placed after the verb. For example:

我再填一遍（表）。

I will fill out the form again. (emphasizing "to fill the whole form out from beginning to end again")

我再填一次（表）。

I will fill out the form one more time. (emphasizing the number of times the action takes place)

In addition, 次 (not 遍) can also follow 这/那，上/下，or numbers to form a phrase functioning as a time word.

| 这次 this time | 那次 that time | 哪次 which time |
| 上次 last time | 下次 next time | |

Examples:

As an adverbial adjunct:

我下次一定去。

I will definitely go next time.

（反正办签证总是要去大使馆两次，）一次办签证，一次取签证。

(Either way, you have to go to the embassy twice for reasons related to your visa,) once to fill out a visa application and once to pick up the actual visa.

*Yonghegong in Beijing.*

Lauren Brown

## 🔲 PRACTICE

Use the following two patterns to make sentences of your own, demonstrating that you understand not only their meanings but also their uses in a sentence.

Subject + 再 + Verb + 一次/遍 + Object

Subject + Verb 了 + 一次/遍 + Object

Suggested verbs or verb phrases:

（次）：打电话, 参加晚会, 尝菜, 签名, 停车, 搬家, 对表, 见面.

（遍）：说, 教, 听新闻, 背单词, 复习课文, 准备功课, 写电邮, 填表格.

# IV. Using the Preposition 离 (Lí)

In the previous lesson, you learned the preposition 从, which is frequently used to indicate a distance between times or places. 从 is often used with directional verbs such as 到, 去, and 来. For example:

| | |
|---|---|
| 从 10点到11点 | from ten o'clock to eleven o'clock |
| 从这儿到那儿 | from here to there |
| 从这儿去宿舍 | to go to the dorm from here |
| 从宿舍来 | to come from the dorm |

Like 从, the preposition 离 can also be used to indicate the distance between times and places. It frequently does this with the help of an adjective or with the verb 有. Unlike 从, it CANNOT be used with directional verbs such as 到, 去, and 来. In summary, 从 is often used in sentences describing movement from one place to another, but 离 is used only in connection with measurement (absolute or relative) of distance. See the examples below.

## A. Distance between Places

| Place 1 | | Place 2 | Distance |
|---|---|---|---|
| **Subject** | 离 | **Noun** | **Adjective or verb 有** |
| 大使馆 | 离 | 我家 | 很近。 |

The embassy is very close to my home.

| | | | |
|---|---|---|---|
| 我家 | 离 | 大使馆 | 很远。 |

My home is very far from the embassy.

| | | | |
|---|---|---|---|
| 大使馆 | 离 | 我家 | 有一英里 (yīnglǐ, mile) 路 (lù, road)。 |

The embassy is a mile from my house.

## B. Distance between Times

| Time 1 | | Time 2 | Distance | |
|---|---|---|---|---|
| **Time word** | 离 | **Noun** | **Adjective or verb 有** | **Time word** |
| 现在 | 离 | 我的生日 | 还有 | 一个星期。 |

My birthday is (still) one week away.

| | | | | |
|---|---|---|---|---|
| 现在 | 离 | 我们去中国 | 还有 | 一个月。 |

Our visit to China is (still) one month away.

*The Forbidden City in Beijing.*

##  PRACTICE

Use each of the two 离 structures to ask questions, e.g., how far is your dorm from the library? How long until your birthday? Is your house far from school? When you're done, provide an answer for each one. Suggested words: 英里 (yīnglǐ, mile) 路 (lù, road).

# Textbook Exercises

## 🎧💻 TASK 1. 课文问答 (KÈWÉN WÈNDÁ) QUESTIONS AND ANSWERS

How well did you understand the text? Check your comprehension by answering the following questions.

1. 办签证都需要带什么东西？
2. 吴文德填签证申请表的时候，细心不细心？为什么？
3. 吴文德办了签证了吗？为什么？
4. 吴文德去了几次中国大使馆？

## TASK 2. 语法练习 (YǓ FǍ LIÀNXÍ) GRAMMATICAL STRUCTURE PRACTICE

### A. Sentence Completion

Complete each of the sentences below by selecting one of the four choices.

1. 我在 (1) 中国的时候，非常喜欢吃鱼 (2)。
    a) Only (1) needs a 了.          b) Only (2) needs a 了.
    c) Both (1) and (2) need a 了.     d) Neither (1) nor (2) needs a 了.

2. 他昨天做 (1) 很多菜，好吃极 (2)。
    a) Only (1) needs a 了.          b) Only (2) needs a 了.
    c) Both (1) and (2) need a 了.     d) Neither (1) nor (2) needs a 了.

3. 我昨天吃 (1) 早饭就去办护照 (2)。
    a) Only (1) needs a 了.          b) Only (2) needs a 了.
    c) Both (1) and (2) need a 了.     d) Neither (1) nor (2) needs a 了.

4. A: 你吃饭 (1) 没有？ B: 我还没有吃饭 (2)。
    a) Only (1) needs a 了.          b) Only (2) needs a 了.
    c) Both (1) and (2) need a 了.     d) Neither (1) nor (2) needs a 了.

5. 你今天早上给我来 (1) 电话的时候，我去取照片 (2)。
    a) Only (1) needs a 了.          b) Only (2) needs a 了.
    c) Both (1) and (2) need a 了.     d) Neither (1) nor (2) needs a 了.

### B. 次 or 遍 Insertion

Insert 次 and 遍 where applicable into the following sentences.

1. 我给他打了几 _____ 电话，他都不在家。

2. 他的留言我听了好几 _____ 。

3. 我上个星期去了两 _____ 大使馆。

4. 他每 _____ 填申请表都有错别字。

5. 这本小说非常好看，所以我看了两 _____ 。

### C. Sentence Construction

Use 了 to rewrite the following sentences.

1. 他今天在大使馆填两张表。

2. 我办签证，但是他还没有办签证。

3. 昨天下课，他就去大使馆。

4. A: 你签字没有？ B: 我签字。

5. 昨天晚上我给你打两次电话，你都不在。

6. 昨天我工作很忙，我朋友给我写的信我只看一遍，今天晚上我还得再看一遍。

7. 今天我朋友没去上课，他去大使馆办签证。他晚上回宿舍的时候，我问他：
"你的签证办没有？"他说没有，因为他忘带照片。

---

## 💻 TASK 3. 翻译 (FĀNYÌ) PARAPHRASING

How well do you remember the grammar and vocabulary we've covered so far? Check yourself by translating the following sentences into Chinese.

1. To get a visa, you need to go to the embassy twice: once to fill out a visa application and once to pick up the visa. (Hint: 次)

2. After picking up my passport yesterday, (Hint: Verb 了) I went to the Chinese Embassy to get a student visa. (Hint: Modal 了) However, I forgot to bring my letter of admission with me. (Hint: Verb 了 + Object + Modal 了) I have to go back again tomorrow (Hint: 次).

3. The embassy is very close to my school (Hint: 离), (so) I got my visa last month. (Hint: Verb + Object + 了) It will be two weeks before I leave for China (Hint: 离). Now I just have to pack the things I'm bringing with me.

4. When I was getting my visa at the embassy, I filled out the visa application form twice with no misspelled words or corrections. (Hint: Verb 了, 遍)

---

## 💻 TASK 4. 情景对话 (QÍNGJǏNG DUÌHUÀ) SITUATIONAL DIALOGUE

**Setting:**     An embassy

**Cast:**        An embassy employee and a student who wants a visa (you)

**Situation:**   You are talking to an embassy officer to get a visa from the embassy. Tell him/her where you want to go, and provide the following information: 1) What is the purpose of your visit to that country? 2) What kind of visa do you want? Make sure to show the officer all the proper documentation, and ask him about anything unusual that is going on in that country. He looks like he's had a long day, so be polite, and impress him with your excellent Chinese.

# 23
# 送人
# Seeing Someone Off

> **In this lesson you will:**
> ■ Check in at the airport.
> ■ Talk about departure and arrival times.
> ■ Wish someone a safe and happy trip.
> ■ Talk about events that will take place in the near future.

李丽莉和吴文德就要去北京了。林笛开车送他们去飞机场。到了飞机场以后，林笛去停车，李丽莉和吴文德去托运行李，取登机牌。吴文德给李丽莉要了一个靠走道的座位，给自己要了一个靠窗口的座位。他们办完了登机手续以后，又去看了一下到港--离港的屏幕，飞机还是准时起飞。他们真的就要离开美国了。下面请看他们在飞机场办手续的小故事。

（在去飞机场的路上）

　　林笛：快要到飞机场了，你们马上就要离开美国了。

吴文德：是啊，我真高兴。我们明天就要到北京了。

　　林笛：我难过极了。真不想让你们走。

李丽莉：别难过了。我们也不想离开你。要不，你跟我们一起走吧。

　　林笛：别开玩笑了，我没有签证，想走也走不了[1]。前边就是进站口了，你们去托运行李，取登机牌，我去停车。我们一会儿在那儿碰头。

（在飞机场）

工作人员：您好，去哪儿？

李丽莉：中国北京。这是我们的护照和机票。

工作人员：托运几件行李？

吴文德：四件。我们换飞机的时候，还要取行李吗？

33

工作人员：不用，行李可以直接到北京。

吴文德：麻烦你给我们一个靠窗口的座位，一个靠走道的座位。好吗？

李丽莉：我有的时候晕机，你能不能给我们两个前边的座位？

工作人员：我查查有没有你们要的座位，请稍等……你们的座位是A6和C6。这是你们的登机牌，请到14号登机口登机。祝你们旅途愉快。

（吴文德看了看时间跟李丽莉说）

吴文德：李丽莉，时间还早，我还想再去买一杯咖啡。你在这儿等等，好不好？

李丽莉：你怎么又要喝咖啡。一会儿又要上厕所，多麻烦啊。你看，林笛来了。

林笛：你们的登机手续都办好了吗？行李都托运了吗？

吴文德：都办了，行李也托运了。我们去候机室等飞机吧。那儿还有咖啡。

林笛：等一等，咱们再看一下到港--离港的屏幕，看看飞机是不是准时起飞。

吴文德：刚才我看了一下儿，飞机还是准时起飞。

林笛：我们再看一下儿嘛。要是飞机晚点，我们还可以再说一会儿话。

……

吴文德：前边就到安全检查口了，林笛你回学校吧。

林笛：好吧，李丽莉我给你买的那些晕机药，你又忘了吃，是不是？上了飞机以后，别再忘了。祝你们一路平安，到了北京，就给我打电话。

李丽莉：一定，谢谢。再见。

（在14号登机口）

吴文德：飞机就要起飞了。我们去排队准备登机吧。

李丽莉：再见了，美国！我们要去北京了。

*Meeting friends at the airport.*

## Notes

1. 想走也走不了  (xiǎng zǒu yě zǒu bù liǎo)
   Even though (I) would like to, I cannot go.

 生词表 (Shēngcí Biǎo)
# Vocabulary

| Character | Pinyin | Part of Speech | English Definition |
|---|---|---|---|
| 1. 送(人) | sòng (rén) | v. (obj.) | to see someone off |
| 他今天要去送人。 | | | |
| 2. 飞机场 | fēijī chǎng | n. | airport |
| 你今天也要去飞机场吗？ | | | |
| 飞 | | v. | to fly |
| 机 | | n. | machine, machinery |
| 飞机 | | n. | airplane |
| 场 | | n. | an area designated for a specific use |
| 3. 托运 | tuōyùn | v. | to check in (luggage) |
| 这几件都要托运吗？ | | | |
| 4. 行李 | xíngli | n. | baggage, luggage |
| 这几件行李都要托运。 | | | |

5. 登机牌     dēngjī pái     *n.*     boarding pass

我的登机牌在哪儿？

登                                 *v.*     to climb, to get on, to board

牌（子）                     *n.*     piece of board, plate, card

6. 靠     kào     *prep.*     next to

请你靠这边走。

                                       *v.*     to lean against, to rely on, to depend on

你不能总是靠你爸爸妈妈？

7. 走道     zǒudào     *n.*     (in a theater, airplane, etc.) walkway, aisle

我喜欢靠走道的座位。

道                                 *n.*     path

8. 座位     zuòwèi     *n.*     seat

那个座位靠走道。

9. 窗口     chuāngkǒu     *n.*     window, wicket

我想要一个靠窗口的座位。

口                                 *n.*     (formal) mouth, opening, gate

10. 手续     shǒuxù     *n.*     procedure

我还要办很多手续。

11. 又     yòu     *adv.*     again (used when talking about formerly recurring events)

你为什么又要去厕所？

12. 到港     dào gǎng     *v. obj.*     to arrive at a port or an airport

港                                 *n.*     port, harbor

你去看一下儿飞机到港的时间。

13. 离港     lí gǎng     *v. obj.*     to depart from a port or an airport

这个离港时间不对吧。

14. 屏幕     píngmù     *n.*     screen (of a television, computer, etc.)

我再去看看那个屏幕。

屏                                 *n.*     screen, shield

幕                                 *n.*     curtain

15. 准时     zhǔnshí     *adj.*     on time, punctual

这个老师上课总是很准时。

                                       *adv.*     in accordance with the schedule

我们的飞机一定能准时到北京。

16. 起飞          qǐfēi              *v.*           (of an airplane) to take off
    你的飞机几点起飞？

17. 离开          líkāi              *v.*           to leave (a place or a person)
    我们上午十点离开，下午三点到。

18. 难过          nánguò            *adj.*         sad
    我朋友去北京了，我非常难过。

19. 进站口        jìnzhànkǒu        *n.*           arrival gate, entrance (where a plane,
    请问，这个飞机的进站口在哪儿？                      train, etc. comes in)
    站                              *n.*           station, stop (for a bus, train, airplane)

20. 机票          jīpiào            *n.*           (abbreviation of 飞机票) plane
    我的机票在你那儿吗？                                ticket

21. 换            huàn              *v.*           to exchange
    你们不用换飞机。

22. 直接          zhíjiē            *adv.*         directly
    你们的飞机是不是直接飞北京？
    直                              *adj.*         straight, direct
    接                              *v.*           to connect, to join

23. 晕机          yùnjī             *n., v. obj.*  motion sickness; to have motion sickness
    我常常晕机、晕车。
    晕                              *v.*           to feel dizzy, to faint
    晕            yūn               *adj.*         dizzy

24. 候机室        hòujīshì          *n.*           airport waiting room
    我们去候机室等吧。
    候                              *v.*           (formal) to wait, to await

25. 要是          yàoshi            *conj.*        if, in case
    要是你不去，我也不去。

26. 晚点          wǎndiǎn           *v.*           to arrive later than expected or
    他说飞机今天晚点。                                  scheduled

27. 安全检查口    ānquán jiǎnchá kǒu  *n. phr.*    security inspection gate
    安全检查口在哪儿？
    安全                            *adj.*         secure, safe
                                   *n.*           security

| 检查 | | *v.* | to inspect, to check |
| | | *n.* | inspection |
| 28. 药 | yào | *n.* | medicine |

你有没有晕机药?

## 补充词汇 (Bǔchōng Cíhuì) Supplementary Vocabulary

| | | | | |
|---|---|---|---|---|
| 1. | 送行 | sòng xíng | *v. phr.* | to see someone off |
| 2. | 降落 | jiàngluò | *v.* | (of an airplane) to descend, to land |
| 3. | 上飞机 | shàng fēijī | *v. obj.* | to board an airplane |
| | 上 | | *v.* | to board / to get on (a vehicle, boat, or airplane) |
| 4. | 下飞机 | xià fēijī | *v. obj.* | to get off an airplane |
| | 下 | | *v.* | to disembark / to get off (a vehicle, boat, or airplane) |
| 5. | 坐飞机 | zuò fēijī | *v. obj.* | to travel by airplane |
| | 坐 | | *v.* | to ride, to go by, to take (public transportation, i.e., airplane, bus, train, etc.) |
| 6. | 搭乘 | dāchéng | *v.* | (formal) to ride (in public transportation) |
| 7. | 班机 | bānjī | *n.* | scheduled flight |
| 8. | 航空 | hángkōng | *adv.* | to travel by air |
| 9. | 按时 | ànshí | *adv.* | to be on time, to go by schedule |

## 口头用语 (Kǒutóu Yòngyǔ) Spoken Expressions

*General Expressions*

1. 要不 　　　 yàobù
   otherwise

2. 碰头 　　 pèngtóu
   to meet informally; to touch heads (lit.)

*Expressions for Saying Goodbye*

1. 祝你们旅途愉快。    Zhù nǐmen lǚtú yúkuài.
   Have a pleasant trip. Bon voyage.

2. 一路顺风！    Yī lù shùn fēng!
   Have a good trip! (Lit.) "May there be favorable winds all the way!"

3. 一路平安。    Yī lù píng ān.
   Have a safe trip.

# 词汇注解 (Cíhuì Zhùjiě) Featured Vocabulary

## 1. 口 *(Kǒu)*

| 口 | (Kǒu) | *n.* | opening, point of entry; (lit. & formal) mouth |
|---|---|---|---|

口 can be used to form many compound nouns. For example:

| 门口 | ménkǒu | doorway, entrance |
|---|---|---|
| 进站口 | jìnzhànkǒu | the entrance gate (of a train, plane, etc.) |
| 路口 | lùkǒu | road intersection |
| 安全检查口 | ānquán jiǎnchá kǒu | security checkpoint |
| 窗口 | chuāngkǒu | (ticket, teller's, etc.) window, wicket |

### *Note*
窗口 is different from 窗户 (chuānghù) and 窗子 (chuāngzi), which refer to windows in a wall to let in air or light.

## 2. 晕 *(Yùn)*

| 晕 | (Yùn) | *v.* | to feel dizzy |
|---|---|---|---|

When 晕 is a verb and placed before the name of a type of vehicle, it suggests that somebody has the feeling of dizziness in the vehicle. For example:

| 晕机 | | airsickness |
|---|---|---|
| 晕车 | | carsickness |
| 晕船 | (chuán, ship) | seasickness |

| 晕 | (Yūn) | *adj.* | dizzy |
|---|---|---|---|

| 我头晕 | I feel dizzy. |
|---|---|

## 3. 要是 *(Yàoshì)*

| 要是 | (Yàoshì) | *conj.* | used to introduce a conditional clause |
|---|---|---|---|

要是 can be placed before or after the subject. It is frequently used with the adverbs 就 or 还 in the structure "要是…还/就." For example:

要是飞机晚点，我们还可以再聊一会儿天。
If the flight is delayed, we can chat for a while.

他要是来，我们就去看电影。

If he comes, we will go to see a movie.

However, 要是 does not function as "whether" or "if" in English. For example:

CORRECT: 你问他来不来。 You ask him if he is coming.

xxx INCORRECT: 你问他要是他来。 xxx

CORRECT: 我们都不知道他来不来。 None of us know if he is coming or not.

xxx INCORRECT: 我们都不知道要是他来。 xxx

*At the check-in counter for China Eastern Airlines at Xi'an Airport.*

 语法(Yǔfǎ)

# Grammar

## I. The Impending Future Aspect

As you learned earlier, Chinese uses aspects to indicate different stages of an action. So far you have learned: 1) the aspect of action in progress (Lesson 18); 2) the Perfect Aspect 了, which indicates the completion of action (Lessons 16 and 21); and 3) the Modal 了, which indicates a change in situation, or, rather, expresses the completion of action with reference to the present situation (Lessons 15 and 22). The impending future aspect, which you are going to learn in this lesson, indicates that an action is going to take place in the near future. Impending actions are expressed with "要…了" where 要 is placed before the verb and 了 appears at the end of the sentence. For example:

| Subject | 要 | Verb | Object 了 |
|---------|---|------|-----------|
| 他 | 要 | 去 | 中国了。 |

Strictly speaking, there is no negative form in the impending future aspect. To give a negative response to a question, you can use "还没(有)呢" or simply say "不" and proceed with the explanation—whichever is appropriate in the context. For example:

| | |
|---|---|
| Questions: | 他要去中国了吗/吧？ |
| | 他要去中国了，是不是？ |
| Positive: | 对/是。他要去中国了。 |
| Negative: | 还没(有)呢。他明年去中国。 |
| | 不。他明年去中国。 |

The "要…了" structure can be modified by time adverbials or attributives, and 快/马上 and 就 are the most frequent of these time modifiers. With 快/马上 you can't have additional adverbs or time adverbials, but with 就 you can.

## A. 要…了 Modified by 快/马上

When 快/马上 modifies the "要…了" structure, 快/马上 is placed before 要, indicating the action is about to happen soon. However, no one knows exactly when the action will take place because NO time word can be used in the "快/马上要…了" structure. In this pattern, 要 is optional. See the examples below.

| | |
|---|---|
| Positive: | 电影快/马上(要)开始了。 |
| | The movie will start soon. |
| Question: | 电影快/马上(要)开始了，是不是？ |
| | Is the movie about to start? |

## B. 要…了 Modified by 就

When used without any time word, the "就要…了" structure carries a similar meaning to the "要…了" and "快要…了" structures. However, "就要…了" carries more immediacy than "要…了" and "快要…了." See the examples below:

电影要开始了。　　　　The movie will start soon.

电影快(要)开始了。　　The movie is about to start.
(More imminent than the sentence with "要…了")

电影就要开始了。　　　The movie will start any minute.
(Even more imminent than the sentence with "快(要)…了")

When the "就要…了" structure is used with time words, it indicates that the action is scheduled to take place by a certain time. It may also imply that the action actually takes place earlier than expected. For example:

| Subject | (Time word) | 就要 | Verb phrase | 了 |
|---|---|---|---|---|
| 他 | 今年九月 | 就要 | 去中国 | 了。|

He is scheduled to leave for China this September.

(This implies that he is leaving for China as early as this September.)

## Compare

他今年九月就要去中国了。　　He is scheduled to leave for China (as early as) this September.

他今年九月要去中国。　　He is going to China this September.

---

## PRACTICE

Try using the "要⋯了," "快/马上要⋯了," and "就要⋯了" structures to ask questions. Then provide a positive or negative response to each one. For example:

问：他们是不是要下课了？

答：不。还有一会儿呢。

问：电影开始了没有？

答：还没呢。快要开始了。

问：飞机什么时候起飞？

答：十分钟以后就要起飞了。

## II. The Perfect Aspect 了 with Repeated Verbs or 一下儿

You have learned that the Perfect Aspect 了 (Verb 了) directly follows the verb to indicate the completion of an action. However, some verbs in Chinese can be repeated or followed by 一下儿 to indicate that the action takes place for a very short period of time. When the verb is repeated or is used with 一下儿, 了 should be placed between the verb itself and the repeated verb, or between the verb and 一下儿. For example:

听了听 ＝ 听了一下儿

看了看时间 ＝ 看了一下儿时间

聊了聊天 ＝ 聊了一下儿天

## Note

了 can neither be placed after the repeated verb, nor before an object.

　　xxx INCORRECT: 聊聊了天 xxx

## ⧉ PRACTICE

Can you come up with any other repeated verbs? Make a list of verb phrases, and include both "Verb 了 Verb" and "了 + 一下儿" phrases. Be creative!

# III. Using the Adverb 又 (Yòu)

The adverb 又 is used to indicate the recurrence of a past action and is often translated as "again" in English. Its structural form is "又 + Verb Phrase," and its negative form is "又没 + Verb Phrase." If it can be understood from context, the previous action is often omitted from the conversation. For example:

|  | (Previous action) | Recurrence of the previous action | |
|---|---|---|---|
|  |  | 又 | Verb phrase |
| Positive: | （他昨天晚上给我打了一个电话，）<br>He called me last night and then again this morning. | 他今天又 | 给我打了一个电话。 |
| Negative: | （他昨天没有来，）<br>He neither came yesterday, nor today. | 他今天又 | 没有来。 |

## *Notes*

1. If an auxiliary verb is used in this structure, 又 is placed BEFORE the auxiliary verb. For example:

   （他昨天给他妈妈打了一个电话，）他今天又想给他妈妈打电话。

2. The primary negative form of 又 is 又没, which means that someone did not do something at all. However, with the verb 在, you could also use 又不 to negate the sentence. For example:

| 他又没在家。 | He is not home again. |
|---|---|
| （他昨天不在家，）他今天又不在家。 | He was not at home yesterday, nor is he at home today. |
| 他今天又不在图书馆。 | He is not in the library today either. |

## ⧉ PRACTICE

Complete the following sentences using 又.

1. 昨天我去了一次大使馆，今天早上 ＿＿＿＿＿＿＿＿＿＿＿＿＿＿＿＿＿＿＿＿。

2. 新语法我复习了几遍，考试前 ＿＿＿＿＿＿＿＿＿＿＿＿＿＿＿＿＿＿＿＿＿＿。

3. 上次飞机晚点，这次 ＿＿＿＿＿＿＿＿＿＿＿＿＿＿＿＿＿＿＿＿＿＿＿＿＿。

4. 上星期我去朋友那儿，他没有收拾房间，今天 ＿＿＿＿＿＿＿＿＿＿＿＿＿＿＿＿。

5. 昨天他没有给我打电话，今天 _____。

6. 半个小时以前托运行李的地方没有人，现在那儿 _____。

# Comparing 又 with 再

In Lesson 19, we introduced the adverb 再, which has many different meanings. It is often used to indicate repetition of an action; thus, it can be translated as "again" in English. In that context, 再 has a similar meaning to 又, which means "again." However, upon closer examination, you will find that the meanings and usage of 又 and 再 are not exactly the same and they are usually NOT interchangeable with each other.

## A. In a Positive Sentence

When 再 is used to indicate "again" in a positive sentence, it means that someone did something and WILL do it again. For example:

| (Previous action) | Action not taken place yet |
|---|---|
| 今天下午我给他打电话，他不在。 | 我明天再给他打电话。 |

I called him this afternoon, but he was not in. I will call him again tomorrow.

(In this case, the second phone call has not yet taken place.)

When 又 is used to indicate "again," in a positive sentence, it means someone did something in the past and has ALREADY done it again.

| (Previous action) | Action already taken place |
|---|---|
| （他昨天晚上给我打了一个电话，） | 他今天又给我打电话了。 |

He called me last night and then again this morning.

(Here, the second phone call has already taken place.)

## B. In a Negative Sentence

又 has two negative forms ("又没 + Verb Phrase" and "又不在 + Place"), while 再 has the following three negative forms:

1. 没再 indicates that someone did something once and has not done it again.

   （我昨天给他打了电话了。）我今天没再给他打（电话）。

   (I called him yesterday); I did not call him again today.

2. 不再 indicates that someone did something but will never do it again.

   （我刚给他打了电话了。）我明天不再给他打（电话）了。

   (I just called him); I will not call him again tomorrow.

3. "再不…就" indicates that if the same action is not repeated, something else will happen.

（我昨天没给他打电话。）我今天再不给他打，他就会很不高兴。

(I did not call him yesterday.) If I don't call him today, he will not be happy.

## C. In a Sentence with an Auxiliary Verb

When a sentence contains an auxiliary verb, 再 and 又 have the same meaning. However, 再 is usually placed AFTER the auxiliary verb, whereas 又 is placed BEFORE the auxiliary verb. For example:

（我昨天给他打了一个电话，）今天想再给他打电话。

(I called him yesterday), and I want to call him again today.

（我昨天给他打了一个电话，）今天又想给他打电话。

(I called him yesterday), and I want to call him again today.

---

## 🎮 PRACTICE

Create sentences using each of the structures above. Be careful to use 再 and 又 correctly.

## IV. Using 别/不要 (Bié/Bú Yào)

别 and 不要 both mean "don't" and are usually used to form a negative sentence in an imperative form. 别 and 不要 are interchangeable due to the similarities in their meanings and usages. However, the meaning of 别 and 不要, when used with the Modal 了, is different from that without Modal 了.

## A. Without Modal 了

When 别 and 不要 are used without the Modal 了 at the end of a sentence, they mean "do not do something."

别/不要看电视。

Don't watch TV.

(The speaker is telling someone NOT to watch TV. The action of watching TV hasn't yet taken place.)

## B. With Modal 了

When the Modal 了 is added at the end of the sentence, it usually indicates the speaker would like to see the listener take an action in order to change the current situation. 别 and 不要 both mean "do not continue to do something."

别/不要看电视了。

Don't watch TV anymore / Stop watching TV.

(The speaker is telling someone who is currently watching TV to stop.)

PRACTICE

Try making some sentences of your own following the examples below.

喝咖啡老要上厕所。所以，别喝咖啡。

你喝了三杯咖啡了，别再喝了。

*Domestic baggage claim instructions.*

# Textbook Exercises

## TASK 1. 课文问答 (KÈWÉN WÈNDÁ) QUESTIONS AND ANSWERS

How well did you understand the text? Check your comprehension by answering the following questions.

1. 李丽莉和吴文德托运了几件行李？

2. 李丽莉吴文德他们怎么去的飞机场？

3. 李丽莉和吴文德办完手续以后，林笛为什么要他们再去检查一下儿飞机起飞的时间？

4. 林笛给李丽莉买了什么？为什么？

## 💻 TASK 2. 语法练习 (YǓ FǍ LIÀNXÍ) GRAMMATICAL STRUCTURE PRACTICE

### A. Fill in the Blanks

Use 又 and 再 where needed to fill in the blank spaces in the sentences below.

1. 这本书很有意思，我昨天看了一遍，今天下午 _____ 看了一遍。

2. 今天上课，他 _____ 没带书，明天 _____ 不带，老师就不让他来上课了。

3. 这家饭馆的菜真好吃！明天我还想 _____ 来，_____ 点我们今天喝的那个鱼汤。

4. 星期一我去看他，他不在家。昨天我 _____ 去了，他还是不在。今天我没 _____ 去找他。我明天也不 _____ 去找他了。

5. 我 _____ 忘了飞机起飞的时间。我们 _____ 看一下儿到港—离港的屏幕吧！

### B. Scrambled Sentences

Add either the "快要…了" or "就要…了" structure to the words in each of the following groups to make complete sentences.

1. 中国　去　九　我　今　们　年　月

2. 机　飞　飞　起

3. 登　我　上　机　马　们

4. 离　国　们　美　开　他

5. 们　上　北　我　晚　京　到

### C. Pick and Choose

In each of the following pairs there is a correct sentence and an incorrect one. Can you tell which one is correct and explain why the other one is incorrect?

1.
a) 我们快要离开中国了，我高兴极了。
b) 我们明天快要离开美国了，我真高兴。

2.
a) 你刚才喝了一杯咖啡，为什么再要喝一杯？
b) 你刚才喝了一杯茶，怎么又要喝一杯？

3.
a) 电影还有十五分钟要开始了。
b) 我们还有五分钟就要登机了。

4.
a) 我刚看了看屏幕，飞机还是准时起飞。
b) 他刚刚看看了飞机到港离港的屏幕。

5.
a) 我不知道要是他们现在到北京了没有？
b) 我想知道他们现在是不是在上海？

---

## 🖥 TASK 3. 翻译 (FĀNYÌ) PARAPHRASING

How well do you remember the grammar and vocabulary we've covered so far? Check yourself by translating the following sentences into Chinese.

1. I'm going to park the car. (Hint: 要···了) If you don't get out of the car, you won't have time to check your baggage. (Hint: 再不···就) Don't forget to wait for me at the boarding gate after you finish the boarding procedures. (Hint: 不要忘···)

2. I just checked the arrival/departure screen. (Hint: Verb + 了 + Verb) The flight is still only 30 minutes delayed. It will not be delayed any longer (Hint: 再). Let's go to the waiting room to wait for the airplane.

3. We are five minutes away from the airport (Hint: 就要···了), and you are about to leave America again (Hint: 又). This time, don't forget your motion sickness pills (Hint: 别再 + Verb 了 + Object), and call me as soon as you arrive in Beijing! (Hint: 就) Have a safe trip!

4. A: When I first got on the airplane, I had a little bit of motion sickness. I stopped getting dizzy after I took my pill (Hint: Verb 了 + Object, 没再), but I'm afraid that it might happen again (Hint: 再). Now I want to take another pill. (Hint: 又)
   B: If you want to take another pill, just take it. (Hint: 要是, 再)

---

## 🖥 TASK 4. 情景对话 (QÍNGJǏNG DUÌHUÀ) SITUATIONAL DIALOGUE

**Setting:**     The airport
**Cast:**         Airport employee, a traveler, a friend of the traveler

**Situation:**    You and your best friend are about to go your separate ways for the summer. You are going to China to study while your friend is going to Japan. Your friend won't be leaving until next week, but he/she has come to the airport to see you off. At the airport, you need to check your bags and get a boarding pass. Make sure you have everything packed, and when you're saying goodbye, don't forget to use the vocabulary and grammar from this lesson!

*Waiting for a bus in Hangzhou.*

# 24

# 到达北京机场
# We Made It!

*In this lesson you will:*

■ Talk about how long it takes you to complete certain tasks.

■ Speak to someone you're picking up at the airport.

■ Fill out the customs form for entering China.

飞机从美国华盛顿特区到北京要飞十几个小时。这是李丽莉和吴文德第一次去中国。他们非常激动，不吃饭也不睡觉，想用飞机上的时间练习中文。飞机快到北京的时候，乘务员给旅客发了入关卡和入境申报表。这些表格可以用中文填写，也可以用英文，但是他们都要用中文填写。你知道他们填表填了多长时间吗？

（在飞机上）

乘务员：请各位旅客注意。我们的乘务员马上就要给大家发入关卡和入境申报表了，如果您填表有困难，我们的乘务员可以给您提供帮助。

……

吴文德：你填表了吗？

李丽莉：我正在填，填了十几分钟，好多字不认识，还要查字典。你呢？

吴文德：我还没填呢。不过，学了好几年的中文了，这种表应该不太难，用七、八分钟就应该能完成任务。

……

李丽莉：时间过得真快呀，我们填表填了一个多小时，才完成任务。吴文德，你怎么不说话，你在想什么呢？

吴文德：我在想我怎么这么笨？填一张表还这么吃力。你要是不帮我，我可能现在还在填表呢。

李丽莉：这是我们第一次填表，我们又填了好几遍，当然要费时间了。飞机已经飞了十几个小时了，每次乘务员送饭你都不吃。你现在饿不饿？

吴文德：有一点儿饿，但是我不想吃飞机上的饭，太难吃了。我们还有两、三个小时就到北京了。我到了北京再好好吃饭。

······

吴文德：到北京了吗？我睡了多长时间？

李丽莉：你真能睡[1]，睡了三个多小时了。

吴文德：飞机晚点了？

李丽莉：听说晚了一个多小时，不过现在飞机已经开始下降了。

吴文德：飞机真的快要到北京机场了。我们准备下飞机吧。咦，我的行李在哪儿？

李丽莉：哎呀，你的行李在上边的行李架子上。你别太激动了。

（下了飞机以后。）

吴文德：李丽莉，你看，那个人的牌子上有我们的名字，接我们的人在那儿。

李丽莉：你好，你是陈小云吧？我是你的笔友李丽莉。

陈小云：你好，李丽莉。我们通了那么多次电话，写了那么多电子邮件，总算见面了。这位一定是吴文德吧。

吴文德：对。我是吴文德，谢谢你来机场接我们。

陈小云：别客气。我们头回生，二回熟，三回成朋友[2]。你们路上辛苦了。

吴文德：路上还可以，挺顺利。但是，我们飞了二十多个小时了，我还没有吃饭，都快饿死了。

陈小云：那我们取了行李，就去吃饭。我请客。

李丽莉：太好了，我们想在中国吃真正的中国饭想了二十多年了。

## Notes

1. 你真能睡。    (Nǐ zhēn néng shuì.)
   You slept for a long time. (Lit.) You are very capable of sleeping.

2. 头回生，二回熟，三回成朋友。　　(Tóu huí shēng, èr huí shú, sān huí chéng péngyou.)
The first time (we meet, we are) strangers; the second time, acquaintances; the third time, friends.

*Waiting to pick up travelers arriving at Xi'an Airport.*

 生词表 (Shēngcí Biǎo)
# Vocabulary

| Character | Pinyin | Part of Speech | English Definition |
|---|---|---|---|
| 1. 到达 | dàodá | *v.* | to arrive (usually referring to formal or long-distance travel) |
| 我们的飞机能准时到达北京吗？ | | | |
| 2. 小时 | xiǎoshí | *n.* | hour (period of time) |
| 从这儿到北京要飞几个小时？ | | | |
| 3. 第 | dì | *pref.* | used before a number to change it into an ordinal number |
| 这是你第一次去中国吗？ | | | |
| 4. 激动 | jīdòng | *adj.* | excited |
| 你太激动了。 | | | |
| 5. 乘务员 | chéngwùyuán | *n.* | flight attendant |
| 你去问问乘务员吧。 | | | |
| 6. 旅客 | lǚkè | *n.* | passenger |
| 这么多旅客都去中国吗？ | | | |

7. 入关卡     rùguān kǎ     *n.*     customs entry card

这是你的入关卡吗？

    入           *v.*     (formal) to enter

    关           *n.*     pass, customs station

    卡           *n.*     card

8. 入境     rù jìng     *v. obj.*     to enter a country

你在哪儿入境？

    境           *n.*     boundary, border, frontier

9. 申报表     shēnbào biǎo     *n.*     customs declaration form

你有申报表吗？

    申报           *v.*     to report (to an authority)

10. 各     gè     *adj.*     each, every

各位老师，你们好。

11. 注意     zhùyì     *v.*     to pay attention to

请大家注意。

12. 如果     rúguǒ     *conj.*     if, in case

如果你不去，我也不去。

13. 提供     tígōng     *v.*     (formal) to provide

我们为大家提供茶和咖啡。

14. 不过     bùguò     *conj.*     however, but

不过，我们现在没有中国茶。

15. 完成     wánchéng     *v.*     to complete, to finish

你想什么时候完成这些工作？

16. 任务     rènwu     *n.*     task, assignment

我看，你今天不能完成任务。

17. 才     cái     *adv.*     only, only when

现在才两点。

18. 已经     yǐjing     *adv.*     already

我们已经到了。

19. 下降     xiàjiàng     *v.*     to descend, to decline

飞机已经开始下降了。

20. 架（子）     jià(zi)     *n.*     shelf, rack

我的东西还在行李架子上呢。

21. 牌子     páizi     *n.*     sign, tablet, plate
那个牌子上写着什么？

22. 接人     jiē rén     *v. obj.*     to pick up someone (from somewhere, e.g., airport, bus station)
你也来接人吗？

23. 通     tōng     *v.*     to go through, to make/let (something) go through
我们现在还常常通电话。

24. 总算     zǒngsuàn     *adv.*     at long last, finally
我们总算到北京了。

25. 路上     lù shang     *n. phr.*     on the road
你们在路上吃饭了没有？

26. 辛苦     xīnkǔ     *adj.*     toilsome, laborious, hard-working, painstaking (often used in polite expressions)
你的工作真辛苦。

27. 真正     zhēnzhèng     *adj.*     authentic
他想吃真正的中国饭。

## 专有名词 (Zhuānyǒu Míngcí) Proper Nouns

华盛顿特区     Huáshèngdùn Tèqū     Washington, D.C.

## 补充词汇 (Bǔchōng Cíhuì) Supplementary Vocabulary

1. 飞行员     fēixíngyuán     *n.*     pilot

2. 海关     hǎiguān     *n.*     customs (at a national border)

3. 免税     miǎnshuì     *adj.*     duty-free

4. 耳机     ěrjī     *n.*     headphones

5. 降落     jiàngluò     *v.*     to land, to descend

6. 出境     chū jìng     *v.*     to leave a country

7. 救生衣     jiùshēngyī     *n.*     life jacket

## 口头用语 (Kǒutóu Yòngyǔ) Spoken Expressions

1. 吃力　　　　　　　　　　chīlì

difficult; (lit.) to eat energy, to be energy-consuming (used to describe something that is very difficult to do physically or mentally)

2. 你怎么了？　　　　　Nǐ zěnme le?

What's wrong with you?

## 词汇注解 (Cíhuì Zhùjiě) Featured Vocabulary

### 1. 一次 (Yī Cì) vs. 第一次 (Dì Yī Cì)

| 一次 | (Yī Cì) | Number + Measure Word | one time, once |
|------|---------|-----------------------|----------------|

一次 is a measure complement and is placed after the verb to indicate the number of times an action has been carried out. For example:

> 他去了一次中国。　　　　He went to China once.

| 第一次 | (Dì Yī Cì) | Ordinal Number + Measure Word | the first time |
|--------|------------|-------------------------------|----------------|

第一次 is placed BEFORE a verb to tell the order of events or actions. For example:

> 这是我第一次去中国。　This is my first time going to China.
> 这是他第三次去日本。　This is his third time going to Japan.

### 2. 提供 (Tígōng)

| 提供 | (Tígōng) | *v.* | to provide |
|------|----------|------|------------|

This verb is frequently used in the pattern "给/为 Somebody 提供 Something," which means "to provide somebody with something." For example:

> 给大家提供帮助　　　　　to provide everyone with assistance

### 3. 好 (Hǎo)

**a.  好 as an Adjective**

> 这本书很好。　　　This book is very good.
> 他最近很好。　　　His health is very good.
> 好吧。我们走吧。　Okay. Let's go.

**b.  好 + Verb to Form Adjectives**

Here it can be translated as "good/easy (to do)."

> 好看 good to look at　　好吃 good to eat　　好听 good to listen to

**c.  好 as an Adverb**

In this case, 好 functions as an intensifier for verbs or adjectives—similar to 很, but more colloquial.

### 1) *Modifying an Adjective*

For example:

| 好多 | 好大 | 好快 | 好慢 |
|------|------|------|------|
| a lot | very big | very fast | very slow |

### 2) *Modifying a Verb*

好 is frequently doubled up to intensify verbs in the pattern "好好 + Verb." For example:

| 我得好好谢谢你。 | I need to find a special way to thank you. |
|------|------|
| 你好好吃饭。 | Concentrate on eating. |
| 他应该好好读书。 | He should work hard on his studies. |

### 3) *Modifying 多/几*

| 好多年 | 好多天 | 好多遍/次 |
|------|------|------|
| 好几年 | 好几天 | 好几遍/次 |
| so many years | so many days | so many times |

### 4) *Modifying Time Phrases*

| 好一会儿 | 好长时间 |
|------|------|
| quite a while | a long time |

## 4. 通 *(Tōng)*

| 通 | (Tōng) | *v.* | to go through, to connect (via a certain means of communication) |
|------|------|------|------|

As "to connect," 通 can be used with many means of communication.

跟 Someone 通信: to communicate with someone via letter

跟 Someone 通电话: to communicate with someone via telephone

As "to go through," 通 is often used in the following context:

电话不通了。   The line is not going through.

# 语法(Yǔfǎ)
# Grammar

## I. Time-duration Words

The time-duration words are noun phrases that indicate the duration of an action or a state. Unlike time words, which should be placed before the verb (Lesson 15), time-duration words are placed after the verb.

| Questions containing duration phrases | Responses |
|------|------|
| 1. 多少年/几年？ | 半年，一年，一年半，两年，两年半··· |
| (Duōshao nián / Jǐ nián?) | (half a year, one year, one and a half years, two years, two |
| How many years? | and a half years...) |

| Questions containing duration phrases | Responses |
|---|---|

2. 多少个月/几个月？
(Duōshao gè yuè / Jǐ gè yuè?)
How many months?

半个月，一个月，一个半月，两个月，两个半月…
(half a month, one month, one and a half months, two months, two and a half months…)

3. 多少星期/几个星期？
(Duōshao xīngqī / Jǐgè xīngqī?)
How many weeks?

半个星期，一个星期，一个半星期，两个星期，两个半星期…
(half a week, one week, one and a half weeks, two weeks, two and a half weeks…)

4. 多少天/几天？
(Duōshao tiān / Jǐ tiān?)
How many days?

半天，一天，一天半，两天，两天半…
(half a day, one day, one and a half days, two days, two and a half days…)

5. 多少小时/几个小时？
(Duōshao xiǎoshí / Jǐgè xiǎoshí?)
How many hours?

半个小时，一个小时，一个半小时，两个小时，两个半小时…
(half an hour, one hour, one and a half hours, two hours, two and a half hours…)

6. 多少分钟/几分钟？
(Duōshao fēnzhōng / Jǐ fēnzhōng?)
How many minutes?

一分钟，两分钟，三分钟，四分钟，五分钟，十几分钟…
(one minute, two minutes, three minutes, four minutes, five minutes, more than ten minutes…)

7. 多长时间/多久？
(Duō cháng shíjiān / Duō jiǔ?)
How long?

Responses include any of those phrases listed above.

## Notes

1. 年 and 天, unlike the nouns 月, 星期, etc., are measure words themselves, so they can follow numbers or question words like 几 or 多少 directly. No other measure words are necessary. For example:

   CORRECT: 一年 (one year), 一天 (one day), 几年？ (How many years?)
   xxx INCORRECT: 一个年, 一个天, 几个年 xxx

2. When 半, which means "half," is used by itself without any numbers, it is placed before the measure words. For example:

   半年 half a year, 半个月 half a month, 半个星期 half a week, 半天 half a day.
   xxx INCORRECT: 一半年 xxx

   When 半 is used with numbers, its pattern is "Number + M.W. + 半" and it means "# and a half." For example:

   两年半        two and a half years
   一个半月      one and a half months

一个半星期    one and a half weeks
两天半    two and a half days

When 半 is used with 天, it means "a half day." 半天 can also be used figuratively to mean "a long period of time." For example:

你读了半天书了，该休息一下了。
You've read for a long time; you should take a break now.

3. Both 多久 and 多长时间 carry the meaning of "how long," but 多久 is more colloquial than 多长时间.

An action verb can take a time-duration word in any of the following time frames: 1) habitual or future events; 2) past events; or 3) actions/events continuing into the present. Time-duration words occur in various structures depending on whether or not the verb has an object. The negative form is rarely used.

## A. Without an Object

When there is no object, the time-duration phrase is placed directly after the verb. For example:

Habitual:    你每天休息多长时间？
    For how long each day do you usually take breaks?

    我每天休息半小时。
    I take a thirty-minute break every day.

Past:    我昨天休息了半小时。
    I took a thirty-minute break yesterday.

Continuing:    我已经休息了半小时了。
    I have taken a thirty-minute break already.

## Note
The first 了 is "Verb 了" indicating the action of 休息 is completed. The second 了 is "Sentence 了," and it refers to the present situation, indicating that that the action 休息 is still going on. This pattern is often used with 已经.

---

## PRACTICE

Now it's your turn! Try using action verbs such as 锻炼, 练习, 准备, 收拾, 走, 玩, and 住 to ask the person sitting next to you in class questions about his or her daily activities. Be sure to use all of the above grammatical structures when asking or responding to the questions. Example:

问：你每天睡几小时？
问：你昨天晚上睡了多长时间？
问：你睡了多长时间了？

## B. With an Object

When the verb takes an object, time-duration words can be used to modify either the verb or the object.

### 1. Modifying a Verb

If a time-duration word modifies a verb, it must be placed after the verb. If an object is in the way, you can either repeat the verb or move the object before the subject. See the examples below.

a. Repeating the Verb

Habitual:        我每天看书总是看半小时。
                 I always read for half an hour a day.

Past:            昨天看书看了半小时。
                 I read for half an hour yesterday.

Continuing:      我看书(已经)看了半小时了。
                 I have been reading for half an hour.

---

## 🔳 PRACTICE

Try using action verbs such as 看电视,买东西,听音乐,做饭,洗澡,坐飞机, and 打电话 to ask the person sitting next to you in class questions about his or her daily activities. Be sure to use all of the above grammatical structures when asking or responding to the questions. Example:

问：你每天晚上读报读多长时间？

问：你昨天晚上读报读了多长时间？

问：你读报读了多长时间了？

Note: Adverbs such as 总是 and 常常 are generally placed before the repeated verb.

b. Placing the Object before the Subject

When the object is a definite noun and has modifiers, it is usually placed at the beginning of the sentence.

Habitual:        中文书我每天总是看三个半小时。
                 I always read Chinese books for half an hour a day.

Past:            中文书我昨天看了半小时。
                 I read the Chinese book for half an hour yesterday.

Continuing:      中文书我已经看了半小时了。
                 I have read that Chinese book for half an hour.

## 🔲 PRACTICE

Let's try using action verbs such as 看电视新闻,买需要吃的东西,听这个好听的音乐, and 做晚饭 to ask the person sitting next to you in class questions about his or her daily activities. Be sure to use all of the above grammatical structures when asking or responding to the questions. For example:

问：中文报你每天晚上读多久？

问：中文报你昨天读了多长时间？

问：中文报你读了多长时间了？

### 2. Modifying an Object

When the objects are short and simple nouns, time-duration words can be used directly to modify the objects, but they cannot be used to modify an object that is a personal pronoun. In this structure, verbs are not repeated.

| | | |
|---|---|---|
| Habitual: | 我每天总是看半小时的书。 | |
| | I always read for half an hour every day. | |
| Past: | 我昨天看了半小时的书。 | |
| | I read for half an hour yesterday. | |
| Continuing: | 我已经看了半小时的书了。 | |
| | I have already been reading for half an hour. | |

## Note

If the object is a personal pronoun, repeat the verb. For example:

我等他等了一个小时。

xxx INCORRECT: 我等了一个小时的他。 xxx

## 🔲 PRACTICE

Try using action verbs such as 看电视,买东西,听音乐,做饭,洗澡,填表, and 打电话 to ask the person sitting next to you in class questions about his or her daily activities. Be sure to use all of the above grammatical structures when asking or responding to the questions. For example:

问：你每天晚上读多长时间的报？

问：你昨天读了几小时的报？

问：你读了几小时的报了？

# II. Comparing 就 (Jiù) with 才 (Cái)

In Lesson 20, you learned that the adverb 就 can be placed before the main verb and after "time," "amount," or "number," to indicate that an action takes place earlier than expected (in this case, 了 is usually placed at the end of the sentence). In this lesson, you will learn more about the adverb 才, which can be placed before the main verb and after a time, an amount, or a number to indicate that an action took place later than expected. We will now compare and contrast 就 and 才. See the examples below.

## A. Simple Sentences

Simple sentences contain two components: subjects and predicates. The following are examples of how to use 就 and 才 in simple sentences.

我五点就到了。 I was here early, at five o'clock.

(The speaker managed to get there earlier than expected.)

我五点才到。 I did not get here until five o'clock.

(The speaker expected to arrive earlier than five o'clock.)

## *Note*

A definite object can be placed at the beginning of the sentence. For example:

这本书我一天就看完了。 I finished reading this book in just one day.

这本书我一个月才看完。 After spending the entire month on it, I finally finished reading this book.

## B. Complex Sentences

Complex sentences are composed of more than one clause; one of them is the main clause and others are dependent clauses, which cannot stand alone. These simple clauses in a complex sentence are connected by a conjunction to indicate the relationship between them. The complex sentences can have one or more subjects. In the case of 就/才, they can be used in conjunction with dependent clauses and are always placed after the second subject.

One Subject:

飞机再飞两个小时，就到北京了。

The plane will arrive in Beijing in two hours.

(This indicates that the plane will arrive earlier than expected.)

飞机还要再飞两个小时，才到北京。

The plane has to fly another two hours before it reaches Beijing.

(It will be another two hours before the plane reaches Beijing.)

Two Subjects:

老师讲了一遍，学生就懂了。

The teacher only had to explain it once, and thestudents immediately understood.

老师讲了很多遍，学生才懂。

Only after the teacher explained it many times did the students finally understand.

## *Note*

就 and 才 should be placed directly after the subject.

CORRECT: 老师讲了一遍，学生就懂了。

xxx INCORRECT: 老师讲了一遍，就学生懂了。 xxx

## ❀ PRACTICE

Use 什么时候, 几点, 多长时间, 多久, and 多少次/遍 to ask questions, and then use 就 and 才 to provide answers. For example:

                                          **Hints**

问：我们还有多久到达北京？     答：（十分钟/两个小时）

问：他几点起床？              答：（六点/十二点）

问：你们用多长时间完成任务？   答：（一，两天/四，五个月）

问：我什么时候会看中文报？     答：（学一年中文/学十年中文）

问：你什么时候跟他谈对象？     答：（做了一个星期的朋友/做了一年的朋友）

问：你怎么认识这个字？         答：（查了一遍词典/查了好几遍）

问：你跟老师面试，预约了几次？  答：（一次/好几次）

## III. Indicating Approximate Numbers

There are several different ways to indicate approximate numbers in Chinese. In this section, we are going to cover the following three basic ways.

### A. Use Two Adjacent Numbers

Two adjacent numbers can often be used to indicate approximate numbers. However, there are certain rules to follow.

1. Numbers between 1 and 9

   一、两位老师        one to two teachers
   两、三张报纸        two to three pages of the newspaper

## *Note*

The number 十 by itself usually does not work with adjacent numbers to form approximate numbers.

   xxx INCORRECT: 九、十位老师 xxx
   xxx INCORRECT: 十、十一位老师 xxx

2. Numbers between 11 and 99

   十一、二本书       approximately a dozen books
   十七、八个学生      seventeen to eighteen students
   二十一、二条裤子    twenty-one to twenty-two pairs of trousers

## *Note*

Do not repeat the number 十. It is incorrect to say "十一、十二本书" or "二十一、二十二本书."

3. Tens

   二、三十顶帽子      approximately twenty to thirty hats
   三、四十张桌子      approximately thirty to forty tables

## *Note*

Do not repeat the number 十. It is incorrect to say "二十、三十顶帽子" or "三十、四十张桌子."

## B. Use 多 (Duō)

When 多 is used to indicate an approximate number, it always means "more than." 多 can take either one of the following two structures, depending on whether the number is greater or less than ten.

1. When the number is less than ten, place 多 after the measure word.

三个多小时    more than three hours (but fewer than four)
九个多月    more than nine months (but fewer than ten)

2. When the number is more than ten, place 多 before the measure word.

These multiples include 十, 百, 千 (qiān, thousand), and 万 (wàn, ten thousand). Please see the examples below.

十多年    more than ten years
三十多个小时  more than thirty hours
一百多本书    more than one hundred books (but fewer than two hundred)

---

## 🈶 PRACTICE

Use 多 to translate the following phrases into Chinese.

| | | |
|---|---|---|
| more than ten weeks | more than twenty years | more than one hundred days |
| more than five months | more than thirty hats | more than forty suits |

## C. Use 几 (Jǐ)

When 几 is used to indicate an approximate number, it means "several." Below are a few examples of how 几 can be used in a sentence.

1. When the number is less than ten, place 几 before the measure word(s).

几天    a few days
几年    a few years
几本书    a few books
几小时    a few hours

2. When the number is a multiple of ten (twenty, thirty, forty, etc.), place 几 between the number 十 itself and the measure word(s).

十几天    more than ten days
三十几本书    more than thirty books
二十几个小时  more than twenty hours

However, if the number focuses on ten itself (or twenty, thirty, forty, etc.) 几 is placed before ten. For example:

几十年    (lit.) "several ten years," indicating a range from more than ten years to less than one hundred years

## *Note*

This structure cannot be used with a number that's not a multiple of ten.

    xxx INCORRECT: 二几个, 三几本 xxx

3. When the number is a multiple of 100 (200, 300, etc.), place 几 before 百, 千, 万, etc.

| | |
|---|---|
| 几百本书 | several hundred books |
| 几千个学生 | several thousand students |

4. When the number contains 零, the approximate number is between 100 and 109; use 零 and 几.

| | |
|---|---|
| 一百零几个人 | (lit.) one hundred and a few people |
| 两百零几本书 | (lit.) one hundred and a few books |

---

## 🔲 PRACTICE

Use 几 to translate the following phrases into Chinese.

| | |
|---|---|
| more than thirty magazines | a few weeks |
| more than twenty nurses | a few years |
| more than forty tables | a few days |
| more than one hundred chairs | a few months |

*In the baggage claim area at Beijing International Airport.*

# Textbook Exercises

## 🎧💻 TASK 1. 课文问答 (KÈWÉN WÈNDÁ) QUESTIONS AND ANSWERS

How well did you understand the text? Check your comprehension by answering the following questions.

1. 李丽莉和吴文德填入境申报表填了多长时间？他们觉得填入境申报表容易不容易？为什么？

2. 李丽莉和吴文德坐飞机坐了多久？在飞机上他们都做了些什么事？

3. 吴文德到了北京以后，最想做的第一件事是什么？为什么？

4. 去机场接李丽莉和吴文德的人是谁？李丽莉和吴文德认识不认识这个来机场接他们的人？为什么？

## 💻 TASK 2. 语法练习 (YǓFǍ LIÀNXÍ) GRAMMATICAL STRUCTURE PRACTICE

### A. Sentence Completion

Use the time-duration word structure and approximate numbers to complete the following sentences.

1. 昨天下午我在音乐大厅门口等我朋友 _____。

2. 吃了早饭以后，我爸爸常常 _____ 的报纸。

3. 我学唱中国歌 _____，可是还是唱得不好听。

4. 那本小说他已经 _____。

5. 这位老师来美国教书 _____。

6. 我妈妈每天晚上十一点睡觉，早上七点起床。她每天 _____。

7. 赵老师九点到飞机场接朋友，现在十点多了，他的朋友还没到。赵老师已经等 _____。

8. 小张去年去了英国，明年回来，他要在英国 _____。

9. 赵老师昨天去北京，飞机上午六点多起飞，晚上八点钟到，他坐 _____。

10. 他从一九八九年就开始学，现在他还在学。他已经 _____。

## B. Pick and Choose

In each of the following pairs there is a correct sentence and an incorrect one. Can you tell which one is correct and explain why the other one is incorrect?

1.

a) 我在这儿等朋友已经等了两个小时了，他还没来。

b) 已经上课了，老师还没来，学生等了一刻钟的他。

2.

a) 大文昨天晚上听音乐听了三个多小时了。

b) 大文今天办入关手续办了一个小时了。

3.

a) 他在这儿坐了一分钟他的朋友才到了。

b) 我跳舞跳了几个小时才累。

4.

a) 这个学校东亚系有几千个学生。

b) 这儿有一百个多中国老师。

5.

a) 他学唱歌没有学几天。

b) 小李学中文没学两个年。

---

## 💻 TASK 3. 翻译 (FĀNYÌ) PARAPHRASING

How well do you remember the grammar and vocabulary we've covered so far? Check yourself by translating the following sentences into Chinese.

1. A: How long does it take you to go through the customs? (Hint: 入境手续, 多久)

   B: It takes about two or three hours. (Hint: Approximate Number, Verb + Time-duration) This is our first time coming to China. (Hint: 次) The customs personnel are very conscientious. (Hint: 可···了) Every piece of luggage has to be thoroughly inspected, which is why it takes so long. (Hint: 遍)

2. A: How long is the flight from Beijing to Shanghai? (Hint: 飞, 多长时间)

   B: It will take more than two hours. (Hint: 要 + Verb + Time-duration, 多) I heard that we might be delayed for at least twenty minutes today, (Hint: 不过,几) but the airplane is already descending. (Hint: 已经) We should get off the plane in twenty to thirty minutes. (Hint: 再 + 过 + Time-duration [approximate number + time words], 就)

3. A: We only have two more hours left before our flight arrives in Beijing (Hint: Verb + Time-duration, 多,就). I'm so excited! (Hint: Exclamatory Sentence)

   B: What? We still have to fly two more hours before we get to Beijing? I can't wait! (Hint: Verb + Time-duration, 才,急 + Exclamatory Sentence)

4. I've been sitting in the airplane for over twenty hours and haven't eaten a thing. (Hint: Verb + Time duration, 几) I'm starving! (Hint: Exclamatory Sentence) After I pick up my luggage, I'm going to go eat immediately. (Hint: 就) I've been thinking about eating authentic Chinese food for more than twenty years, and the opportunity is now here! (Hint: 多, Verb + Object + Time-duration, 才)

5. I have studied Chinese for many years, (Hint: Verb + Time-duration, 好几) and the year before last, I lived in China for a little over a year. (Hint: 前年, Verb + Time-duration + Object, 多) However, when I visited China this time, I had a lot of difficulties filling out the entry card and declaration form for customs. (Hint: 这次) It took me two hours, and I had to fill them out three times! (Hint: Verb + Time-duration, 遍, 才)

*A boarding gate at Beijing International Airport.*

## TASK 4. 情景对话 (QÍNGJǏNG DUÌHUÀ) SITUATIONAL DIALOGUE

**Setting:**      On an airplane

**Cast:**         Two passengers

**Situation:**    One passenger starts to talk with another passenger, who politely engages in the conversation. Construct a dialogue between the two people. Make sure to discuss the flight origin, destination, and duration. Why are these passengers on this flight? Are they visiting family in another country? Going on vacation? On a business trip?

# 25
# 体检
# Getting a Physical Examination

**In this lesson you will:**

- Speak to someone about getting a physical exam or seeing a doctor in China.
- Discuss your health with someone.
- Stay healthy in the same way that people in China typically try to stay healthy.
- Talk about experiences.

很多中国的大学都有自己的医务所。学校的医务所给学生体检，还做简单的治疗。吴文德到学校已经快一个星期了。但是，他总是觉得不舒服，也没精神。学校让新生体检。吴文德因为学习很忙，没有时间去。但是，这几天，他觉得他还是应该去学校的医务所检查一下儿。所以，他给陈小云打了个电话，请她帮帮忙。

（吴文德在给陈小云打电话。）

吴文德：　喂，陈小云，你去过学校的医务所吗？

陈小云：　去过一次，我去那儿做过体检，但是，已经半年多没去了。你有事吗？

吴文德：　我总是觉得没精神，想去医务所检查一下儿。但是不知道医务所在哪儿？

陈小云：　你人生地不熟的[1]，我带你去吧。我明天早上十点下课。下了课五分钟以后，我们在图书馆见面。我们从那儿去医务所，好不好？

吴文德：　太好了。谢谢。明天见。

（在学校医务所）

陈小云：　这就是学校的医务所。学校让新生体检，你做过体检了吗？

吴文德：还没有。前几天很忙，没有时间。

陈小云：先到左边的窗口拿一张体检表。填你的姓名、年龄、性别、国籍……

吴文德：这么长的表格，这么多问题，还要填地址、电话，你以前得过什么病……我最不喜欢填表了。

陈小云：快填吧。别叨叨了。填过表以后，坐在这儿等医生叫你的名字。

……

医　生：吴文德，你好。你刚才量过身高，称过体重了吗？

吴文德：都做过了。这是我的体检表。

医　生：你最近检查过身体吗？

吴文德：来中国以前，我检查过一次，身体很健康。

医　生：你是什么时候离开美国的？

吴文德：我离开美国已经一个多星期了。

医　生：你哪儿不舒服？

吴文德：我这几天头疼，胃疼，不想吃饭，也没有精神。我是不是感冒了？

医　生：来，我给你检查一下儿。你不发烧，心脏、血压也都很正常……我看你这是时差的问题。你刚来中国，还没有习惯，你要多喝水，注意锻炼身体。过一、两个星期就好了。不需要治疗。

吴文德：谢谢。

……

陈小云：怎么样？有什么病吗？医生给你开药方了吗？

吴文德：没有，一切正常。医生说是时差的问题，过几天就好了。

陈小云：现在天气这么热，你应该注意身体，没病应该预防，你吃过姜吗？

吴文德：没吃过，为什么要吃姜？

陈小云：中国有句老话，"冬吃萝卜，夏吃姜，不劳医生开药方[2]"。

吴文德：你吃过姜吗？

陈小云：没吃过，但是我喝过用姜沏的茶，想不想到我家去尝一杯？

吴文德：我还是去锻炼锻炼身体吧。

## Notes

1. 人生地不熟   (Rén shēng dì bù shú.)

Literally, "(One finds) the people (in a particular place) all strangers and the land unfamiliar." This phrase describes someone who finds himself completely new to a place, a stranger in a strange land.

2. 冬吃萝卜，夏吃姜，不劳医生开药方。

(Dōng chī luóbo, xià chī jiāng, bù láo yīshēng kāi yàofāng.)

There is an old saying in China, "If you eat radishes in the winter and ginger in the summer, you don't have to bother a doctor to give you a prescription." It is a piece of folk wisdom that says eating radishes and ginger can keep you healthy.

*A university clinic at Xi'an Science and Technology University.*

## Cultural Note

Chinese people believe that sometimes the right foods can be more useful than medicine in resolving health problems. Certain foods can help to maintain proper balance in the human body, and food is commonly divided into two categories:

I. Food that is "cooling in nature" (凉性 liángxing); e.g., watermelon, green beans, and green tea.

II. Food that is "warming or heating in nature" (热性 rèxing); e.g., ginger, green onions, and black tea.

If your diet includes too much of either "cooling" or "warming" food, your body will suffer from the imbalance, and you may get sick. Traditional Chinese medicine believes that a diet, when properly guided by medicinal principles, could alleviate or even cure many chronic diseases and conditions. Most importantly, traditional Chinese medicine advocates the belief that one can prevent diseases by maintaining balance in diet and lifestyle.

# 生词表 (Shēngcí Biǎo)
# Vocabulary

| Character | Pinyin | Part of Speech | English Definition |
|---|---|---|---|
| 1. 体检 | tǐjiǎn | *n.* | physical examination |
| 你每年都去做体检吗？ | | | |
| 2. 医务所 | yīwùsuǒ | *n.* | clinic |
| 请问，医务所在哪儿？ | | | |
| 医务 | | *n.* | medical service |
| 所 | | *suff.* | institute, office |
| 3. 治疗 | zhìliáo | *n.* | medical treatment |
| 你的病需要一个星期的治疗。 | | | |
| | | *v.* | to treat (a disease), to cure |
| 你在我们医院治疗一下儿吧。 | | | |
| 治 | | *v.* | to regulate, to put in order |
| 疗 | | *b.f.* | to heal, to cure |
| 4. 舒服 | shūfu | *adj.* | comfortable |
| 我今天有一点不舒服。 | | | |
| 5. 精神 | jīngshen | *n.* | energy, vigor, spirit |
| 你今天怎么没有精神？ | | | |
| 6. 新生 | xīnshēng | *n.* | freshman |
| 你是不是新生？ | | | |
| 7. 年龄 | niánlíng | *n.* | age |
| 他年龄多大？ | | | |
| 8. 性别 | xìngbié | *n.* | gender |
| 不要忘了在这儿填你的性别。 | | | |
| 9. 病 | bìng | *n.* | sickness, disease, illness |
| 医生说我没有病。 | | | |
| | | *v.* | to get sick, to have a disease |
| 他今天病了。 | | | |
| 10. 最 | zuì | *pref.* | (a superlative prefix used before adjectives) "the most" |
| 他是这儿最好的医生。 | | | |

11. 量　　liáng　　*v.*　　to measure
你量一下儿桌子有多高？

12. 身高　　shēngāo　　*n.*　　(lit.) the body height (of a person)
请在这儿量一量你的身高。
　　高　　　　*adj.*　　high
　　　　　　*n.*　　height

13. 称　　chēng　　*v.*　　to weigh
你称一下儿那些水果。

14. 体重　　tǐzhòng　　*n.*　　body weight
请在那边称一称体重。
　　重　　　　*adj.*　　heavy

15. 健康　　jiànkāng　　*n.*　　health
你每天这么工作？还要不要你的健康？
　　　　　　*adj.*　　healthy
他现在身体很健康。

16. 头疼　　tóuténg　　*n. phr.*　　headache
我昨天头疼，不能来上课。
　　头　　　　*n.*　　head
　　疼　　　　*n.*　　ache, pain
　　　　　　*v.*　　to hurt

17. 胃　　wèi　　*n.*　　stomach
我现在胃不舒服。

18. 感冒　　gǎnmào　　*v.*　　to catch a cold
医生说我感冒了。
　　　　　　*n.*　　cold
我今天有一点感冒。

19. 发烧　　fāshāo　　*v. obj.*　　to develop a fever
你现在发烧吗？

20. 心脏　　xīnzàng　　*n.*　　the heart
他心脏没有问题。
　　脏　　　　*n.*　　internal organs

21. 血压　　xuèyā　　*n.*　　blood pressure
他今天血压怎么样？
　　血　　　　*n.*　　blood

| 压 | | v. | to hold down, to press |
|---|---|---|---|
| | | n. | pressure |

22. 正常    zhèngcháng    *adj.*    normal
我这两天血压不正常。

23. 时差    shíchā    *n.*    jet lag
我现在还有一点儿时差。

24. 习惯    xíguàn    *v.*    to be accustomed to, to be used to
你哥哥在北京现在习惯不习惯？

                                     *n.*    habit, custom
吸烟不是个好习惯。

25. 开药方    kāi yàofāng    *v. obj.*    to write out a prescription
你看，这是那个医生今天给我开的药方。
    药方                              *n.*    prescription

26. 天气    tiānqì    *n.*    weather
北京现在天气怎么样？
    天                                *n.*    sky, heaven
    气                                *n.*    air, atmosphere, climate

27. 热    rè    *adj.*    (of temperature) hot
现在天气还不太热。

28. 预防    yùfáng    *v.*    to take preventive measures
医生常常跟我说应该预防感冒。

                                       *n.*    prevention
我们学校的预防工作做得很好。
    预                                *b.f.*    beforehand, in advance
    防                                *v.*    to guard against, to take precautions against

29. 沏    qī    *v.*    to steep, to infuse (tea)
请帮我沏一杯茶，谢谢。

## 补充词汇 (Bǔchōng Cíhuì) Supplementary Vocabulary

1. 医院    yīyuàn    *n.*    hospital

2. 药房    yàofáng    *n.*    pharmacy

3. 急诊室    jízhěnshì    *n.*    emergency room

| | | | |
|---|---|---|---|
| 4. 验血 | yàn xiě | *v. obj.* | to do a blood test |
| 5. 验尿 | yàn niào | *v. obj.* | urine test |
| 6. 心电图 | xīndiàntú | *n.* | EKG |
| 7. 透视 | tòushì | *n.* | X Ray |
| 8. 食欲 | shíyù | *n.* | appetite; (lit.) food desire |
| 9. 食物中毒 | shíwù zhòngdú | *n.* | food poisoning |
| 10. 流感 | liúgǎn | *n.* | flu |

*Entrance to the emergency room at a university clinic.*

## 口头用语 (Kǒutóu Yòngyǔ) Spoken Expressions

| | | |
|---|---|---|
| 叨叨 | dāodao | to nag |
| 我看… | wǒkàn… | I think…<br>(to express someone's opinion) |

## 词汇注解 (Cíhuì Zhùjiě) Featured Vocabulary

### 1. 病 (Bìng)

病    *n.*        illness, sickness, disease

The following are a few common ways of using 病:

| 有病 | yǒu bìng | to have a chronic illness or condition |
|---|---|---|

他现在有病，不能来上课。

| 得病 | débìng | to catch/get a disease or illness |
|---|---|---|

Both 得 and 有 can be followed with specific types of illness.

| 他得什么病了？ | What kind of illness did he get? |
|---|---|
| 他得心脏病了。 | He has got heart disease now. |
| 他有心脏病。 | He has heart disease. |

| 生病 | shēngbìng | to become sick, to fall ill |
|---|---|---|

他生病了。

生病 CANNOT be used with a specific illness.

   xxx INCORRECT: 他生心脏病了。 xxx

| 看病 | kànbìng | (of the patient) to go to see a doctor (to have the illness examined) (of the doctor) to see a patient (about his/her illness), used in the pattern "给 Somebody 看病." |
|---|---|---|

我不舒服，得去医院看病。

I am not feeling well, (have to) go to the hospital to have (my) illness examined.

那个医生正在给我妈妈看病。

This doctor is presently examining my mother('s disease).

| 病了 | bìng le | to become ill |
|---|---|---|

This is similar to 生病，but sounds slightly more informal.

## 2. 前几天 (Qián Jǐ Tiān) vs. 几天 (以) 前 (Jǐ Tiān [Yǐ] Qián)

| 前几天 | *phr.* | the past few days |
|---|---|---|
| 几天 (以) 前 | *phr.* | a few days ago |

For example:

| 前几天我很忙。 | Over the past few days I have been very busy. |
|---|---|
| 我几天前去北京了。 | I went to Beijing a few days ago. |

## 3. ···就 + 好/行/可以 + 了 (Jiù + Hǎo/Xíng/Kěyǐ + 了)

| ···就 + 好/行/可以 + 了 | *phr.* | then (it) will/would be all right |
|---|---|---|

This pattern is a truncated version of the conditional sentence "as long as...then (it) would/will be all right."
For example:

| (老师来了) 就好了。 | As long as the teacher comes, it will be all right. |
|---|---|
| (买一本) 就行了。 | As long as you buy a copy, it will be okay. |
| (你去) 就可以了。 | As long as you go, it will be okay. |

In this lesson, 过一个星期就好了 can be translated as, "After a week, all the symptoms will be gone, and you will be okay."

# 语法(Yǔfǎ)
# Grammar

## I. Using 过 (Guò) to Talk about Past Experience

In Lesson 16 you learned the verb 过, which indicates the passing of time. For example:

你准备怎么过你的生日？     How do you want to spend time on your birthday?

时间过得真快啊！     Time is passing so quickly! (Time flies!)

In this lesson, you are going to use 过 not as a verb but as a particle placed after the verb to indicate that an experience did indeed take place in the past. This structure is used with action verbs and not with non-action verbs. See the examples below.

### A. Structure

|  | Subject | | Verb | Aspect | Object | |
|---|---|---|---|---|---|---|
| Positive: | 我 | 以前 | 检查 | 过 | 心脏。 | |
| | I have had my heart checked before. | | | | | |
| Negative: | 我 | 以前 | 没(有)检查 | 过 | 心脏。 | |
| | I have not had my heart checked before. | | | | | |
| | 我 | 还没 | 检查 | 过 | 心脏 | 呢。 |
| | I have not yet had my heart checked. | | | | | |
| Questions: | 你 | 以前 | 检查 | 过 | 心脏 | 吗？ |
| | Have you had your heart checked before? | | | | | |
| | 你 | 以前 | 检查 | 过 | 心脏 | 没有？ |
| | Have you had your heart checked before or not? | | | | | |
| | 你 | 以前 | 检查没检查 | 过 | 心脏？ | |
| | Have you had your heart checked before or not? | | | | | |

## Notes

1. Either 吗 or 没有 can be added to the end of a sentence to form a question.

2. The affirmative-negative question pattern is "Verb + 没 + Verb + 过."

3. In the negative form, 过 MUST remain in the sentence. 没有 and 没 are placed before the verb to negate the sentence, giving the meaning of "have not done something." The sentence's structure should be, "没(有) + Verb + 过 + Object." In addition, "还…呢" may be inserted in the negative sentence for emphasis. It means "not yet."

4. In a sentence with two verbs or two verb phrases in a series, 过 is usually placed after the second verb, as in 我去中国学过中文.

5. Non-action verbs such as 知道, 在, and 是 cannot be used in the 过 structure.
   CORRECT:                    我当过老师。 I have been a teacher before.
   xxx INCORRECT:              我是过老师。 xxx
   CORRECT:                    我去过中国。 I have been to China before.
   xxx INCORRECT:              我在过中国。 xxx

## B. Comparing 过 with 了

Both 了 and 过 can be used alone to indicate that an action has taken place in the past. However, each of them has a different focus in meaning and a different negative form.

### 1. Differences in Meaning

了 indicates that a specific action took place, whereas 过 indicates that an event has been experienced at least once in the past. For example:

了:昨天你们看了那个中国电影没有？

Did you see that Chinese movie yesterday?

(Emphasis is on having watched one specific movie.)

过:去年你们看过中国电影没有？

Did you get a chance to see any Chinese movies last year?

(Emphasis is on the experience of seeing any movie at any time last year.)

## Notes

1. 过 and 了 can also be used in the same sentence, as in 我吃过饭了, "I have already eaten."

2. When 过 and 了 are placed before "Number + 次/遍," there is no significant difference between them. For example:

他去年买的这本书我读过三遍。 = 他去年买的这本书我读了三遍。

I read the book he bought for me last year three times.

### 2. Differences in Negative Forms

Although both 了 and 过 use 没(有) in their negative forms, the 了 MUST be dropped in the negative sentence, and 过 MUST remain in the negative sentence. See the examples below.

了: 昨天我们没(有)看那个中国电影。

We did not see that Chinese movie last night.

过: 去年我们没看过中国电影。

We did not see Chinese movies last year.

他们今年还没在这儿看过电影呢。

They have not seen a movie here yet this year.

## 🎴 PRACTICE

Form pairs and talk about your past experiences by asking and responding (positively or negatively) to each other's questions. For example:

问：你最近得过病吗？（感冒, 发烧, 吃药, 看病）

问：你去过中国没有？（吃中国饭, 看中国电影, 写中文信, 用手机）

问：你今天都做过什么事了？（做作业, 沏姜茶, 填体检表, 量身高）

问：你开过几年的车？（用中文软件, 搞电脑, 教书, 学外语）

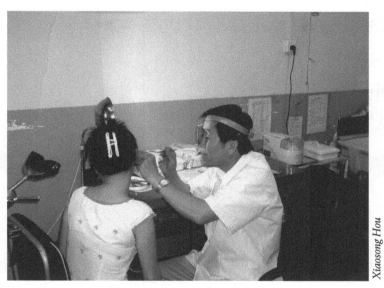

*Getting a physical.*

# II. Using 次/遍 (Cont'd.)

In Lesson 22, you learned how to use 次 and 遍 in a sentence without objects. In this lesson, we will focus on how to use them when a sentence contains "Verb ＋ 过/了" and an object. The structure varies depending on whether the object is a noun or a pronoun. See the examples below.

## A. Nouns as Objects

次：When the object is a noun, it can appear either before or after 次.

| Subject | Verb | Aspect | Number 次 | Object | (Number 次) |
|---------|------|--------|-----------|--------|-------------|
| 我 | 去 | 过/了 | 两次 | 中国。 | |
| I have been to China twice. | | | | | |
| 我 | 去 | 过/了 | | 中国 | 两次。 |
| I have been to China twice. | | | | | |

遍: When the object is a noun, it usually appears after 遍, not before.

| Subject | Verb | Aspect | Number 遍 | (Noun) Object |
|---------|------|--------|-----------|---------------|
| 我 | 听 | 过/了 | 一遍 | 录音。 |

I listened to the recording once (from the beginning to the end).

## 🔲 PRACTICE

Try using phrases such as 检查身体, 得感冒, 量血压, 读这本书, 坐飞机, 开生日晚会, 住宿舍, and 搬家 with the structures given below.

问: 你 Verb 过/了 Object 没有? Verb 过/了几次/遍?

答: 我 Verb 过/了几次/遍。

## B. Pronouns as Objects
When the object is a pronoun, it appears before 次/遍.

| Subject | Verb | Aspect | Pronoun Object | Number 次/遍 |
|---------|------|--------|----------------|--------------|
| 我 | 看 | 过 | 他 | 一次。 |

I have seen him once.

| Subject | Verb | Aspect | Pronoun Object | Number 次/遍 |
|---------|------|--------|----------------|--------------|
| 我 | 问 | 过 | 他 | 好几遍。 |

I have asked him many times.

## 🔲 PRACTICE

Try using the above structure to create some sentences of your own. Suggested phrases: 告诉他, 见她, 说他们, 教你, 请我们.

## C. Long Objects
If the object is too long or complicated, it can be moved before the subject for clarification.

| Long object | Subject | Verb | Number 次/遍 |
|-------------|---------|------|--------------|
| 他去年买的这本书 | 我 | 读过 | 三次/遍。 |

I read the book he bought for me last year three times.

## 🔲 PRACTICE

Try using the above structure to create some sentences of your own. Suggested phrases: 尝妈妈做的菜, 听老师讲的成语故事, 坐靠窗口的座位, 办去中国的签证.

# III. The Time-duration Words (Cont'd.)

As you learned in Lesson 24, the time-duration words functioning as time-measure complements indicate the duration of an action. In this lesson we will introduce two additional structures.

## A. Using the Time-duration Words with Non-continuative Actions

When a time-duration word is used with a verb representing a non-continuative action, it indicates a period of time has passed since the action occurred. Verbs that represent non-continuative actions, such as 来, 去, 到, 离开, 下课, 起飞, and 开始, are frequently used in a structure where the time-duration word is placed after its object and 了 is at the end of the sentence. For example:

| Subject | Verb | Object | Time-duration |
|---|---|---|---|
| 我 | 离开 | 美国 | 已经一个星期了。 |
| I left America a week ago. | | | |
| 我 | 下 | 课 | 十分钟了。 |
| I got out of class ten minutes ago. | | | |
| 他 | 去 | 中国 | 已经两个月了。 |
| It has been two months since he went to China. | | | |

---

## ❧ PRACTICE

Try using phrases such as 到医务所, 来美国, 下中文课, 去图书馆, and 起飞 to ask a question and then to provide an answer. For example:

问：他是什么时候离开家的？

答：他离开家已经一年多了。

## B. Special Negative Structure with Action Verbs

So far you have learned that a time-duration word is usually placed after the verb to indicate the duration of an action. However, you could also use the structure "Subject 有 + Time-duration + 没 + Action Verb + 了," to indicate that an action has not occurred for a given period of time. In this structure, the time-duration word is placed before the action verb. The non-action verb 有 is usually omitted. See the examples below.

| Subject | Time-duration | 没 | Action verb | (Object) 了 |
|---|---|---|---|---|
| 我们（有） | 好几天 | 没 | 见 | 了。 |
| We have not seen each other for several days. | | | | |
| 我（有） | 两年 | 没 | 做 | 体检 了。 |
| I have not had a physical for two years. | | | | |

## *Compare*

The "Subject（有）+ Time-duration + 没 + Action Verb + 了" structure you learned in this lesson is different from the "Subject + 没 + Action Verb + Time-duration" structure introduced in Lesson 24. For example:

我（有）两个小时没看电视了。

It has been two hours since I last watched TV.

(The speaker has not watched any TV for two hours.)

我没看两个小时的电视。

I did not watch TV for two hours.

(The speaker was watching TV but not two hours' worth. The speaker might have watched TV for only an hour.)

---

## 🔳 PRACTICE

Try using the time words to ask questions and then to provide negative answers. Follow the examples given below.

问：你多久/多长时间没喝茶了？

答：我好几个月没有喝了。

问：你去过几次中国饭馆？

答：两，三次。但是我已经有一年没吃中国菜了。

## IV. A Brief Introduction to the "是…的" Structure

The "是…的" structure emphasizes certain elements, such as time, place, manner, or purpose, related to a past action. Thus, it can only be used for an action that took place in the past. While 是 is placed before the word group that is emphasized, 的 frequently appears at the end of the sentence. In this lesson, you will learn how to use the "是…的" structure to emphasize time.

Regular Sentence：我们两个星期以前离开了美国。

We left America two weeks ago.

"是…的" Structure Emphasizing Time：你们是什么时候离开美国的？

When was it that you left America?

我们是两个星期以前离开美国的。

It was two weeks ago that we left America.

*Medicine pick-up window at a university clinic.*

 **Textbook Exercises**

 **TASK 1. 课文问答 (KÈWÉN WÈNDÁ) QUESTIONS AND ANSWERS**

How well did you understand the text? Check your comprehension by answering the following questions.

1. 吴文德找陈小云有什么事？

2. 吴文德以前填过体检表没有？他在体检表上都要填些什么？

3. 吴文德跟医生都说了一些什么？医生说吴文德的身体怎么样？为什么？

4. 小云觉得应该怎么预防病？

**TASK 2. 语法练习 (YǓFǍ LIÀNXÍ) GRAMMATICAL STRUCTURE PRACTICE**

### A. Scrambled Sentences

Add 过 to the words in each of the following groups to make complete sentences.

1. 检查　我　了　　身体　两次　已经　今年
2. 给我　早上　量　一次　今天　血压　医生
3. 看　病　去　你　没　吗　医务所？

4. 没得   得   几年前   心脏病   王老师？
5. 厉害   药   你   很   吃   病得   了没有？
6. 我在   还   工作   但是   没见   已经   三天了   张医生   医务所

## B. Fill in the Blanks

Use 了 or 过 where needed to fill in the blank spaces in the sentences below.

1. 那本小说我看 _____ 两遍 _____ 。

2. 他最近去看 _____ 病，量 _____ 血压吗？

3. 我去那个医务所体检 _____ 三次。

4. 我十几岁的时候，得 _____ 心脏病。

5. 我朋友离开 _____ 他家两年 _____ 。

6. 我好几年没吃 _____ 真正的中国菜 _____ 。

## C. Pick and Choose

In each of the following pairs there is a correct sentence and an incorrect one. Call you tell which one is correct and explain why the other one is incorrect?

1.
a) 我一个多月没称体重了。
b) 他没量身高一个星期了。

2.
a) 李丽莉不在这个医务所量过血压。
b) 吴文德没有在那个医务所检查过身体。

3.
a) 我朋友离开中国已经离开了半年了。
b) 他们下课已经一刻钟了。

4.
a) 他以前当过老师。
b) 在中国的时候，他是过医生。

5.
a) 我只见过他一次。
b) 去美国以前，我看过三次她。

---

## 📖 TASK 3. 翻译 (FĀNYÌ) PARAPHRASING

How well do you remember the grammar and vocabulary we've covered so far? Check yourself by translating the following sentences into Chinese.

1. A: Have you ever filled out the school's physical examination forms before? (Hint: Object, Verb + 过)

   B: Yes, I have filled them out twice. (Hint: Verb + 过 + #遍) The first time when I finished filling out the forms (Hint: #次, 填完), the doctor said that the forms were not filled out clearly and asked me to redo them. (Hint: 再···遍) The forms were too long. After filling in age, gender, and nationality, I still had to fill out my address, phone number, and information about what illnesses I had had before. (Hint: Verb + 过 + Object)

2. Before I came to China, I had a physical exam. (Hint: Verb + 过 + #次 + Object) Everything was all right (with me). Since I came to China, I haven't had a single physical. (Hint: 没有 Verb + 过 + Object) I should get another one in a few days. (Hint: 再, #次)

3. I have been to the school clinic for a physical before. (Verb + 过 + Object) I have had my height and weight measured. (Hint: Verb + 过 + Object) I have also had my blood pressure measured. (Hint: Verb + 过 + Object) But I haven't been there (to the clinic) for the past six months. (Hint: [有] + Time-duration + 没 + Action Verb + 了)

4. A: Have you had a cold recently? (Hint: Verb + 过 + Object)

   B: No. I have been very healthy recently. However, I haven't had a physical for quite a few years. (Hint: Subject [有] + Time-duration + 没 + Action Verb + 了) It's already been five or six years since I left the U.S. (Hint: Subject + Non-continuative Verb 离开 + Object + Time-duration) I went to Japan and studied there for a few years. (Hint: Verb + 过) Now it's already been two weeks since I came to China. (Hint: Verb + Object + Time-duration) (I) don't feel like eating and have no energy. A few days ago, I went to see a doctor. (Hint: Verb + 过 + #次 + Object) The doctor said it was jet lag and required no medical treatment.

---

## 💻 TASK 4. 情景对话 (QÍNGJǏNG DUÌHUÀ) SITUATIONAL DIALOGUE

**Setting:**     Classroom
**Cast:**        A teacher and a student
**Situation:**   The student apologizes to his/her teacher for missing class and explain that it was because of a doctor's appoinment. The student asks the teacher what assignments he/she missed. Construct a dialogue between the student and the teacher. Did the student miss a major test or assignment? What class is this? Is the teacher satisfied with the student's excuse for being absent, or is the teacher suspicious because he/she knows the students likes to skip class?

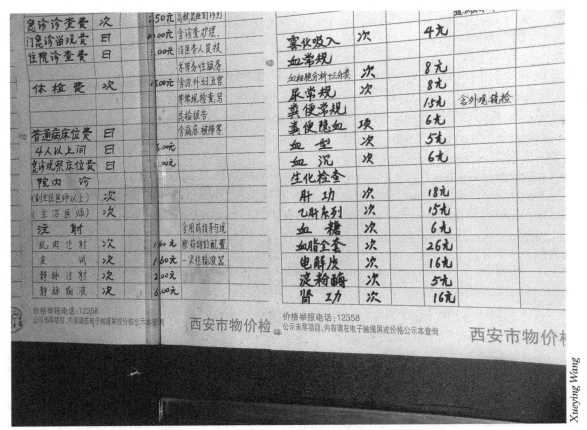

*Hospital fees for various treatments at Xijing Hospital in Xi'an.*

# 26
# 谈季节，谈天气
# *Seasons and the Weather*

**In this lesson you will:**
- Talk about the weather.
- Describe the four seasons.
- Understand the weather forecast over the radio or on TV.

李丽莉和吴文德刚到北京的时候，天气又热又闷。上个星期最热的那一天，气温都达到了摄氏40多度。但是，最近几天天气开始凉快了一些了。李丽莉，吴文德和陈小云觉得这么好的天气，大家应该找个时间去公园玩儿玩儿。陈小云告诉李丽莉和吴文德她昨天晚上听天气预报说星期六是一个晴天，温度不高也不低。可是，天气预报准确不准确呢？下面请看他们那个星期六去公园玩儿的一个小故事。

（在学校图书馆外边）

李丽莉：今天的天气真好。真舒服。

吴文德：是啊。刚到北京的时候，天气太热了。

陈小云：北京六月、七月、八月都热。最热的时候，气温能达到摄氏40多度。

李丽莉：北京是不是一年也有春、夏、秋、冬、四个季节？

陈小云：对。但是春季和秋季短，夏季和冬季长。

吴文德：陈小云，春、夏、秋、冬四季，你最喜欢哪个季节？

陈小云：我最喜欢秋天。北京十月的秋天最好。

李丽莉：为什么？

陈小云：那时候，天气不冷也不热。树叶都红了，又舒服又漂亮。

李丽莉：我觉得春天最好。天气暖和了，花儿都开了，草也绿了……多漂亮啊！

陈小云：不错。但是北京的春天常常刮大风。

吴文德：北京的冬天怎么样？很冷吗？

陈小云：冬天很冷，最低气温能达到零下 20 度，常常下雪。

吴文德：现在应该是秋天了吧？天气不那么热了。

陈小云：八月六号就立秋了，但是有时候秋老虎非常厉害。八月二十一号是处暑，处暑以后天气才开始越来越凉快。

李丽莉：现在天气这么好，我们应该找个时间去公园玩儿玩儿。

陈小云：行啊，天气预报说今天晚上阴天，摄氏二十四度，有小雨。明天星期五多云转晴。星期六晴，有小风。最高温度二十六度。最低温度二十四度。

吴文德：星期六天气很舒服。我们去公园玩儿玩儿吧。

（星期六早上）

李丽莉：天气预报会不会不准确呢？你们看天这么阴，说不定会下雨。我们是不是应该拿一把伞？

陈小云：不用拿伞。昨天天快黑的时候，半个天都是红的。中国人常说："早霞不出门，晚霞行千里[1]。"你们放心吧，我的天气预报不会错。

吴文德：别吹牛了，我的天气预报专家，你看现在开始刮风了，一会儿说不定真有雨呢。

陈小云：你们别杞人忧天[2]了。今天是大晴天，我说没有雨就没雨。

（刚到公园一会儿，就开始下大雨了，李丽莉和吴文德撒腿就跑。）

陈小云：你们别跑呀，前面也有雨。你们谁带伞了？

## Notes

1. 早霞不出门，晚霞行千里。    (Zǎo xiá bù chū mén, wǎn xiá xíng qiān lǐ.)
   This is a proverb predicting the weather. It literally means "If there are red clouds in the morning, don't go out. If there are red clouds in the evening, you can go thousands of miles." This is similar to the English saying, "Red sky in morning, sailors take warning. Red sky at night, sailors delight."

2. 杞人忧天。    (Qǐ rén yōu tiān.)
   This is a 成语故事 about someone in ancient times who constantly worries that the sky is going to fall. The moral of this story is, "Don't worry about something that is not your concern or that is beyond your control."

*Boarding a public bus.*

Alaric Radosh

 生词表 (Shēngcí Biǎo)

# Vocabulary

| Character | Pinyin | Part of Speech | English Definition |
| --- | --- | --- | --- |
| 1. 季节 | jìjié | *n.* | season (of a year) |
| 北京一年有四个季节。 | | | |
| 季 | | *n.* | season (of a year), agricultural season |
| 节 | | *n.* | festival, holiday |
| 2. 闷 | mēn | *adj.* | (of weather) stuffy, (of a room) lacking ventilation |
| 今天天气真闷。 | | | |
| 3. 气温 | qìwēn | *n.* | (of weather) temperature |
| 你看看现在气温是多少。 | | | |
| 温 | | *adj.* | warm, lukewarm |
| | | *n.* | warmth, temperature |
| 4. 达到 | dádào | *v.* | to reach, to achieve (a certain degree, level, etc.) |
| 现在气温已经达到四十度了。 | | | |
| 5. 度 | dù | *m.w.* | degree |
| 明天多少度? | | | |
| 6. 凉快 | liángkuai | *adj.* | pleasantly cool |
| 明天很凉快。 | | | |
| 凉 | | *adj.* | cool, cold |

7. 公园    gōngyuán    *n.*    public park

我们去公园玩儿玩儿吧。

     公        *adj.*    public

     园        *n.*    park

8. 预报    yùbào    *n.*    forecast

天气预报说明天天气怎么样？

9. 晴天    qíngtiān    *n.*    clear weather

明天是晴天。

     晴        *adj.*    (of weather) clear, fine

10. 低    dī    *adj.*    low, down

明天气温也不会低。

11. 准确    zhǔnquè    *adj.*    accurate, precise, to the point

天气预报都不准确。

12. 春夏秋冬    chūn xià qiū dōng    *phr.*    the four seasons; (lit.) spring, summer, fall, and winter

这儿春夏秋冬都很舒服。

13. 短    duǎn    *adj.*    short

北京春天太短了。

14. 冷    lěng    *adj.*    cold, chilly, freezing

那儿冬天冷不冷？

15. 树叶    shùyè    *n.*    tree leaves, foliage

北京秋天树叶很好看。

     树        *n.*    trees

     叶        *n.*    (of plants) leaves

16. 暖和    nuǎnhuo    *adj.*    pleasantly warm, nice and warm

今天外边很暖和。

17. 草    cǎo    *n.*    grass, herbs

这儿的草都不高。

18. 绿    lǜ    *adj.*    green

现在草都绿了。

19. 刮风    guā fēng    *v. obj.*    to be windy; (lit.) to blow wind

外边又开始刮风了。

     刮        *v.*    to scrape, to shave, to spread

     风        *n.*    (of weather) wind

| 20. 零下 | língxià | *n.* | below zero |

现在已经是零下三十度了。

| 21. 下雪 | xià xuě | *v. obj.* | to snow |

北京冬天下雪吗？

| 下 | | *v.* | to drop, to fall (of rain, snow) |
| 雪 | | *n.* | snow |

| 22. 越来越 | yuè lái yuè | *adv.* | more and more |

你看，现在雪越来越大了。

| 23. 阴天 | yīntiān | *n.* | overcast sky, cloudy day |

明天也是阴天。

| 阴 | | *adj.* | cloudy, overcast |

| 24. 下雨 | xià yǔ | *v. obj.* | to rain |

明天会不会下雨？

| 雨 | | *n.* | rain |

| 25. 多云转晴 | duō yún zhuǎn qíng | *phr.* | cloudy turning clear |

明天是多云转晴，不会下雨。

| 多云 | | *phr.* | cloudy; (lit.) a lot of clouds |
| 转 | | *v.* | to shift, change direction |

| 26. 拿 | ná | *v.* | to hold (in hand), to grasp |

你拿着这么多书去哪儿？

| 27. 伞 | sǎn | *n.* | umbrella |

要下雨了。你有伞吗？

| 28. 吹牛 | chuī niú | *v. obj.* | to brag, to boast |

他非常喜欢吹牛。

| 29. 专家 | zhuānjiā | *n.* | expert, specialist |

专家说的话也不是都对。

| 专 | | *adj.* | focusing (on a certain field), specializing (in sth.) |
| 家 | | *suff.* | suffix used to indicate an expert or specialist in a certain field |

## 反义词 (Fǎnyìcí) Antonyms

Studying antonyms and synonyms together is a very convenient way to keep one's vocabulary organized. In this lesson, you have learned the following:

| | | |
|---|---|---|
| 1. 热/冷 | rè/lěng | hot/cold |
| 2. 高/低 | gāo/dī | high/low |
| 3. 暖和/凉快 | nuǎnhe/liángkuai | warm/cool |

Many commonly used compound Chinese words and phrases are composed of antonyms. The following are good examples:

| | |
|---|---|
| 不热 (也) 不冷 | neither too hot, nor too cold |
| 不高 (也) 不低 | neither too high, nor too low |
| 不大 (也) 不小 | neither too big, nor too small |
| 不快 (也) 不慢 | neither too fast, nor too slow |

## 专有名词 (Zhuānyǒu Míngcí) Proper Nouns

| | | |
|---|---|---|
| 1. 摄氏 | Shèshì | Celsius |
| 2. 处暑 | Chùshǔ | the end of the summer; (lit.) "cessation of heat," the fourteenth period of the twenty-four divisions of the traditional Chinese calendar, occurring in late August |
| 3. 立秋 | Lìqiū | the beginning of autumn; (lit.) establishing autumn, the thirteenth of the twenty-four seasonal divisions of the traditional Chinese calendar, usually occurring in early August. |

## 补充词汇 (Bǔchōng Cíhuì) Supplementary Vocabulary

| | | | |
|---|---|---|---|
| 1. 雾 | wù | *n.* | fog |
| 2. 霜 | shuāng | *n.* | frost |
| 3. 冰雹 | bīngbáo | *n.* | hail |
| 4. 湿 | shī | *adj.* | wet |
| 5. 气候 | qìhòu | *n.* | climate |
| 6. 华氏 | huáshì | *n.* | Fahrenheit |
| 7. 冻 | dòng | *v.* | to freeze |
| 8. 多云偶雨 | duō yún ǒu yǔ | *phr.* | cloudy with occasional showers |

## 口头用语 (Kǒutóu Yòngyǔ) Spoken Expressions

| | | |
|---|---|---|
| 1. 秋老虎 | qiū lǎohǔ | (lit.) the autumn tiger, an idiomatic expression for the very hot days in the early fall |
| 2. 半个天 | bàn ge tiān | half the sky |
| 3. 大晴天 | dà qíngtiān | very clear day; (lit.) a big clear sky |
| 4. 撒腿就跑 | sā tuǐ jiù pǎo | to start running immediately; (lit.) let go of one's legs and run |

## 词汇注解 (Cíhuì Zhùjiě) Featured Vocabulary

### 1. 达到 (Dádào) vs. 到达 (Dàodá)

达到    to reach
到达    to arrive (at a certain place)

### 2. 半个天 (Bàn Ge Tiān) vs. 半天 (Bàntiān)

半个天   half of the sky
半天    half a day, a long time

### 3. 开 (Kāi)

开 **to turn on an electronic device**

开电视 to turn on the TV      开电脑 to turn on a computer

开 **to open something**

开门 to open a door       开窗 to open a window
开花 (of plants, trees, etc.) to blossom; (lit.) to "open up the flowers"

### 4. 黑 (Hēi)

黑 **adj.  black**

黑裤子 black pants

黑 **predicate adj.  to turn black/dark**

天黑了 The sky is getting dark.

### 5. 刮风 (Guā Fēng), 下雨 (Xià Yǔ), 下雪 (Xià Xuě)

All of these verb-object phrases can be modified by 大/小. For example:
刮 (大/小) 风      下 (大/小) 雨   下 (大/小) 雪

*A bridge in the city of Suzhou.*

 语法(Yǔfǎ)

# Grammar

## I. Modal Particle 了 (Cont'd.)

You learned in Lessons 16 and 22 that the Modal Particle 了 can be used together with the Perfect Aspect 了 to indicate the completion of an action with a concern for the present situation, as in 我吃了饭了。 The Perfect Aspect 了 that follows the verb 吃 indicates that the 吃 action is completed. The Modal Particle 了 that is placed at the end of the sentence indicates that the subject 我 is no longer hungry. Modal Particle 了 is also used to complete the sentence because the object 饭 is a single word object.

In this lesson, you will learn to use Modal Particle 了 to indicate a change of condition/situation. In this case, 了 is also placed at the end of the sentence. This structure sometimes contains a time word, but if the situation can be understood from the context, the time word can be omitted. The most common negative form of this structure is "不…了," which means "no longer this way." However, if the verb is 有, the negative structure changes to "没有…了". See the examples below.

### A. With Verbs

*1.  Non-Action Verbs: 是, 喜欢, 在, 有, etc.*

| Before | Now | | | | |
|---|---|---|---|---|---|
| | (Time) | Subject | Non-action verb | (Object) | 了 |
| （以前我有钱，） | （现在） | 我 | 没有 | 钱 | 了。 |

I used to have money. I don't have money anymore.

| | | | | |
|---|---|---|---|---|
| （以前我喜欢他，） | 我 | 不喜欢 | 他 | 了。 |

I did like him before. I do not like him now.

| | | | | |
|---|---|---|---|---|
| （以前我是学生，） | 我 | 不是 | 学生 | 了。 |

I was a student before. I am no longer a student.

### 2. Action Verb

| Before | Now | | | | |
|---|---|---|---|---|---|
| | Subject | Time word | Action verb | (Object) | 了 |
| （我以前不做饭，） | 我 | （现在） | 做 | 饭 | 了。 |

I didn't used to cook, but now I do.

| Before | Now | | | | |
|---|---|---|---|---|---|
| （我以前上班，） | 我 | （现在） | 不上 | 班 | 了。 |

I used to work, but I am not working anymore.

### 3. Auxiliary Verb

| Before | Now | | | | |
|---|---|---|---|---|---|
| | (Time) | Subject | Auxiliary verb | Verb | (Object) 了 |
| （以前我姐姐不会开车，） | （现在） | 她 | 会 | 开 | 车了。 |

My sister didn't used to know how to drive, but she can drive now.

| Before | Now | | | | |
|---|---|---|---|---|---|
| （以前他不喜欢跳舞，） | （现在） | 他 | 喜欢 | 跳 | 舞了。 |

He did not like dancing before; he likes dancing now.

| Before | Now | | | | |
|---|---|---|---|---|---|
| （以前他怕问问题，） | （现在） | 他 | 不怕 | 问 | 问题了。 |

He was afraid before, but he is no longer afraid of asking questions.

## B. With a Predicate Adjective

| Before | Now | | | |
|---|---|---|---|---|
| | Time | Subject | Adjective phrase | 了 |
| （以前我的裤子很新，） | （现在） | 我的裤子 | 都旧 | 了。 |

I used to own pants that were new, but now they are all old.

| Before | Now | | | |
|---|---|---|---|---|
| （刚才我很累，） | （现在） | 我 | 不那么累 | 了。 |

I was very tired a moment ago. I am not that tired anymore.

| Before | Now | | | |
|---|---|---|---|---|
| （几年前我们不老，） | （现在） | 我们 | 都老 | 了。 |

We were not old a few years ago. Now we are getting old.

## C. With a Verb Complement of Degree

| Before | Now | | | | |
|---|---|---|---|---|---|
| | Time | Subject | Verb | Verb得 | Adjective | 了 |
| （以前我们写字写得很慢，） | （现在） | 我们 | 写字 | 写得 | 不慢 | 了。 |

We used to write characters slowly, but now we can write quickly.

（以前他中文说得不流利，）　　　（现在）他中文　　说得　很流利了。

Before, he did not speak Chinese fluently, but now he does.

## D. With Verbs Describing Natural Phenomena

| Before | Now | | |
|---|---|---|---|
| | Time | Predicate | 了 |
| （刚才没有下雪，） | （现在） | 下雪 | 了。 |

(It wasn't snowing just then.) It is snowing now.

| （昨天天气不冷，） | （现在） | 天气 冷 | 了。 |
|---|---|---|---|

(It was not cold yesterday.) Now it is very cold.

| （刚才在下雨，） | （现在） | 雨 停 | 了。 |
|---|---|---|---|

(It was raining before.) It has stopped raining now.

## E. With a Nominal Predicate

### 1. Time

| Before | Now | | |
|---|---|---|---|
| | Time | Predicate | 了 |
| （刚才是九点，） | 现在 | 九点半 | 了。 |

(It was just nine o'clock.) It is nine thirty now.

### 2. Age

| Before | Now | | |
|---|---|---|---|
| | Time | Predicate | 了 |
| （他去年七十九岁，） | 今年 | 八十岁 | 了。 |

(He was seventy-nine years old last year.) He is eighty this year.

## ❀ PRACTICE

Try using 了 to complete the following sentences.

1. 我上个星期还没有工作，_____。

2. 我朋友五分钟前还在这儿，_____。

3. 他的感冒昨天还没有好，_____。

4. 九月的时候，天气还很热，十月 _____。

5. 北京的天气我刚来的时候不太习惯，现在 _____。

6. 他以前希望当律师，上大学以后 _____。

7. 昨天我想去参加他星期六的晚会，今天 _____。

8. 夏天的时候，树叶都是绿的，秋天 _____。

9. 我们去年去过一次中国，今年 _____。

10. 她一年以前还不会说中文，现在说得 _____。

## II. Sentences without a Definite Subject

In many situations, a "Verb + Object Phrase" can form a sentence. This kind of subjectless sentence exists because sometimes it is not clear who/what the subject is, or there is no need to specify the subject. For example:

### A. Describing Natural Phenomena

| | | |
|---|---|---|
| Positive: | 下雨了。 | It is raining. |
| Negative: | 不下雨了。 | It is not raining now. |
| Question: | 下雨了没有？ | Has it begun to rain? |
| | 下雨了吗？ | |

### B. Indicating Existence Using 有 (Yǒu)

| | | |
|---|---|---|
| Positive: | 有人请你吃饭。 | Someone is inviting you for dinner. |
| Negative: | 没有人来过这儿。 | No one has been here before. |
| Question: | 有没有人来过这儿？ | Has anyone been here before? |
| | 有人来过这儿吗？ | |

### C. Imperative Sentences

别说话。   Don't talk.

*Buddhist sculptures in Leshan, Sichuan.*

## PRACTICE

Find a partner in class and create a short dialogue by asking or responding to each other's questions. Make sure that your dialogue includes the three structures discussed above.

## III. Using "越来越…" (Yuè Lái Yuè...)

"越来越…" means "getting more" or "becoming more and more" and is used here as an adverb to modify adjectives and certain verbs. "越来越…" must be placed between the subject and the predicate.

| A. Subject | 越来越 | Adjective (了) | |
|---|---|---|---|
| 天气 | 越来越 | 热了。 | The weather is getting hotter and hotter. |
| 他中文说得 | 越来越 | 好。 | His Chinese is getting better and better. |

| B. Subject | 越来越 | Verb phrase (了) | |
|---|---|---|---|
| 我 | 越来越 | 爱唱歌。 | I like to sing more and more. |
| 我 | 越来越 | 不会跳舞了。 | My dancing just gets worse and worse. |

## PRACTICE

Use each of the above two 越来越 structures to create sentences of your own that demonstrate your understanding of their meaning and usage.

## IV. Using "又…又…" (Yòu...Yòu...)

Lesson 23 introduced the adverb 又, which means "again." In this lesson you will learn the "又…又…" structure, which means "both...and...." The "又…又…" structure links either adjectives or verbs, but not noun phrases, to indicate that two or more circumstances or actions exist simultaneously. The two phrases linked by "又…又…" should be either similar or contrasting in meaning. The "又…又…" structure should always be placed after the subject.

### A. Adjective (Phrases)

Predicate adjective

| Subject | 又 Adjective | 又 Adjective |
|---|---|---|
| 那条裤子 | 又舒服 | 又漂亮。 |

These pants are very comfortable, and they look nice, too.

| 我的朋友要走了。我 | 又高兴， | 又伤心。 |
|---|---|---|

My friend is leaving. I am happy, but at the same time very sad.

## *Note*

Some phrases linked by the "又…又…" structure to describe physical appearance are considered to be fixed phrases, such as 又高又大, 又瘦又小, 又白又胖, and 又黑又瘦.

## B. Verb (Phrases)

Predicate verb

| Subject | 又 Verb phrase | 又 Verb phrase |
|---|---|---|
| 今天 | 又刮风， | 又下雨。 |

It is windy and rainy today.

## *Note*

Make sure that the verbs/verb phrases linked by "又…又…" are describing similar situations.

　　CORRECT: 又学中文又学日语

　　xxx INCORRECT: 又不学中文又学日语 xxx

---

## 🔲 PRACTICE

Use each of the above two structures to create as many phrases as you can.

*Braving the weather in Xi'an.*

# Textbook Exercises

## 🎧💻 TASK 1. 课文问答 (KÈWÉN WÈNDÁ) QUESTIONS AND ANSWERS

How well did you understand the text? Check your comprehension by answering the following questions.

1. 春，夏，秋，冬四个季节，小云最喜欢哪个季节？为什么？

2. 李丽莉最喜欢哪个季节？为什么？

3. 李丽莉，陈小云和吴文德为什么星期六去公园？那天的天气好不好？陈小云的天气预报准确不准确？为什么？

4. 你喜欢不喜欢北京的四季？为什么？

## 💻 TASK 2. 语法练习 (YǓ FǍ LIÀNXÍ) GRAMMATICAL STRUCTURE PRACTICE

### A. Sentence Construction

Try constructing your own sentences using the new situation 了. If you need help, look at the hints on the right.

| | Hints |
|---|---|
| 1. 以前, 现在, 秋天 | Do you like autumn? |
| 2. 刚才, 现在, 阴天, 晴天 | What is the weather like? |
| 3. 昨天早上, 昨天下午, 低 | What is the temperature? |
| 4. 去年冬天，今年冬天，冷 | What is the difference between the two winters? |
| 5. 天气预报，没雨，下雨 | Is the weather report correct? |
| 6. 来中国以前，会，天气预报 | Now I listen to the Chinese weather forecast. |

### B. Matching

Match the phrases in the left column with their corresponding phrases on the right to make a complete sentence.

1. 现在是十月了，天气          a)（又累又饿）。

2. 现在是晚上十二点了，我   b)（又凉快又舒服）。

3. 现在夏天了，天气          c)（又暖和又漂亮）。

4. 现在是九月了，学习        d)（又热又闷）。

5. 现在花儿开了，外边        e)（又紧张又辛苦）。

---

## 💻 TASK 3. 翻译 (FĀNYÌ) PARAPHRASING

How well do you remember the grammar and vocabulary we've covered so far? Check yourself by translating the following sentences into Chinese.

1. It was dark and cloudy a moment ago, (Hint: 又…又…) and now it's pouring! (Hint: Verb + Object + 了) The weather is cooling down. (Hint: 越来越…) The weather forecast says the rain is going to stop tomorrow morning. (Hint: Verb + 了) After it has cleared up around noon, let's go to the park and have some fun! (Hint: Adjective + 了)

2. Spring is my favorite season (Hint: 最), because the weather gets warmer and warmer (Hint: 越来越…), the flowers all come into bloom, and the grass becomes green again. (Hint: Adjective + 了, Verb + 了) I think fall is nice, too. The weather is not that warm, the leaves turn red, and it is very comfortable and beautiful. (Hint: Adjective + 了, 又…又…)

3. I dislike the winters here most (Hint: 最). The temperatures go lower and lower, and the weather gets colder and colder. (Hint: 越来越…) One minute it snows; the next, it's windy. (Hint: 一会儿, Verb + Object + 了) No one can go to the park in the winter. (Hint: 没有人)

4. I used to really dislike the summer; I always found it hot and stuffy. (Hint: 又…又…) At its hottest the temperature can go over forty degrees Celsius. (Hint: 最, 达到) But now that I'm getting older, (Hint: Adjective + 了) maybe I am getting used to the weather here. (Hint: Verb + 了) I don't dislike the summer that much anymore. (Hint: 不 + 不 + Verb + 了)

---

## 💻 TASK 4. 情景对话 (QÍNGJǏNG DUÌHUÀ) SITUATIONAL DIALOGUE

**Setting:**      A news station

**Characters:**   One or two weather forecasters

**Topic:**        Using the website www.yahoo.com.cn for simplified characters and www.tw.yahoo.com for traditional characters, get this week's weather information for a city in China. (Hint: Type in 天气预报 and then search for information.) Then present a report as if you were a weather forecaster on television, either alone or in conjunction with one other weather forecaster, with whom you can discuss the week's outlook. Tell us if we should expect rain or shine for the upcoming week. Snow? High winds? A cold front? A heat wave? A hurricane? What should the public do to prepare for and/or enjoy the week ahead?

# 27

# 去邮局

# Mail and the Post Office

> **In this lesson you will:**
> ■ Address an envelope in Chinese.
> ■ Speak to people about mailing a letter and buying items in a post office.
> ■ Describe where things are located in a room.

中国的邮局服务项目很多，可以寄东西，可以打电话，可以买信封、邮票、明信片，还可以买杂志、报纸。在中国寄包裹要填包裹单，寄挂号信，要填挂号单。在美国寄信、寄包裹的时候信封的左上边写着寄件人的地址，信封的中间写着收件人的地址。在中国寄东西，左上边应该写收件人的地址，右下边写寄件人的地址。吴文德觉得自己学了好几年的中文了，写中文地址应该没有问题。但是他会不会在包裹上写中文地址呢？下面是吴文德寄包裹的一个小故事。

（在宿舍楼外面，李丽莉笑着问吴文德）

李丽莉：吴文德，你去哪儿？你手里拿着什么？

吴文德：一个包裹。我去邮局给我家寄东西。

李丽莉：你知道地址怎么写吗？

吴文德：学了这么长时间的中文，写地址还能不会？小菜一碟儿[1]。你放心吧。

（在邮局里面）

吴文德：这个邮局开着这么多窗口，每个窗口上都挂着一个牌子，我的眼睛都看花了。

营业员：每个窗口都有自己的服务项目。有的窗口可以寄包裹；有的窗口可以买邮票、信封。您是不是要寄包裹？

吴文德：是啊。我应该去哪个窗口呢？

营业员：寄东西要填包裹单。您先坐着慢慢地填，然后去一号窗口。

吴文德：取包裹在哪个窗口？

营业员：(营业员指着一号窗口的牌子说)您看，一号窗口的牌子上面写着"包裹"。寄包裹、取包裹都在那儿。

吴文德：谢谢。

(在一号窗口前)

吴文德：你好。我想给美国纽约寄一个包裹。这是我填的包裹单。

营业员：您带证件了吗？

吴文德：我有学生证，学生证也是证件吧？

营业员：对，我来称一下包裹的重量。您要寄航空还是海运？

吴文德：哪种好？

营业员：寄航空快，两个星期就到了。寄海运要两、三个月，但是便宜。

吴文德：寄海运吧。你这儿也卖邮票和明信片吗？

营业员：买邮票，买明信片都在三号窗口。您看三号窗口的牌子上写着"航空信-挂号信-邮票"。左边的柜台里放着十几种明信片，您慢慢地选吧。

吴文德：谢谢！

(李丽莉在吴文德宿舍学习，有人在外面叫吴文德的名字。)

邮递员：吴文德的包裹，请签字。

吴文德：好，谢谢。咦，这个包裹怎么这么面熟。

李丽莉：哎呀，吴文德，你地址写反了，这是你要寄纽约的包裹，怎么寄到自己这儿了呢²？在中国寄东西，左上边应该写收件人的地址，右下边写寄件人的地址。

吴文德：我去寄包裹的那天早上你为什么不告诉我呢？

## Notes

1. 小菜一碟儿  (xiǎo cài yī diér)
   no big deal, a piece of cake

2. 怎么寄到自己这儿了？   (Zěnme jì dào zìjǐ zhèr le?)
   How come you mailed it to yourself?

*Package pick-up and inspection window at the post office in Xi'an.*

 生词表 (Shēngcí Biǎo)

## Vocabulary

| Character | Pinyin | Part of Speech | English Definition |
|---|---|---|---|
| 1. 邮局 | yóujú | *n.* | post office |
| 请问，邮局在哪儿？ | | | |
| 邮 | | *n.* | mail |
| 局 | | *n.* | office, bureau |
| 2. 服务项目 | fúwù xiàngmù | *n. phr.* | services offered; (lit.) service items |
| 这个邮局很小，服务项目不多。 | | | |
| 服务 | | *n.* | service |
| | | *v.* | to serve |
| 项目 | | *n.* | item, project |
| 3. 寄 | jì | *v.* | to send by mail |
| 你想寄什么？ | | | |
| 4. 信封 | xìnfēng | *n.* | envelope |
| 你们有没有大信封？ | | | |
| 封 | | *m.w.* | measure word for letters |
| 5. 邮票 | yóupiào | *n.* | stamps |
| 我想买两张邮票。 | | | |

6. 明信片      míngxìnpiàn      *n.*      postcard

他从北京给我寄的明信片很漂亮。

7. 包裹单      bāoguǒdān      *n.*      form for mailing a parcel

请你给我一张包裹单，好吗？

包裹      *n.*      parcel, package

单      *n.*      list, sheet

8. 挂号信      guàhàoxìn      *n.*      registered mail

你要不要寄挂号信？

挂号      *v. obj.*      (lit.) to register a number (for something)

9. 着      zhe      *part.*      a grammatical component indicating the status of an action

你拿着这个包裹去哪儿？

10. 寄件人      jìjiànrén      *n.*      the sender (of a letter, parcel, etc.)

寄件人是什么意思？

件      *n.*      item, piece

11. 收件人      shōujiànrén      *n.*      the recipient (of a letter, parcel, etc.)

收件人就是收信的人。

12. 挂      guà      *v.*      to hang (something on a wall, etc)

你看，那儿挂着一个牌子。

13. 眼睛      yǎnjing      *n.*      (human) eyes

你眼睛好不好？

14. 营业员      yíngyèyuán      *n.*      shop assistant

那个营业员说他们明天不营业。

营业      *v. obj.*      (of a business or shop) to be open, to do business

     *n.*      business

15. 先…然后      xiān...ránhòu      *conj.*      first...then

我想先去商店，然后去邮局。

先      *adv.*      first, before

然后      *conj.*      afterwards, thereupon

16. 地      de      *part.*      attached to an adjective to make an adverbial expression

请你慢慢地说。

17. 指      zhǐ      *v.*      to point (with a finger) to/at
他指着牌子跟我说："你看，他们不营业。"

18. 证件      zhèngjiàn      *n.*      certificate, ID
对不起，我没有证件。

19. 重量      zhòngliàng      *n.*      weight
这个包裹的重量是多少？

20. 航空      hángkōng      *n.*      aviation, air transportation, airmail
这个包裹你想寄航空吗？
     航      *n.*      navigation
     空      *n.*      air

21. 海运      hǎiyùn      *n.*      sea transportation
这个包裹我想寄海运。
     海      *n.*      sea
     运      *n.*      motion, transportation

22. 便宜      piányì      *adj.*      inexpensive, cheap
寄海运很便宜。

23. 卖      mài      *v.*      to sell
这儿不卖邮票。

24. 柜台      guìtái      *n.*      counter
请问，寄挂号信的柜台在哪儿？
     台      *n.*      table, desk, platform

25. 放      fàng      *v.*      to release, to let go, to send off/away, to leave (sth. at a certain place)
我的信你放哪儿了？

26. 选      xuǎn      *v.*      to choose, to select, to elect
我选这本书。

27. 邮递员      yóudìyuán      *n.*      mail-delivery worker, postal worker, letter carrier
今天邮递员来了吗？
     递      *v.*      to hand over, to pass on (sth.), to deliver

28. 签字      qiān zì      *v. obj.*      to sign
请您在这儿签字。

29. 反      fǎn      *adj.*      in the opposite direction, backwards
你的地址写反了。

*Xueying Wang*

## 专有名词 (Zhuānyǒu Míngcí) Proper Nouns

| | | |
|---|---|---|
| 纽约 | Niǔyuē | New York |

## 补充词汇 (Bǔchōng Cíhuì) Supplementary Vocabulary

| | | | |
|---|---|---|---|
| 1. 寄平信 | jì píngxìn | *v. obj.* | to send by ordinary mail |
| 2. 收信人 | shōuxìnrén | *n.* | addressee, recipient (of a letter) |
| 3. 寄信人 | jìxìnrén | *n.* | sender (of a letter) |
| 4. 信纸 | xìnzhǐ | *n.* | letter paper, stationery |
| 5. 纪念邮票 | jìniàn yóupiào | *n.* | commemorative stamp |
| 6. 快递 | kuàidì | *n.* | (lit.) quick delivery, express mail |
| 7. 邮政编码 | yóuzhèng biānmǎ | *phr.* | zip code |

## 口头用语 (Kǒutóu Yòngyǔ) Spoken Expressions

| | | |
|---|---|---|
| 1. 都看花了 | dōu kàn huā le | There are so many things and you don't know where to look. |
| 2. 面熟 | miànshú | (usually of a person) to look familiar |

这个人怎么这么面熟?

## 词汇注解 (Cíhuì Zhùjiě) Featured Vocabulary

### 有的 *(Yǒude)*

有的, just like 这 or 那, can be used to modify a noun. However, unlike 这 or 那, there is no need for a measure word between 有的 and the noun. For example:

这本书/那本书

有的书

When a noun functions as an object, "有的 + Noun" should be placed at the beginning of the sentence. 有的 is frequently used more than once in the parallel pattern "有的…有的…." The noun after the second 有的 can be omitted if the context makes clear what that noun refers to. For example:

Modifying Subject: 　有的学生学习日文。
Some students are studying Japanese.

有的学生学习很认真，有的(学生)学习不认真。
Some students study hard, and some don't.

Modifying Object: 　有的学生我认识，有的(学生)我不认识。
Some students I know, and some I don't.

 ## 语法(Yǔfǎ)
# Grammar

## I. The Continuing Aspect Particle 着 (Zhe)

You have already learned that the "正在 Verb Phrase + 呢" structure can be used to describe an action in progress (Lesson 18). You have also learned that the Perfect Aspect 了 can be used to indicate the completion of an action. In this lesson, you are going to learn how to use the Continuing Aspect Particle 着 to indicate the continuation of an action or the continuation of a result of an action. The structure is "Verb 着 (+ Object)." Note that 着 is placed directly after the verb and before the object (if there is one). To form a negative sentence, place 没(有) before the verb. For questions, add either 吗 or 没有 at the end of the sentence. Below are some examples of how this structure can be used.

### A. Continuation of an Action

#### 1. Describing the Current State of an Action

When there is only one verb in a sentence, 着 is placed directly after it and before the object. Its pattern is "Verb 着…呢," which functions very much like the progressive aspect pattern "正在 Verb…呢." It can also be used together with "正在 Verb…" in a sentence to further emphasize an action in progress. For example:

我上着课呢。= 我正在上课呢。

I am taking a class right now.

For further emphasis: 我正在上着课呢。

## Note

Certain adjective predicates such as 忙 can also be used in this structure.

我忙着呢。= 我正在忙呢。

For further emphasis: 我正在忙着呢。

---

## ⧈ PRACTICE

Try using verb phrases such as 跳舞, 唱歌, 做饭, and 看电视 with 着 to make sentences of your own.

### 2. Describing the Manner in Which an Action Is Performed

When 着 is used in a sentence with two verbs, the first verb describes the manner in which the main verb, the second verb, is carried out. 着 should be placed between the first verb and the first object (if there is one). Below are two patterns, one in which the first verb has no object and one in which it does.

**When the First Verb Has No Object**

| | Descriptive action | | Main action | |
|---|---|---|---|---|
| Subject | Verb1 | 着 | Verb2 | (Object) |
| 李丽莉 | 笑 | 着 | 说 | |

Li Lili smiles and says...

| | | | | |
|---|---|---|---|---|
| 张老师 | 喜欢坐 | 着 | 教 | 课。|

Zhang Laoshi likes to sit while teaching classes.

## Notes

1. In this context, 怎么 is frequently used to ask a question concerning the second verb. For example:

   Question:   他怎么教课？

   How does he teach? (Lit.) In what manner does he teach class?

   Response:   他坐着教课。

   He sits while he teaches class.

2. You can also use 还是 to ask a question. For example:

   他站 (zhàn, to stand) 着教课还是坐着教课？

**When the First Verb Has an Object**

| | | Descriptive action | | Main action | |
|---|---|---|---|---|---|
| | Subject | Verb1 | 着 | Object1 | Verb2 | Object2 |
| Positive: | 李丽莉 | 唱 | 着 | 歌 | 开 | 车。|

Li Lili sings while driving.

| | | | | | | |
|---|---|---|---|---|---|---|
| Negative: | 李丽莉 | 没(有)唱 | 着 | 歌 | 开 | 车。|

Li Lili does not sing while driving.

Question:     李丽莉     怎么              开     车？
                    How does Li Lili drive?

                     李丽莉     是不是唱    着     歌      开     车？
                    Does Li Lili sing while driving?

## *Compare*

"Verb1 + 着 + Object1 + Verb2 + Object2" is different from the "Verb + 的时候" phrase. For example:

唱着歌开车                   The first verb, 唱歌, describes how the second verb is carried out.

他开车的时候, 总是喜欢唱歌    The actions 唱歌 and 开车 take place at the same time.

---

## 🔲 PRACTICE

Find a partner in class and ask each other questions using the following two question patterns. Do not forget to provide responses to each other's questions. For example:

问1： 你常常怎么做作业？

答1： 我常常看着电视做作业。

问2： 你们老师坐着还是站着上课？

答1： 站着上课。

## B. Continuation of the Result of an Action

In this context, the action is already completed but the result of the state brought about by the action is still continuing.

### 1. Describing the Ongoing Result of a Person's Action

When 着 describes the ongoing result of an action that somebody performed, only certain verbs, such as 穿 (chuān), 坐 (zuò), 拿 (ná), and 指 (zhǐ) can be used in combination with 着. In the following example, we will use 穿 to demonstrate this structure.

|  | Subject | Verb | 着 | Object |
|---|---|---|---|---|
| Positive: | 她 | 穿 | 着 | 一件大衣。 |

She is wearing a coat.
(The action of 穿 is completed, but the person is still wearing the coat she put on.)

| Negative: | 她 | 没（有）穿 | 着 | 一件大衣。 |
|---|---|---|---|---|

She is not wearing a coat.

| Question: | 她 | 穿 | 着 | 什么？ |
|---|---|---|---|---|

What is she wearing?

## *Compare*

Here the function of 着 is different from that of 正在, which describes an action in the process of being carried out.

她正在穿大衣。 She is putting on her coat.

---

## PRACTICE

Use "Verb 着" to ask a question and provide a response. For example:

问：你拿着什么？（指着，穿着）

答：我手里拿着一杯咖啡。

### 2. Describing the Current State of a Thing

In this context, the object (a thing) functions as the subject. The verbs that are frequently used in this pattern are 开 (kāi) and 关 (guān). 呢 is frequently used in the positive statement. We will use 开 to demonstrate how to use this pattern. For example, in the following situation, the action 开 has already been completed, but the door is still open.

|           | Thing | Verb    | 着    |        |                       |
| --------- | ----- | ------- | ----- | ------ | --------------------- |
| Positive: | 门     | 开       | 着呢。  |        | The door is open.     |
| Negative: | 门     | 没（有）开  | 着。    |        | The door is not open. |
| Question: | 门     | 开       | 着     | 没有？    | Is the door open or not? |

---

## PRACTICE

Find a partner in class and try using 电视,电脑,电灯,手机,大门,房间里的窗户, and 邮局的窗口 to ask each other questions. Do not forget to answer each other's questions.

### 3. Describing a Scene Where a Person or a Thing Is Located

"Verb 着" can be used to describe a scene where a person or a thing is found at a certain location. Here are some examples:

| Location | Verb 着 | Person/Thing |                                          |
| -------- | ------ | ------------ | ---------------------------------------- |
| 教室里      | 坐着     | 几个学生。        | There are a few students in the classroom. |
| 桌上       | 放着     | 一本书。         | There is a book placed on the table.     |

## Compare

When "Verb 着" is used to describe where a person or a thing is located, it carries a similar meaning as 有. However, "Verb 着" is more descriptive than 有. It describes the result of an action while 有 only indicates the existence of something. For example:

桌上有一本书。      There is a book on the table.

桌上放着一本书。      There is a book placed on the table.

("The book that is now on the table" is the result of the action of 放.)

---

## 🔲 PRACTICE

Try using the following to describe a person or an object.

Verbs: 坐,站,停,住,放,挂,写

Places: 机场上,墙上,信封上,门口,桌子上,客厅里,大学前边

# II. Using the Subordinating Particle 地 (De)

There are three subordinating particles in the Chinese language: 的,得, and 地. Although these three particles all have the same pronunciation (de), they each function differently in a sentence.

You learned how to use 的 and 得 in the previous lessons. Here is a brief review:

的: 的 indicates possession or describes a noun. It appears between an attributive modifier and the noun of a sentence (Attributive Modifier + 的 + Noun). For additional information, see Volume 1, Lesson 5, and Volume 2, Lesson 13 and 14.

得: Following a predicate verb or a predicate adjective, 得 introduces the complement of degree, where the 得 appears between a verb/adjective predicate and a complement (Verb/Adjective + 得 + Complement) and describes the extent to which something is done. For additional information, see Volume 2, Lesson 19.

## A. Introducing 地

地 is an adverb modifier describing the manner in which an action is performed. 地 can follow an adjective phrase or a phrase functioning as an adjective to modify a predicate verb. Also, the adjective preceding 地 must always be multisyllabic. If the adjective is monosyllabic, repeat it (e.g., "快快地," NOT "快地") or add 很 (e.g., 很慢地 + Verb). As an adverbial modifier, 地 should always be placed before the verb.

| | | |
|---|---|---|
| Current action: | 他认真地听课。 | He listens attentively in class. |
| Future action: | 我们要高高兴兴地玩儿。 | We will play happily. |
| Suggestion: | 他应该认真地学习中文。 | He should study Chinese seriously. |

## B. Comparing 地 with 得

Of the three subordinating particles, 的, 地, and 得, it is relatively easy to distinguish between 的 and 地/得, because 的 is the only one of the three that can modify a noun. As a noun modifier, 的 is always placed before the noun. For example: 他是一个很好的学生。 On the other hand, 地 and 得 always have something to do with the verb. Therefore, it is important to be able to differentiate between 地 and 得. The adjective and 地 should always be placed before the verb (Adjective + 地 + Verb) to indicate the manner in which the action takes place. As a particle that connects a verb to its complement, 得 should be placed before the adjective and after the verb (Verb + 得 + Adverb + Adjective) to indicate the result of an action. For example:

### 1. Positive Statements

地：我要认真地学习。          I am going to study seriously.

得：他总是学习得很认真。      He always studies seriously.

### 2. Negative Forms

In the negative form, if a sentence contains 地, 没 is used to negate the adjective. If a sentence has 得, 不 is used to negate the adjective. For example:

地：我今天没认真地学习。

得：他学习得很不认真。

### 3. Questions

Sentences with 地 can add 吗 or 没有 at the end of a sentence to form a question. However, they cannot form affirmative-negative questions. Sentences with 得 cannot use 没有 to form a question.

地：你今天认真地学习了吗/没有？

得：你学习得认真不认真？

　　他学习得很认真吗？

---

## ⚇ PRACTICE

Use each of the structural particles 的, 得, and 地 to make at least five different sentences. Be sure to demonstrate that you know how to use them correctly!

## III. Describing a Sequence of Events with "先⋯再/然后" (Xiān..., Zài/Ránhòu)

In Lesson 24, you learned that simple sentences contain two components, a subject and a predicate, whereas complex sentences contain more than one simple sentence. In this lesson, you learn more complex sentences connected by the adverbial structure "先⋯,再然后⋯," which can be translated as "first..., then...." This structure describes two actions that are happening sequentially.

## A. 先···，再

The two clauses introduced by "先···再" can have two separate subjects or just one. 先 should be placed after the first subject, and 再 should go after the second subject (if there is one).

| First clause | Second clause |
|---|---|
| 我先填包裹单， | （我）再到一号窗口去。 |

I will fill out the package form first and then go to the first window.

| | |
|---|---|
| 你先给我一张包裹单， | 我再到一号窗口去，好不好？ |

Could you please give me the package form first; I will then go to the first window, okay?

## B. 先···，然后

The two clauses introduced by "先···然后" can only have one subject. 然后 can only be used in a sentence with one subject, and it is usually placed before the verb in the second clause.

| First clause | Second clause |
|---|---|
| 你先填包裹单， | 然后到一号窗口去。 |

You will first fill out the package form and then go to the first window.

## C. 先···，然后再

The two clauses introduced by "先···然后再" carry a similar meaning as those introduced by "先···然后" but place more emphasis on "after someone does something, THEN he/she does something else." This structure can only have one subject.

| First clause | Second clause |
|---|---|
| 你先填包裹单， | 然后再到一号窗口去。 |

You will first fill out the package form and then go to the first window.

---

## ❏❏ PRACTICE

Try using each of the three patterns to make a sentence describing what you have done today. Here are some phrases that might be useful: 做体检, 寄包裹, 入境, 登记, 办签证, 复习考试, 申请学校, and 请客.

*A mailbox outside a Xi'an post office.*

*Book displays in a Chinese bookstore.*

 # Textbook Exercises

## 🎧💻 TASK 1. 课文问答 (KÈWÉN WÈNDÁ) QUESTIONS AND ANSWERS

How well did you understand the text? Check your comprehension by answering the following questions.

1. 吴文德会不会写中国地址？为什么？

2. 在中国寄东西应该办什么手续？

3. 吴文德寄包裹为什么寄海运？

4. 吴文德在邮局还做了什么事情？

## 💻 TASK 2. 语法练习 (YǓFǍ LIÀNXÍ) GRAMMATICAL STRUCTURE PRACTICE

### A. Fill in the Blanks

Read the following phrases and sentences and choose the best word to fill in each blank.

1. 地    得    的

雨下 _____ 很大          收件人 _____ 名字

细心 _____ 填表          邮票卖 _____ 很快

学习 ＿＿＿＿＿＿ 很认真      闷热 ＿＿＿＿＿＿ 天气

认真 ＿＿＿＿＿＿ 修课      个人简历写 ＿＿＿＿＿＿ 整齐

2. 放着　开着　指着　坐着　穿着

他 ＿＿＿＿＿＿ 包裹对我说这是李丽莉给你寄来的。

营业员今天 ＿＿＿＿＿＿ 一件新衬衫。

邮局的门 ＿＿＿＿＿＿ ，我想邮局今天一定营业。

房间里 ＿＿＿＿＿＿ 几个学生，他们都在学写信封。

柜台里 ＿＿＿＿＿＿ 一些邮票和一些明信片。

## B. Sentence Construction

Complete the following sentences using 着 and then turn each of the sentences into a question.

1. 邮局的三号窗口的牌子 ＿＿＿＿＿＿＿＿＿＿＿＿＿＿＿＿＿＿ 。

2. 他喜欢听音乐 ＿＿＿＿＿＿＿＿＿＿＿＿＿＿＿＿＿＿＿＿＿＿ 。

3. 柜台上 ＿＿＿＿＿＿＿＿＿＿＿＿＿＿＿＿＿＿＿＿＿＿＿＿＿ 。

4. 墙 (qiáng, wall) 上 ＿＿＿＿＿＿＿＿＿＿＿＿＿＿＿＿＿＿＿＿＿ 。

5. 挂号信上 ＿＿＿＿＿＿＿＿＿＿＿＿＿＿＿＿＿＿＿＿＿＿＿＿ 。

## C. Pick and Choose

In each of the following pairs there is a correct sentence and an incorrect one. Can you tell which one is correct and explain why the other is incorrect?

1.
a) 他不笑着给营业员他的身份证。
b) 柜台上没有放着邮票。

2.
a) 他先去寄包裹，然后再去买邮票。
b) 他太太先去拿了一张包裹单，他然后再寄包裹。

3.
a) 他在慢慢地选明信片。
b) 他总是好地学习，是个好学生。

4.
a) 你应该看书看得很认真。
b) 你应该认真地填收件人和寄件人的姓名和地址。

5.
a) 有的人在寄包裹，有的人在寄航空信。
b) 我爱吃有的点心，我不爱吃有的点心。

---

## 💻 TASK 3. 翻译 (FĀNYÌ) PARAPHRASING

How well do you remember the grammar and vocabulary we've covered so far? Check yourself by translating the following sentences into Chinese. Try to use the particle 着 wherever you can.

1. He is busy writing letters in Chinese with total concentration. (Hint: 正忙着,认真地) He is afraid of making mistakes; thus, (he) writes very slowly. (Hint: 得)

2. Do (you) want to mail a package? First you (have to) fill out the parcel form, then come and weigh (it). (Hint: 先···再) Take your time in filling out the form. (Hint: 地) If you do it too quickly, (you can) easily make mistakes. (Hint: 得)

3. Smiling, Li Lili asked me, "There are several stamps on the table—are they yours?" (Hint: 笑着, 放着)

4. He pointed at the stamps in my hand (Hint: 指着) and said, "You are holding mine in your hand." (Hint: 拿着) The stamps on the table probably belong to Wu Wende. (Hint: 放着)

5. A: You are wearing your overcoat. (Hint: 穿着) Can you help me by going to see if the door of the post office across a street is open? (Hint: 开着)

   B: The door of the post office is open. (Hint: 开着) Their business hours are posted on a sign outside the post office. (Hint: 写着)

---

## 💻 TASK 4. 情景对话 (QÍNGJĬNG DUÌHUÀ) SITUATIONAL DIALOGUE

| | |
|---|---|
| **Setting:** | The post office |
| **Cast:** | A clerk and a student |
| **Situation:** | The student wants to mail a package but isn't used to sending mail in China. Construct a dialogue between the student and the clerk, as the student tries to figure out what he/she needs to do. Can the clerk help the student understand the process? Does the student have enough money to mail this package? Where is it going, and what does it contain? |

# 28

## 找路

# Knowing Where to Go

> **In this lesson you will:**
> - Ask for and give directions in Chinese.
> - Discuss how to take a bus, subway, or taxi from one place to another.
> - Work toward understanding the announcements made on a Chinese bus.

在中国，自己有车的人不多。出门常坐出租车有些贵。所以，很多人都坐公共汽车或地铁。如果你在中国没乘过公共汽车或坐过地铁，有机会的时候，一定要去试试。吴文德在中国已经好几个星期了。但是他没有坐过公共汽车。有一天，吴文德要去购物中心给他妈妈买礼物，他觉得中国的公共汽车那么多，坐公共汽车一定也很容易。所以，他让李丽莉陪他一起坐公共汽车去。下面请看吴文德带李丽莉坐公共汽车去购物中心的小故事。

（星期六早上吃过早饭以后，吴文德到李丽莉的宿舍来找李丽莉。）

吴文德：我妈妈的生日快到了，我得去购物中心买个礼物。上次我寄包裹闹了一个大笑话。这次去购物中心不能再出丑了。你陪我去购物中心吧。

李丽莉：好吧。我和陈小云上次坐出租车去，十分钟就到了。坐地铁可能也很方便。

吴文德：但是地铁路线我还不熟悉，打的又太贵。我们坐公交去吧。

李丽莉：你坐过公交吗？

吴文德：我没坐过公交，但是我知道公交的路线。先在学校门口坐 22 路车，再换 9 路车就到了。咱们走吧。

（在学校门口）

李丽莉：来了好几辆公共汽车，怎么都不是 22 路？

吴文德：是啊，等了十几分钟了。我去问问。请问 22 路汽车什么时候来？

一位老师：22 路？22 路车站在学校的南门外。这是北门。你们出错大门了。但是离这儿不远的地方也有一个 22 路车站。你们从这儿往左边拐，到第二个有红绿灯的路口往右拐，再走十几分钟就能看见那个 22 路车站了。

吴文德：谢谢。（吴文德对李丽莉说）刚才是一个小小的失误，咱们走错大门了，现在应该不会再有错了。

（在 22 路车上）

吴文德：怎么样，李丽莉，这次咱们坐对车了吧。你先往里边走。我去买票。

售票员：下一站就是终点站，请各位乘客拿好票，准备下车。

李丽莉：吴文德，售票员说大家都要下车了，我没听错吧？

吴文德：她说什么我没听见，我去问一下儿。（对售票员说）请问，您刚才说什么？

售票员：下一站是终点站，请带好自己的东西准备下车。

吴文德：就要到终点站了？请问我们去购物中心，在哪儿能换 9 路车呢？

售票员：你们坐错方向了。你们应该坐往西开的 22 路车。这是往东开的，是开往北京医院的 22 路车。

吴文德：那我们从这儿怎么才能到 9 路车站呢？

售票员：你们在终点站下车，下车以后过马路，换往西开的 22 路车。在北京图书馆站下车，下车以后往前走，过了十字路口就能看见 9 路车站了。

李丽莉：吴文德，你听懂了吗？

吴文德：这次我听清楚了，你放心吧。

李丽莉：我们还是细心一点儿好。办坏一件事太容易了。再出"南辕北辙[1]"这种事，购物中心就要关门了。

吴文德：你乐观一点儿好不好？购物中心不是还没关门吗？

*Bus routes.*

## Note

1. 南辕北辙 (nán yuán běi zhé)

   If you're not going in the right direction, you're wasting your time and effort. (Lit.) The carriage that needs to go to the south is set on a northbound track.

# 生词表 (Shēngcí Biǎo)
# Vocabulary

| Character | Pinyin | Part of Speech | English Definition |
|-----------|--------|----------------|--------------------|
| 1. 出门 <br> 他们明天要出门了。 | chū mén | *v. obj.* | to go out, to leave home |
| 2. 出租车 <br> 他出门总是坐出租车。 | chūzū chē | *n.* | taxi |
| 出租 | | *v.* | to rent (out) |
| | | *n.* | rental |
| 3. 贵 <br> 这儿的东西贵不贵？ | guì | *adj.* | expensive |

4. 公共汽车     gōnggòng qìchē     *n.*     public bus
公共汽车也叫公交。

    公共               *adj.*     public, communal
    汽车               *n.*     automobile, vehicle

5. 地铁     dìtiě     *n.*     subway, metro
我想坐地铁去你那儿。

6. 可能     kěnéng     *adv.*     maybe, probably, possibly
我今天晚上可能会去看电影。

7. 乘     chéng     *v.*     to ride, to take (a bus, train, taxi, or boat)
从你那儿乘车来很快。

8. 购物中心     gòuwù zhōngxīn     *n.*     shopping center, mall
那个购物中心有很多商店。

    购物               *v. obj.*     to purchase things, to go shopping
    中心               *n.*     center

9. 陪     péi     *v.*     to accompany, to keep (somebody) company
我明天陪你去，怎么样？

10. 路线     lùxiàn     *n.*     route, itinerary
这条路线车太多。

    线               *n.*     line, thread

11. 熟悉     shúxī     *adj.*     familiar
这儿的商店我都不太熟悉。

12. 辆     liàng     *m.w.*     measure word for vehicles
这辆车是不是你的？

13. 车站     chēzhàn     *n.*     station, stop (for buses, trains)
车站在我们家的对面。

14. 东南西北     dōng nán xī běi     *n.*     the four directions
我已经不知道哪儿是东南西北了。

    东               *n.*     east
    南               *n.*     south
    西               *n.*     west
    北               *n.*     north

15. 往　　　　　　wǎng　　　　　v.　　　to go toward
这是开往我们学校的车。

　　　　　　　　　wàng　　　　　prep.　　toward
你应该往南走。

16. 拐　　　　　　guǎi　　　　　v.　　　to make a turn, to change direction
我应该往右拐还是往左拐？

17. 红绿灯　　　　hónglǜdēng　　n.　　　traffic light; (lit.) red-green light
你应该在红绿灯那儿往西拐。

　　灯　　　　　　　　　　　　　n.　　　light

18. 路口　　　　　lùkǒu　　　　　n.　　　street intersection
你在哪个路口等我？

19. 失误　　　　　shīwù　　　　　n.　　　fault (in ball games), error, mistake
那是我的失误。对不起。

　　失　　　　　　　　　　　　　n.　　　loss

　　误　　　　　　　　　　　　　n.　　　error, mistake

20. 售票员　　　　shòupiàoyuán　n.　　　ticket seller
你去问问那个售票员吧。

　　售　　　　　　　　　　　　　v.　　　to sell

21. 终点　　　　　zhōngdiǎn　　　n.　　　terminal point
请问，这是终点站吗？

　　终　　　　　　　　　　　　　n.　　　end (as opposed to beginning)

22. 乘客　　　　　chéngkè　　　　n.　　　passengers
这些乘客都是去北京的。

23. 方向　　　　　fāngxiàng　　　n.　　　direction, orientation
你们家在哪个方向？

24. 医院　　　　　yīyuàn　　　　　n.　　　hospital
我明天去医院看病。

　　院　　　　　　　　　　　　　n.　　　courtyard, yard, institute, academy

25. 马路　　　　　mǎlù　　　　　　n.　　　street, avenue
我们在这儿过马路吧。

26. 十字(路口)　　shízì (lùkǒu)　n.　　　crossroads; (lit.) an intersection that is
我们家就在那个十字路口那儿。　　　　　　shaped like the Chinese character 十

　　十字　　　　　　　　　　　　n.　　　the character 十

27. 关      guān      *v.*      to close a door/gate, (of a business) to be closed
商店现在已经关门了。

28. 坏      huài      *adj.*      broken, bad, evil
我的车今天坏了。

29. 乐观      lèguān      *adj.*      (having) a joyful outlook, optimistic
他这个人总是很乐观。

## 补充词汇 (Bǔchōng Cíhuì) Supplementary Vocabulary

1. 劳驾      láojià      *phr.*      excuse me
2. 火车      huǒchē      *n.*      train
3. 转弯      zhuǎn wān      *v. obj.*      to make a turn
4. 司机      sījī      *n.*      driver
5. 悲观      bēiguān      *adj.*      pessimistic
6. 转车      zhuǎn chē      *v. obj.*      to transfer (vehicles)
7. 拐弯      guǎi wān      *v. obj.*      to make a turn, to turn a corner
8. 电车      diànchē      *n.*      trolley

## 口头用语 (Kǒutóu Yòngyǔ) Spoken Expressions

1. 出丑      chū chǒu      to make a fool of oneself; (lit.) to let out one's foolishness

2. 打的      dǎ dī      to take a taxi (a very colloquial expression)

3. 公交      gōng jiāo      colloquial expression for 公共汽车

4. 出那种事      chū nà zhǒng shì      for that kind of thing to happen; (lit.) to make that kind of thing come out

## 词汇注解 (Cíhuì Zhùjiě) Featured Vocabulary

### 1. 乘车 (Chéng Chē) and 坐车 (Zuò Chē)
乘车 and 坐车 both mean "to take a bus." They are interchangeable, but 坐车 is more colloquial than 乘车.

### 2. 过 (Guò)
So far you have learned three ways of using 过:

**A. As a particle: expressing the idea of having had a certain experience**

我去过图书馆了。      I have been to the library.

**B. As a verb: to pass (a period of time), to celebrate**

| | |
|---|---|
| 过日子 | to live (from day to day); (lit.) to pass/spend days |
| 过生日 | to celebrate a birthday |

**C. As a verb: to cross (the street, etc.), to pass by**

| | |
|---|---|
| 过马路 | to cross a street |
| 过了十字路口 | to pass an intersection |

## 3. 上／下 (Shàng/Xià)

You have learned that 上 and 下 can be used in the following ways:

**A. As a short form of 上边／下边 after a noun, indicating relative position:**

| | |
|---|---|
| 桌子上 | on top of the table |
| 桌子下 | under the table |

**B. As a demonstrative particle indicating relative position in time, space, or in a sequence of things:**

| | |
|---|---|
| 上个月 last month | 下个月 next month |
| 上个星期 last week | 下个星期 next week |
| 上午 morning | 下午 afternoon |
| 上（一）次 last time | 下（一）次 next time |
| 上（一）课 last lesson | 下（一）课 next lesson |
| 上（一）站 last stop | 下（一）站 next stop |

**C. As a verb:**

| | |
|---|---|
| 上车 to get in/on a car/bus | 下车 to get out/off of a car/bus |
| 上飞机 to get on an airplane | 下飞机 to get off an airplane |
| 上课 to go to a class | 下课 to end a class |
| 上楼 to go upstairs | 下楼 to go downstairs |

## 4. 出 (Chū)

出 is a verb with several meanings: to come/go out, to make (something) come out, to emerge, or to happen.

| | |
|---|---|
| 出门 | to go out; (lit.) to step out of the door |
| 出丑 | (lit.) (of a person) to accidentally show someone's foolish side |
| 出事 | to have an accident; (lit.) to bring out an accident |
| 出错 | to make a mistake; (lit.) to bring out a mistake |

## 5. 关／开 (Guàn/Kāi)

**A. to turn off / to turn on**

关电视 (to turn off the TV)    开电视 (to turn on the TV)

**B. to close / to open**

关门 (to close the door)          开门 (to open the door)

关窗户 (to close the window)    开窗户 (to open the window)

## 6. 出门/进门 (Chū Mén / Jìn Mén)

出门     to go out; (lit.) to step out the door

进门     to come in; (lit.) to enter through the door

Xueying Wang

 语法(Yǔfǎ)
Grammar

## I. The Resultative Complement (Cont'd.)

You have already learned that the resultative complement follows an action verb to show the result of that action, and that the complement can be either a verb or an adjective (Volume 2, Lesson 18). The "Verb + Complement" structure forms a compound word functioning as one verb unit. So far you have only learned 打错 and 写反 (adjective as complement) and 打完 (verb as complement). The Verb Particle 了 and the object are usually placed after the complement. In this lesson you will learn more verb and adjective complements.

### A. Verbs as Resultative Complements

In Chinese, certain verbs frequently serve as resultative complements when they follow the action verb. See the examples below.

| Verb | Verb complement | |
|------|------|------|
| 看/听 | 见 (jiàn) | see/hear something |
| 看/听 | 懂 (dǒng) | understand after watching or listening |
| 学 | 会 (huì) | be able to do (something) after studying it |
| 看/听 | 完 (wán) | finish watching/listening |

## *Compare*

| | |
|---|---|
| 我学了。 | I studied. |
| 我学会了。 | I studied and fully grasped (what was to be learned). |

看/听 and 看见/听见 are different:

| 看 | to look | 看见 | to see, to perceive through sight |
|---|---|---|---|
| 听 | to listen | 听见 | to hear, to perceive through hearing |

The following are examples of how the verb functions as a resultative complement in the sentence.

| Positive: | 他看见汽车站了。 | He saw a bus station. |
|---|---|---|
| Negative: | 他没看见汽车站。 | He did not see a bus station. |
| Question: | 他看见汽车站了吗/没有？ | Did he see a bus station or not? |

## *Notes*

1. A verb and its resultative complement must be adjacent to one another in a sentence.

2. If the object is very long, it can be placed before the subject. For example:

    昨天老师教的那些语法我都学会了。

    I understand the grammar rules the teacher taught us yesterday.

---

## ◫ PRACTICE

Use each of the given phrases and the verb complements 见, 懂, 会, and 完 to create a question and a response of your own. Suggested phrases: 成语故事, 北京机场, 新语法, 老师说的话, 他唱的歌, 中文小说, 我做的菜, 那个日本电影, 中文软件, and 他的留言.

## B. Adjectives as Resultative Complements

Just as a verb can form a resultative complement, adjectives can also be used to express the result of an action verb.

| Verb | Adjective complement | |
|------|---------------------|---|
| 写 | 错 (cuò) | write something incorrectly |
| 回答 | 对 (duì) | answer correctly |
| 听 | 清楚 (qīngchu) | hear clearly |
| 用 | 坏 (huài) | use (something) abusively so that it breaks |
| 学 | 好 (hǎo) | learn well |

## Note

好 as a complement has two meanings: One refers to quality of what has been done and one refers to completion. When 好 is used to indicate the completion of an action, it sometimes can be used interchangeably with 完, but there is a slight difference. 好 as a verb complement indicates that the action has been successfully completed. 完 as a verb complement indicates that the process is completed, either successfully or unsuccessfully.

## Compare

| | |
|---|---|
| 这辆车我修好了。 | I have successfully repaired this car. |
| 这辆车我修完了，但是没修好。 | I finished working on this car, but I cannot repair it. |

The following are examples of how an adjective can function as a resultative complement in the sentence.

| Positive: | 我们坐错车了。 | We took the wrong bus. |
|---|---|---|
| Negative: | 我们没(有)坐错车。 | We did not take the wrong bus. |
| Question: | 你们坐错车了没有/吗？ | Did you take the wrong bus or not? |

## ◪ PRACTICE

Use each of the adjective complements we learned in this lesson (错, 对, 清楚, 好 and 坏) and phrases such as 乘飞机, 坐公共汽车, 走方向, 带礼物, 填表, 用电脑, 开新车, 租房子, 认人 and 看牌子上的字 to create sentences of your own.

## II. Using 往

往 can function either as a verb complement or a preposition. As the former, it means "moving toward." As the latter, it means "to go in the direction of." See the examples below.

### A. 往 (Wǎng) as a Verb Complement

| Verb | Complement |
|------|-----------|
| 开 | 往北京的飞机快要起飞了。 |

The flight to Beijing is about to take off.

## B. 往 (Wàng) as a Preposition

| | Preposition | Verb |
|---|---|---|
| 你从这儿 | 往 | 东 走。 |

From here, you go east.

### PRACTICE

Try to make a sentence using 往 first as a verb complement and then as a preposition.

As a verb complement: 开往, 飞往

As a preposition: 往（东/西/南/北/前/后/里/外/左/右/上/下）

*A designated taxi stand.*

# III. Asking for and Giving Directions

## A. Asking for Directions

The following three patterns are commonly used to ask for directions:

### 1. *Where Is That Place?*

| | Place | 在哪儿 |
|---|---|---|
| 请问， | 16路公共汽车站 | 在哪儿？ |

Would you please tell me where the stop for Bus 16 is?

| | Place | 在哪儿 |
|---|---|---|
| 请问， | 图书馆 | 在哪儿？ |

Would you please tell me where the library is?

### 2. How to Get There?

|  | 到/去 | Place | 怎么走 |
|---|---|---|---|
| 请问， | 到 | 图书馆 | 怎么走？ |

Would you please tell me how to get to the library?

| 请问， | 去 | 医院 | 怎么走？ |
|---|---|---|---|

Would you please tell me how to get to the hospital?

### 3. Is This the Right Place to Take Transportation to...?

|  | 去 | Place | | 等/上/换车 |
|---|---|---|---|---|
| 请问， | 去 | 图书馆 | 是在这儿 | 等车吗？ |

Excuse me, is this the right place to wait for the bus to the library?

| 请问， | 去 | 医院 | 是在这儿 | 上车吗？ |
|---|---|---|---|---|

Excuse me, is this the right place to get on the bus to the hospital?

| 请问， | 去 | 机场 | 是在这儿 | 换车吗？ |
|---|---|---|---|---|

Excuse me, is this the right place to transfer to the bus to the airport?

## B. Giving Directions

So far, you have learned three key words to use when giving directions: 从 (+ Place) + 往 (+ Position Word) + 到 (+ Place). Position words that are frequently used in this structure are 前, 后, 回, 左, 右, 东, 南, 西, and 北. For examples of how to use these words, see the patterns below.

|  | 从 | Place | 往P.W. | Verb | 就到(Place)了 |
|---|---|---|---|---|---|
| 你 | 从 | 这儿 | 往东 | 走，(过一个十字路口) | 就到(医院)了。 |

From here you go east, go through an intersection, and it will be right there.

| 你 | 从 | 这儿 | 往前 | 走十几米， | 就到(医院)了。 |
|---|---|---|---|---|---|

You go straight for more than ten meters, and it will be right there.

| 你 | 从 | 这儿 | 往回 | 走，(过两个红绿灯) | 就到(医院)了。 |
|---|---|---|---|---|---|

From here you go back, pass two traffic lights, and it will be right there.

| 你 | 从 | 这儿 | 往右 | 拐，(走五分钟) | 就到(医院)了。 |
|---|---|---|---|---|---|

From here you turn right, walk for five minutes, and it will be right there.

---

## ❧ PRACTICE

Take a few minutes to draw a simple map. Tell the class where you are on the map, where you want to go, and how you are going to get there (by taking a bus, subway, taxi, or simply walking).

## IV. 如果（要是）…就 (Rúguǒ (Yàoshi)...Jiù)

The pattern "如果（要是）…就" means "if...then...." 如果 may appear either before or after the subject of the first clause. 就 must be placed between the subject and the verb in the second clause. In this structure, 如果 can replace 要是. The only difference between 如果 and 要是 in this structure is that 如果 is more formal than 要是. For example:

### A. With One Subject

| First clause | Second clause |
| --- | --- |
| 如果你每天都锻炼， | 就会很健康。 |
| 你如果每天都锻炼， | 就会很健康。 |

If you exercise every day, then you will be very healthy.

### B. With Two Subjects

| 1st clause | 2nd clause |
| --- | --- |
| 如果他不跟你去跳舞， | 我就跟你去。 |
| 他如果不跟你去跳舞， | 我就跟你去。 |

If he does not go dancing with you, I will.

## *Notes*

1. If the content is obvious, either 如果 or 就 can be omitted.

   （如果）明天天气好，我们就去公园。

   If the weather is nice tomorrow, we will go to the park.

   如果有钱，我（就）一定会去中国玩儿。

   If I have the money, I will definitely travel to China for fun.

2. Although 如果 can be translated as "if," it does not function as "if," where "if" implies "whether," in English. For example:

   In English: I don't know IF he is Chinese.

   CORRECT: 我不知道他"是不是"中国人。

   xxx INCORRECT: 我不知道他"如果是"中国人。 xxx

---

## ❄ PRACTICE

Use the "如果…就" structure to create two sentences: one with one subject and the other with two subjects. Be sure to demonstrate that you understand the meaning and usage of this structure!

*Deciding which bus to take.*

# Textbook Exercises

## 🎧💻 TASK 1. 课文问答 (KÈWÉN WÈNDÁ) QUESTIONS AND ANSWERS

How well did you understand the text? Check your comprehension by answering the following questions.

1. 吴文德为什么去找李丽莉？

2. 从李丽莉和吴文德的学校到购物中心可以怎么去？

3. 李丽莉和吴文德坐了几次 22 路车才到购物中心？为什么？

4. 李丽莉和吴文德怎么才能从 22 路车上 9 路公共汽车？

## 💻 TASK 2. 语法练习 (YǓFǍ LIÀNXÍ) GRAMMATICAL STRUCTURE PRACTICE

### A. Word Selection

Select the choice that best completes each sentence.

1. 准备下车的乘客请带 _____ 自己的东西。

   错　对　好　　坏

2. 我没听 _____ 那个售货员说的话。你知道他说的是什么意思吗？

   见　懂　会　　完

3. 在中国，收信人的地址应该写在上边，咱们都写在下边了。所以，
我们写 ＿＿＿＿＿＿＿ 了。

　　错　对　好　坏

4. 我刚才在医院南门外看 ＿＿＿＿＿＿＿ 李丽莉了。

　　见　懂　会　完

5. 那个电影没意思，我没看 ＿＿＿＿＿＿＿ 就回家了。

　　见　懂　会　完

## B. Sentence Completion

Use "Verb + Complement" to complete the following sentences.

1. 坐在我旁边的那个学生不是吴文德，你 ＿＿＿＿＿＿＿ 了。

2. 对不起，星期三没有 ＿＿＿＿＿＿＿ 北京的飞机。

3. 这条路已经修了好几个月了，什么时候才能 ＿＿＿＿＿＿＿ ？

4. 牌子上的字我 ＿＿＿＿＿＿＿ 了，但是没 ＿＿＿＿＿＿＿ 。

5. 这辆公共汽车 ＿＿＿＿＿＿＿ 北京医院，我们这次 ＿＿＿＿＿＿＿ 方向了。

## C. Pick and Choose

In each of the following pairs there is a correct sentence and an incorrect one. Can you tell which one is correct and explain why the other one is incorrect?

1.
a) 他刚才在医务所看见吴文德了。
b) 我看李丽莉了，她正在上课。

2.
a) 这本书太难了，他没有看懂。
b) 老师说话说得太快了，我没听见。

3.
a) 你们坐错方向了，这是开往北京图书馆的车。
b) 你要去购物中心，应该走往南。

4.
a) 我们不知道要是我们坐错车了。
b) 我们要是再坐错车，购物中心就要关门了。

5.

a) 如果出租车太贵，就我们坐公交吧。

b) 出租车如果要的钱太多，我们就坐公共汽车吧。

---

## 💻 TASK 3. 翻译 (FĀNYÌ) PARAPHRASING

How well do you remember the grammar and vocabulary we've covered so far? Check yourself by translating the following sentences into Chinese.

1.  A: Excuse me, (may I ask,) how (can I) get to the metro station please? (Hint: 怎么,走)

    B: You turn right from here, then keep walking towards the west, (and you) will arrive at the metro station in five minutes. (Hint:从,往, and 到)

    A: (We) have already been walking for quite a few minutes now. How come we still haven't seen the metro station? (Hint: 看见) Could it be that (we) walked in the wrong direction? (Hint: 走错)

2.  A: Just now I didn't hear clearly what the ticket-seller was saying. Did you hear clearly? (Hint: 听清楚)

    B: Yes, I did hear clearly. However, I didn't understand (her). (Hint: 听懂) She said: "Everybody please make sure that (you) have your belongings with you, and be prepared to get off the bus." What does it mean to "make sure that (you) have your belongings?" (Hint: 带好)

3.  A: Excuse me; is this the right place for one to get on the bus to the Bank of China? (Hint: 上车)

    B: If you get on the bus here, you will need to transfer to another bus. (Hint: 如果) But if you walk east from here for a few minutes and go through an intersection, there's the Bus 22 stop. (Hint: 要,是,从,往, and 过) If you get on the bus there, you won't need to transfer to another bus. (Hint: 就)

4.  A: Excuse me; is this Bus 9, which goes to Beijing Hospital? (Hint: 开往)

    B: This is (indeed) the Number 9 bus. However, you are taking (the bus that) goes in the opposite direction. (Hint: 坐反) You should take the bus that goes north. (Hint: 往) The next stop is the last stop. After you arrive at the last stop, cross the street, walk not far, and you will see the Number 9 bus stop where the bus goes north. (Hint: 过,就, and 看见)

---

## 💻 TASK 4. 情景对话 (QÍNGJǏNG DUÌHUÀ) SITUATIONAL DIALOGUE

**Setting:**      On the street

**Cast:**      Two friends

**Situation:**    After running to catch a bus, two friends realize they've boarded the wrong one. They decide to get off and take a subway to their destination. Construct a dialogue between the two confused friends. How did they make the mistake? Do they know how to get to their destination by subway? Are they frustrated? Mad? Does each friend blame the other for getting on the wrong bus? Do they have someplace to be? Or was the whole situation an exciting adventure?

# 29

# 买礼物

# Choosing a Gift

> **In this lesson you will:**
> - Purchase things in China.
> - Describe which items you would like to buy for an occasion and why.
> - Compare things in Chinese.

在中国，一般百货大楼里每个柜台都有卖东西的营业员，但是这些营业员不收钱，他们给顾客回答问题或者拿东西给顾客看。如果顾客要买东西，营业员马上给顾客开一张发票。顾客拿着发票到收款台交钱。收款台的服务员收到钱以后，在发票上盖红章。顾客拿着盖好红章的发票，再到营业员那儿取东西。下面是李丽莉和吴文德去购物中心买东西的一个小故事。

（在购物中心）

李丽莉：如果我们没坐错车，我们早就到了。还好，购物中心还没关门。时间不多了。我们快给你妈妈买礼物吧。

吴文德：我们今天没白跑。你看这儿的东西真的比学校旁边的百货商店的东西多。三楼卖国画，我们先去三楼看看吧。

李丽莉：好啊。那儿有电梯，坐电梯比走楼梯快。买完了礼物，我觉得我们应该骑自行车回学校。你给咱们买两辆自行车吧。

吴文德：为什么？骑自行车没有坐公共汽车快。

李丽莉：今天这个南辕北辙的故事你怎么这么快就忘了。我们如果再坐错车，坐公交就可能真的要比骑自行车更慢呢。

吴文德：你现在一天比一天厉害，不停地揭我的短。吃一堑，长一智[1]。我们不会再走错方向了，你放心吧。

……

（在三楼购物中心）

售货员：请问，你们想买什么？

吴文德：我们想看看国画。哪种国画比较好？

售货员：国画有人物画、山水画和花鸟画三种。我喜欢山水画。您看这张山水画画得多漂亮啊。要不要买一张？

李丽莉：吴文德，国画不好寄。我们去看看那边的纱巾，好吗？我听说中国的真丝又有名，质量又好。

吴文德：国画是没有纱巾好寄，但是，给我妈妈送真丝纱巾是不是有点儿太轻了？

李丽莉：千里送鸿毛，礼轻情意重[2]嘛。我们去看看吧。

……

李丽莉：这么多种纱巾，一条比一条漂亮。吴文德，你看那条更漂亮，上面还有国画呢。

吴文德：那条纱巾比其它的都漂亮。质量也好，我妈妈一定会喜欢。请问，那条纱巾多少钱一条？

售货员：一条一百六十五块八毛钱。

吴文德：真不贵，比在美国买便宜。麻烦你给我拿一条。

售货员：好。我给您开一张发票，请到前边的收款台交钱，然后再来取货。

（在收款台）

吴文德：我没有零钱，这是二百块。

收款员：找您三十四块两毛。这是您的发票，请收好，你买的东西如果有问题，可以凭收据来退换。

吴文德：谢谢。再见！

*The Pearl Market in Beijing.*

## Notes

1. 吃一堑，长一智   (Chī yī qiàn, zhǎng yī zhì)
   You can learn from every mistake. (Lit.) Every time you fall into a ditch, your wisdom grows by that much.

2. 千里送鸿毛，礼轻情意重。   (Qiānlǐ sòng hóngmáo, lǐ qīng qíngyì zhòng.)
   This proverb comes from a Chinese 成语故事. This sentence is usually used to express one's appreciation for a gift. It literally means, "You carry a feather thousands of miles. Even though it's light, its meaning is significant." For the full story behind the phrase, see 读写练习 Task 3.

 生词表 (Shēngcí Biǎo)
## Vocabulary

| Character | Pinyin | Part of Speech | English Definition |
|---|---|---|---|
| 1. 百货大楼 你下午想不想去百货大楼看看？ | bǎihuò dàlóu | *n.* | department store |
| 百货 | | *n.* | general merchandise; (lit.) a hundred goods |
| 大楼 | | *n.* | a big multistoried building |

2. 一般　　　yībān　　　*adv.*　　　generally speaking
你一般每个月要付多少钱。

　　　　　　　　　　　　　　 *adj.*　　　ordinary, common

这个饭馆的菜很一般。

3. (收)钱　　(shōu) qián　*v. obj.*　　to collect money
我不收钱。

钱　　　　　　　　　　　　 *n.*　　　money, cash

4. 顾客　　　gùkè　　　　*n.*　　　customer
这个饭馆晚上顾客总是很多。

5. 回答　　　huídá　　　 *v.*　　　to answer
你怎么不回答我的问题？！

6. 或者　　　huòzhě　　　*conj.*　　or (used in a statement)
晚上去商店或者去看电影都可以。

7. 开发票　　kāi fāpiào　*v. obj.*　　to write out a receipt
请您给我开一张发票，好吗？

发票　　　　　　　　　　　 *n.*　　　receipt, bill, invoice

8. 收款台　　shōukuǎntái　*n.*　　　cashier's counter
请问，收款台在哪儿？

收款　　　　　　　　　　　 *v. obj.*　　to receive/collect money

9. 盖章　　　gài zhāng　　*v. obj.*　　to stamp a seal (usually as a
我在这儿给你盖一个红章。　　　　　sign of approval by an authority)

盖　　　　　　　　　　　　 *v.*　　　to cover, to put a lid on

10. 比　　　　bǐ　　　　　*prep.*　　compared with, compared to
你的书比我的新。

11. 画　　　　huà　　　　　*n.*　　　painting, drawing
你喜欢这张画吗？

　　　　　　　　　　　　　　 *v.*　　　to paint, to draw

你会不会画画？

12. 电梯　　　diàntī　　　 *n.*　　　elevator; (lit.) electric stairs
请问，电梯在哪儿？

梯　　　　　　　　　　　　 *b.f.*　　　stair, ladder

13. 楼梯　　　lóutī　　　　*n.*　　　stairs in a multistoried building
今天电梯坏了，我们走楼梯吧。

14. 骑      qí      *v.*      to ride astride (e.g., a horse, a bike)

你会不会骑自行车？

15. 自行车      zìxíngchē      *n.*      bike

那辆自行车是谁的？

16. 更      gèng      *adv.*      even more

这本书很贵，但是那本更贵。

17. 比较      bǐjiào      *v.*      to compare

我们来比较一下儿这两家商店的东西。

                                           *adv.*      comparatively, relatively

这儿的饭馆比较贵。

18. 纱巾      shājīn      *n.*      scarf made of silk or silk-like fabric

这条纱巾太漂亮了。

     纱                               *n.*      gauze, gauze-like material

     巾                               *n.*      kerchief, scarf, turban

19. 丝      sī      *n.*      silk

这些纱巾都是真丝的吗？

20. 有名      yǒu míng      *adj.*      well-known, famous

他的书在中国很有名。

21. 质量      zhìliàng      *n.*      quality

这些纱巾质量怎么样？

     质                               *n.*      original nature, character, quality

     量                               *n.*      amount

22. 轻      qīng      *adj.*      light (weight)

今天你的行李怎么这么轻？

23. 其它      qítā      *adj.*      other, the rest

您还想买些其他的东西吗？

24. 块      kuài      *m.w.*      unit of Chinese currency (its amount is the same as 元, but it is more colloquial than 元); (lit.) a piece or a lump

你还有几块钱？

25. 毛      máo      *m.w.*      one-tenth of a yuan

我只有两毛钱。

26. 取货          qǔ huò        *v. obj.*     to pick up merchandise
    你去那边取货吧。

27. 零钱          língqián      *n.*          small change, pocket money
    你有零钱吗？
    零                          *num.*        zero

28. 凭            píng          *v.*          to depend on, to rely on
    别忘了，你取货要凭这张发票。

29. 收据          shōujù        *n.*          receipt
    这是您的收据。

30. 退换          tuìhuàn       *v.*          to return and/or exchange something
    对不起，这种纱巾不能退换。                    bought
    退                          *v.*          to go backwards, to reverse, to return
    换                          *v.*          to exchange

**Chinese Brush Painting Related Vocabulary**

1. 国画          guóhuà                      traditional-style Chinese painting

2. 人物画        rénwù huà                   portrait painting

3. 山水画        shānshuǐ huà                landscape painting

4. 花鸟画        huāniǎo huà                 flower-and-bird painting

## 补充词汇 (Bǔchōng Cíhuì) Supplementary Vocabulary

1. 人民币        Rénmínbì      *n.*          Chinese currency; (lit.) People's
                                            currency

2. 美元          Měiyuán       *n.*          U.S. dollar

3. 日元          Rìyuán        *n.*          Japanese yen

4. 欧元          Ōuyuán        *n.*          Euro

5. 英镑          Yīngbàng      *n.*          English pound

6. 台币          Táibì         *n.*          Taiwanese currency

7. 兑换率        duìhuàn lǜ    *n.*          exchange rate

## 口头用语 (Kǒutóu Yòngyǔ) Spoken Expressions

| | | |
|---|---|---|
| 1. 白跑 | bái pǎo | to make a trip in vain |
| 2. 揭我的短 | jiē wǒ de duǎn | to expose my weaknesses (揭短 is to reveal someone's shortcomings.) |

## 词汇注解 (Cíhuì Zhùjiě) Featured Vocabulary

### 1. 还是 (Háishi) vs. 或者 (Huòzhě)

| 还是 | *conj.* | used in a QUESTION or indirect quote to introduce options |
|---|---|---|
| 你想喝茶还是咖啡？ | | What do you want, tea or coffee? |
| 他问我想喝茶还是咖啡。 | | He asks me what I want, tea or coffee. |

| 或者 | *conj.* | used in a STATEMENT to introduce options |
|---|---|---|
| 我想喝一点水或者茶。 | | I want some water or tea. |

### 2. 交 (Jiāo)

| 交 | *v.* | to turn or hand something in; to interact |
|---|---|---|
| 交朋友 (Lesson 19) | *v. obj.* | to make friends |
| 交钱 (this lesson) | *v. obj.* | to hand in money |

### 3. 白 (Bái)

| 白 | *adj.* | white, clear, plain |
|---|---|---|
| 白色 (white color), 白水 (plain water) | | |

| 白 | *adv.* | (to do something) in vain |
|---|---|---|
| 我们白干了。 | | What we did was in vain. |

### 4. 零钱 (Língqián) vs. 找钱 (Zhǎo Qián)

| 零钱 | *n.* | loose change or "pocket money" (in coins or paper) |
|---|---|---|
| 找 (Someone) 钱 | *v. obj.* | to give the proper amount of change to somebody |

A: 你还没有找我钱呢。 You haven't given me change.

B: 找你一块钱。 Here is your one yuan.

*Paying for a purchase in a department store.*

# 语法(Yǔfǎ)

# Grammar

## I. Chinese Currency

人民币 is the currency of the People's Republic of China. The units of the currency are 元/块 (yuán/kuài), 角/毛 (jiǎo/máo), and 分 (fēn), respectively. 块 is more colloquial than 元, and 毛 is more colloquial than 角. Amounts of money are expressed in phrases that begin with the largest unit and decrease step by step to the smallest. See if you can read the following correctly.

|          | 块        | 毛    | 分    |      |
|----------|-----------|-------|-------|------|
| ¥.05     |           |       | 五分  | (钱) |
| ¥.10     |           | 一毛  |       | (钱) |
| ¥.25     |           | 两毛  | 五分  | (钱) |
| ¥1.00    | 一块      |       |       | (钱) |
| ¥4.99    | 四块      | 九毛  | 九分  | (钱) |
| ¥380.05  | 三百八十块 | 零    | 五分  | (钱) |

## Notes

1. 钱 is frequently omitted.

2. 分 (except when it is the only unit as in 五分) is also frequently omitted. For example: 一毛五.

## A. Relationship between Units

The units of Chinese currency have the same unit relation to each other as do the American dollar, dime, and cent. For example:

*1.* *1毛/角 = 10分*

An amount of ten fen is read as 一毛, NOT 十分钱.

Twenty fen is 两毛, NOT 二十分钱.

*2.* *1块/元 = 10毛/角*

Ten mao is read as 一块, NOT 十毛.

*3.* 三百八十块零五分(钱)

When one unit is missing (in this case, 毛), 零 (which means "and" but can be read as "zero") is added to fill in for the missing unit.

---

## 🔲 PRACTICE

Try reading the following Chinese currency aloud.

¥341.05     ¥200.09     ¥99     ¥44.15     ¥105.25     ¥.25

## B. Asking the Price

Both of the following phrases mean "how much." They are the most commonly used phrases for asking the price of something.

多少钱 (for general use)

几块钱 (only used if the estimated cost is less than ten yuan)

The following patterns will help you to get started.

*1. Number + Measure Word + (Noun)* 多少钱/几块(钱)？

For example: How much is one (shirt)?

一件(衬衫)多少钱？

一件(衬衫)几块(钱)？

*2. (Noun) +* 多少钱/几块(钱) *Number + Measure Word?*

For example: How much is one (shirt)?

(衬衫)，多少钱/几块(钱)一件？

*3.* 这/那 *+ Measure Word + (Noun)* 多少钱/几块(钱)？

For example: How much is this (shirt)?

这件(衬衫)多少钱？

这件(衬衫)几块(钱)？

*4.* 这/那种 + *(Noun)* 多少钱/几块（钱）+ *Number + Measure Word?*

For example: How much does this type of bike cost?

这种自行车多少钱一辆？

## C. Recognizing Chinese Currency

You have already learned the Chinese numbers (Volume 1, Lesson 9). There are also some Chinese characters that represent numbers. Learning these characters will help you read Chinese currency.

| 壹 | 贰 | 叁 | 肆 | 伍 | 陆 | 柒 | 捌 | 玖 | 拾 | 佰 |
|---|---|---|---|---|---|---|---|---|---|---|
| yī | èr | sān | sì | wǔ | liù | qī | bā | jiǔ | shí | bǎi |
| 一 | 二 | 三 | 四 | 五 | 六 | 七 | 八 | 九 | 十 | 百 |
| 1 | 2 | 3 | 4 | 5 | 6 | 7 | 8 | 9 | 10 | 100 |

# II. Making Comparisons with the Preposition 比 (Bǐ)

Some statements with one subject and an adverb indicating degree—such as 比较 (bǐjiào), 更 (gèng), and 最 (zuì)—imply comparison, as in the examples below:

她的衣服漂亮。（我的不漂亮。）  Her clothes are pretty.

她的衣服比较漂亮。  Her clothes are rather pretty.

她的衣服更漂亮。  Her clothes are prettier.

她的衣服最漂亮。  Her clothes are the prettiest.

In this lesson, you'll learn how to make comparisons between two items by using the preposition 比. Adverbs such as 很, 非常, 太, and 最 should NEVER be used when making comparisons using 比. To form a negative sentence, you may use 不比. However, the negative form 不比 is rarely used for any purpose other than emphasis. To form a question, you may use "比…吗." 比 can be used with a predicate adjective, a predicate verb, or a verb complement.

## A. Comparing with a Predicate Adjective

In the predicate adjective structures with 比, the adverbs 更 and 还 may be placed before the predicate adjective to indicate the degree of comparison.

| | Subject1 | 比 | Subject2 | Predicate adjective |
|---|---|---|---|---|
| Positive: | 我看的书 | 比 | 他（看的书） | （更/还）多。 |
| | I read more than he does. | | | |
| Question: | 你看的书 | 比 | 他 | （更/还）多吗？ |
| | Do you read even more books than he does? | | | |

## *Notes*

1. The repeated phrases in the second subject can be omitted. For example:

   我看的书比他(看的书)多。= 我看的书比他多。

2. When an adverb such as 总 is used, it should be placed before 比.

   他总比我们努力。

3. 比 cannot be used to form an affirmative-negative question.

---

## ❖ PRACTICE

Compare some of your hobbies or favorite activities with those of your best friends, using the patterns given in this lesson.

## B. Comparing with a Predicate Verb

Some verbs such as 了解 (liǎojiě) and 注意 (zhùyì), or auxiliary verbs such as 喜欢 (xǐhuan), 想 (xiǎng), 要 (yào), 爱 (ài), and 会 (huì) can be used in this pattern. In this structure, the adverbs 更 and 还 may be placed before a predicate verb to indicate the degree of comparison.

|  | Subject1 | 比 | Subject2 | Predicate adjective |
|---|---|---|---|---|
| Positive: | 我 | 比 | 他 | (更/还)喜欢看中国电影。|
| | I like watching Chinese movies (even) more than he does. | | | |
| Question: | 你 | 比 | 他 | (更/还)喜欢看中国电影吗？|
| | Do you like watching Chinese movies (even) more than he does? | | | |

---

## ❖ PRACTICE

Use the above patterns and the phrases given here (了解中国文化, 注意身体健康, 想去旅游, 会搞电脑, 爱喝茶, and 能吃能睡) to compare yourself with your friends.

## C. Comparing with the Verb Complement of Degree

These structures vary depending on where the "Prepositional Phrase 比 + Subject2" is placed.

### *1. Without an Object*

The "Prepositional phrase 比 + Noun" can be placed either before the verb or before the complement. For example:

Before the verb:           他比我来得早。   He got here before I did.

Before the complement:     他来得比我早。   He got here before I did.

## 🔲 PRACTICE

Use one of the patterns above to ask someone a question comparing his/her habits to someone else's. When you're done, try the other pattern. Suggested phrases: 走得快, 吃得多, 离开得晚, 复习得好, and 穿得少.

### 2. With an Object

The "Prepositional Phrase 比 + Subject2" can be placed in one of the following three places. Since there is no significant difference between the three patterns, you only need to remember one of the three.

| | | |
|---|---|---|
| Before the main verb: | 他比我看书看得多。 | He reads more books than I do. |
| Before the repeated verb: | 他看书比我看得多。 | He reads more books than I do. |
| Before the complement: | 他看书看得比我多。 | He reads more books than I do. |

## 🔲 PRACTICE

Use one of the three patterns above to ask someone a question comparing his/her habits to someone else's. When you're done, switch roles and try it again! Suggested phrases: 买东西, 卖东西, 找路, 考试, 修课, 听录音, 洗澡, and 开车.

## D. Comparing with Time or Location Words

Sometimes the 比 structure is used in a one-subject sentence comparing different points in time or location. 比 is placed between the two time words or the two location words. Adverbs 更 and 还 are frequently used in this structure.

With time words:

| | |
|---|---|
| 他现在比以前还忙。 | Now he is busier than before. |
| 他现在比以前更认真了。 | He is more serious now than before. |

With location words:

| | |
|---|---|
| 他在饭馆比在家吃得多。 | He eats more in a restaurant than at home. |
| 他在家比在图书馆学得更认真。 | He studies better at home than in the library. |

## 🔲 PRACTICE

Ask someone a question using the above pattern. Your partner should answer using both positive and negative forms. Then switch roles, and try it again. Suggested topics: 学习习惯, 天气, and 价格.

## III. Making Comparisons with the Verb 有 (Yǒu) / 没有 (Méi Yǒu)

The comparative structure that uses the verb 有 is similar in function but different in form and meaning to the structure that uses 比. When comparing two subjects that are very different from each other, 比 is often used, while 有 is used to compare two subjects that are very similar. When translating sentences using 比, "than" is frequently used. When translating sentences using 有, people usually use "as (adjective) as." In addition, when 有 or 没有 is used, the condition of Subject2 is known and Subject1 is measured against Subject2. The only adverbs indicating degree that can be used in the comparative structures 有 and 没有 are 这么 and 那么. We will talk more about the usage of 有 and 没有 in the next lesson.

| | Subject1 | 有 | Subject2 | 那么 | Adjective |
|---|---|---|---|---|---|
| Positive: | 我 | 有 | 他 | 那么 | 高。 |
| | I am as tall as he is. | | | | |
| Negative: | 我 | 没有 | 他 | 那么 | 高。 |
| | I am not as tall as he is. | | | | |
| Question: | 我 | 有没有 | 他 | 那么 | 高？ |
| | Am I as tall as he is or not? | | | | |
| | 我 | 有 | 他 | 那么 | 高吗？ |
| | Am I as tall as he is? | | | | |

## Notes

1. The positive form with 有 is used less frequently than the positive form with 比.

2. The negative form using 没有 is frequently used in the 比 structure. 不比 is rarely used unless for emphasis.

## 🔊 PRACTICE

Pick two items and think of an adjective that can be used to describe the differences between the items. One person should ask a question comparing the items, and the other should answer in both a negative and a positive form. Then switch roles. For example:

Question:　　中文有日文那么难学吗？

Answer:　　　中文没有日文那么难学。

## IV. The Adverbial Structure "一 Measure Word 比 (Bǐ) 一 Measure Word"

### A. Indicating "Every One of..."
This structure has the same meaning as "每 + Measure Word + 都" but is more emphatic.

| Subject | 一M.W. | 比一M.W. | Predicate adjective |
|---|---|---|---|
| 你的裤子 | 一条 | 比一条 | 瘦。 |
| Every pair of your pants is tighter than the last. | | | |
| 你的衬衫 | 一件 | 比一件 | 好看。 |
| Every one of your shirts looks nicer than the last. | | | |

你的学生　　　一个　　　　比一个　　　认真。

Every one of your students is more serious than the other.

我看的书　　　一本　　　　比一本　　　有意思。

Every book I read is more interesting than the last.

## B. Indicating the Progressive Development of a Changing Situation

This structure indicates a continuous change associated with the passing of time and takes the following form: "一 Measure Word 比一 Measure Word + Adjective/Verb." The measure words in this structure are usually time expressions such as 一天比一天 and 一年比一年. This structure is usually followed by an adjective, but sometimes it may also be followed by a verb, such as 喜欢, 希望, 想, 会, 了解, etc.

### 1. An Adjective (Phrase) as a Predicate

| Subject | 一 M.W. | 比一 M.W. | Predicate adjective |
|---------|---------|-----------|---------------------|
| 天气 | 一天 | 比一天 | 热了。 |

It is getting hotter and hotter each day.

### 2. A Verb (Phrase) as a Predicate

| Subject | 一 M.W. | 比一 M.W. | Predicate verb |
|---------|---------|-----------|----------------|
| 我 | 一天 | 比一天 | 爱跳舞。 |

I like dancing more and more each day.

| | | | |
|---------|---------|-----------|----------------|
| 我 | 一天 | 比一天 | 想家。 |

I miss my family more and more each day.

## Notes

1. If the noun 月 or 星期 is used in this pattern, measure words are needed. For example:
   一个月比一个月
   一个星期比一个星期

2. A clock-time expression such as 一分钟比一分钟 also contains the measure word 分 and the noun 钟.

## ❈ PRACTICE

Have a short conversation with a partner, using the "一 Measure Word 比一 Measure Word" structure as many times as possible during the dialogue. Try to incorporate the vocabulary from this lesson into your conversation.

## V. The Adverbial Structure "早就…了" (Zǎo jiù...le)

The adverbial structure "早就…了" emphasizes that something happened a long time ago or earlier than expected. It can be used with either an adjective predicate or a verb predicate. See the examples below.

### A. With an Adjective Predicate

| Subject | 早就 | Adjective predicate | 了 |
|---|---|---|---|
| 我的车 | 早就 | 坏 | 了。|

My car broke down long ago.

| | | | |
|---|---|---|---|
| 菜 | 早就 | 不热 | 了。|

The food has been cold for a long time.

### B. With a Verb Predicate

| Subject | 早就 | Verb predicate | 了 |
|---|---|---|---|
| 我 | 早就 | 吃完饭 | 了。|

I finished eating a long time ago.

| | | | |
|---|---|---|---|
| 我 | 早就 | 不喜欢跳舞 | 了。|

I haven't liked dancing for a long time.

---

## PRACTICE

Try to use the above patterns with the suggested phrases to create sentences of your own. Suggested phrases: 电梯, 百货商店, 乘客, 公共汽车, 包裹, 信封, 血压, 签证, 飞机, and 面试的时间.

*Tang dynasty-style clothing for sale at a local store in Xi'an.*

# Textbook Exercises

## 🎧📖 TASK 1. 课文问答 (KÈWÉN WÈNDÁ) QUESTIONS AND ANSWERS

How well did you understand the text? Check your comprehension by answering the following questions.

1. 李丽莉和吴文德是怎么去购物中心的？为什么？

2. 吴文德给他妈妈买什么生日礼物？为什么？

3. 李丽莉为什么要让吴文德买自行车？

4. 发票收据有什么用？

## 📔 TASK 2. 语法练习 (YǓFǍ LIÀNXÍ) GRAMMATICAL STRUCTURE PRACTICE

### A. Sentence Construction

Using the words in parentheses, construct new single-clause sentences that incorporate the meaning of the two clauses for each sentence below.

1. 她有两辆自行车，我只有一辆自行车。(比, 多/少)

2. 这个百货大楼大，那个百货大楼小。(比, 大/小)

3. 我骑车骑得很快，他骑得不快。(比 for positive, 没有 for negative)

4. 那张国画很有名，这张更有名。(比 for positive, 没有 for negative)

5. 李丽莉是今天早上八点来的。吴文德是早上八点半来的。(比 for positive, 没有 for negative)

### B. Sentence Completion

1. Use the comparative expression to the right of each incomplete sentence and add a noun or pronoun to complete the sentence.

a. 他骑自行车骑得很慢，我比……还……。

b. 我不喜欢吃日本饭，……没有……。

c. 我知道你很想买那件毛衣。……比……更想……。

d. 我常常去百货大楼买东西，……比……多。

e. 你哥哥能不能穿你爸爸的衬衫？……有没有……高？

2. Use the phrases given to complete the sentences below.

a. 上个月去上海的飞机票还是$800，这个月已经$900多了，_____。
   （一个月比一个月）

b. 春天到了，草_____。
   （一天比一天）

c. 他的书很多，_____。
   （一本比一本）

d. 下个星期中文课要考试了，修汉语课的学生_____。
   （一个比一个）

e. 我那位去中国留学的朋友每个星期都给我写信，_____。
   （一封比一封）

---

## 📖 TASK 3. 翻译 (FĀNYÌ) PARAPHRASING

How well do you remember the grammar and vocabulary we've covered so far? Check yourself by translating the following sentences into Chinese.

1. Riding a bus is faster than riding a bike, (Hint: 比) but it's not convenient. (Hint: 没有) Therefore, I prefer to ride a bike. (Hint: 比较)

2. Shopping in China is more troublesome than shopping in the U.S. (Hint: 比) Customers first look at the sample of the goods, then take a receipt given by the salesclerk to the cashier's counter. (Hint: 先…然后再) After paying, they bring the stamped receipt back to the salesclerk to pick up their goods. (Hint: 以后再)

3. These silk scarves are prettier than the one I bought last time for my mother's birthday gift. (比) What a pity that I mailed the gift to her a long time ago. (Hint: 但是,早就…了)

4. A: Do you like to take the elevator or walk up the stairs? (Hint: 还是)
   B: I think that walking up the stairs is healthier than taking the elevator. (Hint: 比…更 + Adjective)

5. A: How much is this Chinese painting? (Hint: 一张)
   B: It's eighty yuan and fifty-five fen.
   A: This is a one hundred. I don't have change.
   B: No problem. I'll give you change—nineteen yuan and forty-five fen.

# 📓 TASK 4. 情景对话 (QÍNGJǏNG DUÌHUÀ) SITUATIONAL DIALOGUE

**Setting:**   At a department store

**Cast:**   A clerk and a customer

**Situation:**   The customer cannot decide which merchandise to buy and seeks advice from the clerk. Construct a dialogue between the clerk and the customer. What is the customer looking for? Can the clerk help, or is he/she confused and dealing with his/her first day on the job? Don't forget to use comparative structures!

*Women's clothes for sale at Kaiyuan Shopping Mall in Xi'an.*

# 30
# 逛夜市

# Browsing at the Night Market

*In this lesson you will:*
- Understand the proceedings at the Chinese night market.
- Use your bargaining skills to lower prices.
- Talk in detail about the similarities and differences between things.

中国夜市非常热闹。每天晚上天快黑的时候，小贩就在夜市的街道两边摆起了小摊子，开始卖东西。夜市的东西比商店的便宜，顾客还可以讨价还价。但是在夜市里买的东西不能保证质量，买了以后一般不能退换。讨价还价的最好方法是用本地话。如果你是外地人，小贩就会想办法跟你多要钱。下面请看李丽莉和吴文德逛夜市的故事。

（在李丽莉的房间。）

吴文德：李丽莉，我们今天晚上去逛逛夜市吧，练一练讨价还价的本领。

李丽莉：我看咱们别去了。夜市的小贩跟商店的营业员不一样，他们太油了。我们不会讲价钱，去了一定会吃亏。

吴文德：我们只去看看热闹，不买东西，怎么会吃亏呢？咱们走吧。早一点儿去夜市，人会少一些。

（吴文德和李丽莉到夜市的时候，小贩们已经在忙着卖东西了。）

小　贩：先生，今天我的东西大降价，打八折。我这儿有毛衣，有西服；要不，您买一件衬衫吧。您看这件衬衫多好啊，百分之百真丝的。比您身上穿的那件帅多了。

吴文德：我们不买东西，只是看一看。

小　贩：你们不会说本地话，一定是外地人吧？

李丽莉：我们是美国人。

小　贩：可是你们说的中国话跟美国人说的不一样。你们的中文说得真棒！

李丽莉：哪里，哪里。你过奖了。

　小贩：美国人最喜欢买我的牛仔裤。我这儿长的、短的、肥的、瘦的都有。您要不要买一条？穿多大公分的？您要是再晚来半小时，就没有了。

李丽莉：谢谢。牛仔裤我不想买。这种夹克多少钱一件？都有什么颜色的？

　小贩：三百五十块一件。我这儿有蓝的、有黑的、也有深红色的。质量很好，是全棉的。您试试吧。如果您买两件，三百块一件。每件便宜五十块。

吴文德：李丽莉，小心上当受骗[1]。这儿的东西可都是金玉其外，败絮其中[2]。

‥‥‥‥

　小贩：小姐，您不胖，不瘦，长得苗条，上次来的一个姑娘穿这种夹克就没有您穿着好看。这两件夹克就跟给您订做的一样，长短、肥瘦正合适。您穿这两件，就跟电影明星一样。

李丽莉：这件黑色夹克跟那件蓝色夹克有什么不一样？

　小贩：一样。您穿这件黑色的跟穿那件蓝色的一样好看。

李丽莉：可是，这两件不一样长。这件黑色的比蓝色的长一点儿。

　小贩：差不多，只长三厘米。要不，您再少给十块钱吧，我今天要赔本儿了。

李丽莉：这两件夹克我都想买。但是，蓝色的三百块，黑色的两百九十块。一共五百九十块。太贵了！能不能便宜一点儿？五百五十块，你卖不卖？

　小贩：不能再便宜了。我真的没赚上几个钱。

吴文德：李丽莉，你讲价钱没有小贩讲得那么油，小心吃亏。你看，这件夹克上边的颜色比下边的要深得多。算了吧。别买了。

　小贩：那是一种新样式。好吧。您交五百五十块。唉，我这次赔本赔大了。

李丽莉：好。这是六百块。麻烦你给我找五十块。

## Notes

1. 上当受骗   (shàng dàng shòu piàn)
   To be tricked or fooled and suffer a loss.

2. 金玉其外，败絮其中   (jīn yù qí wài, bài xù qí zhōng)
   (Lit.) gold and jade on the outside, but spoiled cotton filling (of a cushion, etc.) inside. For the full story behind the phrase, see 读写练习, Task 3.

*Shopping for trinkets at the night market in the Muslim Quarter of Xi'an.*

 生词表 (Shēngcí Biǎo)
# Vocabulary

| Character | Pinyin | Part of Speech | English Definition |
|-----------|--------|----------------|--------------------|
| 1. 逛<br>我们去逛商店，你去不去？ | guàng | *v.* | to take a stroll in (a store, market, etc.) |
| 2. 夜市<br>你一定要去看看那儿的夜市。 | yèshì | *n.* | night market |
| 3. 热闹<br>那儿怎么那么热闹？<br><br>我们也去看看热闹吧。 | rènao | *adj.*<br><br>*n.* | bustling with excitement, lively; (lit.) warm and loud<br>a lively scene |

| 闹 | nào | *adj.* | noisy |
| | | *v.* | to make noise, to make a lively scene |
| 4. 小贩（子） | xiǎofàn(zi) | *n.* | street vendor |

那个小贩（子）说得不对。

| 5. 街道 | jiēdào | *n.* | street |

那条街道很小，商店不多。

| 6. 摆（起） | bǎi(qǐ) | *v. (comp.)* | to set (up) |

他们在那儿摆（起）了一个柜台。

| 7. 摊子 | tānzi | *n.* | street vendor booth |

那个小摊子上的东西太贵了。

| 8. 讨价还价 | tǎo jià huán jià | *v. phr.* | to negotiate a price, to bargain; (lit.) to make a (price) offer and to counter a (price) offer |

你总喜欢跟我讨价还价。

| 9. 保证 | bǎozhèng | *v.* | to guarantee |

我保证以后不去那儿买东西。

| 10. 本地话 | běndì huà | *n.* | local dialect |

你会我们本地话，你也是北方人吧。

| 11. 外地人 | wàidì rén | *n.* | person from another region |

他们都知道你是外地人。

| 12. 本领 | běnlǐng | *n.* | ability, skills |

你有这么大的本领，我怎么不知道？

| 13. 一样 | yīyàng | *adj.* | identical; (lit.) of one shape |

这个小摊子和那个小摊子不太一样。

| | | *adv.* | similarly, in the same way |

这件和那件一样贵。

| 14. 讲价钱 | jiǎng jiàqian | *v. obj.* | to bargain a price |

你真会讲价钱！

| 价钱 | | *n.* | price |

| 15. 吃亏 | chī kuī | *v. obj.* | suffer a loss |

你去一定不会吃亏。

| 16. 降价 | jiàng jià | *v. obj.* | to discount or lower the price |

请您再给我降一点儿价吧。

17. 打折      dǎ zhé      *v. obj.*      to sell at a discount, to take off a percentage (of the original price); (lit.) to make a break in the price
这些衣服已经打折了，已经打了三折了！

18. 毛衣      máoyī      *n.*      sweater (usually knit of wool or wool-like yarn)
这件毛衣我穿好看吗？

19. 百分之百      bǎi fēn zhī bǎi      *phr.*      100 percent; (lit.) one hundred out of one hundred divisions
这是百分之百的中国货。

20. 牛仔裤      niúzǎikù      *n.*      jeans; (lit.) cowboy pants
你不应该在那家商店买牛仔裤。

     牛仔           *n.*      cowboy

21. 肥      féi      *adj.*      (of human beings or animals) fat, (of clothing) loose
那条裤子你穿肥不肥？

22. 公分      gōngfēn      *m.w.*      centimeter
这条裤子是多少公分？

23. 夹克      jiákè      *n.*      jacket
你穿那件夹克很好看。

24. 棉      mián      *n.*      cotton
这件是全棉的吗？

25. 小心      xiǎoxīn      *adj.*      careful, cautious, wary
你去夜市买东西，应该小心一点儿。

26. 苗条      miáotiao      *adj.*      (usually of a woman's figure) slender
你现在怎么这么苗条？

27. 合适      héshì      *adj.*      suitable
这件你穿正合适。

28. 明星      míngxīng      *n.*      (movie, pop, etc.) star
我想当一个大明星。

29. 厘米      límǐ      *m.w.*      centimeter
这件夹克比那件长三厘米。

30. 赔本      péi běn      *v. obj.*      to lose money on a sale, to make less money than what you invested
那个小贩总是说他赔本儿了。

31. 一共      yīgòng      *adv.*      totally, altogether
你一共买了几件？

32. 赚      zhuàn      *v.*      to make money, to earn (a profit from), (derogatory) to rip off
他赚了你多少钱？

## 补充词汇 (Bǔchōng Cíhuì) Supplementary Vocabulary

| | | | |
|---|---|---|---|
| 1. 价格 | jiàgé | *n.* | price |
| 2. 优惠 | yōuhuì | *adj.* | preferential, favorable |
| | | *n.* | preferential treatment |
| 3. 折扣 | zhékòu | *n.* | discount |
| 4. 杀价 | shā jià | *v. obj.* | to slash the price |
| 5. 大拍卖 | dà pāimài | *phr.* | clearance sale, auction sale |
| 6. 价廉物美 | jià lián wù měi | *phr.* | high-quality products at bargain prices |

# 口头用语 (Kǒutóu Yòngyǔ) Spoken Expressions

## A. General Terms

| | | |
|---|---|---|
| 1. 太油了 | tài yóu le | (derogatory) too slick, too much of a smooth-talker |
| 2. 你过奖了。 | Nǐ guòjiǎng le. | You flatter me. (Lit.) You overly praise me. |
| 3. 算了 | suàn le | forget it, drop it, let it go |

## B. Bargaining Techniques

It's good to hone your bargaining skills before visiting a night market. Here are some long-standing techniques that you may find helpful.

### 1. The Fault-finding Technique

You can find fault with any merchandise you like and use that as a basis for bargaining.

那条牛仔裤的质量不错，但是样式太老了，颜色也太深了。便宜一点儿，行不行？

Nà tiáo niúzǎikù de zhìliàng bú cuò, dànshì yàngshì tài lǎo le, yánsè yě tài shēn le. Piányi yīdiǎnr, xíng bù xíng?

That pair of jeans is okay in terms of quality, but in terms of style it is too old, and in terms of color it is also too dark. Lower the price a little bit, would you?

这件夹克大小合适，但是质量没有那件好。你能给我便宜十块吗？

Zhè jiàn jiākè dàxiǎo héshì, dànshì zhìliàng méiyǒu nà jiàn hǎo. Nǐ néng gěi wǒ piányi shíkuài ma?

This jacket suits me in terms of size, but in terms of quality it is not as good as the other one. Would you take off ten yuan for me?

## 2. The "Buy in Quantity" Technique

Usually the more you buy, the easier it is to bring the price down, because the street vendors do not want to lose your business.

两件四十你卖吗？

Liǎng jiàn sìshí nǐ mài ma?

Would you sell two for forty yuan?

我想买三个，你给我打九折，行吗？

Wǒ xiǎng mǎi sān ge, nǐ gěi wǒ dǎ jiǔ zhé, xíng ma?

I am thinking of buying three; give me ten percent off, would you?

## 3. The "Not Enough Money" Technique

When you've found something you like, name your own price, and let the vendor know that you are not going to spend more than that.

这件毛衣挺好看，但是我只有八十四块钱，你卖不卖？

Zhè jiàn máoyī tǐng hǎokàn, dànshì wǒ zhǐyǒu bāshísì kuài qián, nǐ mài bú mài?

This sweater looks pretty good, but I have only eighty-four yuan. Would you sell (at that price)?

二十块你卖我就买，不卖就算了。

Ershí kuài nǐ mài wǒ jiù mǎi, bú mài jiù suàn le.

If you sell for twenty yuan, I'll buy. If you don't, then forget it.

## 4. The "Bad Cop" Technique

If you have your friend there with you, ask your friend to play the "bad cop."

Customer: 这件毛衣多少钱？

Zhè jiàn máoyī duōshao qián?

How much is this sweater?

Street Vendor: 一百块一件。

Yībǎi kuài yī jiàn.

One hundred yuan for one piece.

Bad Cop: 你有那么多毛衣，怎么又想买毛衣了？别买了。

Nǐ yǒu nàme duō máoyī, zěnme yòu xiǎng mǎi máoyī le? Bié mǎi le.

You have so many sweaters, why do you want to buy more? Forget it. (Lit.), Stop buying it.

Customer: 便宜一点儿，好不好？

Piányi yīdiǎnr, hǎo bù hǎo?

Lower the price a little, okay?

Street Vendor: 九十块，不能再低了。

Jiǔshí kuài, bù néng zài dī le.

Ninety yuan, no lower than that.

Bad Cop: 九十块不值。咱们走吧。

Jiǔshí kuài bù zhí. Zánmen zǒu ba.

It's not worth ninety yuan. Let's go.

Customer: 七十（块），你卖不卖？

Qīshí (kuài), nǐ mài bù mài?

Seventy, would you sell?

Street Vendor: 八十块怎么样？

Bāshí kuài zěnme yàng?

How about eighty?

*Traditional Chinese fans for sale at the night market.*

# 词汇注解 (Cíhuì Zhùjiě) Featured Vocabulary

## 1. 长 (Cháng) vs. 长 (Zhǎng)

| 长 (cháng) | *adj.* | long |
|---|---|---|

这件毛衣太长了。    This sweater is too long.

| 长 (zhǎng) | *v.* | to grow |
|---|---|---|

他长高了。    He has grown taller.

## 2. 打折 (Dǎ Zhé)

| 打折 | *v. obj.* | to take a certain percentage off (the original price) |
|---|---|---|

The number inserted between 打 and 折 indicates not the percentage to be discounted but the discounted price. For example:

| 打三折 | 70% off | 打五折 | 50% off |
|---|---|---|---|
| 打七折 | 30% off | 打九折 | 10% off |

## 3. 厘米 *(Límǐ) vs.* 公分 *(Gōngfēn)*

Both 厘米 and 公分 are measure words for centimeter. But 厘米 is an official measurement while 公分 is colloquial.

| 厘米 | *m.w.* | centimeter | 一厘米 |
|------|--------|------------|--------|
| 公分 | *m.w.* | centimeter | 多少公分 |

# 语法(Yǔfǎ)
# Grammar

## Review of Resultative Complement Construction

In Lessons 18 and 28, you learned about the resultative complement construction. We have come across three resultative complements in this lesson. Do you know what they are? If you need help, please refer to your multimedia CD-ROM.

### 1. 摆起 *(Verb + Verb Complement)*

街道的两边摆起了小摊子。　　　Along both sides of the street, vendors have set up their booths.

### 2. 说好 *(Verb + Adjective Complement)*

我们今天不是说好不买东西吗？　Didn't we agree we wouldn't buy anything today?

### 3. 赚上 *(Verb + Verb Complement)*

我真是没赚上几个钱。　　　　　I didn't make much of a profit.

## I. Making Comparisons with "跟…一样" (Gēn...Yīyàng)

In Lesson 29, you learned to compare two items that are different using 比 and 有/没有. In this lesson you will learn the "跟…一样" construction, which compares items that are similar. This kind of comparative construction can take the following three forms:

### A. With a Predicate Adjective

The negative 不 should be placed before 一样, not before the adjective.

Positive:　　　他跟他弟弟一样高。
　　　　　　　He and his brother are the same height.

Negative:　　　他跟他弟弟不一样高。
　　　　　　　He and his brother are not the same height.

Questions:　　他跟他弟弟一样高吗？
　　　　　　　Are they (he and his brother) of the same height?

他跟他弟弟一样不一样高？
Are they (he and his brother) the same height?

Positive Response:   一样。
Yes.

Negative Response:   不一样。他比他弟弟高。
No. He is taller than his brother.

## Note

The difference between "跟⋯一样" and the 有 comparative structure:

A跟B一样高。    A and B are identical. (A and B are of the same height.)
A有B那么高。    A is measured against B. (A is as tall as B.)

## B. Comparing with a Predicate Verb

Positive:   他跟我一样喜欢吃中国饭。
He likes Chinese food, just as I do.

Question:   他跟你一样喜欢吃中国饭吗？
Does he like Chinese food as much as you do?

Positive Response:   一样。
Yes.

Negative Response:   不一样。我比他更喜欢吃中国饭。
No. I like Chinese food more than he does.

## C. With a Verb Complement of Degree

### 1. Without an Object

"跟 + Subject2" can be placed either before the main verb or before 一样. 一样 is always placed before the adjective. For example:

我跟他写得一样快。          I write as quickly as he does.
我写得跟他一样快。          I write as quickly as he does.

### 2. With an Object

When the sentence has an object, "跟 + Subject2" can be placed before any of the following three places.
1) the main verb, 2) the repeated verb or 3) 一样. All three patterns have identical meanings. 一样 should
be placed before the adjective.

我跟他写信写得一样快。      I write as quickly as he does.
我写信跟他写得一样快。      I write as quickly as he does.
我写信写得跟他一样快。      I write as quickly as he does.

## Note

The object can also be placed either before or after the subject. In both cases, the verb does not need to be repeated. For example:

| | |
|---|---|
| Object after the subject: | 他书看得跟我一样快。 |
| Object before the subject: | 书他看得跟我一样快。 |

---

## 🔲 PRACTICE

Ask someone a question using each of the above patterns. Your partner should answer in both positive (a full sentence) and negative forms. When you've finished, switch roles. For example:

| | |
|---|---|
| Question: | 中文跟英文一样难吗？ |
| Positive: | 中文跟英文一样难。 |
| Negative: | 不一样，中文比英文难。 |
| Question: | 你跟他一样爱睡觉吗？ |
| Positive: | 我跟他一样爱睡觉。 |
| Negative: | 不一样，我比他睡得少。 |
| Question: | 你睡得跟他一样晚吗？ |
| Positive: | 我睡得跟他一样晚。 |
| Negative: | 不一样，我比他睡得早。 |
| Question: | 你讲价讲得跟他一样好吗？ |
| Positive: | 我讲价讲得跟他一样好。 |
| Negative: | 不一样，他比我讲得好。 |

## II. Making Comparisons with the Preposition 比 (Cont'd.)

In this section, you will learn how to use 比 to indicate the difference between two items.

### A. Indicating a Slight Difference

In this form, 一点／一些 is placed after a predicate adjective to indicate that there is a slight different between Subject1 and Subject2. The structure "比… Adjective + 一点" is rarely used in negative forms.

| | |
|---|---|
| Question: | 你比你妹妹高一些吗？ |
| | Are you slightly taller than your sister? |
| Positive: | 我比我妹妹高一点。 |
| | I am slightly taller than my sister. |

## 🔲 PRACTICE

Ask someone a question using one of the above structures. When you're done, switch roles and try it again. Suggested words: 长, 短, 肥, 瘦, 贵, 便宜, 轻, 重, 热闹, and 有名.

## B. Indicating an Emphatic Difference

得多 or 多了 can be placed after a predicate adjective to indicate that there is a significant difference between Subject1 and Subject2. 多了 is rarely used in a question or a negative form.

他的工作比你的好得多。　　His job is much better than yours.

他的工作比你的好多了。　　His job is much better than yours.

## 🔲 PRACTICE

Ask someone a question using one of the above structures. When you're done, switch roles and try it again. Suggested words: 长, 短, 肥, 瘦, 贵, 便宜, 轻, 重, 热闹, and 有名.

## C. Quantity Complement Providing Specific Information

The quantity complement usually appears after the predicate to provide information related to money (块, 毛, 分⋯), age (岁⋯), time (年, 天, 星期⋯), or measurement (公分⋯). The negative form is rarely used in this structure.

Money:　　　　这件毛衣比那件贵五块。
This sweater is five dollars more expensive that that one.

Age:　　　　他太太比他小十岁。
His wife is ten years younger than he is.

Time:　　　　我的表比你的快半个小时。
My watch is half an hour faster than yours.

Measurement:　这条牛仔裤比那条长一厘米。
This pair of jeans is one centimeter longer than that pair.

## 🔲 PRACTICE

Try using money, time, or measurement to ask a question, and then provide an appropriate answer.

## III. Making Comparisons with the Verb 有/没有 (Cont'd.)

In Lesson 29, you learned to make comparisons using the verb 有/没有 with a predicate adjective. The adverb 那么 is usually used in this structure. For example:

我有他那么高。

I am as tall as he is.

In this lesson, you will learn to make comparisons using the 有/没有 comparative structure with a predicate verb or a verb complement of degree.

## A. Comparing with a Predicate Verb

The adverb 那么 is usually used to modify a predicate verb in this construction.

Positive:    我有他那么喜欢吃中国饭。

I like Chinese food as much as he does.

Negative:    我没有他那么喜欢吃中国饭。

I don't like Chinese food as much as he does.

Questions:   你有没有他那么喜欢吃中国饭？

Do you like to eat Chinese food as much as he does?

你有他那么喜欢吃中国饭吗？

Do you like to eat Chinese food as much as he does?

## *Compare*

我比他喜欢吃中国饭。        I like Chinese food more than he does.

(This implies that although 我 likes Chinese food, 他 may not like Chinese food.)

我没有他那么喜欢吃中国饭。    I don't like Chinese food as much as he does.

(This implies that both 我 and 他 like the Chinese food. 我 may like the Chinese food a little less than 他 does.)

## *Note*

In the "比···" structure, the negative form 不比 is rarely used unless for emphasis. In the "有/没有···" structure, the positive form 我有他那么喜欢吃中国饭 is used much less than the negative form.

## B. Comparing with a Verb Complement of Degree

Only 这么 and 那么 can be used before the adjective. No other adverb may be used in this structure.

### *1. 有/没有 + Subject2 Are Placed before the Main Verb*

| Subject1 | 有/没有 | Subject2 | Main Verb | Object | Repeated Verb + 得 | Complement |
|---|---|---|---|---|---|---|
| 你 | 没有 | 他 | 开 | 车 | 开得 | 快。 |

You don't drive as fast as he does.

### *2. 有/没有 + Subject2 Are Placed before the Repeated Verb*

| Subject1 | Main Verb | Object | 有/没有 | Subject2 | Repeated Verb + 得 | Complement |
|---|---|---|---|---|---|---|
| 你 | 开 | 车 | 没有 | 他 | 开得 | 快。 |

You don't drive as fast as he does.

**3.** 有/没有 + *Subject2 Are Placed before the Complement*

| Subject1 | Main Verb object | Repeated Verb + 得 | 有/没有 | Subject2 | (Adv.) Complement |
|---|---|---|---|---|---|
| 你 | 开车 | 开得 | 没有 | 他 | （这/那么）快。 |

You don't drive as fast as he does.

## C. Comparing the 有 Structure with the "比…" Structure

我开车开得不比他快。  I do not drive faster than he does.

我开车开得没有他快。  I don't drive as fast as he does.

---

## ❀ PRACTICE

Use each of the above two comparative structures to ask someone a question. Then switch so that your partner asks and you answer. Suggested verbs: 写, 修, 读, 看, 买, 赚, and 花. Of course, there are other verbs that can be used as well. How many can you come up with?

# IV. Using 早 (Zǎo), 晚 (Wǎn), 多 (Duō), and 少 (Shǎo) in Comparative Sentences

In comparisons, 早 or 晚 can be used to indicate relative difference in time, and 多 or 少 can be used to indicate relative difference in quantity. When 早, 晚, 多, and 少 appear in comparison structures with quantity complements, they should be placed before the verb. The object in this structure is usually a place or a thing. If the object is a place, it is usually placed after the verb. If the object is a thing, it is usually placed at the end of the sentence. 了 can be used in this structure to indicate the completion of an action and should be placed after the verb.

## A. Without 比

In this structure, 早, 晚, 多, and 少 appear between the subject and the verb.

| Subject | 早/晚/多/少 | Verb (了) (Object) | Number + M.W. | (Object) |
|---|---|---|---|---|
| 我明天 | 早/晚 | 来学校 | 一刻钟。 | |

I will come fifteen minutes earlier/later tomorrow morning.

| | | | | |
|---|---|---|---|---|
| 你 | 少/多 | 喝 | 一点儿 | 茶吧。 |

You should drink a little bit less/more tea.

## B. With 比

In this structure, 早, 晚, 多, and 少 appear between the second subject and the verb.

| Subject1 比 Subject2 | 早/晚/多/少 | Verb (了) (Object) | Number + M.W. (Object) |
|---|---|---|---|
| 我比他 | 早/晚 | 到 | 半小时。 |

I arrived thirty minutes earlier/later than him.

| | | | |
|---|---|---|---|
| 我比他 | 多/少 | 看了 | 两本书。 |

I read two more/fewer books than he did.

## ▨ PRACTICE

Use each of the above structures to create two sentences of your own. Try to use vocabulary from this lesson in both of your sentences. Suggested phrases: 买毛衣, 花钱, 收信, 到机场, 入境, 下课, 背单词, and 托运行李.

# V. A Summary of How to Use 多

So far you have learned four different ways of using 多: 1) to indicate "many," 2) to make an exclamatory sentence, 3) to express an approximate number, and 4) to ask "how much." The 多 in each of these categories carries a different meaning, each of which is summarized in the table below.

## Table: Uses of 多

| | Part of speech | Definition | Pattern | Example |
|---|---|---|---|---|
| 1. | Adjective | Many | Adverb + 多 | 夜市里有很多小贩。At the night market there are lots of street vendors. |
| 2. | Adverb | Emphatic marker | 多 + Adjective + 啊 | 中国的夜市多热闹啊。How bustling the Chinese night market is! |
| 3. | Marker of a number | Several | # + 多 + Noun | 我们系有一百多个学生。There are over one hundred students in our department. |
| 4. | Question word | How much | 多 + Adjective | 夜市有多大？How big is the night market? |

## ▨ PRACTICE

Try using each of the above patterns to create sentences of your own.

*Xueying Wang*

*Shopping for trinkets at the night market.*

Textbook Exercises

## 🎧💻 TASK 1. 课文问答 (KÈWÉN WÈNDÁ) QUESTIONS AND ANSWERS

How well did you understand the text? Check your comprehension by answering the following questions.

1. 吴文德为什么要去逛夜市？李丽莉想不想去？为什么？
2. 夜市的小贩用什么方法叫李丽莉和吴文德买他的东西？吴文德买没买小贩的东西？为什么？
3. 李丽莉在夜市买了什么东西？一共多少钱？是不是少花了一百一十块钱？为什么？
4. 中国的夜市和商店有什么不一样？

## 💻 TASK 2. 语法练习 (YǓFǍ LIÀNXÍ) GRAMMATICAL STRUCTURE PRACTICE

### A. Sentence Construction

Use the structures given in parentheses to rewrite the following sentences.

1. 我认识十几个汉字，他认识九百多个汉字。（比…多/少 + 得多）
2. 这个荤菜十五块钱，那个素菜十四块多。（比…贵/便宜 + 一点儿）
3. 我朋友看过十次中国电影，我看过五次。（比…多/少 + Verb + Amount）
4. 她穿六号的衣服，我穿八号的衣服。（跟…不一样 Adjective, 比…大/小 + Measure Word）
5. 李老师今年五十五岁，李老师的先生已经快六十五岁了。（跟…不一样 Adjective, 比…大/小…）
6. 他非常喜欢逛夜市，我不太喜欢。（没有）但是这个月我逛了两次夜市，他只逛了一次。（比…少 + Amount）
7. 我姐姐订做了一件夹克，很漂亮。我也想去订做一件。（跟…一样）
8. 我想星期六早上九点跟我朋友去逛街。我朋友叫我早上八点三刻去。（早 + Verb + Quantity）

### B. Sentence Completion

Read the following prompts and complete the sentences with the given words or phrases.

1. 我姐姐新买的衬衫，…跟…一样 Adjective。
2. 我的个子比我朋友高，但是…没有…。

3. 我想买那件蓝色的，…比… Adjective一点儿。

4. 我这个星期学了十个汉字，…比… Adjective + # + Measure Word…。

5. 我这个月赚了九百多块，…没有…。

6. 我买东西常常吃亏，但是…跟…不一样…。

## C. Pick and Choose

In each of the following pairs there is a correct sentence and an incorrect one. Can you tell which one is correct and explain why the other one is incorrect?

1.

a) 夜市卖的东西没有百货商店的便宜。

b) 小摊子卖的菜比商店的不便宜。

2.

a) 这件衬衫比那件不一样合适，这件短两公分。

b) 他跟他弟弟不一样高，他高五公分。

3.

a) 这件黑毛衣的价钱比那件白的贵一些。

b) 这套西装的价钱比那套很贵。

4.

a) 我妹妹比我多穿一件夹克。

b) 她比我买衣服买得少一件。

---

## 💻 TASK 3. 翻译 (FĀNYÌ) PARAPHRASING

How well do you remember the grammar and vocabulary we've covered so far? Check yourself by translating the following sentences into Chinese.

1. Buying things from a street vendor is very different from buying them in a department store. (Hint: 跟…不一样) With the street vendor, we can bargain for a better price. My brother's price negotiating skills are a lot better than mine, (Hint: 比…+ Adjective + 多了) so if I go with him to browse the night market, I will not be cheated out of any money. (Hint: 吃亏)

2. The blue jeans he bought at the night market are the same color and style as those that I bought from the department store, (Hint: 跟…一样) but the quality of his jeans is not as good as mine. (Hint: 没有…+ Adjective)

3. Yesterday my friend and I bought all-silk shirts at a night market, but I bought one more than he did (Hint: 比…+ Adjective + M.W.), because that silk shirt was a lot cheaper than the cotton one I bought at the department store a few days ago. (Hint: 比…+ Adjective + 一些)

4. The jacket you tried on fits you perfectly. (Hint: 正合适) It's not too loose or too tight. (不 + Adjective + 也不 + Adjective) It looks like it was specially made for you. (Hint: 跟···一样) When you wear it, you look like a movie star. (Hint: Verb + 着, 跟···一样) You should buy it.

5. A: What's the difference between these black pants and those blue pants? (Hint: 有···不一样)
   B: They're not the same length or the same size. The black ones are one size bigger and two centimeters longer. (Hint: 比···+ Adjective + 一号, 比···+ Adjective + 厘米)

---

## 💻 TASK 4. 情景对话 (QÍNGJǏNG DUÌHUÀ) SITUATIONAL DIALOGUE

**Setting:**     At a night market
**Cast:**        A street vendor and a student
**Situation:**   A student is negotiating the price of some clothes that he or she is interested in buying. Bargaining is a useful skill for anyone who wants to shop at the night market. Can the student haggle his/her way down to a reasonable amount, or will the street vendor make money because of the student's lack of bargaining experience? Does the street vendor somehow trick the student into paying more than the original price? Construct a dialogue between the student and the street vendor.

*Traditional Chinese clothes for sale at the night market.*

# 31

# 去银行

# Opening a Bank Account

> **In this lesson you will:**
> - Learn to open a bank account and conduct financial transactions in China.
> - Read about the difference between Chinese debit and credit cards.
> - Find out which methods of payment are accepted at stores in China.

在中国，每家银行的利息都是一样的，外汇的兑换率也是一样的。中国的银行有大有小，大的银行有叫号机，顾客不用站在窗口前边排队。进了银行以后，先拿一个号码，然后坐在椅子上等叫号机在屏幕上显示自己的号码。等轮到你的时候，叫号机会告诉你去几号窗口。小的银行因为没有叫号机，所以顾客得站在柜台前排队，一般也没有外汇服务项目。外国学生在中国开银行帐户的时候，不用拿号，可直接去外汇窗口。下面请看吴文德和李丽莉去银行存钱、取钱的小故事。

（一辆出租车在银行门口停住了。李丽莉和吴文德下了车，就进了银行。）

吴文德：这个银行这么大，开着这么多窗口，我应该去哪个窗口呢？

李丽莉：存美金去外汇窗口。我先去问一下儿在哪儿能办外卡取现，一会儿见。

（在银行的一个办公室里。）

李丽莉：你好。我听说在你们这个银行我可以用美国的信用卡取一些人民币，对吗？

营业员：对。这种手续叫外卡取现。今天美金和人民币的兑换率是 1 比 8.4[1]。您想取多少？

李丽莉：我取两百五十块。谢谢。

（外汇窗口）

吴文德：你好。麻烦你给我开一个银行帐户。

营业员：您要存多少钱？想存定期，还是活期？

吴文德：我想存五百美金。你给我开一个活期的帐户吧。

营业员：这么多美金都存活期，不值得。活期利息很低。

吴文德：定期利息高吗？

营业员：定期利息虽然也不高。但是比活期高一些。

吴文德：好极了。麻烦你帮我把这张两百美元的旅行支票存在活期帐户里，把这张三百美元的私人支票存在定期帐户里，好不好？

营业员：旅行支票是银行支票。我可以马上给您存。但是私人支票要等钱到银行后，才能给您开定期存款单。

吴文德：那我要等多长时间？

营业员：要等二到四个星期。等钱到了银行，我们会给您打电话。这是您的活期帐号的存折。您以后每次存钱、取钱都会记录在这个存折上。

吴文德：太好了！有了存折，我就能记住我银行里还有多少钱了。

营业员：有了银行帐户，您现在可以申请办借记卡或者信用卡了。

吴文德：借记卡和信用卡哪种好？

营业员：都好。但是借记卡容易办，可是不能超支。信用卡可以超支。但是办信用卡不但自己在银行要有帐户，而且还要有人担保才能办。

吴文德：这么麻烦！你给我办一张借记卡吧。我这个人总是丢三落四的[2]。我要是把现金丢了，那就太可惜了。

⋯⋯

李丽莉：看你那个高兴的样子，你的银行帐户一定办好了。

吴文德：我不但银行帐户办好了，而且还办了一个借记卡。我以后任何时候都能从门口外边的自助机里取钱、存钱、查帐号。方便不方便？

李丽莉：方便！你现在有卡了，就不应该一毛不拔[3]了吧？现在越来越多的商店都可以刷卡了，很多饭馆也收借记卡。我们现在去吃饭，你请客怎么样？

## *Notes*

1. 8.4 is read as "bā diǎn sì."

2. 丢三落四的   (diū sān là sì de)
   Literally, "lose three (items), and leave behind four (other items)." This is a vivid way to describe someone who is always losing things.

3. 一毛不拔   (yī máo bù bá)
   Literally, "(a person who) does not allow a single hair to be pulled (from his or her body, even if that would benefitthewholeworld)."Itcomesfroma    成语故事, and is used to describe someone who is extremely miserly. To read the story behind this four-character set phrase, see Reading/Writing Task 2 in the Workbook.

*A Bank of China branch.*

 生词表 (Shēngcí Biǎo)
# Vocabulary

| Character | Pinyin | Part of Speech | English Definition |
|---|---|---|---|
| 1. 银行 | yínháng | *n.* | bank |
| 这个银行很大。 | | | |
| 2. 利息 | lìxī | *n.* | (of a monetary account) interest |
| 现在你们银行的利息是多少？ | | | |
| 3. 外汇 | wàihuì | *n.* | foreign currency |
| 你有外汇吗？ | | | |

4. 兑换率　　　　duìhuàn lǜ　　　*n.*　　　exchange rate
   今天人民币和美金的兑换率是多少？

5. 叫号机　　　　jiàohàojī　　　*n.*　　　(lit.) number-calling machine
   叫号机正在叫三十二号。

6. 站　　　　　　zhàn　　　*v.*　　　to stand
   你别站在那儿。

7. 显示　　　　　xiǎnshì　　　*v.*　　　(usually on a screen) to display
   叫号机的屏幕怎么还不显示我的号码！？

8. 轮到　　　　　lún dào　　　*v. comp.*　　　to be someone's turn
   怎么还不轮到我。

9. 帐户　　　　　zhànghù　　　*n.*　　　account
   你想在这儿开个帐户吗？

10. 存钱　　　　　cún qián　　　*v. obj.*　　　to deposit money
    我要去银行存钱，你去不去？

11. 取钱　　　　　qǔ qián　　　*v. obj.*　　　to withdraw money
    我还要去银行取一点钱。

12. 信用卡　　　　xìnyòngkǎ　　　*n.*　　　credit card
    你们这儿收不收信用卡？
    信用　　　　　　　　　　*n.*　　　credibility, trustworthiness

13. 人民币　　　　Rénmínbì　　　*n.*　　　Chinese currency
    我现在没有人民币。

14. 定期　　　　　dìngqī　　　*attr.*　　　(lit.) a fixed period
    你想存定期存款吗？

15. 活期　　　　　huóqī　　　*attr.*　　　(lit.) a non-fixed period
    我想存活期存款。

16. 值得　　　　　zhídé　　　*v.*　　　to deserve, to be worth
    这件衣服太贵，不值得买。
    　　　　　　　　　　　　*adj.*　　　worth, merit
    这件衣服非常值得。

17. 虽然…但是…　suīrán...dànshì...　*conj.*　　　although...but/still/yet...
    虽然我现在没有人民币，但是我有一些美金。

18. 旅行　　　　　lǚxíng　　　*v.*　　　to travel
    我想去旅行。

|  |  | n. | travel |

他喜欢旅行。

| 19. 支票 | zhīpiào | n. | check |

你有支票吗？

| 20. 私人 | sīrén | adj. | personal, private |

我们这儿用私人支票的人不多。

| 21. 存款单 | cúnkuǎndān | n. | deposit slip |

这是你的存款单。

| 款 |  | b.f. | fund, sum of money |

| 22. 存折 | cúnzhé | n. | bank book |

我的这张存折上已经没有钱了。

| 23. 记录 | jìlù | n. | record |

你每次在这儿存的钱都有记录。

|  |  | v. | to record |

你每次存的钱都记录在这儿。

| 24. 借记卡 | jièjìkǎ | n. | debit card |

在中国，借记卡很容易办。

| 25. 超支 | chāo zhī | v. obj. | to overdraw one's bank account |

借记卡不能超支。

| 超 | chāo | v. | to surpass, to exceed |

| 26. 不但…而且… | búdàn…érqiě… | conj. | not only…but also… |

我不但有借记卡，而且还有美金。

| 而且 |  | conj. | moreover, furthermore, on top of |

| 27. 担保 | dānbǎo | v. | to guarantee, to vouch for |

在中国办信用卡一定要有人给你担保。

| 28. 现金 | xiànjīn | n. | cash |

我现在没有现金，你们收不收借记卡？

| 29. 丢 | diū | v. | to lose, to discard, to put aside |

你丢了什么？

| 30. 可惜 | kěxī | adj. | (it's) a pity, too bad, a shame |

你明天不能去，太可惜了。

|  |  | conj. | It is a pity that… |

这本书真好，可惜不是我的。

31. **任何**  rènhé  *adj.*  any

这种信用卡在任何地方任何时候都可以用。

32. **自助机**  zìzhùjī  *n.*  ATM machine

那边有一个自助机，我去取一点钱。

33. **刷卡**  shuā kǎ  *v. obj.*  (lit.) to swipe card; to accept a credit

现在中国很多商店都可以刷卡。 or debit card

**刷**  shuā  *v.*  (lit.) to swipe

*Using an ATM machine.*

## 补充词汇 (Bǔchōng Cíhuì) Supplementary Vocabulary

1. 贷款  dài kuǎn  *v. obj.*  to get a loan
2. 利率  lìlǜ  *n.*  interest rate
3. 还清  huán qīng  *v. comp.*  to pay off (debt)
4. 欠债  qiàn zhài  *v. obj.*  to owe money
5. 开户头  kāi hùtóu  *v. obj.*  to open an account

## 口头用语 (Kǒutóu Yòngyǔ) Spoken Expressions

| | | |
|---|---|---|
| 1. 外卡取现 | wài kǎ qǔ xiàn | to withdraw cash from a foreign credit card |
| 2. 我这个人 | wǒ zhè ge rén | I myself; (lit.) I, this person |
| 3. 看你那个高兴的样子。 | Kàn nǐ nà ge gāoxìng de yàngzi. | Look how happy you are. |

## 语法 (Yǔfǎ) Grammar

## I. Verb Resultative Complements (Cont'd.)

In Lesson 18, you learned that the resultative complement follows an action verb to show the result of the action verb. So far you have learned how to use verbs (such as 见, 往, 懂, 会, and 完) and adjectives (such as 对, 错, 清楚, 好, and 坏) as complements. In this lesson, you will learn a few more verbs that are frequently used as complements. These verbs are 到, 住, 在, and 开.

### A. With/Without an Object

#### 1. 住 (Zhù): Fixed in a Certain Place or Position

| Verb | Complement | (Object) | |
|---|---|---|---|
| 站 | 住 | | to stand still, to freeze |
| 停 | 住 | | to stop |
| 记 | 住 | 生词 | to memorize vocabulary |
| 留 | 住 | 客人 | to have guests stay |

#### 2. 开 (Kāi): To Open or Depart from a Previous Place or State

| Verb | Complement | (Object) | |
|---|---|---|---|
| 走 | 开 | | to walk away |
| 离 | 开 | 美国 | to leave America |
| 拿 | 开 | | to take away |
| 打 | 开 | 电视/书 | to turn on the TV / to open a book |
| 开 | 开 | 窗户 | to open a window |

### 3. 到 (Dào)

a. Successfully Completing an Action

| Verb | Complement | Object | |
|------|-----------|--------|---|
| 找 | 到 | 一本故事书 | found a storybook |
| 收 | 到 | 一本故事书 | received a storybook |
| 看 | 到 | 一本故事书 | (same as 看见) saw a storybook |
| 听 | 到 | 一个故事 | (same as 听见) heard a story |
| 买 | 到 | 一本故事书 | bought a storybook |

b. About

| Verb | Complement | Object | |
|------|-----------|--------|---|
| 谈 | 到 | 这件事 | to talk about this issue |
| 想 | 到 | 这个问题 | to think about this issue |

*The Industrial and Commercial Bank of China in Xi'an.*

Xueying Wang

## ⊞ PRACTICE

Now that you know the meaning of verb complements 开, 住, and 到, can you make sentences using each of them? Be sure to indicate that you understand their meaning and usage, and remember to include the different meanings of 开, 住, and 到.

*A sign indicating the business hours of the Bank of China.*

## B. With Places or Time Words

The verbs 到 and 在 are frequently used in this structure.

### 1. 在 *(Zài): Located at a Certain Place or Position*

在 must be followed by a word indicating a place.

| Verb | Complement | Place | |
|------|-----------|-------|---|
| 放 | 在 | 桌子上 | to put on the table |
| 挂 | 在 | 墙 (qiáng) 上 | to hang on the wall |
| 站 | 在 | 柜台前 | to stand in front of a counter |
| 写 | 在 | 信封上 | to write on an envelope |

## *Note*

Please don't confuse the verb 在 with the preposition 在. Chinese prepositions are usually placed before the verb, as in the structure "在 + Place + Verb," e.g., 他现在在北京学习。 The second 在 in this sentence is a preposition, not a verb.

### 2. 到 *(Dào):*

a. Reaching a Certain Point (of Time, Number, or Amount)

| Verb | Complement | Time/Number/Amount | |
|------|-----------|--------------------|---|
| 工作 | 到 | 三点 | worked until three o'clock |
| 学习 | 到 | 一点 | studied until one o'clock |
| 学 | 到 | 第三十九课 | learned up to Lesson 39 |

b. Arriving at a Place

| Verb | Complement | Place | |
|------|-----------|-------|---|
| 回 | 到 | 座位 | to return to one's seat |
| 走 | 到 | 宿舍 | to walk to the dorm |
| 飞 | 到 | 机场 | to arrive at the airport (by airplane) |

## Note

Please do not confuse the verb 到 and with the preposition 到. When 到 is used as a preposition, it is frequently used in the following two patterns:

1. 到 + Place 去

2. 从…到…

*The Agricultural Bank of China in Xi'an.*

## ✖ PRACTICE

Now that you know the meaning of verb complements 到 and 在, can you make sentences using each of them? Be sure to indicate that you understand their meaning and usage, and remember to include the different meanings of 到 and 在.

## II. Brief Introduction to the 把 (Bǎ) Construction

You learned in Lesson 7 that the object of a verb in Chinese can be placed at the beginning of a sentence to place emphasis on the object itself. In this case, the object is usually a definite noun that is already known to the listener or speaker. In this lesson, we will introduce how the preposition 把 is used to move the object in front of the main verb. This kind of sentence focuses on what has happened to the object and how the object is dealt with or handled by the subject. The structure of the 把 construction is "Subject 把 + Object + Verb + Other Element." Please note that the main verb in the 把 construction must be followed by at least one additional element. For example:

| Subject | 把 | Object | Verb | Other element |
|---|---|---|---|---|
| 我 | 把 | 现金 | 丢 | 了。 |

I lost my cash.

When an object is in a sentence that contains a verb complement, the most natural and commonly used structure in Chinese incorporates the 把 pattern. For example:

| Subject | | Object | Verb | Complement | Other elements |
|---|---|---|---|---|---|
| 我 | 把 | 书 | 放 | 在 | 桌子上了。 |

I put the book on the table.

| 我 | 把 | 客人 | 留 | 住 | 了。 |
|---|---|---|---|---|---|

I let the guest stay.

You will learn more about the 把 construction in Lesson 36.

## III. Conjunctions and Complex Sentences

Conjunctions are words that link other words, phrases, or clauses. Sometimes conjunctions appear in the sentences as single words, and sometimes they appear in pairs. So far you have learned the following kinds of conjunctions:

***Simple Conjunctions:*** 和, 或, 但是

| 你和我 | you and me |
|---|---|
| 爸爸和妈妈 | dad and mom |
| 喝水或喝咖啡 | to drink water or coffee |
| 我很忙，但是很快乐。 | I am very busy, but very happy |

***Conjunctions in Pairs:*** 要是/如果⋯就⋯ ***If...then... (Lessons 25 & 28)***

你要是不想去，就别去。
If you don't want to go, then don't go.

如果你叫我去跳舞，我就去。
If you ask me to go dancing, I will go.

***Adverbial Conjunctions:*** 才 *and* 就 *(Lesson 24)*

我看了好几遍，才看懂。
Only after I had read it many times did I understand it.

我明天下了课，就去图书馆。
As soon as I finish class tomorrow, I will go to the library.

### *Adverbial Conjunctions in Pairs That Link Phrases or Clauses*

#### 又…又… *(Lesson 26)*

大家昨天晚上又唱歌又跳舞，高兴极了。
Everyone was singing and dancing last night; they were so happy.

#### …先…，再/然后… *...First..., then... (Lesson 27)*

| | |
|---|---|
| 我想先吃饭，再学习。 | I want to eat first and then study. |
| 我想先吃饭，然后去看电影。 | I want to eat first and then go to see a movie. |
| 你先填包裹单，然后再到一号窗口去。 | Fill out the package form first, and then go to the first window. |

You have also learned in Lesson 27 that complex sentences consist of more than one clause. In this lesson, you will learn three new paired conjunctions used in constructing complex sentences.

## A. 因为…所以…    (Yīnwèi...Suǒyǐ...)

The paired conjunctions "因为…所以…" means "because...therefore...." They are used to link two clauses indicating a causative relationship. In this structure, the first clause starting with 因为 usually states the reason for doing something, while the second clause (introduced by 所以) provides information on the effect. In English, you only need to use "because" or "therefore," but in Chinese, 因为 and 所以 are frequently used in tandem. See the examples below.

### 1. With One Subject

When two clauses have the same subject, the subject can be placed either before 因为 or right after 因为.

| First clause | | | | | Second clause |
|---|---|---|---|---|---|
| **Subject** | 因为 | **(Subject)** | **Predicate1** | 所以 | **Predicate2** |
| 我 | 因为 | | 需要钱， | 所以 | 在找工作。 |

I need money, so I'm looking for a job.

| | 因为 | 他 | 不肯多吃东西， | 所以 | 不胖。 |
|---|---|---|---|---|---|

He doesn't gain weight because he is reluctant eat very much.

### 2. With Two Different Subjects

If the subjects are different, the first subject is placed after 因为 and the second subject is placed after 所以.

| First clause | | | | Second clause | |
|---|---|---|---|---|---|
| 因为 | **Subject** | **Predicate1** | 所以 | **Subject** | **Predicate2** |
| 因为 | 他 | 需要钱， | 所以 | 我 | 在帮他找工作。 |

I'm helping him look for a job because he needs money.

Sometimes when the situation is very clear, either 因为 or 所以 can be omitted. Here are a few variations of the "因为…所以…" structure.

…所以…    他不肯多吃东西，所以不胖。

He is reluctant to eat much. Therefore, he has not gained any weight.

…是因为…    他不胖是因为他不肯多吃东西。

He has not gained any weight because he is reluctant to eat much.

…因为…    我昨天没来，因为太忙了。

I didn't come yesterday, because (I) was too busy.

## 🔲 PRACTICE

Now it's your turn. Try to ask each other questions, following the examples given below. Use "因为…所以…" to provide answers. Examples:

你怎么不去夜市买东西？

你昨天为什么去银行了？

## B. 虽然…但是/可是…    (Suīrán…Dànshì/Kěshì…)

The paired conjunctions "虽然…但是/可是…" carry the meaning of "although or but." They are used to link two clauses that are contradictory statements.

### 1. With One Subject

When two clauses have the same subject, it can be placed either before 虽然 or right after 虽然.

| First clause | | | | Second clause | | |
|---|---|---|---|---|---|---|
| Subject | 虽然 | (Subject) | Predicate1 | 但是 | Subject | Predicate2 |
| 他 | 虽然 | （他） | 没记住生词， | 但是 | 他 | 不错。 |

Although he didn't memorize the new vocabulary, he did well on the test.

### 2. With Two Different Subjects

If the subjects are different, 虽然 should be placed before the first subject, while 但是 (or 可是) should be placed at the beginning of the second clause.

| First clause | | | Second clause | | |
|---|---|---|---|---|---|
| 虽然 | Subject | Predicate1 | 可是 | Subject | Predicate2 |
| 虽然 | 老师 | 教了这课， | 可是 | 学生 | 都没听懂。 |

The teacher went over the lesson, but the students did not understand.

## Note

虽然 is often omitted in this structure. However, 可是 and 但是 are rarely omitted.

## ⊞ PRACTICE

Try asking questions of your own by following the examples below, then use "虽然…但是/可是" to provide an answer. For example:

问：购物中心的东西怎么这么贵？

答：东西虽然很贵，但是质量好。

问：现在商店都可以刷卡，你担心什么？

答：虽然可以刷卡，但是我还是喜欢用现金。

## C. 不但…而且…    (Búdàn…Érqiě…)

The paired conjunctions "不但…而且…" carry the meaning of "not only…but also…" They are used to link two similar statements.

### 1. With One Subject

When 不但 and 而且 use the same subject, it should be placed before 不但.

| | | First clause | | | Second clause |
|---|---|---|---|---|---|
| Subject | 不但 | Predicate1 | 而且 | Predicate2 | |
| 他 | 不但 | 是我的老师， | 而且 | 也是我的好朋友。 | |

He is not only my teacher, but also a good friend.

| 我 | 不但 | 有借记卡， | 而且 | 也有信用卡。 |

I not only have a debit card, but also a credit card.

### 2. With Two Different Subjects

When 不但 and 而且 have two different subjects, the first subject should be placed after 不但 and the second after 而且.

| | | First clause | | | Second clause | |
|---|---|---|---|---|---|---|
| 不但 | Subject1 | Predicate1 | 而且 | Subject2 | Predicate2 | |
| 不但 | 中国人 | 喜欢这位数学家， | 而且 | 外国人 | 也喜欢他。 | |

It's not just the Chinese who like this mathematician; foreigners like him, too!

## ⊞ PRACTICE

Use the "不但…而且…" structure to describe a bank, post office, department store, or restaurant you are familiar with.

# Textbook Exercises

## 🎧💻 TASK 1. 课文问答 (KÈWÉN WÈNDÁ) QUESTIONS AND ANSWERS

Check your comprehension of the text by responding to the following questions.

1. 中国大银行的服务和小银行有什么不一样的地方？

2. 借记卡和信用卡一样不一样？为什么？

3. 吴文德开了什么帐户？为什么？

4. 吴文德以后用现金方便不方便？为什么？

## 💻 TASK 2. 语法练习 (YǓFǍ LIÀNXÍ) GRAMMATICAL STRUCTURE PRACTICE

### A. Word Selection

Select the choice that best completes each sentence.

1. 昨天吴文德跟我 _____ 了他去银行办信用卡的事。

   a) 放在          b) 记住          c) 谈到          d) 打开

2. 那个银行地址，他只告诉了我一次，我就 _____ 了。

   a) 放在          b) 记住          c) 谈到          d) 打开

3. 他 _____ 电脑以后，就开始工作了。

   a) 放在          b) 记住          c) 谈到          d) 打开

4. 你的支票，我 _____ 桌子上了。

   a) 放在          b) 记住          c) 谈到          d) 打开

5. _____ 信用卡很方便，_____ 办手续太麻烦，不值得。

   a) 因为…所以…      b) 虽然…但是…      c) 不但…而且…      d) 如果…就…

6. _____ 他在银行有帐户，_____ 他可以申请借记卡。

   a) 因为…所以…      b) 虽然…但是…      c) 不但…而且…      d) 如果…就…

7. _____ 你们这的利息高，我 _____ 在这儿开帐户。

   a) 因为…所以…      b) 虽然…但是…      c) 不但…而且…      d) 如果…就…

8. 用自助机 _____ 可以直接存钱、取钱，_____ 也可以查自己银行的帐户。

   a) 因为…所以…    b) 虽然…但是…    c) 不但…而且…    d) 如果…就…

## B. Sentence Completion

Use a "Verb + Complement" to complete the following sentences.

1. 他每天做作业都要 _____ 晚上12：00点，但是他不觉得累。

2. 我们家的地址你 _____ 了没有？

3. 林医生的信你 _____ 哪儿了？我找了一个小时也没有 _____。

4. 我给他打了几次电话叫他别走，但是没有 _____ 他。他现在已经坐飞机 _____ 北京了。

## C. Sentence Construction

Answer the following questions by writing sentences that use as many conjunctions as possible. Don't forget to include the "虽然…但是…," "因为…所以…," "如果…就…," and "不但…而且…" patterns you learned in this lesson!

1. 你为什么在夜市买东西？

2. 你为什么不陪我去银行？

3. 你为什么不办信用卡？

4. 他为什么没拿到签证？

---

## 💻 TASK 3. 翻译 (FĀNYÌ) PARAPHRASING

Translate the following sentences into Chinese.

1. Because the large banks in China have number-calling machines, the clients who deposit money to (or) withdraw money from a big bank do not have to stand in line in front of the (teller's) windows. (Hint: 因为…所以…, 站 + Complement 在) You take a number at the door, return to your seat and sit down (in the waiting area), and wait there. That's all you have to do! (Hint: 回 + Complement 到, 就行了) When your turn comes, the machine will show your number on the screen (Hint: 轮 + Complement 到)

2. If you live in China, you will know that many stores, post offices, and restaurants take credit cards. (Hint: 住 + Complement 在, 借记卡) Thus, when you go out, you should not only bring cash, but also your debit card. (Hint: 所以, 出门, 不但…而且…) It is easy to obtain a debit card, but it cannot withdraw more than the account balance. (Hint: 虽然, 申请 + Complement 到) If you can find someone to be your guarantor, you shouldn't be afraid of going through the trouble of applying for a credit card. (Hint: 要是, 找 + Complement 到, 担保人)

3. A: After I received a check from my family last week, I went to the bank and deposited the money immediately. (Hint: 收 + Complement 到) You open our bank book and check how much money we are supposed to have now. (Hint: 打 + Complement 开) Where is the bank book? (Hint: 放 + Complement 在)

B: (You) don't have to look (for it). I have memorized (it) all. (Hint: 记 + Complement 住) If the money has been deposited into the bank, we will not overdraw from our debit account tomorrow. (Hint: 存 + Complement 到, 超支)

---

## 💻 TASK 4. 情景对话 (QÍNGJǏNG DUÌHUÀ) SITUATIONAL DIALOGUE

**Setting:**　　A bank in China

**Cast:**　　　 A bank employee and a foreign student

**Situation:**　A foreign student goes to the Bank of China to open an account. In order to do so, however, he/she needs to talk to a bank teller. Construct a short dialogue between the student and the teller as the student tries to explain why he/she needs the account. What exactly does the student want to do at the bank? Deposit money? Withdraw money? Apply for a debit or credit card? Is the transaction successful? Why or why not? Be creative, and remember to use the grammar from this lesson!

# 32
# 订火车票
# Taking the Train

> **In this lesson you will:**
> ■ Make a travel plan that includes places to visit and things to see.
> ■ Learn to schedule a train trip.
> ■ Learn how and where to buy train tickets.

在中国，很多人出去旅游的时候，都喜欢乘火车，因为火车比飞机便宜。乘火车可以选硬座、软座、硬卧和软卧。硬座最便宜，软卧最贵最舒服。火车票可以直接在火车站的售票处买，也可以在火车站代售点买。有些地方还可以上网，或打电话预订。李丽莉和吴文德想乘火车到西安去玩玩儿。他们会不会买火车票？买的是哪种火车票？下面请看他们买火车票的故事。

（李丽莉在宿舍看书，外边有人敲门。）

李丽莉：进来。

吴文德：来北京这么长时间，还没到外地玩儿过。现在要放长假了，我们出去到外地逛一逛，见见世面，好不好？我们再不出去，就快成井底之蛙[1]了。

李丽莉：好是好，可是我们去哪儿玩呢？

吴文德：我一直想到西安去看看，那儿有著名的兵马俑。我听说那些兵和马都跟真人真马一样。你想不想去看看？

李丽莉：想是想，可是谁带我们去呢？陈小云还没有从上海回来呢。

吴文德：不要紧。你听说过塞翁失马[2]的故事吗？陈小云不在，我们自己坐火车去，既学了本领，又见了世面。这不是坏事变成好事吗？

李丽莉：那我们得赶快订火车票，我听说火车票很难买。既不能上网预订，也不能打电话预订。

吴文德：那是老皇历了，现在火车票比以前好买多了。你就等着我的好消息吧。

（第二天早上，吴文德在火车站售票处）

吴文德：我想买两张下个晚上从北京去西安的火车票。都有几点的火车？

售票员：列车时刻表在墙上挂着呢。晚上从北京出发去西安的是 K81 次特快，晚上 7:50 分出发，第二天早上 9:30 分到。

吴文德：这趟车时间很方便，请你给我买两张来回票。

售票员：您要买什么票？硬座、软座还是卧铺？硬卧、软卧？

吴文德：硬座、软座不能睡觉，短途还可以，长途太累，软卧又太贵了。麻烦您给我两张硬卧吧。

售票员：对不起，没有下铺了。上铺、中铺行不行？

吴文德：可以。谢谢。

（吴文德从火车站回来以后就给李丽莉打电话。）

吴文德：我给咱们买了两张下个星期四去西安的硬卧票。你想过来取票，还是让我给你送去。

李丽莉：我正忙着呢，你给我送来好吗？

吴文德：好吧。下铺没有了，我买了一张上铺，一张中铺。你想要哪张？

李丽莉：上铺上来下去很不方便。你给我一张中铺吧。

吴文德：好，一会儿见。

（在李丽莉的宿舍。）

吴文德：我明天给咱们定一个旅游计划。我当导游，带你去参观西安的名胜古迹。照一些漂漂亮亮的风景照片，给你家寄去，你家里的人一定会很羡慕你。

李丽莉：你也没去过西安，怎么当导游呢？

吴文德：我买了一本西安旅游指南，还有一张大大的西安地图。我当导游没问题。

李丽莉：吴文德，你当导游，要是我能在西安火车站照几张相给我爸爸妈妈寄去，我就满足了。

吴文德：哎，你这个人太悲观了。

## Notes

1. 井底之蛙 (jǐng dǐ zhī wā)

   Literally, "a frog in the bottom of the well." It comes from a 成语故事, and is used to describe someone who doesn't see much, someone who is narrow-minded. To read the story behind the phrase, see Reading/Writing Task 1 in the Workbook.

2. 塞翁失马 (sài wēng shī mǎ)

   Literally, "the old man at the border loses his horse." This is also a 成语故事. It is used to remind people that good things can come from bad situations and bad things can come from good situations. For the full story behind the phrase, see Reading Task 3.

*Buying train tickets.*

# 生词表 (Shēngcí Biǎo)
# Vocabulary

| Character | Pinyin | Part of Speech | English Definition |
|-----------|--------|----------------|--------------------|
| 1. 火车 | huǒchē | *n.* | train |

他想坐火车去北京。

| Character | Pinyin | Part of Speech | English Definition |
|-----------|--------|----------------|--------------------|
| 2. 硬 | yìng | *adj.* | stiff, inflexible, hard |

这种座位很硬，很不舒服。

| Character | Pinyin | Part of Speech | English Definition |
|-----------|--------|----------------|--------------------|
| 3. 软 | ruǎn | *adj.* | soft |

你想坐硬座还是软座？

| Character | Pinyin | Part of Speech | English Definition |
|-----------|--------|----------------|--------------------|
| 4. 售票处 | shòupiàochù | *n.* | ticket office |

这儿有火车票售票处吗？

5. 代售点     dàishòudiǎn     *n.*     a place to be commissioned to sell something (e.g., train tickets)
这有一个火车票代售点。

   代售         *v. phr.*     to sell on behalf of..., to sell as a substitute

   点         *n.*     a place

6. 上网     shàng wǎng     *v. obj.*     to go online
你应该上网去买。

7. 预订     yùdìng     *v.*     to place an order, book ahead
我想预订一个房间。

8. 敲     qiāo     *v.*     to knock
有人敲门。

9. 放假     fàng jià     *v. obj.*     (of institutions) to give a vacation; (of individuals) to have a vacation
你们什么时候放假?

   假         *b.f.*     vacation

10. 出去     chū qù     *v. comp.*     to go out
我们这个周末出去玩儿玩儿吧。

11. 一直     yīzhí     *adv.*     all the way through, all along
我一直想去看看他。

12. 著名     zhùmíng     *adj.*     famous
他是一位著名的中国作家。

13. 既…也/又     jì...yě/yòu     *conj.*     not only...but also
他这个人既不爱看电 影也不爱看书。

14. 变成     biàn chéng     *v. comp.*     to change into, to turn into
坏事都能变成好事。

   变         *v.*     to change

15. 赶快     gǎnkuài     *adv.*     quickly
我们赶快去吧。

16. 消息     xiāoxi     *n.*     information
你今天这么高兴，有什么好消息?

17. 时刻表     shíkèbiǎo     *n.*     (of buses, trains, planes) timetable, schedule
我们去拿一张火车时刻表吧。

   时刻         *n.*     time

18. 墙      qiáng      *n.*      wall

火车时刻表都在墙上，你去看看吧。

19. 出发      chūfā      *v.*      to set out, to start out

我们明天什么时候出发？

20. 趟      tàng      *m.w.*      (of trips) the number of times, (of trains, buses, planes, etc.) number, code, flight, etc.

你们来晚了，那趟车已经走了。

21. 来回票      láihuípiào      *n.*      round-trip ticket

我买一张北京上海的来回票。

22. 卧铺      wòpù      *n.*      sleeping berth (in a train)

我没有买到卧铺票。

铺      *n.*      bed

23. 定      dìng      *v.*      to decide, to determine

我们定一个旅游计划吧。

24. 计划      jìhuà      *n.*      plan

你应该定一个旅游计划。

*v.*      to plan

我们计划今年四月去西安旅游。

25. 导游      dǎoyóu      *n.*      tour guide

我们要不要找一位导游？

26. 名胜古迹      míngshèng gǔjì      *phr.*      famous ancient sites (for tourists)

北京有很多名胜古迹。

27. 风景      fēngjǐng      *n.*      scenery

那儿风景很漂亮。

28. 羡慕      xiànmù      *v.*      to envy, to admire

你明天就去中国，我真羡慕你！

29. 指南      zhǐnán      *n.*      guidebook, guide

我们应该去买一本旅游指南。

30. 地图      dìtú      *n.*      map

这是哪儿的地图？

31. 满足                 mǎnzú         *adj.*        content, satisfied

你怎么还不满足？

                        *v.*          to be satisfied

谁能满足你的需要？

32. 悲观                 bēiguān       *adj.*        pessimistic

他对这件事情很悲观。

## 专有名词 (Zhuānyǒu Míngcí) Proper Nouns

1. 西安                  Xī'ān                       a city in China

2. 兵马俑                 Bīngmǎyǒng                  Terracotta Soldiers

3. K81 次特快            K81 cì tèkuài               Super-express Train K81 (次 is a m.w.)

## 补充词汇 (Bǔchōng Cíhuì) Supplementary Vocabulary

1. 铁路                  tiělù         *n.*          railroad

2. 交通                  jiāotōng      *n.*          traffic

3. 车厢                  chēxiāng      *n.*          compartment of a train

4. 火车头                 huǒchētóu     *n.*          locomotive

5. 铁轨                  tiěguǐ        *n.*          rail

6. 旅游车                 lǚyóuchē      *n.*          tour bus

7. 景点                  jǐngdiǎn      *n.*          scenic spot

8. 候车室                 hòuchēshì     *n.*          waiting room

## 口头用语 (Kǒutóu Yòngyǔ) Spoken Expressions

1. 见世面                 jiàn shìmiàn                to see the world

2. 不要紧                 bú yàojǐn                   It does not matter.

3. 老皇历                 lǎo huánglì                 very old; (lit.) very old imperial calendar

## 词汇注解 (Cíhuì Zhùjiě) Featured Vocabulary

### 1. 放假 (Fàng Jià)

假 means "vacation" and is frequently used with the verb 放. It also takes adjective modifiers. For example: 放长假 (long weekend), 放寒假 (winter break), 放暑假 (summer break), or 放春假 (spring break).

### 2. 上网 (Shàng Wǎng) vs. 网上 (Wǎngshàng)

| 上网 | *v. obj.* | to go online |
| 网上 | *n.* | on the Web |

### 3. 满足 (Mǎnzú) vs. 满意 (Mǎnyì)

| 满足 | ***v.*** | to satisfy |
| --- | --- | --- |
| 这个饭馆的菜不能满足顾客的需要。 | | The food in this restaurant does not satisfy the customers' needs. |

| 满足 | ***adj.*** | to be satisfied or content |
| --- | --- | --- |
| 我能照几张相，我就满足了。 | | I will be satisfied if I can take a few pictures. |

| 满意 | ***adj.*** | to be satisfied or to be pleased |
| --- | --- | --- |
| 李丽莉对她的导游很满意。 | | Li Lili is very pleased with her tour guide. |

*A restaurant catering to train travelers.*

 语法(Yǔfǎ)

# Grammar

## I. 来 and 去 as Simple Complements of Direction

来 and 去, which indicate the direction of movement, can function as directional complements. In this lesson, you will learn the verbs 来 and 去 as simple directional complements. The 来 or 去 complement is placed after the motion or an action verb to indicate the direction of the action in relation to the speaker. 来 (come) indicates that an action moves toward the speaker, while 去 (go) indicates that an action moves away from the speaker (see pictures). For example:

我们进去吧！大家都在里边儿。

Let's go in; everyone is inside.

你进来吧！

Please come in!

Now that you are familiar with this usage of 来 and 去, we will introduce seven basic motion verbs that take the simple directional complement. These seven motion verbs form the following thirteen pairs:

| Motion Verb | Directional Complement | Example | English |
| --- | --- | --- | --- |
| 上 | 来/去 | 上来/去吧。 | Come/go up. |
| 下 | 来/去 | 下来/去吧。 | Come/go down. |
| 进 | 来/去 | 进来/去吧。 | Come/go in. |
| 出 | 来/去 | 出来/去一下儿。 | Come/go out. |
| 过 | 来/去 | 过来/去一下儿。 | Come/go over. |
| 回 | 来/去 | 回来/去吧。 | Come/go back. |
| 起 | 来 | 起来吧。 | Get up. |

In addition to these seven basic motion verbs, other action verbs such as 走, 跑, 带, 送, 寄, 买, 借, and 拿 can take directional complements.

## Note

The verb 起 can only use 来, NOT 去, as its complement.

---

## 🖳 PRACTICE

Look at the following pictures and describe each one using appropriate phrases from the thirteen pairs given above.

## A. Without an Object

When there are no objects in the sentence, the verb complements 来 and 去 are placed directly after the main verb. If 了 is used, it must be placed after 来 or 去. To form a negative sentence, use 没有 before the predicate verb. Remember that 了 is omitted at the end of a negative sentence.

| | Subject | Verb | Directional complement 来/去 | |
|---|---|---|---|---|
| Positive: | 他哥哥 | 回 | 来了。 | His brother came back. |
| Negative: | 他哥哥 | 没有回 | 来。 | His brother did not come back. |
| Question: | 他哥哥 | 回 | 来了吗？ | Did his brother come back? |

## Note

The prepositional phrase "从 + Place" can be placed before the main verb to indicate the point where the movement originates. For example: 他哥哥从法国回来了。

*Exit gate of the Xi'an train station.*

## 🔲 PRACTICE

With a partner, ask a question using the structure above along with the phrases given, and have the other student answer in both positive and negative forms. Suggested phrases: 从外边进来, 从教室里出去, 从前边过来, 从学校回去, 从楼下上来, 从电影院出来.

## B. With a Person/Thing as an Object

If the object is a noun referring to a person or a thing, it can be placed either before or after the complement (来/去).

### 1. When the Object Is before 来/去

In this structure, the object can be either a specific or a non-specific noun. If the object is a specific noun, you can also use the 把 structure.

*Waiting for train departures in Xi'an.*

| | Subject | Verb | Person/Thing Object | Directional complement 来/去 |
|---|---|---|---|---|
| Non-specific: | 他 | 想带 | 一个朋友 | 来。 |
| | He wants to bring a friend here. | | | |
| | 我 | 要给他寄 | 一本书 | 去。 |
| | I want to mail him a book. | | | |
| Specific: | 他 | 想带 | 他弟弟 | 来。 |
| | He wants to bring his brother here. | | | |
| | 我 | 要给他寄 | 那本书 | 去。 |
| | I want to mail him that book. | | | |

Now let's change the above two sentences containing the specific objects into the 把 structure:

他想把他弟弟带来。

我要把那本书给他寄去。

If 了 is used in this structure, it can be placed either after the main verb or after the complement. For example:

他给我寄了一本书来。　　He mailed me a book.

他带那本书来了。　　He brought that book.

## 2. When the Object Is after 来/去

In this structure, the object tends to be a non-specific noun.

|  |  | Directional complement | Person/Thing |
|---|---|---|---|
| **Subject** | **Verb** | 来/去 | **Object** |
| 他 | 要带 | 来 | 一个朋友。 |

He wants to bring a friend.

| 他 | 要寄 | 来 | 一本书。 |
|---|---|---|---|

He wants to mail a book.

If 了 is used in this structure, it is usually placed directly after the verb complement 来/去. For example:

他带来了一个朋友。    He brought a friend.

他带来了一本书。    He brought a book.

---

## PRACTICE

Now it's your turn! Using verbs such as 寄, 拿, 送, 带, 请, 买来, 借来, and 请来 create sentences demonstrating that you know the correct usage of the above structures. For example:

你带来了什么？

你带什么去了？

你带谁来/去了？

你带书来了吗？

## C. With a Place/Location Word as an Object

When the object is a place/location word, it MUST be placed between the main verb and the complement (来 or 去). Verbs such as 上, 下, 进, and 回 are frequently used in this structure. If 了 is used in this structure, it should be placed after the verb complement. In the negative form, 了 is dropped. For example:

|  |  |  | Place/Location | Complement |  |
|---|---|---|---|---|---|
|  | **Subject** | **Verb** | **Object** | 来/去 |  |
| Positive: | 他哥哥 | 上 | 楼 | 去了。 | His brother went upstairs. |
| Negative: | 他哥哥没有 | 上 | 楼 | 去。 | His brother did not go upstairs. |
| Question: | 他哥哥 | 上 | 楼 | 去了吗？ | Did his brother go upstairs? |
|  | 他哥哥 | 上 | 哪儿 | 去了？ | Where did his brother go? |

## PRACTICE

Use the verbs 上, 下, 进, and 回 to ask a question with a place/location word as an object. When you're done, answer the question in both positive and negative forms. For example:

你昨天上哪儿去了？

他下楼去了吗？

# II. Verb 来 Verb 去

The pattern "Verb 来 Verb 去" indicates a back and forth movement or repetition of an action. The two verbs in this pattern are usually the same.

## A. Indicating Back and Forth Movement

| Verb | 来 | Verb | 去 | |
|------|-----|------|-----|---|
| 走 | 来 | 走 | 去 | to walk back and forth |
| 跑 | 来 | 跑 | 去 | to run back and forth |
| 拿 | 来 | 拿 | 去 | to bring (something) here and there |

## Note

Sometimes verbs in this pattern may also be complementary, as in 上来下去 (up and down).

## B. Indicating Repetition of an Action

| Verb | 来 | Verb | 去 | |
|------|-----|------|-----|---|
| 看 | 来 | 看 | 去 | looking at this, looking at that; repeatedly looking |
| 吃 | 来 | 吃 | 去 | eating this, eating that; repeatedly eating |
| 听 | 来 | 听 | 去 | listening to this, listening to that; repeatedly listening |
| 尝 | 来 | 尝 | 去 | taste this, taste that; to taste again and again |
| 想 | 来 | 想 | 去 | thinking about this, thinking about that; to think over many times |

## PRACTICE

Try using each of the patterns given above to ask a question, and then provide a response. For example:

问：你为什么走来走去？

答：因为我很紧张，所以走来走去。

问：你看来看去，到底要买哪本书？

答：我看来看去，不知道应该买哪本书。

# III. The Reduplication of Adjectives

Reduplication is a morphological process in which all or part of a word is copied. Verbs can be reduplicated to indicate the repetition of an action, to give the action a casual, informal feeling, or to stress the verb. As you learned in Lesson 6, verb reduplication takes the following forms.

| Monosyllabic | Reduplicated | Disyllabic | Reduplicated |
|---|---|---|---|
| A | AA | AB | ABAB |
| 说 | 说说 | 休息 | 休息休息 |
| 听 | 听听 | 介绍 | 介绍介绍 |

In this lesson, you will learn about the reduplication of adjectives, which can create a more lively and poetic effect. Adjectives can be reduplicated in the following forms.

| Monosyllabic | Reduplicated | Disyllabic | Reduplicated |
|---|---|---|---|
| A | AA | AB | AABB |
| 大 | 大大 | 高兴 | 高高兴兴 |
| 高 | 高高 | 清楚 | 清清楚楚 |

However, not all adjectives can be reduplicated. In this lesson we will introduce a handful of words that are commonly reduplicated. Reduplication of monosyllabic and disyllabic adjectives can occur before 的 to modify the noun. See the examples below.

**Reduplicated**

| Adjective | 的 | Noun | |
|---|---|---|---|
| 大大 | 的 | 客厅 | big living room |
| 高高 | 的 | 桌子 | tall table |
| 高高大大 | 的 | 房子 | big, tall house |

The reduplicated monosyllabic and disyllabic adjectives can also occur before 地 to modify verbs. See the examples below.

**Reduplicated**

| Adjective | 地 | Verb | |
|---|---|---|---|
| 慢慢 | 地 | 说 | to speak slowly |
| 好好 | 地 | 写 | to write carefully |
| 认认真真 | 地 | 写 | to write carefully |

The reduplicated disyllabic adjectives usually occur after 得 to modify the verb. See the examples below.

**Disyllabic reduplicated**

| Verb | 得 | Adjective | |
| --- | --- | --- | --- |
| 说 | 得 | 清清楚楚 | to speak clearly |
| 玩儿 | 得 | 高高兴兴 | to play happily |

## PRACTICE

Try reduplicating the following adjectives, and then form your own sentences with the words 的, 地, and 得.

Adjective + 的 + Noun:    软    胖    短    热    黑

Adjective + 地 + Verb:    轻    冷    早    快    慢

Verb + 得 Adjective:    热闹  高兴  清楚  快乐  紧张

# IV. Using the Adverbial Conjunction 既 (Jì)…又/也…

"既…又/也…" ("not only…but also…") connects two parallel clauses or components to indicate the simultaneous existence of two situations. This structure can only have one subject, which is shared by two clauses. "既…又/也…" must be placed after the subject.

| Subject | 既 | Verb/Adjective | 又/也 | Verb/Adjective |
| --- | --- | --- | --- | --- |
| 你 | 既 | 学了本领， | 又 | 见了世面。 |

You not only learn new skills, but also get to see the outside world.

| | | | | |
| --- | --- | --- | --- | --- |
| 我们 | 既不能 | 上网预订， | 也 | 不能打电话预订。 |

We cannot make reservations online or by phone.

### *Note*
The "既…又/也…" structure is similar to the "又…又…" structure, but it is more formal.

## PRACTICE

Use the "既…又/也…" structure to complete the following tasks:

1. Describe the recent weather, the gift you bought, or the clothes you're wearing.

2. Tell the audience what you need to do when you are getting ready for an exam, applying for a visa, or preparing for an interview.

# V. Adjective/Verb + 是 + Adjective/Verb, 可是…

The "Adjective +是 + Adjective, 可是…" or "Verb +是 + Verb, 可是…" structure indicates partial agreement with someone else's opinion, but goes on to make a critical or contrary statement or another related point. See the example below.

## A. Adjective + 是 + Adjective, 可是...

| First clause | | Second clause (contrary statement) |
|---|---|---|
| (Subject) | Adjective 是 Adjective， | 可是 + Clause |
| （去玩） | 好是好， | 可是我们去哪儿呢？ |

It's OK to go out, but where are we going?

| | | |
|---|---|---|
| 软卧的票 | 贵是贵， | 可是舒服得多。 |

The sleeper car in a train is certainly expensive, but it is more comfortable.

| | | |
|---|---|---|
| 他回答得 | 清楚是清楚， | 可是回答错了。 |

He did give a clear answer, but his answer is wrong.

## B. Verb +是 + Verb, 可是...

| First clause | | | | | Second clause (contrary statement) |
|---|---|---|---|---|---|
| Object | (Subject) | Verb | 是 | Verb， | 可是 + Clause |
| 那个电影 | 我 | 看 | 是 | 看过， | 可是没看懂。 |

I saw that movie, but I did not understand it.

| | | | | | |
|---|---|---|---|---|---|
| 晚饭 | | 吃 | 是 | 吃了， | 可是没吃饱。 |

Although I had supper, I did not eat enough.

| | | | | | |
|---|---|---|---|---|---|
| 我 | | 想 | 是 | 想， | 可是谁带我们去呢？ |

I want to (go), but who is going to take us there?

---

## 🔲 PRACTICE

Working with a partner, use each of the structures (Adjective + 是 + Adjective, 可是…; Verb + 是 + Verb, 可是…) to talk about your upcoming plans and past experiences. Be sure your sentences demonstrate that you understand the meaning, form, and usage for each one. For example:

问：你去买火车票了没有？

答：我去是去了，可是没买到。

# Textbook Exercises

## 🎧💻 TASK 1. 课文问答 (KÈWÉN WÈNDÁ) QUESTIONS AND ANSWERS

Check your comprehension of the text by responding to the following questions.

1. 吴文德放长假想去哪儿玩儿？为什么？

2. 吴文德买的是哪次班车？几点出发？几点到？

3. 吴文德买的是哪种火车票？为什么？

4. 吴文德买的两张火车票一样不一样？李丽莉要的是哪张票？为什么？

## 💻 TASK 2. 语法练习 (YǓFǍ LIÀNXÍ) GRAMMATICAL STRUCTURE PRACTICE

### A. Fill in the Blanks

Use 来 or 去 where needed to fill in the blank spaces in the sentences below.

1. A: 谁给你寄 ＿＿＿＿＿＿ 了这么多照片？

   B: 我妹妹。她上个星期带她的几个朋友 ＿＿＿＿＿＿ 西安旅游的时候，照了不少照片。

2. A: 我同学要看的杂志你带 ＿＿＿＿＿＿ 了吗？

   B: 对不起，我忘了到图书馆 ＿＿＿＿＿＿ 借了。

   A: 没关系，他明天在宿舍，你借了以后再给他送 ＿＿＿＿＿＿ 吧！

3. A: 今天天气真不错。我们可以出 ＿＿＿＿＿＿ 玩玩儿。

   B: 好啊。可是我们到哪儿 ＿＿＿＿＿＿ 呢？

   A: 对面的公园里花都开了。我们进 ＿＿＿＿＿＿ 看看吧。

   B: 好。但是我们不要回 ＿＿＿＿＿＿ 得太晚了，因为我明天还得回学校 ＿＿＿＿＿＿上课呢！

### B. Word Selection

Select the choice that best completes each sentence.

1. 我在上铺休息的时候，我朋友说：你 ＿＿＿＿＿＿ 跟我们一起看地图吧。
   a) 下去          b) 下来          c) 上去          d) 上来

2. 我跟我妈妈在火车站售票处的外边等我妹妹，我妈妈说我们先 ＿＿＿＿＿＿＿＿＿ 买
   票吧。
   　　a) 进去　　　　　b) 进来　　　　　c) 出去　　　　　d) 出来

3. 外面站着很多人，挺热闹的，我们快 ＿＿＿＿＿＿＿＿＿ 看看吧。
   　　a) 进去　　　　　b) 进来　　　　　c) 出去　　　　　d) 出来

4. 我在学校照了很多风景照片，明天就给我住在西安的爸爸妈妈 ＿＿＿＿＿＿＿＿＿。
   　　a) 看去　　　　　b) 看来　　　　　c) 寄去　　　　　d) 寄来

5. 喂，你的火车时刻表在不在？你能不能 ＿＿＿＿＿＿＿＿＿ 让我看看？
   　　a) 拿去　　　　　b) 拿来　　　　　c) 走去　　　　　d) 走来

## C. Sentence Completion

Read the following prompts and complete the sentences with the correct words or phrases.

1. 你在地图上找到39路汽车站了没有？（看来看去）

   这张地图，＿＿＿＿＿＿＿＿＿＿＿＿＿＿＿＿＿＿＿＿＿＿＿＿＿＿。

2. 这几天他忙什么？（跑来跑去）

   他 ＿＿＿＿＿＿＿＿＿＿＿＿＿＿＿＿＿＿＿＿＿＿＿＿＿＿＿＿＿＿。

3. 你买到牛仔裤了吗？听说牛仔裤很难买到。（买来买去）

   是啊，我 ＿＿＿＿＿＿＿＿＿＿＿＿＿＿＿＿＿＿＿＿＿＿＿＿＿＿＿＿。

4. 你想不想去西安？（Verb 是 Verb）

   ＿＿＿＿＿＿＿＿＿＿＿＿＿＿＿＿＿＿＿＿＿＿＿＿＿＿＿＿＿＿＿＿＿＿。

5. 我们买软卧票，好不好？（Adjective 是 Adjective）

   ＿＿＿＿＿＿＿＿＿＿＿＿＿＿＿＿＿＿＿＿＿＿＿＿＿＿＿＿＿＿＿＿＿＿。

6. 你为什么要去西安旅游？（既…又…）

   去西安旅游，＿＿＿＿＿＿＿＿＿＿＿＿＿＿＿＿＿＿＿＿＿＿＿＿＿＿。

---

## 💻 TASK 3. 翻译 (FĀNYÌ) PARAPHRASING

Translate the following sentences into Chinese.

1. I always wanted to go out (Hint: Verb + Complement 来 or 去) to see the world. Now that school is over, could you take me (Hint: Verb + Complement 来 or 去) to Xi'an to see the famous historical site?

2. Now it is very convenient to purchase train tickets in China. You can book the tickets online or over the phone, (Hint: 既…又…) you can also go to (Hint: 到…来 or 去…) the ticket office in the train station to get them.

3. That map would be useful but I don't have it with me, so I can't function as your tour guide. (Hint: Verb 是 Verb, 可是; Verb + Complement 来 or 去)

4. When I travel, I will surely take pictures of the beautiful scenery (Hint: Reduplication of Adjective). I will send them (Hint: Verb + Complement 来 or 去) to my friends and they will be so envious of me.

5. A: Would you please help me get two round-trip tickets? When you get back with the tickets, (Hint: 把 + Object + Verb + Complement 来 or 去), please bring them (Hint: Verb + Complement 来 or 去) to my house.

   B: Could you please come over (Hint: Verb + Complement 来 or 去) and pick them up by yourself?

---

## 💻 TASK 4. 情景对话 (QÍNGJǏNG DUÌHUÀ) SITUATIONAL DIALOGUE

| | |
|---|---|
| **Setting:** | At a train ticket office |
| **Cast:** | A sales agent and a customer |
| **Situation:** | The customer wants to buy a round-trip ticket and is speaking to a sales agent. Carry out this conversation. Be sure to discuss where he/she is going, when he/she is leaving and returning, what kind of train he/she wants to take, and what type of seat the customer wants to buy. |

# 33

# 风味小吃

# A Taste of China

> **In this lesson you will:**
> - Learn how to order dishes in a local specialty restaurant.
> - Practice commenting on the food you ordered.
> - Talk about Chinese snacks.

小吃店跟饭馆不太一样。小吃店一般比饭馆便宜。小吃店吃的东西一般是一种地方风味的。有些小一点儿的小吃店，没有菜单。小吃的名字和价格都写在牌子上。有的小吃店没有服务员。点菜要到柜台去点。西安的回民小吃很有名。所以，李丽莉和吴文德到了西安以后，第一件事就是去尝尝西安的回民小吃。下面请看他们在小吃店吃小吃的故事。

（从火车站出来）

李丽莉：坐了一晚上的火车，我现在又累又饿，我们先去吃一点儿东西吧。

吴文德：好啊，西安的羊肉泡馍很有名，离这儿不远有一家回民小吃店。我带你去尝尝吧。

（李丽莉和吴文德从火车站对面那条马路穿过去，走过两条街，十几分钟后，就走进了一家回民小吃店。一个服务员走了过来。）

服务员：几位？

李丽莉：两位。

服务员：楼下已经满了，请跟我来，我带你们上楼去。楼上还有好几张桌子。

吴文德：这家小吃店的小吃一定不错，你看，顾客很多，差不多都没有空位了。

......

吴文德：我一走进来就觉得饿了，快坐下来点菜吧。

李丽莉：劳驾，你们有菜单吗？

服务员：没有。墙上挂着价格表。我们店有二十多种风味小吃，有甜的、有咸的、有酸的、有辣的、有热的、也有冷的……你们先看看再点吧，一定有适合你们口味的。

（几分钟以后，服务员又走了过来。）

服务员：你们想来一点儿什么？

吴文德：我们是第一次来这儿。你给我们推荐几个菜吧。

服务员：我们这儿羊肉泡馍非常有名，味道纯正，要不要尝尝？

吴文德：我饿极了，给我两碗吧。对不起，我口淡，请不要放太多盐。

服务员：好。小姐，您想吃一点儿什么？

李丽莉：我想吃一点儿素的。

服务员：我们这是回民小吃。吃的东西都是素的。我们这儿的油饼都是用素油炸的，香喷喷的。豆浆也是刚刚煮好的，热腾腾的。保证让你吃得乐呵呵的。想不想尝一尝？

李丽莉：好，我听你的。给我两个油饼，一碗豆浆，豆浆请不要加糖，我不喜欢吃甜的。

服务员：请稍等几分钟，我很快就给你们送过来。

吴文德：怪不得这家小吃店生意这么好，你看这儿的服务员服务得多周到。我们应该多给一些小费来感谢他。

李丽莉：在中国吃饭，一般都不用给小费。

……

服务员：来了，二位点的小吃都到齐了，要是不够可以再点。

吴文德：真香。我一闻到香味，就更饿了。我一会儿可能还得再要一碗。

……

李丽莉：吴文德，你第一碗几分钟就吃完了，怎么第二碗吃了这么长时间还在吃？你是不是眼大肚子小[1]，吃不完了？

吴文德：谁说吃不完？我吃得完。这饭实在是好吃。你耐心地等一会儿。让我慢慢吃。

李丽莉：饱了就别再使劲吃了。肚子撑破了不值得[2]。要不，咱们把剩
下的打包，带回旅馆去，晚上再吃。咱们走吧。

吴文德：我太撑了！现在已经站不起来了，怎么能走得到旅馆去呢？
等一会儿再走，好不好？

## Notes

1. 眼大肚子小　(Yǎn dà dùzi xiǎo)

   Literally, "my eyes are bigger than my stomach." This is used when someone has taken more food than he/she can eat.

2. 肚子撑破了不值得。　(Dùzi chēng pò le bù zhíde.)

   Literally, "If your stomach bursts, it isn't worth it." This is used to tell people to stop eating if they are full.

 生词表 (Shēngcí Biǎo)
## Vocabulary

| Character | Pinyin | Part of Speech | English Definition |
|---|---|---|---|
| 1. 风味 | fēngwèi | *n.* | flavor or style of food |
| 这儿的饭馆都有自己的风味。 | | | |
| 2. 羊肉泡馍 | yángròu pàomó | *n.* | bread soaked in mutton soup |
| 3. 小吃店 | xiǎochīdiàn | *n.* | a bistro-style restaurant that serves local specialties |
| 这些小吃店都不错，你应该每个都试一试。 | | | |
|    小吃 | | *n.* | local specialties (food/dishes) |
| 4. 菜单 | càidān | *n.* | menu |
| 这个菜怎么不在菜单上？ | | | |
| 5. 价格 | jiàgé | *n.* | price |
| 那些小吃价格都不贵。 | | | |
| 6. 点菜 | diǎn cài | *v. obj.* | to order dishes |
| 你们来点菜好吗？ | | | |
|    点 | | *v.* | to order (dishes) |
| 7. 满 | mǎn | *adj.* | full, filled |
| 来这儿吃饭的人很多，你看，楼上楼下都满了。 | | | |

| | | | |
|---|---|---|---|
| 8. 差不多 | chàbuduō | *phr.* | almost there; (lit.) missing by not very much |
| 我们差不多已经吃完了。 | | | |
| 9. 空位 | kòngwèi | *n.* | empty seat |
| 你们还有空位吗？ | | | |
| 10. 甜 | tián | *adj.* | sweet |
| 我今天不想吃甜的。 | | | |
| 11. 咸 | xián | *adj.* | salty |
| 我想吃一点咸的。 | | | |
| 12. 酸 | suān | *adj.* | sour |
| 你爱吃酸的吗？ | | | |
| 13. 辣 | là | *adj.* | hot and spicy |
| 四川人都爱吃辣的，是不是？ | | | |
| 14. 适合 | shìhé | *v.* | to fit, to be suitable |
| 这个菜对我不适合。 | | | |
| 15. 口味 | kǒuwèi | *n.* | taste |
| 你尝尝，看这个菜合不合你的口味。 | | | |
| 16. 味道 | wèidào | *n.* | flavor of a dish/food |
| 这个菜味道不错。 | | | |
| 17. 纯正 | chúnzhèng | *adj.* | pure, authentic |
| 这个菜是纯正的四川风味。 | | | |
| 18. 碗 | wǎn | *m.w.* | bowl |
| 请你给我们来三碗饭。 | | | |
| | | *n.* | bowl |
| 我买了三个大碗。 | | | |
| 19. 口淡 | kǒu dàn | *phr.* | (lit.) mouth preferring mild flavors |
| 我口淡。 | | | |
| 淡 | | *adj.* | (of flavor) mild, not strong |
| 20. 盐 | yán | *n.* | salt |
| 这个菜你放盐放得太多了。 | | | |
| 21. 炸 | zhá | *v.* | to deep-fry |
| 我不爱吃炸的东西。 | | | |

| 22. 油饼 | yóubǐng | *n.* | deep-fried cake |
|---|---|---|---|

| 23. 香喷喷 | xiāngpēnpēn | *phr.* | (of food) so delicious smelling that it hits one in the face |
|---|---|---|---|

这个菜刚做好，香喷喷的，你快吃吧。

| 24. 豆浆 | dòujiāng | *n.* | soy milk |
|---|---|---|---|

| 25. 煮 | zhǔ | *v.* | to boil |
|---|---|---|---|

这个菜不是炸的，是煮的。

| 26. 热腾腾 | rètēngtēng | *phr.* | (lit.) so steaming hot that vapor can still be seen (rising from the object) |
|---|---|---|---|

这碗饭还是热腾腾的，你要不要？

| 27. 乐呵呵 | lèhēhē | *phr.* | smiling happily |
|---|---|---|---|

他这个人总是乐呵呵的，一定不会生气。

| 28. 加 | jiā | *v.* | to add |
|---|---|---|---|

那儿的人做菜都喜欢加糖。

| 29. 怪不得 | guàibude | *phr.* | no wonder |
|---|---|---|---|

这个菜做得那么好，怪不得大家都爱吃。

| 30. 周到 | zhōudào | *adj.* | complete, all-encompassing |
|---|---|---|---|

这家饭馆服务很周到。

| 31. 小费 | xiǎofèi | *n.* | tip |
|---|---|---|---|

在中国饭馆吃饭，不用给小费。

| 32. 到齐 | dàoqí | *v. comp.* | to arrive in completion |
|---|---|---|---|

菜都到齐了，请你们点一点。

| 33. 闻 | wén | *v.* | to smell, to listen |
|---|---|---|---|

你闻闻，这个菜还能吃吗？

| 34. 实在 | shízài | *adv.* | truly, indeed |
|---|---|---|---|

这个饭馆实在太好了。

| 35. 剩下 | shèngxia | *v. comp.* | left over |
|---|---|---|---|

剩下的饭我吃。

| 36. 撑 | chēng | *v.* | to prop up |
|---|---|---|---|

你撑着这边，我去撑那边。

| 37. 破 | pò | *adj.* | broken, damaged |
|---|---|---|---|

你的衬衫怎么破了？

## 专有名词 (Zhuānyǒu Míngcí) Proper Nouns

| | | |
|---|---|---|
| 回民 | Huímín | A Muslim ethnic group in China |

## 补充词汇 (Bǔchōng Cíhuì) Supplementary Vocabulary

| | | | | |
|---|---|---|---|---|
| 1. | 冷盘 | lěngpán | *n.* | cold dishes |
| 2. | 小菜 | xiǎocài | *n.* | appetizer |
| 3. | 正餐 | zhèngcān | *n.* | entrée |
| 4. | 四菜一汤 | sì cài yī tāng | *phr.* | four dishes and a soup |
| 5. | 蒸 | zhēng | *v.* | to steam |
| 6. | 炒 | chǎo | *v.* | to stir-fry |
| 7. | 胡椒 | hújiāo | *n.* | pepper |
| 8. | 酱油 | jiàngyóu | *n.* | soy sauce |
| 9. | 麻油 | máyóu | *n.* | sesame oil |
| 10. | 调料 | tiáoliào | *n.* | seasoning |

## 口头用语 (Kǒutóu Yòngyǔ) Spoken Expressions

| | | | |
|---|---|---|---|
| 1. | 劳驾 | láojià | excuse me, may I trouble you |
| 2. | 我听你的 | wǒ tīng nǐ de | I will listen to you. |
| 3. | 打包 | dǎ bāo | to wrap/pack a doggy bag |
| 4. | 使劲 | shǐ jìng | to make an effort, to exert oneself |

## 词汇注解 (Cíhuì Zhùjiě) Featured Vocabulary

### 1. 地方 (Dìfang)

You learned in Lesson 14 that 地方 means "a place." In this lesson, 地方 means "local." For example: 地方风味小吃, local flavor of food.

### 2. 一晚上 (Yī Wǎnshang)

一晚上 consists of "一 + Time Word" and indicates "the whole time."

| | | | |
|---|---|---|---|
| 一晚上 | the whole night | 一上午 | the whole morning |
| 一下午 | the whole afternoon | 一天 | the whole day |

When 一 is used with measure words and nouns, sometimes it carries the meaning of "entire." For example: 一家人, the entire family.

## 3. 来 (*Lái*) vs. 点 (*Diǎn*)

Both 来 and 点 can be used to order food in a restaurant.

| 来: a very informal way to ask for food | | |
|---|---|---|
| Waiter: | 你们想来一点儿什么？ | What do you want to order? |
| Customer: | 来三个包子吧。 | (We want to) order three dumplings. |

| 点: to describe the process of ordering | | |
|---|---|---|
| Customer: | 点菜了吗？ | Did you order any dishes? |
| Customer: | 还没有。我们点菜吧。我都快饿死了。 | Not yet. Let's order now. I am starving. |

## 4. 穿 (*Chuān*)

| 穿 | *v.* | to wear | 穿衣服 |
|---|---|---|---|
| 穿 | *v.* | to cross | 穿过马路 |

## 5. 怪不得 (*Guàibùdé*)

| 怪不得 | *phr.* | no wonder |
|---|---|---|

怪不得 indicates that the speaker understands the reason for an action/behavior. The phrase 怪不得, which usually presents a fact, should always be placed before the clause containing the action/behavior. The second clause that explains the reason can precede or follow the clause introduced by 怪不得.

> 怪不得这家小吃店生意这么好，你看这儿的服务员服务得多周到。
> No wonder this 小吃店 has such good business; the waiters here provide very good service.

> 外面下雪了，怪不得今天这么冷。
> No wonder today is so cold; it is snowing outside.

## 6. 适合 (*Shìhé*) vs. 合适 (*Héshì*)

| 合适 | *adj.* | fit, suitable |
|---|---|---|
| 这件衣服你穿很合适。 | | These clothes fit you perfectly. |

| 适合 | *v.* | to fit |
|---|---|---|
| 这种菜一定会适合你的口味。 | | You will like this type of dish. (Lit.) This type of dish must fit your taste. |

## 7. 口味 (*Kǒuwèi*) vs. 味道 (*Wèidao*) vs. 味口 (*Wèikǒu*)

| 口味 | *n.* | to describe someone's taste |
|---|---|---|
| 我们的菜一定有适合你们口味的。 | | Our dishes must fit your taste. |

| 味道 | *n.* | to describe the flavor of food |
| --- | --- | --- |

我们的菜味道很好。　　　　Our dishes taste wonderful.

| 味口 | *n.* | appetite |
| --- | --- | --- |

我今天没有味口。　　　　I don't have any appetite today.

# 语法(Yǔfǎ)
# Grammar

## I. The Compound Directional Complement

In the previous lesson you learned the simple directional complement 来/去, which can be attached to a motion or an action verb to indicate the direction of an action in relationship to a speaker. In this lesson you will learn the compound directional complement.

The structure of a compound directional complement is composed of three components: V1 + V2 + V3.

- V1 is an action verb that specifies the manner in which the motion or action is carried out.
- V2 is a motion verb.
- V3 is the directional complement (来/去).

V2 + V3 = the structure of simple directional complement that you learned in the previous lesson. Again, 来 (to come) indicates that an action moves toward the speaker, while 去 (to go) indicates that an action moves away from the speaker.

*A local flavor restaurant in Xi'an.*

Xueying Wang

| Action | Motion | Direction | Example |
|--------|--------|-----------|---------|
| Verb1 | Verb2 | Verb3 | |
| 拿 | 上 | 来/去 | 拿上来/拿上去 |
| 送 | 下 | 来/去 | 送下来/送下去 |
| 带 | 进 | 来/去 | 带进来/带进去 |
| 走 | 出 | 来/去 | 走出来/走出去 |
| 寄 | 回 | 来/去 | 寄回来/寄回去 |
| 跑 | 过 | 来/去 | 跑过来/跑过去 |
| 拿 | 起 | 来 | 拿起来 |

## *Note*

As the simple directional complement, the verb 起 can only use 来 as its complement.

*A menu of Muslim specialties in Xi'an.*

## A. Without an Object

The action or the predicate verb in this structure has no object, and the pattern is very simple. For example:

| | Action verb | Motion verb | Complement |
|---|-------------|-------------|------------|
| Subject | Verb1 | Verb2 | 来/去 |
| 他 | 跑（了） | 上 | 来/去了。 |

He ran upstairs.

| | | | |
|---|---|---|---|
| 他 | 走（了） | 进 | 来/去了。 |

He walked in.

## *Note*

If the model 了 is used, it can be placed either after the first verb or after 来/去. Sometimes there can be two 了 at the same time.

## ✇ PRACTICE

Translate the following phrases into Chinese and then use these phrases to make sentences of your own. Phrases: walk in, run out, sit down, drive (towards the speaker), jump down, stand up, fly away (from the speaker), and walk over here.

## B. With a Person/Thing as an Object

The object can take four possible positions in a sentence, thus creating multiple structures. See the following for details.

### 1. Object after the Action Verb1

In this pattern, the object can be either specific (definite) or non-specific (indefinite).

|  | Action | Someone/Something | Motion | Complement |
|---|---|---|---|---|
| **Subject** | **Verb1** | **Object** | **Verb2** | **来/去** |
| 他明天 | 陪 | （他的）女朋友 | 回 | 去。 |

He will accompany his girlfriend back tomorrow.

|  |  |  |  |  |
|---|---|---|---|---|
| 他 | 要带 | （一）瓶酒 | 出 | 来。 |

He will take out a bottle of wine.

### 2. Object after 来/去

The object in this pattern should be non-specific.

|  | Action | Motion | Complement | Something |
|---|---|---|---|---|
| **Subject** | **Verb1** | **Verb2** | **来/去** | **Object** |
| 他 | 想给我们送 | 过 | 来 | 一瓶酒。 |

He wants to send us a bottle of wine.

*Traditional Beijing cuisine sold at a restaurant at the Beijing Airport.*

*Enjoying hotpot in Chengdu.*

### 3. Object after the Motion Verb2

The object in this pattern should represent a thing, rather than a person, and it should also be non-specific.

|  | Action | Motion | Something | Complement |
|---|---|---|---|---|
| Subject | Verb1 | Verb2 | Object | 来/去 |
| 他要给我们 | 寄 | 回 | 一瓶酒 | 来。 |

He wants to send us a bottle of wine by mail.

### 4. Object before the Subject

In the following pattern, the object is placed before the subject for emphasis. However, the object must be a specific noun.

| Thing |  |  | Action | Motion | Complement |
|---|---|---|---|---|---|
| Object |  | Subject | Verb1 | Verb2 | 来/去 |
| 这本书， | 请 | 你 | 送 | 过 | 去。 |

Please send over this book.

| 那瓶酒， | 请 | 他 | 带 | 回 | 去。 |
|---|---|---|---|---|---|

Please ask him to take this bottle of wine back with him.

## Note

Again because the object in the above pattern is a specific noun, the sentences can be rewritten using the 把 structure. For example:

> 请你把这本书送过去。
> 请他把那瓶酒带回去。

## C. The Position of 了

When 了 is used in a sentence with the compound Directional Complement, it can be placed either after the main action verb or after verb complement 来/去, if the object is a non-specific noun. If the object is a specific noun, it is usually placed at the end of the sentence. For example:

### 1. Object as a Non-specific Noun

| | |
|---|---|
| 他带了一个朋友回来。 | He brought a friend back. |
| 他带了一瓶酒回来。 | He brought back a bottle of wine. |
| 他给我们送过来了一本书。 | He sent a book over to us. |

### 2. Object as a Specific Noun

| | |
|---|---|
| 那瓶酒，他带回去了。 | He took back the bottle of wine. |
| 他把那瓶酒带回去了。 | (The 把 structure) |
| 他带他的女朋友回来了。 | He brought his girlfriend back. |
| 他把他的女朋友带回来了。 | (The 把 structure) |
| 他带那本书回来了。 | He brought that book back. |
| 他把那本书带回来了。 | (The 把 structure) |

## 🔲 PRACTICE

Try using each of the above patterns to create a few sentences of your own.

## D. With a Place/Location Word as an Object

When the object represents a place or location, it should be placed BEFORE 来/去, not after. If 了 is used to indicate past action, it should be placed after 来/去.

| | Action | Motion | Place/Location | Complement |
|---|---|---|---|---|
| Subject | Verb1 | Verb2 | Object | Verb来/去 |
| 老师 | 走 | 进 | 教室 | 来了。 |

The teacher walked into the classroom.

## 🔲 PRACTICE

Translate the following phrases into Chinese and then use these phrases to make sentences of your own. Phrases: to drive into a parking lot, to walk across a street, to walk into a park, to run upstairs, and to buy something and bring it home.

# II. Using the Adverbial Conjunction "一⋯就⋯" (Yī...Jiù...)

The adverbial conjunction "一⋯就⋯" has the following two meanings.

## A. Indicating Actions in a Series

The adverbial conjunction "一⋯就⋯" here indicates that the second action takes place immediately after the first action.

|  | First clause | | | Second clause | | | |
|---|---|---|---|---|---|---|---|
|  | Subject1 | 一 | Verb | Object | (Subject2) | 就 | Verb | Object |
| One subject: | 他 | 一 | 吃完 | 早饭， |  | 就 | 去上 | 课了。 |

As soon as he finished the breakfast, he went to class.

| Two subjects: | 老师 | 一 | 说 | 下课，学生 |  | 就 | 都跑 | 出去了。 |

The minute the teacher dismissed the class, the students ran out.

## B. Indicating Cause and Effect

In this structure, the second action is always caused by the first action.

|  | First clause | | | Second clause | | |
|---|---|---|---|---|---|---|
|  | Subject1 | 一 | Verb | Object | (Subject2) | 就 | Predicate verb/adj. |
| One subject: | 他 | 一 | 看见 | 他朋友 |  | 就 | 高兴地笑了。 |

He smiled happily as soon as he saw his friend.

| Two subjects: | 老师 | 一 | 说 | 要考试， | 学生 | 就 | 紧张。 |

Students get very nervous the minute the teacher says he wants to give a quiz.

## *Note*

Both 一 and 就 are adverbs and should appear before the verb and after the subject.

    CORRECT: 一下课我就回家。

    xxx INCORRECT: 一下课就我回家。 xxx

## ❀ PRACTICE

Answer the following questions using the "一⋯就⋯" structure:

你每天一回到家，就做什么？

学生一下课，就去哪儿？

顾客一走进饭馆，服务员就做什么？

学生一打开书，就怎么样？

你一闻到饭馆的香味，你就会怎么样？

## III. Adjectives Followed by Particles

You have learned in Lesson 6 and Lesson 32 that verbs and adjectives can be reduplicated to soften the tone or make language more colorful and expressive. In this lesson, you will find that some adjectives can be followed by repeated particles to describe the sound, manner, and situation of the object. This pattern also makes the language more lively and vivid. However, the combination of the adjective and particles is usually considered to be a fixed phrase, so you should avoid creating such combinations yourself. For example:

| Adjective | Particles | |
|---|---|---|
| 热 | 腾腾 | Something is so hot that you can see vapor rising from it. |
| 香 | 喷喷 | The delicious smell from the food is coming directly into your nose. |
| 乐 | 呵呵 | Someone is smiling from ear to ear. |

## 🔲 PRACTICE

Try using the phrases above to make a few sentences of your own.

# IV. A Brief Introduction to the Potential Complement

The potential complement indicates an action's potential result, which may or may not be accomplished. It uses 得 or 不 to indicate whether it is possible to achieve a result through an action. In this structure, 得 or 不 is inserted between the verb and its resultative complement or directional complement. It takes the following forms:

| | Subject | Action Verb | 得/不 | Resultative/Directional Complement | |
|---|---|---|---|---|---|
| Resultative: | 我 | 吃 | 得 | 完。 | Positive |
| | 我 | 吃 | 不 | 完。 | Negative |
| | I can(not) finish eating it. | | | | |
| Simple directional: | 我 | 走 | 得 | 到旅馆去。 | Positive |
| | 我 | 走 | 不 | 到旅馆去。 | Negative |
| | I can(not) walk to the hotel. | | | | |
| Compound directional: | 我 | 站 | 得 | 起来。 | Positive |
| | 我 | 站 | 不 | 起来。 | Negative |
| | I can(not) stand up. | | | | |

# Textbook Exercises

## 🎧💻 TASK 1. 课文问答 (KÈWÉN WÈNDÁ) QUESTIONS AND ANSWERS

Check your comprehension of the text by answering the following questions.

1. 吴文德觉得那家小吃店的饭好吃不好吃？为什么？
2. 你知道吴文德和李丽莉吃饭的那家小吃店都有什么吃的东西？
3. 吴文德不喜欢吃什么？李丽莉不喜欢吃什么？
4. 吴文德第二碗羊肉泡馍吃完了没有？为什么？

## 💻 TASK 2. 语法练习 (YǓFǍ LIÀNXÍ) GRAMMATICAL STRUCTURE PRACTICE

### A. Fill in the Blanks

1. Fill in the blanks by taking words from below and placing them into the appropriate places in the sentences. When you are done, translate the sentences into English.

    带回去　　开过去　　　跑出去　　　拿出来　　　寄出去

    a) 一下课，学生们就 ＿＿＿＿＿＿＿＿ 了。
    b) 你昨天写好的信 ＿＿＿＿＿＿＿＿ 了没有？
    c) 没吃完的菜我们可以打包 ＿＿＿＿＿＿＿＿ 。
    d) 他从书房里 ＿＿＿＿＿＿＿＿ 两本杂志。
    e) 现在是绿灯了，快一点 ＿＿＿＿＿＿＿＿ 吧。

2. Use 过去, 过来, 下去, 回来, 下来, and 出来 where needed to fill in the following blanks.

    我妈妈上次来我这儿的时候，从菜店买 ＿＿＿＿＿＿＿＿ 了很多菜，在我的宿舍里做饭。做好了以后，她拿 ＿＿＿＿＿＿＿＿ 了一些，让我给我宿舍对面的那个朋友送 ＿＿＿＿＿＿＿＿ 。我那个朋友以为是我做的菜，他高兴地说："你做的菜这么香！你能不能搬 ＿＿＿＿＿＿＿＿ 给我当室友？"我回到宿舍以后，我妈妈又让我给我楼下的朋友也送 ＿＿＿＿＿＿＿＿ 一些。我楼下的那个朋友尝了尝我妈妈做的菜，也以为是我做的，高兴地对我说：你这么会做菜，你搬 ＿＿＿＿＿＿＿＿ 跟我一起住吧。

## B. Sentence Completion

1. Use the appropriate "Verb + Directional Complement" to complete the following sentences.

   a) 别站在那儿，快坐 ＿＿＿＿＿＿＿＿ 喝杯茶吧。

   b) 你看，前边有一条大马路，你一穿 ＿＿＿＿＿＿＿＿ 就能看到那家饭馆了。

   c) 他从墙上取 ＿＿＿＿＿＿＿＿ 了那张旧画以后，又挂 ＿＿＿＿＿＿＿＿ 了一张新的。

   d) 我的朋友坐在车站着等我。他一看见我下车，就马上站了 ＿＿＿＿＿＿＿＿，跑 ＿＿＿＿＿＿＿＿ 帮我拿行李。

2. Use "一···就···" to complete the following sentences.

   a) 服务员一看见我，＿＿＿＿＿＿＿＿＿＿＿＿＿＿＿＿＿＿＿＿＿＿＿＿＿＿＿。

   b) 天气一热，我＿＿＿＿＿＿＿＿＿＿＿＿＿＿＿＿＿＿＿＿＿＿＿＿＿＿＿＿＿。

   c) 他早上一起床，＿＿＿＿＿＿＿＿＿＿＿＿＿＿＿＿＿＿＿＿＿＿＿＿＿＿＿。

   d) 我一闻到香味，肚子＿＿＿＿＿＿＿＿＿＿＿＿＿＿＿＿＿＿＿＿＿＿＿＿＿。

   e) 他一收到学校发的录取通知书，他＿＿＿＿＿＿＿＿＿＿＿＿＿＿＿＿＿＿＿＿。

## C. Scrambled Sentences

Rearrange the words in each of the following groups to make complete sentences.

| 1. 了 | 一张菜单 | 给他们 | 饭馆的 | 师傅 | 送过来 | | |
|---|---|---|---|---|---|---|---|
| 2. 回去 | 这些菜 | 带 | 请他 | | | | |
| 3. 她弟弟 | 了 | 送 | 李小英 | 回家 | 去 | | |
| 4. 马上 | 那家小吃店 | 他们 | 去了 | 走进 | 你看 | 就要 | |

---

## 🖥 TASK 3. 翻译 (FĀNYÌ) PARAPHRASING

Translate the following sentences into Chinese.

1. The minute you cross the street, you can see the famous restaurant that serves local specialties. (Hint: 一···就···, Verb + 过去) As soon as you walk in, you will smell that delicious aroma (Hint: Adjective + Particles) and you won't be able to leave. (Hint: 一···就···, Verb + 进去, Verb + 不出来)

2. The minute we sat down in that restaurant, the waiter came over with two menus. (Hint: 一···就···, Verb + 下来, Verb + 过来) Shortly after that, he came over to again to ask us what we wanted to order. (Hint: Verb + 过来) No wonder they have such good business; their service is very prompt! (Hint: 怪不得, 周到)

3. A: These fried cakes that smell so delicious have just been fried. (Hint: Adjective + Particle, Verb + Complement). Can you finish eating them? (Hint: Verb + 得 + Complement)

   B: I can't eat them all. (Hint: Verb + 不 + Complement) I'm so full, I feel like I might burst. (Hint: Verb + 死). I cannot even stand up! (Hint: Verb + 起来) Let's get a doggy bag and take it home. (Hint: Verb 回去)

4. A: The price list is hanging on the wall. We have all kinds of local specialties. (Hint: 各种小吃) Which one do you want to order? (Hint: 来一点儿)

   B: I want something that doesn't have meat in it. (Hint: Verb + 一点儿, 素) I don't like anything too salty. (Hint: 口淡) Could you please recommend a few dishes?

---

## 📖 TASK 4. 情景对话 (QÍNGJǏNG DUÌHUÀ) SITUATIONAL DIALOGUE

| | |
|---|---|
| **Setting:** | At a snack bar |
| **Cast:** | A waiter and two friends |
| **Situation:** | Two friends at a snack bar are ordering food. A waiter is eagerly serving them. |
| **Topic:** | Construct a dialogue (at least twelve sentences) between the two tired friends and the waiter. Pick a role and perform the task in class. Make sure the conversation includes the discussion of food and how to order food. |

# 34
# 住旅馆
# Staying in a Hotel

*In this lesson you will:*
- Learn the dos and don'ts when staying in Chinese hotels.
- Learn the check-in and check-out procedures.
- Know what to watch out for when taking a taxi.

去中国旅游，订旅馆可以上网预订也可以打电话预订，如果你不知道旅馆的电话号码，可以打114查电话号码。在中国住旅馆一定要有证件。只有好一些的旅馆才允许招待外国人。能招待外国人的旅馆里，一般每个房间里都有纯净水，因为中国的自来水不能喝。现在很多的旅馆还有给顾客订飞机票和火车票的服务项目。下面是李丽莉和吴文德在西安住旅馆的小故事。

（从小吃店出来）

吴文德：这家小吃店真不错，我下火车的时候还担心我们找不到这个小吃店呢。

李丽莉：你这个导游当得够水平。这家小吃店的地址你记下来了吗？我们在离开西安以前，你再带我过来一次，好不好？

吴文德：没问题。我保证让你吃个够。我们现在打的去旅馆吧。

李丽莉：打的？我听说有些出租车司机可会"宰"人了，开着出租车在街上绕圈子。你要是问司机，他会告诉你这条路开不进去，那条路走不出来。

吴文德：这种事现在越来越少。就是真的"宰"了我们，也没事。他的计程表旁边有行车执照，抄下来他的执照号码，有事可以告他。

（吴文德在马路边上挥了挥手，开过来了一辆出租车。）

（在旅客登记处）

吴文德：你好，我叫吴文德，她叫李丽莉。我们预订了两个单人间。

服务员：请稍等，我查一下……找到了。你们打算住几个晚上？

吴文德：两个晚上，星期天上午退房。

服务员：一个人一个晚上 120 块。一共 480 块。每个房间还要交 100 块钱押金。

吴文德：交押金？为什么？

服务员：我看出来了，你们从来没有在中国住过旅馆。

吴文德：是啊。这是我们第一次住旅馆，麻烦你给我们解释一下。

服务员：在中国住旅馆一般都要交押金。在您退房间的那天，如果您没打长途电话，也没有损坏东西，押金会全部退还给您。这是您房间的钥匙，有问题请给我们前台打电话。

（李丽莉在自己的房间给吴文德打电话。）

李丽莉：吴文德，我的房间有一些饮料，你过来我们一起喝吧。

吴文德：那些饮料你可千万不要喝。贵得要死。在我们退房的时候，服务员就会上来检查，少一件东西就要交一件东西的钱。每件东西的价格都贵得吓人。

李丽莉：幸亏我还没有喝。我还给你泡了一杯香喷喷的茶。你要不要我给你送过去？

吴文德：来不及了。还有 40 分钟，旅游车就要出发了。半个小时以后咱们在一楼大厅见面的时候，你给我带下来，好不好？

李丽莉：好吧。一会儿见。

（李丽莉和吴文德在大厅里等旅游车。）

李丽莉：导游先生，你走来走去的，在想什么呢？是不是在想明天我们应该去哪儿参观？

吴文德：看起来你挺了解我。我想来想去，总算想出来了一个好主意。我们明天去尝尝西安著名的饺子宴，怎么样？

李丽莉：我早就想跟你说吃饺子宴的事了。但是，你是导游，我不敢班门弄斧[1]。

*Note*

1. 班门弄斧 (bān mén nòng fǔ)

This comes from a 成语故事. Literally, it means "to show off one's skills in using the axe (as a carpenter) right in front (the greatest carpenter) Lu Ban's door." It is used to describe someone who shows off his or her limited skills before an expert. For the story behind this 成语, see Reading/Writing Task 3 in the Workbook.

 生词表 (Shēngcí Biǎo)

## Vocabulary

| Character | Pinyin | Part of Speech | English Definition |
|---|---|---|---|
| 1. 旅馆 | lǚguǎn | *n.* | hotel |
| 那儿的旅馆贵不贵？ | | | |
| 2. 允许 | yǔnxǔ | *v.* | to permit, to allow |
| 他爸爸不允许他们吸烟。 | | | |
| 3. 招待 | zhāodài | *v.* | to act like a host, to entertain (guests, customers, etc.) |
| 你去做饭，我来招待客人。 | | | |
| 4. 纯净水 | chúnjìng shuǐ | *n.* | purified or filtered water; (lit.) pure clean water |
| 你们这儿有没有纯净水？ | | | |
| 纯净 | | *adj.* | pure |
| 5. 自来水 | zìláishuǐ | *n.* | tap water |
| 在中国，自来水一定要煮了才能喝。 | | | |
| 6. 担心 | dān xīn | *v. obj.* | to be anxious, to worry; (lit.) to lift up one's heart |
| 这件事儿我会办，你担什么心？ | | | |
| 7. 够 | gòu | *v.* | to reach, to attain |
| 这家饭馆的服务不够水平。 | | | |
| | | *adj.* | enough, adequate, sufficient |
| 我的衣服够了。 | | | |
| 8. 水平 | shuǐpíng | *n.* | standard; (lit.) water level |
| 你这个导游很够水平。 | | | |

9. 司机          sījī          *n.*          chauffeur, (professional) driver

你刚才挥手，司机没看见。

10. 计程表        jìchéngbiǎo   *n.*          taxi meter; (lit.) distance-calculating

请问，司机先生，你的计程表对吗？                    meter

11. 行车执照      xíng chē zhízhào  *n. phr.*  license for operating a vehicle

请给我看看你的行车执照！

行车                          *v. obj.*     to drive a vehicle

执照                          *n.*          license

12. 抄            chāo          *v.*          to copy, to write down

你抄下他的行车执照号码了没有？

13. 告            gào           *v.*          to tell on (somebody), to accuse

我们去他的公司告他。

14. 挥（手）      huī (shǒu)    *v. obj.*     to wave (hand)

车来了，你快挥挥手！

挥                            *v.*          to wave

15. 登记处        dēngjìchù     *n.*          registration desk, front desk; (lit.)

我去上厕所，你去登记处登记吧。                      record-entering place

登记                          *v.*          to enter a record

16. 单人间        dānrénjiān    *n.*          single room

我们现在只有单人间。

单                            *b.f.*        single, a sheet

17. 打算          dǎsuàn        *v.*          to plan

你打算住几天？

                             *n.*          plan

你有什么打算？

18. 退房          tuì fáng      *v. obj.*     to check out (of a hotel)

我们星期六退房。

19. 押金          yājīn         *n.*          deposit

要不要交押金？

20. 从来（不/没）  cónglái       *adv.*        never
                 (bù/méi)

我从来不喜欢住旅馆。

21. 解释 jiěshì *v.* to explain
请你给我们解释一下儿。

*n.* explanation, interpretation
这是他的解释。

22. 损坏 sǔnhuài *v. comp.* to damage, to break
我没有损坏房间里的东西，为什么不还我押金？

23. 全部 quánbù *adv.* all, in total
我的押金你们应该全部还给我！

24. 退还 tuìhuán *v.* to return (something to its original owner), to give back
你退房的时候，我们就退还你的押金。

25. 钥匙 yàoshi *n.* key
这是您的房间钥匙。

26. 前台 qiántái *n.* front desk
您有事儿，可以给我们前台打电话。

27. 饮料 yǐnliào *n.* soft drinks
你想喝什么饮料？

28. 千万 qiānwàn *adv.* making sure (usually followed by a warning); (lit.) ten million
你千万别去住那儿的旅馆。

29. 吓（人） xià (rén) *v.* to scare (someone)
那儿的东西价格贵得吓人。

30. 幸亏 xìngkuī *adv.* luckily
幸亏你告诉我，要不我一定会去住那儿的旅馆。

31. 来不及 lái bu jí *v. comp.* to not have enough time
我们现在去火车站已经来不及了。

32. 大厅 dàtīng *n.* lobby
你去大厅等我吧。

33. 参观 cānguān *v.* to visit
你去那儿参观了什么名胜古迹？

34. 饺子宴 jiǎoziyàn *n.* dumpling banquet

## 补充词汇 (Bǔchōng Cíhuì) **Supplementary Vocabulary**

| | | | | |
|---|---|---|---|---|
| 1. | 标准房间 | biāozhǔn fángjiān | *n.* | standard room |
| 2. | 豪华间 | háohuájiān | *n.* | deluxe room |
| 3. | 绕路 | rào lù | *v. obj.* | to circle around |
| 4. | 套房 | tàofáng | *n.* | suite |
| 5. | 内宾 | nèibīn | *n.* | Chinese guest |
| | 外宾 | wàibīn | *n.* | foreign guest |
| 6. | 旅行社 | lǚxíngshè | *n.* | travel agency |
| 7. | 驾车执照 | jià chē zhízhào | *n.* | driver's license |
| 8. | 计程车 | jìchéngchē | *n.* | taxi (Taiwan usage) |
| 9. | 酒店 | jiǔdiàn | *n.* | restaurant or hotel |
| 10. | 宾馆 | bīnguǎn | *n.* | guesthouse, hotel |

*The Yong Ning Gong Hotel in Xi'an.*

## 口头用语 (Kǒutóu Yòngyǔ) Spoken Expressions

1. 吃个够     chī gè gòu     to eat as much as you want, to eat until you are full

2. 宰人     zǎirén     By itself, 宰 usually means "to slaughter, to butcher." In the colloquial language, 宰人 means "to rip someone off."

3. 绕圈子     rào quānzi     (lit.) to move in a circle; to take a detour

4. 没事 (儿)／有事     méishì / yǒushì     In colloquial Chinese, 没事 is frequently used to say "no problem" while 有事 means either "there is something to do," or "there is a problem…"

5. 要死     yàosǐ     (lit.) to be on the verge of death; similar to 极了.

## 词汇注解 (Cíhuì Zhùjiě) Featured Vocabulary

### 1. 够 (Gòu)

| | | |
|---|---|---|
| a. Predicate Adjective | 我的钱不够了。 | I don't have enough money. |
| b. Adjective as a Complement | 我吃够了。 | I ate enough. |
| c. Adverb | 我的钱够花一个月。 | I have enough money to last a month. |
| d. Verb | 那个饭馆的服务够水平。 | Service is very good at that restaurant. |

### 2. 打算 (Dǎsuan) vs. 计划 (Jìhuà)

打算 and 计划 are interchangeable due to their similar functions and meanings. However, 打算 is more personal and more informal than 计划.

| 计划 | *v.* | to plan |
|---|---|---|
| 你计划什么时候去中国学习？ | | When do you plan to study in China? |

| 计划 | *n.* | plan |
|---|---|---|
| 你今年夏天有什么计划？ | | What is your plan for the summer? |

| 打算 | *v.* | to plan (more personal and informal, and provides more information than 计划) |
|---|---|---|
| 我打算今年夏天去中国。 | | I plan to go to China this summer. |

| 打算 | *n.* | plan |
|------|------|------|

你今年夏天有什么打算？    What is your plan for the summer?

## 3. 从来 (Cónglái) vs. 总是 (Zǒngshì)

| 从来 | *adv.* | always, all the time |
|------|--------|----------------------|

从来 is frequently used in conjunction with a negative to indicate that one never does something or has never done something. 从来 emphasizes that an action or an event took place in the past and has continued to the present. 就 or 都 is frequently used with 从来.

从来不 + Predicate Adjective

我考试从来不心慌。    I never get anxious when I take exams.

从来不 + Auxiliary Verb

我从来就不会唱歌。    I never could sing.

从来没 + Predicate Verb

我从来没吃过中国饭。    I have never had Chinese food.

| 总是 | *adv.* | always, all the time |
|------|--------|----------------------|

总是 can be used in both positive and negative forms. It describes an action or event in general terms with a focus on the present.

他总是吃中国饭。    He always eats Chinese food.

他总是不学习。    He never studies.

*The Bell Tower Hotel in Xi'an.*

*The Da Hua Hotel in Xi'an.*

## 语法(Yǔfǎ)
## Grammar

## I. Special Compound Directional Complement

In the previous lesson you learned the structure of the Compound Directional Complement, which consists of "Action Verb + Motion Verbs + Directional Complement 来 or 去." All the components of this structure use their literal meanings, which indicate the direction of the movement. However, the directional complement of 来 or 去 may change depending on the position of the speaker. For example: 跑过来 means that someone is running towards the speaker, while 跑过去 means that someone is running away from the speaker.

In this lesson, you will learn some special compound directional complements. These complements are often used as idioms. They are all fixed phrases, so you should not try to change them or create your own. See below for more information.

## A. Verb/Adjective + 起来 (Qǐlái)

### 1. Indicating the Beginning of an Action

Verb 起来 (No object)

| | | |
|---|---|---|
| 笑起来 | 她高兴得笑起来了。 | She was so happy that she started to laugh. |

Adjective 起来

| | | |
|---|---|---|
| 忙起来 | 要考试了，学生开始忙起来了。 | Exams are coming, and the students are starting to get busy. |

Verb 起 Object 来 (An object is always placed between 起 and 来.)

| | | |
|---|---|---|
| 谈起话来 | 他们一见面，就谈起话来。 | The minute they saw each other, they started to chat. |
| 下起雨来 | 外面下起雨来了。 | It started raining outside. |
| 唱起歌来 | 他高兴地唱起歌来了。 | He started singing happily. |
| 跳起舞来 | 她高兴地跳起舞来了。 | She started dancing happily. |

---

## 🎴 PRACTICE

Try using verbs/adjectives such as 叫, 热, 热闹, 悲观, and 苗条 along with 起来 to make sentences of your own. When you're done, use the verb-object phrases 点菜, 挥手, 花钱, 讲价, 下雪, and 逛夜市 to make a few additional sentences. Be sure to demonstrate that you understand their meanings and usages!

### 2. Meaning "When It Comes to Doing Something..."

When the "Verb 起来" structure is used in this context, it usually does not take an object.

听起来   这话听起来很不舒服。
These words sound unpleasant. (Lit., when it comes to listening...)

看起来   这件事看起来容易, 做起来难。
This task may look easy, but it is actually very difficult to do. (Lit., when it comes to doing...)

闻起来   什么东西闻起来这么香？
What is it that smells so delicious? (Lit., when it comes to smelling...)

吃起来   这饭吃起来很好吃。
When you taste this, you will see that it is very good. (Lit., when it comes to eating...)

穿起来   这条裤子穿起来不舒服。
These pants aren't comfortable. (Lit., when it comes to wearing...)

*The Ning Ning Hotel in Xi'an.*

## ❧ PRACTICE

Use the "Verb + 起来" structure to complete the following sentences.

1. 这家小吃店的菜，_____。(吃)

2. 这个单人间，_____。(住)

3. 这碗豆浆的味道，_____。(尝)

4. 我的自行车，_____。(骑)

5. 这瓶饮料，_____。(喝)

6. 我新买的手机，_____。(用)

### 3. Indicating "to Remember" or "to Recall"

Only the verb 想 can be used with 起来 in this context. The verb phrase 想起来 can take an object, or it can stand on its own. See the examples below:

| | | |
|---|---|---|
| No Object: | 我想起来了，您是导游。 | Now I remember. You are the tour guide! |
| Object: | 我想不起他的名字来了。 | I can't think of his name. |

## ❧ PRACTICE

Try using "想 + 起来" to create two sentences, one with an object and one without.

## B. Verb + 出来 (Chūlái)

### 1. Indicating That Something Is Made or Created by the Subject

Verb 出来 Object

| | | |
|---|---|---|
| 写出来 | 她写出来了一本书。 | She just finished writing a book. |
| 煮出来 | 我刚刚煮出来了一壶咖啡。 | I just made a pot of coffee. |

Verb 出 Object 来

| | | |
|---|---|---|
| 想出来 | 我刚想出一个好主意来。 | I just came up with a good idea. |

## ❧ PRACTICE

Try using the patterns above to make a few sentences of your own. Here are some suggested verbs: 想, 变, 炸, 选, 回答.

### 2. Indicating "To Figure out Something"

Verb 出来 Sentence

| | |
|---|---|
| 看出来 | 我看出来了，你们没住过旅馆。 |
| | Now I can see that you have never stayed in a hotel before. |

| 听出来 | 我听出来了，你们是中国人。 |
|---|---|
| | After listening to you speak, I can tell that you are Chinese. |
| 闻出来 | 我闻出来了，你做的是中国饭。 |
| | I could tell you were cooking Chinese food from the smell. |

## ❧ PRACTICE

Use the verbs 看, 听, 闻, 摸, 尝 to create your own sentences containing the "Verb + 出来" structure.

## C. Verb + 下去 (Xiàqu)

### 1. Indicating "to Keep on Doing Something"

| | Object | Subject | Verb | 下去 |
|---|---|---|---|---|
| 看下去 | 这个电影 | 我 | 看不下去了。 | |
| | I can't watch any more of this movie. | | | |
| 学下去 | 这一课 | 你 | 学得下去吗？ | |
| | Can you finish learning this lesson? | | | |
| 说下去 | 请 | 你 | 听我说下去。 | |
| | Please listen to what I'm going to say. | | | |
| 听下去 | 他的故事， | 我 | 听不下去了。 | |
| | I can't listen to his stories anymore. | | | |

### 2. Indicating That Something Is Eaten or Swallowed

| | Object | Subject | Verb | 下去 |
|---|---|---|---|---|
| 吃下去 | 药 | 我 | 吃下去了。 | |
| | I took the medicine. | | | |
| 喝下去 | 水 | 我 | 喝下去了。 | |
| | I drank the water. | | | |

## ❧ PRACTICE

Try creating your own sentences, using the nouns 考试, 房间, 咖啡, 饭, 报纸, and 日语 as objects for the "Verb + 下去" structure.

## D. Verb + 下来 (Xiàlái)

下来 indicates something is retained through the action of the verb.

|  | Object | Subject | Verb | 下来 |
|---|---|---|---|---|
| 写下来 | 这家饭馆的地址 | 我 | 写下来了。 | |
|  | I wrote down the address of that restaurant. | | | |
| 记下来 | 这家饭馆的地址 | 我 | 记下来了。 | |
|  | I memorized the address of the restaurant. | | | |
| 留下来 | 客人 | 我 | 留下来了。 | |
|  | I convinced the guests to stay. | | | |

## ❧ PRACTICE

Create a few sentences of your own, using the verbs 抄, 写, 记 containing the "Verb + 下来" structure.

## II. The Potential Complement

In the previous lesson, we briefly introduced the potential complement. Before we start providing further information on the potential complement, you should know that the resultative complement you learned in Lessons 18 and 28 indicates the result of an action while the directional complement you learned in Lessons 32 and 33 indicates actual direction in relationship to the speaker. The potential complement indicates whether it is possible to achieve a result through an action. In this structure, 得 (de) is placed between the verb and complement to indicate the possibility of achieving a result. In the same way, 不 can be used (in place of 得) to indicate the impossibility of achieving the result. The pattern of an affirmative-negative question is "Verb + 得 + Complement + Verb + 不 + Complement." The potential complement may be either a resultative complement or a directional complement. In this lesson, we will cover the potential complement in greater detail.

### A. Using the Potential Complement in a Sentence

|  | Subject | Verb | 得 | Complement | (Object) | |
|---|---|---|---|---|---|---|
| Positive: | 我 | 听 | 得 | 懂 | 中文。 | (Resultative complement) |
|  | I can understand Chinese. | | | | | |
|  | 我 | 想 | 得 | 出来 | 一个好主意。 | (Directional complement) |
|  | I can think of a good idea. | | | | | |

|  | Subject | Verb | 不 | Complement | (Object) | |
|---|---|---|---|---|---|---|
| Negative: | 我 | 听 | 不 | 懂 | 他说的话。 | (Resultative complement) |
|  | I cannot understand what he said. | | | | | |
|  | 我 | 想 | 不 | 出来 | 一个好主意。 | (Directional complement) |
|  | I cannot think of a good idea. | | | | | |

| | Subject | Verb 得 Complement | Verb 不 Complement | (Object) |
|---|---|---|---|---|
| Question: | 你 | 听得懂 | 听不懂 | 中文？ |
| | | Can you understand Chinese or not? | | (Resultative complement) |
| | 你 | 想得出来 | 想不出来 | 一个好主意？ |
| | | Can you think of a good idea or not? | | (Directional complement) |

| | Subject | Verb | 得 | Complement | (Object) 吗？ | |
|---|---|---|---|---|---|---|
| | 你 | 听 | 得 | 懂 | 中文吗？ | (Resultative complement) |
| | | Can you understand Chinese? | | | | |
| | 你 | 想 | 得 | 出来 | 一个好主意吗？ | (Directional complement) |
| | | Can you think of a good idea? | | | | |

## Notes

1. When the object is short, it is generally placed after the potential complement.

2. When the object is very long or complicated, it is often placed at the beginning of the sentence. For example: 他说的话，我听不懂。

## B. Using 得/不 with the Resultative Complement to Form a Potential Complement

You can form the potential complement structure by combining 得/不 with a resultative complement. The following tables illustrate the differences between the actual resultative complement structure and the potential resultative complement structure. Please also pay special attention to the differences between the negative forms:

| Actual resultative complement | | Potential resultative complement | |
|---|---|---|---|
| **Positive** | **Negative** | **Positive** | **Negative** |
| 听懂 | 没听懂 | 听得懂 | 听不懂 |
| 学会 | 没学会 | 学得会 | 学不会 |
| 找到 | 没找到 | 找得到 | 找不到 |
| 做完 | 没做完 | 做得完 | 做不完 |
| 记住 | 没记住 | 记得住 | 记不住 |
| 收到 | 没收到 | 收得到 | 收不到 |
| 修好 | 没修好 | 修得好 | 修不好 |

## 🔲 PRACTICE

1. Use the potential resultative complements listed above to construct your own sentences, then choose one or two sentences and turn them first into questions and next into negative forms.

2. Can you think of several more words that use 得 with resultative complements? (For example, 看见 and 用坏)

## C. Using 得/不 with the Directional Complement to Form a Potential Complement

You can also form the potential directional complement structure by combining 得/不 with a directional complement. The following tables illustrate the differences between the actual directional complement and the potential directional complement using 得/不 with directional complements. Be sure to note the differences between the negative forms as well.

| Actual directional complement | | Potential directional complement | |
|---|---|---|---|
| Positive | Negative | Positive | Negative |
| 下来 | 没下来 | 下得来 | 下不来 |
| 进来 | 没进来 | 进得来 | 进不来 |
| 过来 | 没过来 | 过得来 | 过不来 |
| 走回来 | 没走回来 | 走得回来 | 走不回来 |
| 爬上去 | 没爬上去 | 爬得上去 | 爬不上去 |
| 开出去 | 没开出去 | 开得出去 | 开不出去 |
| 飞过去 | 没飞过去 | 飞得过去 | 飞不过去 |
| 站起来 | 没站起来 | 站得起来 | 站不起来 |

## 🔲 PRACTICE

1. Use two or three of the above phrases to construct a sentence, then turn the sentence into a question and negative form.

2. Can you think of several more words that use 得 with a directional complement? Here are a few that we came up with: 看出来, 想起来, 喝下去, 问出来, and 穿上去. Try using these complements to make sentences of your own.

## D. Potential Complement vs. Auxiliary Verb 可以 (Kěyǐ) / 能 (Néng)

Remember that both the potential complement form and the verb 能 indicate ability to do something. However, when asking for permission, you should use only auxiliary verbs, not the potential complement.

For example:

| | | |
|---|---|---|
| Potential complement: | Only indicates ability. | |
| | 你吃得完吗？ | Will you be able to finish it? |
| Auxiliary verb 可以/能: | May be used to indicate permission as well as ability. | |
| | 我能/可以吃完吗？ | May I finish it? (Permission) |
| | 我能/可以吃完。 | I can (am able to) finish. (Ability) |

The auxiliary verbs 可以 and 能 can be used along with the potential complements for emphasis. For example:

| | |
|---|---|
| 我能看得懂中文。 | I can read Chinese. |
| 我怎么可以看得完这么多的书呢？ | How can I finish reading all of these books? |

## E. Potential Complement vs. Complement of Degree

In Lesson 19 you learned the complement of degree, which looks similar to the potential complement in that they both use 得. However, the two are very different in their meanings and structures. The following will help you distinguish between the potential complement and the complement of degree.

### 1. Positive Sentence

In a positive statement, the potential complement can take an object directly. In the complement of degree, if the object follows the verb, that verb has to be repeated. Otherwise, the object must be placed before the predicate verb or at the beginning of the sentence. See the examples below:

| | **Subject** | **Verb 得** | **Complement** | **Object** |
|---|---|---|---|---|
| Potential complement: | 他 | 学得 | 好 | 中文。 |

He is able to learn Chinese well. (The object 中文 follows 得 + adjective.)

| | **Subject** | **Verb + Object** | **Verb 得** | **Complement** |
|---|---|---|---|---|
| Complement of degree: | 他 | 学中文 | 学得 | 很好。 |

He studies Chinese well. (The verb 学 is repeated.)

| | **Subject** | **Object** | **Verb 得** | **Complement** |
|---|---|---|---|---|
| | 他 | 中文 | 学得 | 很好。 |

(The object 中文 is placed before the verb.)

| **Object** | **Subject** | **Verb 得** | **Complement** |
|---|---|---|---|
| 中文 | 他 | 学得 | 非常好。 |

(The object 中文 is placed before the subject.)

## Note

Another difference is that the potential complement cannot use adverbial modifiers such as 很, 非常, etc., while the complement of degree can.

CORRECT: 他学得好中文。

xxx INCORRECT: 他学得非常好中文。 xxx

---

## PRACTICE

Try using each of the above structures along with the suggested words below to create sentences of your own.

Suggested Verbs: 解释, 收拾, 写, 说, 煮.

Suggested Adjective: 清楚, 干净, 整齐, 流利, 熟.

### 2. Negative Sentence

The position of 不 changes in the negative form, depending on whether it is a potential complement or a complement of degree. In the potential complement, 得 is dropped and 不 is placed between the verb and the resultative complement. In the complement of degree, 不 is placed between 得 and the adjective. See the examples below.

|  | Subject | Verb 不 Complement |  | Object |
|---|---|---|---|---|
| Potential complement: | 他 | 学不好 |  | 中文。 |
|  | He cannot learn Chinese. |  |  |  |

|  | Subject | Verb + Object | Verb 得 | Complement |
|---|---|---|---|---|
| Complement of degree: | 他 | 学中文 | 学得 | 不好。 |
|  | He didn't learn Chinese very well. |  |  |  |

---

## PRACTICE

Try forming your own negative sentences, using each of the structures given above with the suggested words below.

Suggested Verbs: 解释, 收拾, 写, 说, 煮.

Suggested Adjective: 清楚, 干净, 整齐, 流利, 熟.

### 3. Question

Affirmative-negative questions are also different, depending on whether you are using a potential complement or a complement of degree. For the potential complement, the structure for affirmative-negative question is: "Positive Verb + 得 + Adjective + Negative Verb + 得 + Adjective," while the structure for the complement of degree is "Positive Adjective + Negative Adjective." For more detailed information, see the following examples.

|  | Subject | Verb得Adjective | Verb不Adjective | Object |
|---|---|---|---|---|
| Potential complement: | 他 | 学得好 | 学不好 | 中文？ |
|  | Can he learn Chinese or not? |  |  |  |

| | Subject | Object | Verb得 | Adjective不Adjective |
|---|---|---|---|---|
| Complement of degree: | 他 | 中文 | 学得 | 好不好？ |

How well did he learn Chinese?

## 🔖 PRACTICE

Try using each of the structures above with the suggested words below to form both affirmative and negative questions.

Suggested Verbs: 解释, 收拾, 写, 说, 煮.

Suggested Adjectives: 清楚, 干净, 整齐, 流利, 熟.

## III. The Complement of Extent

You have learned that the complement of degree uses an adjective to describe the degree of an action. For example:

| | Predicate | | Complement of Degree |
|---|---|---|---|
| **Subject** | **Verb** | **得** | **Adjective** |
| 他 | 写信写 | 得 | 很好。 |

In this lesson you will learn the complement of extent, which uses a verb phrase or a sentence to describe the extent of an action or a situation, and includes the following two structures:

### A. Predicate Verbs

This structure is similar to the structure of the complement of degree (see above) in that it has a predicate verb. However, the complement of extent uses a verb phrase or a clause, NOT an adjective, to indicate the extent of the action. See the examples below:

| | Predicate | | Complement |
|---|---|---|---|
| **Subject** | **Verb** | **得** | **Verb phrase/sentence** |
| 我 | 说 | 得 | 都不想再说了。 |

I talked so much that I don't want to talk anymore.

| | | | |
|---|---|---|---|
| 我 | 写信写 | 得 | 手都累了。 |

I've been writing letters so much that my hand is tired.

## 🔖 PRACTICE

Try creating a few sentences of your own using the "Verb + 得" structure with verbs such as 跑, 吃, 睡, and 羡慕.

## B. Predicate Adjectives

The predicate adjective in this structure is followed by "得 + Verb Phrase/Sentence." This structure uses a predicate adjective, NOT a predicate verb, to describe an extreme situation. For example:

| | Predicate | | Complement of Degree |
|---|---|---|---|
| **Subject** | **Adjective** | **得** | **Verb phrase/sentence** |
| 东西的价格 | 贵 | 得 | 吓人。 |

The price of that thing is so expensive it is scary.

| | | | |
|---|---|---|---|
| 我 | 忙 | 得 | 没时间睡觉。 |

I was so busy that I didn't even have time to sleep.

| | | | |
|---|---|---|---|
| 那间房子 | 乱 | 得 | 要命。 |

That room is so messy that I almost died!

---

 PRACTICE

Try using the structure above along with the suggested adjectives to create a few sentences of your own. Suggested adjectives: 高兴, 激动, 伤心, 香, 紧张, 重, 难, and 饿.

# Textbook Exercises

## TASK 1. 課文問答 (KÈWÉN WÈNDÁ) QUESTIONS AND ANSWERS

Check your comprehension of the text by answering the following questions.

1. 吴文德和李丽莉是怎么从小吃店到旅馆去的？

2. 吴文德和李丽莉以前在中国住过旅馆吗？你怎么知道？

3. 吴文德为什么不让李丽莉吃旅馆房间里的东西？

4. 吴文德准备明天带李丽莉去哪儿？为什么？

---

## TASK 2. 语法练习 (YǓFǍ LIÀNXÍ) GRAMMATICAL STRUCTURE PRACTICE

### A. Word Selection

Select the choice that best completes each sentence.

1. 出租车司机的行车执照号码，你都抄 _____ 了吗？

   a) 起来    b) 出来    c) 下去    d) 下来

2. 我想 _____ 了，我的钥匙留在家里的桌上了。

    a) 起来    b) 出来    c) 下去    d) 下来

3. 这个旅馆太贵，我不想再住 _____ 了。

    a) 起来    b) 出来    c) 下去    d) 下来

4. 我看得 _____ 你从来没住过旅馆。

    a) 起来    b) 出来    c) 下去    d) 下来

5. 我撑死了，实在吃不 _____ 了。

    a) 起来    b) 出来    c) 下去    d) 下来

6. 我尝不 _____ 这是什么地方风味的小菜。

    a) 起来    b) 出来    c) 下去    d) 下来

7. 你把这条路线记 _____ ，下一次就不会走丢了。

    a) 起来    b) 出来    c) 下去    d) 下来

8. 借记卡用 _____ 不但方便，而且很便宜。

    a) 起来    b) 出来    c) 下去    d) 下来

## B. Scrambled Sentences

Rearrange the words in each of the following groups to make complete sentences.

1. 不清楚    解释    得    老师    清楚    语法

2. 找不到    得    火车站    到    我们    找

3. 唱    难听    得    歌    极了    他

4. 出来    得    好主意    想    你    什么    能

5. 他聪明    他都懂    得    什么    老师说    要命

---

## 💻 TASK 3. 翻译 (FĀNYÌ) PARAPHRASING

Translate the following sentences into Chinese.

1. It looks like he wouldn't listen to us even if we explained that matter to him today. (Hint: Verb + 起来, Verb + 不下去)

2. I can't stay in that single room anymore. (Hint: Verb + 不下去) I want to check out, but the employee at the front desk does not understand what I'm talking about. (Hint: Verb + 不懂)

3. Did you think of someplace that is worth a visit? (Hint: Verb + 出来) If you cannot think of something soon, then we will stay in the hotel. (Hint: Verb + 不出来, Verb + 下去)

4. I wrote down that driver's license number, but now I can't find it. (Hint: Verb + 下来, Verb + 不到) I can't remember that driver's name either. (Hint: Verb + 不起来)

5. A: Can you remember the name and the address of the hotel where we are going to stay tomorrow? (Hint: Verb + 得 + 住)

   B: No, I can't remember, (Hint: Verb + 不 + 住) but I wrote it down. (Hint: Verb + 下来) The name of the hotel is too difficult to remember. (Hint: Verb + 得 + 要命)

---

## 💻 TASK 4. 情景对话 (QÍNGJǏNG DUÌHUÀ) SITUATIONAL DIALOGUE

**Setting:**    A hotel lobby
**Cast:**    A clerk and customer
**Situation:**    The customer is checking out of the hotel, and he/she needs to turn in the key at the front desk. Before the customer can leave, however, the clerk has to fill out some paperwork. Did the customer make any long distance phone calls? Has the bill been paid? Did the customer get his/her deposit back? Don't let the customer leave until everything has been taken care of!

# 35

## 锻炼身体
# Keep Fit!

---

***In this lesson you will:***

■ Talk about your favorite athlete.

■ Talk about sports you are interested in.

■ Talk about a sports meet/competition.

---

在中国，很多大学每年都要开一次运动会，学生想参加比赛，就可以报名参加，比赛成绩好的运动员，又可以代表自己的学校参加省里的大学生运动会。学校运动会一般要开两、三天，学校那几天也不上课了。不参加比赛的学生也都去为自己的朋友加油。大学生运动会很热闹。李丽莉自从到中国以后就很注意锻炼身体，这次学校的运动会，她也参加了比赛。

（在学校的操场）

吴文德：陈小云，今天李丽莉也要参加比赛。她自从来中国以后，就天天跑步锻炼身体。

陈小云：我知道，这次运动会，她参加了短跑和长跑比赛。吴文德，你参加比赛了没有？

吴文德：没有参加。我喜欢游泳，打篮球。但是大学生运动会没有这些项目。不过，我参加了太极拳表演。

陈小云：你是什么时候开始学打太极拳的？

吴文德：我是两个月以前开始学的。太极拳课有初级班也有中级班，我一个月修一门太极拳课。

陈小云：你真不简单，都修到中级班了。我以前也学过太极拳，学了几天就没有耐心了。你是跟谁学的？

吴文德：我是跟王老师学的。想不想让我给你表演一下？

陈小云：免了，免了。你是中级班的学生，一定打得很象一回事儿。

吴文德：你参加比赛了吗？

陈小云：我这个人跑不动，参加不了比赛。我今天是来给李丽莉加油的。我还想给她照几张照片。

吴文德：这么远，你能照得上吗？

陈小云：照得上。李丽莉能赢就好了。

吴文德：你放心。她输不了。你看运动会开始了。

陈小云：李丽莉跑在最前边。就要到终点了。加油！加油！李丽莉加油！

……

陈小云：李丽莉太棒了！得了个第一名，还打破了学校记录。

吴文德：运动会真带劲儿。你看观众比运动员还激动呢。所有的观众都站起来了，过了这么长时间还在鼓掌。陈小云，你给李丽莉照相了吗？

陈小云：没照上。刚才我一着急，就打不开镜头了。

广播员：现在太极拳表演就要开始了，请太极班的同学到操场东边集合，准备排队入场。

陈小云：吴文德，这回该你露一手了。快去吧。

吴文德：唉呦，你看多不凑巧，我刚要走，左脚就扭了。疼得我实在站不起来了。

陈小云：你怎么这么不小心，该参加表演了，脚突然又扭了。让我给你看看。

吴文德：你看我的右脚肿得多厉害。我走不了路了。不能去表演了。

陈小云：吴文德，你到底是哪个脚扭了？怎么自相矛盾[1]！一会儿是左脚疼，一会儿是右脚肿的？

吴文德：不瞒你说，我是有点儿怯场了。我虽然很喜欢打太极拳，但是总是学不会。学了前边忘后边，现在一紧张，就都忘了。

陈小云：你别太紧张了。你要是打太极拳打得不好，怎么能从初级班升到中级班呢？你应该有一些自信心。

吴文德：哎，我上的两个班都是初级班。

## Note

### 1. 自相矛盾 (zì xiāng máo dùn)

This is a four-character set phrase that comes from a 成语故事, and is used to describe self-contradiction. For the story behind this phrase, see Reading/Writing Task 2 in the Workbook.

*Students playing soccer.*

 生词表 (Shēngcí Biǎo)

## Vocabulary

| Character | Pinyin | Part of Speech | English Definition |
|-----------|--------|----------------|--------------------|
| 1. 运动会 | yùndònghuì | *n.* | sports meet |
| 我们这儿每年都开运动会。 | | | |
| 运动 | | *n.* | sports |
| | | *v.* | to exercise |
| 2. 比赛 | bǐsài | *n.* | competition |
| 今年你参加比赛吗？ | | | |
| | | *v.* | to compete |
| 今天你跟谁比赛？ | | | |
| 3. 报名 | bào míng | *v. obj.* | to register, to sign up |
| 你这次报名参加比赛了吗？ | | | |
| 报 | | *v.* | to report |

4. 成绩　　　　　chéngjì　　　　*n.*　　　　achievement, score, results
你今天的比赛成绩怎么样？

5. 运动员　　　　yùndòngyuán　　*n.*　　　　athlete
昨天来参加比赛的运动员多不多？

6. 省　　　　　　shěng　　　　　*n.*　　　　province
今天哪个省的运动员成绩最好？

7. 加油　　　　　jiā yóu　　　　*v. obj.*　　to cheer (someone) on; (lit.) to add oil
我们明天一定去给你加油。
　加　　　　　　　　　　　　　*v.*　　　　to add
　油　　　　　　　　　　　　　*n.*　　　　oil

8. 自从…就　　　zìcóng…jiù　　　*conj.*　　(ever) since
他自从学中文以后，就一直想去北京看看。

9. 操场　　　　　cāochǎng　　　　*n.*　　　　sports ground
你看这个操场大不大？

10. 跑步　　　　　pǎo bù　　　　　*v. obj.*　　to run, to jog
你每天都跑步吗？
　跑　　　　　　　　　　　　　*v.*　　　　to run
　步　　　　　　　　　　　　　*n.*　　　　step

11. 游泳　　　　　yóu yǒng　　　　*v. obj.*　　to swim
我每天都去游泳。

12. 打篮球　　　　dǎ lánqiú　　　　*v. obj.*　　to play basketball
你喜不喜欢打篮球？
　篮球　　　　　　　　　　　　*n.*　　　　basketball

13. 表演　　　　　biǎoyǎn　　　　*v.*　　　　to perform
你们再给我表演一次，怎么样？

　　　　　　　　　　　　　　　*n.*　　　　performance
今天你们的表演真不错。

14. 初级　　　　　chūjí　　　　　*n.*　　　　elementary level
我去年参加的是初级班。
　初　　　　　　　　　　　　　*b.f.*　　　elementary
　级　　　　　　　　　　　　　*n.*　　　　grade, level, rank

15. 中级　　　　　zhōngjí　　　*n.*　　　　intermediate level
今年我想参加中级班。

16. 门　　　　　　mén　　　　　*m.w.*　　　measure word for courses
这门课有意思吗?

17. 赢　　　　　　yíng　　　　　*v.*　　　　to win
今天的比赛谁赢了?

18. 输　　　　　　shū　　　　　　*v.*　　　　to lose
他们今天输了!

19. 得(第一)名　dé (dìyī) míng　*v. obj.*　　to earn (first) place
今天我得了第一名。
得　　　　　　　　　　　　　*v.*　　　　to earn, to obtain, to achieve

20. 打破记录　　dǎpò jìlù　　　*v. obj.*　　to break a record
今天我打破了世界纪录!
打破　　　　　　　　　　　　*v.*　　　　to break, to smash

21. 观众　　　　　guānzhòng　　*n.*　　　　spectator
今天去看比赛的观众多不多?

22. 所有　　　　　suǒyǒu　　　　*adj.*　　　all
所有的人都来了。

23. 鼓掌　　　　　gǔ zhǎng　　　*v. obj.*　　to applaud
大家都给他鼓掌。
鼓　　　　　　　　　　　　　*n.*　　　　drum
　　　　　　　　　　　　　　*v.*　　　　to beat
掌　　　　　　　　　　　　　*n.*　　　　palm

24. 照相　　　　　zhào xiàng　　*v. obj.*　　to take a photo
来,你给我们大家照一张相吧。

25. 镜头　　　　　jìngtóu　　　　*n.*　　　　lens
这个镜头不太好。

26. 广播员　　　　guǎngbōyuán　*n.*　　　　radio announcer
广播员说运动会现在开始。
广播　　　　　　　　　　　　*v.*　　　　to broadcast
　　　　　　　　　　　　　　*n.*　　　　a broadcast

27. 集合　　　　　jíhé　　　　　*v.*　　　　to assemble
我们应该去那边集合。

28. 入场 rù chǎng *v. obj.* to enter a stadium or a field of play
我们应该从哪儿入场？

29. 凑巧 còuqiǎo *adv.* by coincidence
你去看比赛，凑巧我也去。我们一起去吧。

30. 脚 jiǎo *n.* foot, ankle
我用脚走路。

31. 扭 niǔ *v.* to twist, sprain
啊呀，我的脚扭了。

32. 突然 tūrán *adv.* suddenly
他突然又不想去参加比赛了。

33. 怯场 qièchǎng *v. obj.* to have stage fright
他一定是怯场了。

34. 升 shēng *v.* to rise
我现在已经升到中级班了。

35. 自信心 zìxìnxīn *n.* self-confidence
他那个人很有自信心。
信心 *n.* confidence

36. 太极拳 tàijíquán traditional Chinese shadow boxing

## 补充词汇 (Bǔchōng Cíhuì) Supplementary Vocabulary

1. 体操 tǐcāo *n.* gymnastics

2. 体育馆 tǐyùguǎn *n.* gym

3. 助威 zhù wēi *v. obj.* to cheer someone on

4. 踢足球 tī zúqiú *v. obj.* to play soccer

5. 奥运会 Àoyùnhuì *prop. n.* the Olympic Games

6. 裁判员 cáipànyuán *n.* referee, umpire

7. 平了记录 píng le jìlù *v. obj.* to tie a record

8. 打网球 dǎ wǎngqiú *v. obj.* to play tennis

9. 爬山 pá shān *v. obj.* to climb a mountain

10. 美式足球 měishì zúqiú *n.* American football

## 口头用语 (Kǒutóu Yòngyǔ) Spoken Expressions

| | | |
|---|---|---|
| 1. 免了<br>免 | miǎn le | That's OK, you don't have to do it.<br>to spare, exempt |
| 2. 像一回事儿 | xiàng yīhuíshìr | to look like "something," to be quite good |
| 3. 带劲儿 | dài jìnr | energetic, energizing; (lit.) bringing energy |
| 4. 不瞒你说 | bù mán nǐ shuō | to tell you the truth |

## 词汇注解 (Cíhuì Zhùjiě) Featured Vocabulary

### 1. 回 (Huí)

回 can function as a verb and as a measure word. As a verb it means "to go back to," "to go home to," e.g., 回家 or 回学校. As a measure word, it functions as 次 but it is more colloquial. For example, in this lesson you learn 这回该你露一手了, where 这回 means "this time."

### 2. 自信心 (Zìxìnxīn)

有自信心 can be used as a noun meaning "self-confidence":

    我很有自信心。

对…有信心：有信心 can also be used with the preposition 对 to mean "to have confidence in someone or in doing something."

*Morning exercises in a Beijing school.*

*A ping-pong court on a college campus.*

Xueying Wang

# 语法(Yǔfǎ)
# Grammar

## I. The 是…的 Structures

In Lesson 25, we provided a brief introduction of the "是…的" structure, which carries the meaning of "It is…that…" The "是…的" structure can only be used for an action that takes place in the past. While 是 is placed before the word group that is emphasized (indicating time, place, manner, purpose, etc.), 的 appears at the end of the sentence. For example:

我是昨天晚上去跳舞的。        It was last night I went to dance.

我是昨天下午去图书馆的。      It was yesterday afternoon I went to library.

However, if the object is a noun, 的 may be put either before or after the object.

我是晚上八点去跳的舞。        It was eight o'clock that I went to dancing.

我是昨天下午去的图书馆。      It was yesterday afternoon that I went to the library.

If an object is a pronoun, 的 has to be placed at the end.

我是来看他的。                 It is him that I came to see.

xxx INCORRECT: 我是来看的他。  xxx

Sometimes in spoken language, 是 can be omitted if the sentence is short. For example:

你怎么来的？                   How did you come?

The negative form of the sentence is 不是…的.

我不是来看他的。               It was not him that I came to see.

| 我不是晚上去跳的舞。 | It was not at night that I went dancing. |
|---|---|

The affirmative-negative form of the sentence is 是不是…的.

| 你是不是来看我的？ | Is it me that you are coming to see? |
|---|---|
| 你是不是昨天下午去图书馆的？ | Was it yesterday afternoon that you went to the library? |

As you may know by now, the "是…的" structure is used to emphasize a certain element related to a past action. The sentence below contains various types of components. We will show you how to use the "是…的" structure to emphasize each of these components.

**Regular sentence**

| Subject | Time | Place | Manner | Manner | Purpose |
|---|---|---|---|---|---|
| 我 | 二〇〇四年 | 从美国 | 跟我的朋友 | 一起坐飞机 | 去中国学中文。 |

In 2004, I flew from America to China with a friend to study Chinese.

## A. With Emphasis on Time

| | | | Emphasis | |
|---|---|---|---|---|
| Subject | 是 | Time | Verb predicate | 的 |
| 你 | 是 | 哪年 | 去中国 | 的？ |

What year did you go to China?

| | | | | |
|---|---|---|---|---|
| 我 | 是 | 二〇〇四年 | 去中国 | 的。 |

It was 2004 that I went to China.

## *Note*

Since 中国 is a noun, 的 can be placed before 中国. For example: 我是二〇〇四年去的中国。

---

🔲 PRACTICE

With a partner, try using the "是…的" structure along with the suggested phrases below to ask about each other's backgrounds. For example: 问：你是什么时候（生）的？ Suggested phrases: 来美国, 开始学中文, 认识你的对象.

## B. With Emphasis on Place

| | | | Emphasis | |
|---|---|---|---|---|
| Subject | 是 | Place | Verb predicate | 的 |
| 你 | 是 | 从哪儿 | 去中国 | 的？ |

Where did you leave from (to get to China)?

| | | | | |
|---|---|---|---|---|
| 我 | 是 | 从美国 | 去中国 | 的。 |

I went from America to China.

*Statue of Huai Su, a famous calligrapher in the Tang dynasty.*

|  |  | **Emphasis** |  |  |  |
|---|---|---|---|---|---|
| **Subject** | **是** | **Place** | **Verb** | **Object** | **的** |
| 你 | 是 | 在哪儿 | 学 | 中文 | 的？ |

Where did you go to study?

| 我 | 是 | 在中国 | 学 | 中文 | 的。 |
|---|---|---|---|---|---|

It was China where I studied Chinese.

### *Note*

的 can also be placed before 中文. For example: 你是在哪儿学的中文？

## PRACTICE

With a partner, try using the "是···的" structure along with the suggested phrases below to ask each other a few questions concerning your backgrounds. For example: 问：你在哪儿（生）的？
Suggested phrases: 上大学, 学中文, 认识你朋友, 找到工作.

### C. With Emphasis on Manner (How the Action Was Carried Out)

|  |  | **Emphasis** |  |  |
|---|---|---|---|---|
| **Subject** | **是** | **Manner** | **Verb predicate** | **的** |
| 你 | 是 | 怎么 | 去中国 | 的？ |

How did you get to China?

| 我 | | 是 | 坐飞机 | 去中国 | 的。 |

I took an airplane to China.

| | | | **Emphasis** | | |
| **Subject** | | 是 | **Manner** | **Verb predicate** | 的 |
| 你 | | 是 | 跟谁 | 去中国 | 的？ |

With whom did you go to China?

| 我 | | 是 | 跟我的朋友 | 去中国 | 的。 |

I went to China with my friend (not alone).

## PRACTICE

With a partner, try using the "是…的" structure along with the suggested phrase below to ask a few questions concerning the way or manner in which something is done. For example:

How: 你是怎么(认识你朋友)的？

Suggested phrases: 买火车票, 订旅馆, 去那家饭馆, 听到这个消息.

In which manner: 你是不是(用中文写电邮)的？

Suggested words: 给, 跟, 从, 请.

## D. With Emphasis on Purpose

When the "是…的" structure is used to emphasize the purpose of coming/going/returning somewhere, the 是 is used in front of the directional verb 来, 去, or 回.

| | | | **Emphasis** | | |
| **Subject** | | 是 | **Verb** | **Purpose** | 的 |
| 你 | | 是 | 去中国 | 做什么 | 的？ |

It was for what purpose that you went to China?

| 我 | | 是 | 去 | 学习 | 的。 |

I went to study.

## PRACTICE

Try using the "是…的" structure along with the suggested phrases to ask a question and then provide an answer. Suggested phrases: 来办公室, 去银行, 去操场, 来图书馆, 回国.

## E. With Emphasis on Subject

When using the "是…的" structure to emphasize the subject, the object may sometimes be placed at the beginning of the sentence. For example:

| (Object) | 是 | Subject | Verb predicate + 的 | Object |
|---|---|---|---|---|
| | | | **Emphasis** | |
| | 是 | 谁 | 买的 | 飞机票？ |

Who bought the airplane ticket?

| | 是 | 我朋友 | 买的 | 飞机票。 |
|---|---|---|---|---|

It was my friend who bought the airplane ticket.

| 飞机票 | 是 | 我朋友 | 买的。 |
|---|---|---|---|

(The object 飞机票 is placed before the subject.)

---

## PRACTICE

Try using the "是···的" structure along with the phrases below to ask a question and then provide an answer. For example:

问1：是谁教你中文的？（回答问题，搞翻译，给你照相，打破记录···）

问2：这本书是谁写的？（这些菜，那个手机，短跑的记录，旅馆的房间···）

# II. Potential Verb Complement Cont'd.

In this lesson, you will learn a new kind of potential complement, which uses certain idiomatic verbs as its complement. Each of these idiomatic verbs functions as a fixed potential complement; it takes on its own specific meaning. See the examples below.

## A. 了 (Liǎo): Indicating the Ability to Do or Complete Something

The "Verb + 得/不 + 了" structure functions as a fixed phrase. Thus, 了 may be placed after either 得 or 不, but never after the verb.

### 1. Indicating the Ability to Do Something

| **Positive** | | | **Negative** | | |
|---|---|---|---|---|---|
| Verb | 得 | 了 | Verb | 不 | 了 |
| 去 | 得 | 了 | 去 | 不 | 了 |
| 来 | 得 | 了 | 来 | 不 | 了 |
| 走 | 得 | 了 | 走 | 不 | 了 |
| 忘 | 得 | 了 | 忘 | 不 | 了 |

Example: 我今晚去不了。I am not able to go tonight.

## 🔲 PRACTICE

Create a situation and then use the above structure to ask a question with verbs such as 来, 走, 做, 赢, 参加, 翻译, and 回答. When you are done, provide a negative response. For example:

问：今晚有一个电影晚会，你去得了去不了？

答：我有事儿，去不了。

### 2. *Indicating the Ability to Complete Something*

| Positive | | | Negative | | |
|---|---|---|---|---|---|
| **Verb** | 得 | 了 | **Verb** | 不 | 了 |
| 用 | 得 | 了 | 用 | 不 | 了 |
| 吃 | 得 | 了 | 吃 | 不 | 了 |
| 花 | 得 | 了 | 花 | 不 | 了 |

Example: 这么多钱，我花不了。 I can't spend that much money.

## 🔲 PRACTICE

Create your own situations and use the potential complement to ask questions with verbs such as 花, 吃, 喝, 看, and 干. When you're done, provide a negative response to each question. For example:

问：我给你两百块钱，你用得了吗？

答：用不了。一百块钱就够了。

## B. 动 (Dòng): Indicating the Ability to Make Someone or Something Move

The "Verb + 得/不 + 动" structure functions as the fixed phrase. Thus, 动 may be placed after the 得 or 不, but never after the verb.

| Positive | | | Negative | | |
|---|---|---|---|---|---|
| **Verb** | 得 | 动 | **Verb** | 不 | 动 |
| 拿 | 得 | 动 | 拿 | 不 | 动 |
| 搬 | 得 | 动 | 搬 | 不 | 动 |
| 骑 | 得 | 动 | 骑 | 不 | 动 |
| 走 | 得 | 动 | 走 | 不 | 动 |
| 跑 | 得 | 动 | 跑 | 不 | 动 |

Example: 我太累了，走不动了。 I am too tired to walk.

## ◉ PRACTICE

Create your own situations, and ask questions with verbs such as 走, 跑, 游泳, 跳舞, 拿, 开车, and 骑. When you're done, provide a response to each question. For example:

问：这张桌子，你一个人搬得动搬不动？

答：我搬得动。

## C. 起 (Qǐ): Indicating the Ability to Afford Something

The "Verb + 得/不 + 起" structure functions as a fixed phrase. Thus, 起 may be placed after either 得 or 不, but never after the verb.

| Positive | | | Negative | | |
|---|---|---|---|---|---|
| **Verb** | 得 | 起 | **Verb** | 不 | 起 |
| 买 | 得 | 起 | 买 | 不 | 起 |

(to not) be able to afford to buy (something)

| | | | | | |
|---|---|---|---|---|---|
| 吃 | 得 | 起 | 吃 | 不 | 起 |

(to not) be able to afford to eat (in that restaurant)

| | | | | | |
|---|---|---|---|---|---|
| 住 | 得 | 起 | 住 | 不 | 起 |

(to not) be able to afford living in (that place)

我们住不起这么贵的旅馆吧！

We can't afford to stay in such an expensive hotel!

### *Note*

看得起/看不起 is idiomatic, and therefore, different from the group above. 看得起 means "to respect someone" and 看不起 means "to look down upon someone."

## ◉ PRACTICE

Create sentences of your own using the "Verb + 得/不 + 起" structure with verb phrases such as 开车, 住公寓, 穿衣服, 听音乐会, 吃饭馆, 喝酒, and 用中文软件. For example: 这个东西很便宜，我买得起。

## D. 下 (Xià): Indicating the Capacity to Contain or Hold Something

| Positive | | | Negative | | |
|---|---|---|---|---|---|
| **Verb** | 得 | 下 | **Verb** | 不 | 下 |
| 站 | 得 | 下 | 站 | 不 | 下 |
| 住 | 得 | 下 | 住 | 不 | 下 |
| 停 | 得 | 下 | 停 | 不 | 下 |
| 挤 | 得 | 下 | 挤 | 不 | 下 |

Example: 这间屋子住得下十个人。There is enough space for ten people to live in this room.

## Note

The verb complement 下, when used to indicate capacity to contain, is not followed by the directional complement 去/来. When 下 is combined with the directional complement 去/来, the meaning changes.

## Compare

| Potential complement | | | Directional complement | | |
|---|---|---|---|---|---|
| Verb | 得/不 | 下 | Verb | 得/不 | 下去/来 |
| 写 | 得 | 下 | 写 | 得 | 下去 |
| enough space for writing | | | to be able to write | | |
| 放 | 不 | 下 | 放 | 不 | 下　去/来 |
| not enough space to put something | | | unable to put it down | | |

### Example:

1. 这张表格写得下写不下十个学生的名字？
   Can we write down ten names of students on this form?

2. 这个考试太难了。我实在写不下去了。
   This test is so difficult. I really cannot write anything any more.

## 🔲 PRACTICE

Try using the above structures to ask questions with verbs such as 站, 躺, 住, 停, 挤, 吃, 喝, and 放, and then provide responses. For example:

问：你的车坐得下几个人？　答：坐得下五个人。

问：坐得下坐不下六个人？　答：坐得下。

## E. 开 (Kāi): Indicating the Ability to Move an Object Away from Its Original Position

| Positive | | | Negative | | |
|---|---|---|---|---|---|
| Verb | 得 | 开 | Verb | 不 | 开 |
| 开 | 得 | 开 | 开 | 不 | 开 |
| 打 | 得 | 开 | 打 | 不 | 开 |
| 走 | 得 | 开 | 走 | 不 | 开 |

Example: 你打得开，打不开这个窗子？ Will you be able to open this window?

## *Note*

开 can also be used after the verb as a resultative complement. For example: 打开窗子.

---

## 🔲 PRACTICE

Try using this structure with the following verb phrases to create sentences of your own. Suggested verb phrases: 开开, 打开, 走开, 跑开, 拿开, 搬开.

## F. 上 (Shàng): Indicating the Ability to Fit Something into a Space

| Positive | | | Negative | | |
|---|---|---|---|---|---|
| **Verb** | **得** | **上** | **Verb** | **不** | **上** |
| 照 | 得 | 上 | 照 | 不 | 上 |
| 穿 | 得 | 上 | 穿 | 不 | 上 |

Example: 前边的教室楼，你照得上吗？ Can you fit that whole classroom building in the picture?

## *Note*

上 can also be used after the verb as a resultative complement meaning "on." For example: 穿上衣服。

---

## 🔲 PRACTICE

Try using this structure with the following verb phrases to create sentences of your own. Suggested verb phrases: 照上, 穿上, 贴上, 挂上.

## III. 自（从）…（以后），就… (Zì[cóng]…[Yǐhòu], Jiù…)

This prepositional structure indicates that an action or state began sometime in the past and has continued until now. It is equivalent to "ever since" in English. In this structure, 从 and 以后 are optional.

| First clause | Second clause |
|---|---|
| 她自从有了借记卡， | 她就没有用过现金。 |

Since she got her debit card, she has not used cash.

自从上次从西安回来以后，（她）就病了。
Since she got back from Xi'an last time, she has been sick.

---

## 🔲 PRACTICE

Try using the "自从…（以后），就…" structure to talk about a past experience that you have had.

Textbook Exercises

🎧💻 TASK 1. 课文问答 (KÈWÉN WÈNDÁ) QUESTIONS AND ANSWERS

Check your comprehension of the text by answering the following questions.

1. 李丽莉参加了什么比赛？比赛成绩怎么样？

2. 吴文德觉得李丽莉能不能赢？为什么？

3. 吴文德准备参加什么项目？他参加了没有？为什么？

4. 陈小云知道不知道吴文德是假装脚扭了？为什么？

💻 TASK 2. 语法练习 (YǓ FǍ LIÀNXÍ) GRAMMATICAL STRUCTURE PRACTICE

### A. Sentence Construction

Use the "是…的" structure to rewrite each of the following sentences to emphasize the conditions given below.

1. 小张的妈妈 1980 年在中国生了小张。

   Time:

   Place:

2. 王老师跟两个朋友一起坐火车从北京到西安去了。

   How:

   With whom:

   Place:

3. 我一个人去操场练太极拳了。

   Manner:

   Purpose:

4. 100 米短跑运动员打破了记录。

   Subject:

## B. Sentence Completion

Use a "Verb + 得 + Complement" or a "Verb + 不 + Complement" to complete the sentences.

1. 爸爸每个月给我的钱太多了，我根本就（花）＿＿＿＿＿＿＿＿那么多钱。

2. 虽然这些行李很重，但是我还是（拿）＿＿＿＿＿＿＿＿。

3. 办公室的工作太多太忙，我实在（走）＿＿＿＿＿＿＿。

4. 风这么大，天气这么热，我真的（骑）＿＿＿＿＿＿＿自行车了。

5. 这家旅馆的价格很便宜，我们（住）＿＿＿＿＿＿＿。

6. 明天运动会就开始了，但是我得准备考试。恐怕（去）＿＿＿＿＿＿＿了。

7. 这个壁柜非常小，你怎么（放）＿＿＿＿＿＿＿这么多东西啊？

8. 我已经吃了一大碗饭了，这些点心我真的（吃）＿＿＿＿＿＿＿了。

9. 这个教室（坐）＿＿＿＿＿＿＿一百个学生？ (affirmative-negative)

10. 你帮我们照个相吧，后边的运动场（照）＿＿＿＿＿＿＿？ (affirmative-negative)

## C. Scrambled Sentences

Rearrange the words in each of the following groups to make complete sentences.

1. When did she come to China?

是　　的　　来　　　中国　　去年　　她

2. Why is she here?

来　　表演　　我们　　　是　　她　　的　　看

3. Since when did he start to participate in taijiquan performance?

就　　常常　　打太极拳　　学会了　　太极拳　　参加　　表演　　他　　自从

4. Will he lose?

会　　赢　　输　　　一定　　他　　不了

5. Will he be able to come today?

我　　他　　不下　　得了　　真　　放　　来　　心　　吗

---

## 📓 TASK 3. 翻译 (FĀNYÌ) PARAPHRASING

Translate the following sentences into Chinese.

1. Today our school had a swimming contest. I rode my bike to the school. (Hint: 是 + Manner + 的) I didn't come to participate in the swimming contest, but to take pictures of my friend. (Hint: 是 + Purpose + 的) He first learned how to swim two years ago, when he started taking lessons from Professor

Wang. (Hint: 是 + Time + 的, 是 + from Whom + 的) At the beginning he couldn't swim forward, (Hint: 游不动) and now he's swimming like a professional. (Hint: 像一回事) He should be able to win first place today, but I am not sure if he will be able to break the school record. (Hint: Affirmative-Negative)

2. Ever since I caught a cold a few days ago, I have been worried about whether I'll be able to participate in today's basketball game. (Hint: 自从, Verb + 不了) But here I am today. I came to represent our school to participate in this basketball game. (Hint: 是 + Manner + 的) This year, our school has won more basketball games and has lost only a few. (Hint: Verb + 的 + Adjective) More and more spectators come to cheer us on. Look, the sports ground does not seem to have enough space for so many people to stand there. (Hint: 站不下) I wanted to take pictures of all the spectators, but I couldn't open my camera lens. (Hint: 打不开) Also I did not know how I could fit that many people into a single frame. (Hint: 照得上)

---

## 💻 TASK 4. 情景对话 (QÍNGJǏNG DUÌHUÀ) SITUATIONAL DIALOGUE

**Setting:**     In the dorm
**Cast:**        Two roommates
**Situation:**   Two roommates started talking about sports after dinner. Which sports do they play? What do they like and dislike? Is there a particular team they are rooting for? Construct a dialogue (at least twelve sentences) between the two. Make sure to use vocabulary and grammar structures learned in this lesson.

# 36

# 我生病了

# I Don't Feel Well...

> *In this lesson you will:*
> ■ Learn how to describe your illness.
> ■ Follow a doctor's instructions.
> ■ Recognize different forms used by Chinese doctors.

在中国看病跟在美国看病不太一样，中国的医生一般都在医院的门诊部给病人看病。病人看病不需要预约时间，早上到医院的挂号处挂号，拿一个号码。等轮到自己的号码的时候，病人才能看病。看完病，交钱取药也在医院的药房里。一天晚上李丽莉觉得全身发冷，身上没劲儿。她用从美国带来的体温表给自己量了一下儿体温，才知道自己发高烧了。第二天早上李丽莉还是病得很厉害，吴文德不得不把李丽莉带到医院去看病。

（李丽莉和吴文德来到了内科门诊的服务台。）

吴文德：我的朋友发高烧了，体温 104 度。请医生先给她看看吧。

护　士：你开什么玩笑，100 度水都开了。请你们先去挂号处挂号。

吴文德：我没开玩笑，她真的是 104 度。你看，这是我用的那个体温表。

护　士：噢，我把你说的华氏当成摄氏了。华氏的 104 度也就是摄氏的 40 度。你马上去挂号处给她挂急诊。

吴文德：挂号处在哪儿？

护　士：出了这个门诊大楼，往右一拐就有一座楼，一进门就是挂号处。

（在急诊室，医生正在给李丽莉看病。）

医　生：李丽莉，你在发高烧，你还觉得哪儿不舒服？

李丽莉：我头疼得厉害，嗓子疼，胸也疼，还咳嗽。

医生：你把嘴张开一下儿，让我先检查一下儿你的嗓子，嗓子有点红肿。我听一听你的肺和心脏，都很正常。可是你应该先到二楼 205 室去透视，再到 208 室把血验一验。

……

医生：李丽莉，你得了重感冒。先叫护士给你打一下儿针，再去药房取药。退烧的药一天吃三次，每次一片，饭后半小时吃。止咳糖浆早晚各一次，空腹吃，每次一勺。

李丽莉：我还以为我得了流感或非典了呢。感冒不传染。我可以回家了吗？

医生：可以，我给你开了五天的药，要是吃了药，打了针，高烧还不退，你就不能不住院治疗了。

吴文德：李丽莉，你在这儿等我一下儿，我先去药房把药取了，再送你回宿舍。

（第二天，李丽莉正躺着休息。她看见吴文德走进来就坐了起来。）

吴文德：李丽莉，怎么这么客气，不把我当作朋友了，赶快躺下。药吃了没有？

李丽莉：医生的话我可不敢不听。我不但把药吃完了，而且把今天的针也打了，现在觉得好多了。你帮我把医生开的假条交给老师了吗？

吴文德：我一忙就把这事儿忘了，实在对不起，我一会儿就把你的假条送到老师的办公室去。你的咳嗽好像好一些了。头还疼吗？

李丽莉：我的头已经不疼了。你别把我这一点儿小病当成大病，好不好？

吴文德：昨天我没把体温的事说清楚，闹了一个小笑话。中国用摄氏，不用华氏。我说你体温 104 度。把护士吓了一大跳。她以为你烧到摄氏 104 度了。

李丽莉：发烧发到摄氏 104 度，没有人不害怕。吃一堑，长一智。下次再生病咱们就能把体温的事说得清楚一点儿了。

吴文德：你可别乱说，生病可不是开玩笑的事。多亏那个医生挺棒的，对症下药[1]，一下子就把你的病治好了。不过，你要想早点儿恢复健康，你就非按时吃药不可。不吃药可不行。

李丽莉：听见了，吴医生。我也希望自己早点儿恢复健康。对了，我
　　　　还要麻烦你把陈小云的笔记还给她，你可别忘了。

吴文德：你放心吧。我现在就去。再见。

## *Note*

### 1. 对症下药  (duì zhèng xià yào)

This comes from a 成语故事. It means, "to prescribe medicine based on the diagnosis of the disease." It can also be applied figuratively to any situation where an appropriate solution is used to solve a particular problem. For the story behind this 成语, see Reading/Writing Task 3 in the Workbook.

*Xueying Wang*

*The outpatient center at Gao Xing Hospital, located in an economic development zone of Xi'an.*

 生词表 (Shēngcí Biǎo)
## Vocabulary

| Character | Pinyin | Part of Speech | English Definition |
|---|---|---|---|
| 1. 门诊部 | ménzhěnbù | *n. phr.* | outpatient center |
| 我们门诊部每天都开门。 | | | |
| 门诊 | | *phr.* | treatment of patients |
| 部 | | *n.* | unit, department, ministry |
| 2. 挂号处 | guàhàochù | *n. phr.* | hospital registration office |
| 你应该先到挂号处挂一个号。 | | | |

挂号      *v. obj.*      to register, to sign in
处      *n.*      place, office

3. 药房      yàofáng      *n.*      drugstore, pharmacy
我们去药房取药吧。

4. 全      quán      *adj.*      entire
我全身都疼。

     *adv.*      the whole, entirely
我们全走了。

5. 体温表      tǐwēnbiǎo      *n.*      clinical thermometer
你有没有体温表？
体温      *n.*      body temperature

6. 内科      nèikē      *n.*      internal medicine
你应该去看内科。

7. 急诊      jízhěn      *n.*      emergency treatment
你发高烧了，应该马上去看急诊。

8. 嗓子      sǎngzi      *n.*      throat
你嗓子还疼吗？

9. 胸      xiōng      *n.*      chest
我这几天胸有一点儿疼。

10. 咳嗽      késòu      *v. obj*      to cough
你晚上咳嗽不咳嗽？

11. 张开      zhāngkāi      *v. comp.*      to open up
请你张开嘴让我看看。

12. 红肿      hóngzhǒng      *adj.*      red and swollen
医生说你嗓子红肿，我怎么看你的嗓子不红也不肿？

13. 肺      fèi      *n.*      lungs
你去检查肺了没有？

14. 透视      tòushì      *v.*      to have an X Ray
医生让你马上去透视。

15. 验血      yàn xiě      *v. obj.*      to do a blood test
你去验一下儿血吧。
验      *v.*      to examine, to check
血      *n.*      blood

16. 打针    dǎ zhēn    *v. obj.*    to give or receive an injection

你每天来打两针，上午一针，下午一针。

17. 退烧    tuì shāo    *v. obj.*    to alleviate a fever

你吃一点儿退烧药吧。

18. 片    piàn    *m.w.*    piece, tablet

这种药每天早上吃一片。

19. 各    gè    *adj.*    each, every

各人做各人的事。

   *adv.*    each, every

那种药每天早晚各吃两片。

20. 腹    fù    *b.f.*    stomach

这种药你应该吃饭前空腹吃。

21. 勺    sháo    *m.w.*    spoonful

这种药你每天睡觉前吃一勺。

   *n.*    spoon

他买勺(子)去了。

22. 流感    liúgǎn    *n.*    flu

现在得流感的人很多。

23. 传染    chuánrǎn    *v.*    to be contagious

这种病传染得很快。

24. 住院    zhù yuàn    *v. obj.*    to be hospitalized

你的病不重，不用住院。

25. 躺    tǎng    *v.*    to lie down

你在家躺两天，病就好了。

26. 假条    jiàtiáo    *n.*    a written excuse for being absent

请您给我写一张假条好吗？

27. 好像    hǎoxiàng    *adv.*    it seems that...

他好像没有病。

28. 多亏    duōkuī    *adv.*    thanks to (someone/something for...)

多亏我去看了急诊。

29. 恢复    huīfù    *v.*    to recover, rehabilitate

我现在已经恢复健康了。

| 30. 非···不可 | fēi...bùkě | *conj.* | must; it is not permissible unless |
|---|---|---|---|

我看你今天非去医院看急诊不可。

| 31. 按时 | ànshí | *adv.* | on time |
|---|---|---|---|

你一定要按时吃药。

| 32. 止咳糖浆 | zhǐké tángjiāng | *n.* | cough syrup |
|---|---|---|---|

## 专有名词 (Zhuānyǒu Míngcí) Proper Nouns

| 1. 华氏 | Huáshì | | Fahrenheit |
|---|---|---|---|
| 2. 非典 | Fēidiǎn | | SARS |

## 补充词汇 (Bǔchōng Cíhuì) Supplementary Vocabulary

| 1. 候诊室 | hòuzhěnshì | *n.* | hospital waiting room |
|---|---|---|---|
| 2. 耳鼻喉科 | ěrbíhóukē | *n.* | Otolaryngology Department |
| 3. 放射科 | fàngshèkē | *n.* | Radiology Department |
| 4. 外科 | wàikē | *n.* | Surgery Department |
| 5. 妇科 | fùkē | *n.* | Gynecology Department |
| 6. 小儿科 | xiǎoérkē | *n.* | Pediatrics Department |
| 7. 喉咙 | hóulóng | *n.* | throat |
| 8. 拉肚子 | lā dùzi | *v. obj.* | to have diarrhea |
| 9. 发炎 | fā yán | *v. obj.* | to become inflamed |
| 10. 开刀 | kāi dāo | *v. obj.* | (of a patient) to be operated on (of a doctor) to operate |

## 口头用语 (Kǒutóu Yòngyǔ) Spoken Expressions

| 1. 这就 | zhè jiù | Literally, "as early as this very moment"; right away, right now. For example: 我这就去给她挂号. I will go and register for her right now. |
|---|---|---|
| 2. 吓一跳 | xià yí tiào | Literally, "to jump from fright" or "to make someone jump from fright." It is usually used to describe a big scare. |
| 3. 乱说 | luàn shuō | to speak irresponsibly, to talk nonsense |

4. 挺棒　　　　tǐng bàng　　　pretty good

5. 一下子　　　yīxiàzi　　　a short duration or a single occurrence

# 词汇注解 (Cíhuì Zhùjiě) Featured Vocabulary

## 1. 开 (Kāi)

| 开 | v. | to boil |
|---|---|---|

　水开了。　The water is already boiling.

| 开水 | n. | boiling or boiled water |
|---|---|---|
| 开花 | v. obj. | to bloom (flowers) |
| 开药方 | v. obj. | to write a prescription |
| 开电视 | v. obj. | to turn on the TV |
| 张开 | v. comp. | to open up (eyes, mouth, etc.) |
| 打开 | v. comp. | to turn on (computer, lights); to open up (door, window) |

## 2. 全 (Quán)

| 全 | *adj.* | entire, all, complete, total |
|---|---|---|
| 全 + Noun | | 全国 entire country, 全身 entire body |
| 全 + Measure Word | | 全家人 entire family, 全班学生 entire class |

| 全 | *adv.* | entirely completely, totally |
|---|---|---|
| 全 + Verb | | 全吃完 to eat the entire thing |
| 全 + Adjective | | 全红了 (to turn) completely red |

## 3. 各 (Gè)

各 means "each and every."

| 各 + Noun | 各国 every country, 各人 everyone |
|---|---|
| 各 + Measure Word | 各个学生 every student, 各种药 every kind of medicine |
| 各 + Verb | 各吃一片 one pill each |

## 4. 一下子 (Yīxiàzi) vs. 一下儿 (Yīxiàr)

| 一下子 | *adv. phr.* (usually placed before the verb) |
|---|---|
| 医生一下子就把他的病治好了。 | The doctor immediately cured his disease. |

| 一下儿 | **time complement (usually placed after the verb)** |
|---|---|
| 我先检查一下儿你的嗓子。 | I will quickly check your throat first. |

## 5. 多亏 (Duōkuī), 幸亏 (Xìngkuī) and 吃亏 (Chī kuī)

| 多亏 | *v.* | thanks to so-and-so |
|---|---|---|
| 多亏你，我们才做完了。 | | Thanks to you, we finished our work. |
| 多亏 | *adv.* | luckily |
| 多亏他来了。 | | Luckily, he came. |
| 幸亏 | *adv.* | luckily (It is exchangeable with the adverb 多亏.) |
| 幸亏他来了。 | | Luckily, he came. |
| 吃亏 | *v. obj.* | to get less than he/she should, to be cheated or put at a disadvantage |
| 今天我吃大亏了。 | | I suffered a big loss today. |

# 语法(Yǔfǎ)
# Grammar

## I. The 把 (Bǎ) Construction

In Lesson 31 in this volume, we briefly introduced the 把 construction. In this lesson, we provide more details. The primary difference between the regular sentence and the 把 sentence is that the regular "Subject + Verb + Object" sentence focuses on the action and the 把 sentence focuses on what has happened to the object or how the object is dealt with or handled by the subject. For example:

| Regular Sentence | 把 Sentence |
|---|---|
| Subject + Verb + Object | Subject + 把 + Object + Verb + Other element |
| 他吃了一些甜点。 | 他把甜点吃完了。 |
| He ate some dessert. | He finished eating the dessert. |
| (This sentence focuses on the action 吃.) | (This sentence focuses on what happened to the 甜点.) |

## A. Overview of the 把 Construction

The positive, negative, imperative, and question forms of the 把 construction are presented below.

**Type of Sentence**

| | Subject | 把 | Object | | Verb | Other element |
|---|---|---|---|---|---|---|
| Positive: | 我 | 把 | 甜点 | 都 | 吃 | 完了。 |
| | I finished eating all the dessert. | | | | | |
| Negative: | 我 | 没把 | 甜点 | 都 | 吃 | 完。 |
| | I didn't finish eating all the dessert. | | | | | |

Imperative:　　　　你　　　　别把　　　　甜点　　　都吃完了。
Don't finish all the dessert.

Question:　　　　　你　　　　把　　　　甜点　　　都吃完了没有/吗？
Have you finished eating all the dessert?

## Notes

1. The negative word 没 is usually placed before 把 to form a negative sentence. However, if the sentence also contains an auxiliary verb, 不 + auxiliary verb is placed before 把 to form a negative sentence. In positive as well as negative sentences, the auxiliary verb is always placed before 把.

   我不想把甜点都吃了 I don't want to eat all the dessert.

2. The adverb 都 is usually placed before the action verb. Other adverbs frequently used with the 把 structure include 也, 总, and 常, and they are always placed before 把.

   我把甜点都吃完了。你也把甜点都吃完了。

## B. Requirements for Forming a 把 Construction

Any sentence using the 把 construction must conform to the following requirements:

### 1. Objects in the 把 Construction

The object must be a DEFINITE OBJECT (a specific thing or person). For example:

   CORRECT: 我把菜吃完了。

   xxx INCORRECT: 我把一个菜吃完了。 xxx

### 2. Verbs in the 把 Construction

a) Only transitive action verbs may be used in the 把 construction.

b) The verb predicate must contain ONE EXTRA ELEMENT such as a complement, 了, etc. You cannot use 把 if the predicate is only a simple verb.

   xxx INCORRECT: 我把菜吃。 xxx

*Practicing taijiquan to keep healthy.*

### 3. Verbs that Cannot Be Used in the 把 Construction

| | |
|---|---|
| a) Verbs of existence: | 有, 在, 是 |
| b) Verbs of sense or emotion: | 喜欢, 觉得, 知道 |
| c) Motion Verbs: | 來, 去, 回, 离开 |
| d) Certain verbs with resultative complement: | 看见, 听到 |
| e) Verbs with potential complement: | Verb + 得/不 + Complement |

## C. Elements Commonly Used after the Verb in the 把 Construction

You have already learned that the main verb in the 把 construction must be followed by at least one additional element. The following are the elements that can be used in the 把 construction.

### 1. Perfective 了

了 here indicates completion of an action.

| Subject | 把 | Object | Perfective<br>Verb | 了 |
|---|---|---|---|---|
| 我 | 把 | 他的电话号码 | 忘 | 了。 |

I forgot his telephone number.

### 🎴 PRACTICE

Use the 把 construction with the perfective 了 and create sentences of your own that contain the following verb-object phrases: 丢钱, 喝饮料, 忘地址, 还书, and 吃药.

### 2. Resultative Complement

| Subject | 把 | Object | Resultative<br>Verb | Complement |
|---|---|---|---|---|
| 请你 | 把 | 窗户 | 开 | 开。 |
| 请你 | 把 | 钱 | 准备 | 好。 |

Please open the window.

Please get your money ready.

### 🎴 PRACTICE

Use the 把 construction with the resultative complement and create sentences of your own that contain the following verb-object phrases: 开电视, 关窗户, 做作业, 记生词, 穿大衣, 治病, and 修车.

### 3. *Directional Complement*

| Subject | 把 | Object | Directional Verb | Complement |
|---|---|---|---|---|
| 我 | 得先把 | 我东西 | 放 | 下来。 |

I have to put my stuff down first.

---

### ⊞ PRACTICE

Use the 把 construction with the directional complement and create sentences of your own that contain the following verb-object phrases: 寄信, 存钱, 停車, 搬东西, 挂照片, and 带朋友.

### 4. *Complement of Degree*

| Subject | 把 | Object | Degree Verb | Complement |
|---|---|---|---|---|
| 请你 | 把 | 字 | 写 | 得整齐一点儿。 |

Please write the characters more neatly.

---

### ⊞ PRACTICE

Use the 把 construction with the complement of degree and create sentences of your own that contain the following verb-object phrases: 收拾房间, 洗衣服, 讲语法, and 填申请表.

### 5. *Measure Complement*

| Subject | 把 | Object | Measure Verb | Complement |
|---|---|---|---|---|
| 请你 | 把 | 这件衬衫 | 洗 | 一下儿。 |

Please wash this shirt.

| 我 | 把 | 我的练习 | 检查 | 了两遍。 |
|---|---|---|---|---|

I checked my exercises twice.

| 学生 | 把 | 课文 | 念 | 了几遍。 |
|---|---|---|---|---|

Students read the lesson several times.

---

### ⊞ PRACTICE

Use the 把 construction with the measure complement and create sentences of your own that contain the following verb-object phrases: 写名字, 查生词, 量血压, and 秤体重.

### 6. Reduplication of the Verb

In a request or command that involves a monosyllabic verb, reduplicating the verb softens the tone of the command.

| Subject | 把 | Object | Verb | Reduplicated Verb |
|---------|----|--------|------|-------------------|
| 你 | 把 | 这件衬衫 | 洗 | （一）洗。 |
| Wash this shirt. | | | | |
| 他 | 把 | 那个地图 | 看 | （了）看。 |
| He looked at the map. | | | | |

### ✺ PRACTICE

Use the 把 construction with verb reduplication and create sentences of your own that contain the following verb-object phrases: 讲故事, 洗手, 量体温, and 听录音.

### 7. Indirect Object

| Subject | 把 | Direct Object | Verb | Indirect Object |
|---------|----|---------------|------|-----------------|
| 我 | 把 | 这件事 | 告诉 | 他了。 |
| I told him about that matter. | | | | |

### ✺ PRACTICE

Use the 把 construction with the indirect object and create sentences of your own that contain the following verbs: 告诉, 还, 借, 送, and 给.

*The pharmacy window at Xi Jing Hospital in Xi'an.*

### 8. Continuous Aspect 着 (Zhe)

This pattern is limited to some verbs and some idiomatic phrases.

|  |  |  |  | Continuous aspect |
| --- | --- | --- | --- | --- |
| **Subject** | 把 | **Object** | **Verb** | **着** |
| 你 | 把 | 这些钱 | 拿 | 着。 |

Please hold on to the money.

## 🔲 PRACTICE

Use the 把 construction with 着 and create sentences of your own that contain the verbs 拿, 带, and 留.

## D. Situations Where the 把 Construction Is Usually Required in a Sentence

The following situations usually require the use of the 把 construction:

1) When the verb is followed by a locative complement "在/到 + Place."

2) When the verb is followed by a complement describing the transformation of the object, such as "Verb + 成" or "Verb + 作."

3) When the verb is followed by "给 + Indirect Object."

### 1. 把⋯Verb 在/到 + Place

In this structure, 在 means "in," "on," or "at" and 到 means "to (a place)."

|  |  |  |  | Locative complement |
| --- | --- | --- | --- | --- |
| **Subject** | 把 | **Object** | **Verb** | 在/到 + Place |
| 他 | 把 | 笔 | 放 | 在 桌子上了。 |

He put the pen on the table.

|  |  |  |  |  |
| --- | --- | --- | --- | --- |
| 我们 | 把 | 孩子们 | 送 | 到 公共汽车站去了。 |

We sent the children to the bus station.

## 🔲 PRACTICE

Try using the 把 construction with each of the verb phrases 停在, 放在, 写在, 记在, 搬到, 送到, and 开到 to create sentences of your own.

### 2. 把⋯Verb 作 (Zuò) / 成 (Chéng) + Noun

In this structure, 作 means "as" and 成 means "into."

|  |  |  |  | Resultative complement |
| --- | --- | --- | --- | --- |
| **Subject** | 把 | **Object** | **Verb** | 成/作 + Noun |
| 陈小云的妈妈 | 把 | 李丽莉 | 当 | 作 自己的女儿。 |

Chen Xiaoyun's mother treats Li Lili as her own daughter.

请你们　　　　把　这个句子　翻译　成　　英文。

Please translate this sentence into English.

## Note

Sometimes "把… Verb 成 + Noun" can mean "by mistake" or "mistakenly," e.g., 我把他当成吴文德了, I thought he was Wu Wende by mistake. (I mistakenly thought he was Wu Wende.)

---

## 🔅 PRACTICE

Try using the 把 construction with each of the verb phrases 看成, 听成, 念成, 写成, 当成, 想成, 翻译成, 看作, 当作, and 选作 to create sentences of your own.

### 3. 把... *Verb* 给 *(Gěi) + Noun*

In this structure, 给 means "to (a person)."

|  |  |  |  | Indirect object |
|---|---|---|---|---|
| **Subject** | 把 | **Object** | **Verb** | 给 + Noun |
| 他 | 把 | 书 | 送 | 给他的老师了。 |

He gave his book to his teacher.

| 我 | 把 | 一百块钱 | 借 | 给朋友了。 |
|---|---|---|---|---|

I lent 100 kuai to a friend.

---

## 🔅 PRACTICE

Try using the 把 construction with each of the verb phrases 送给, 交给, 带给, 拿给, 寄给, and 介绍给 to create sentences of your own.

## II. Double Negative for Emphasis

When two negative words are used in a sentence, it emphasizes a strong positive meaning. It is usually used to intensify the speaker's point. In this lesson, you will learn the following four structures:

### A. Using 不 + Auxiliary Verb + 不 (Bù... Bù)

The "不 + Auxiliary Verb + 不" structure is a double negative that functions as an adverbial adjunct. In this structure, the double negative words are placed after the subject.

| 不 | **Auxiliary verb** | 不 |  |
|---|---|---|---|
| 不 | 得 | 不 | 我不得不送李丽莉去医院。 |
|  |  |  | I have no choice but to send her to a hospital. |
| 不 | 能 | 不 | 我们不能不给他帮忙。 |
|  |  |  | We have no choice but to help him. |

| | | | |
|---|---|---|---|
| 不 | 敢 | 不 | 你的话，我不敢不听。 |
| | | | I do not dare not listen to you. |
| 不 | 该 | 不 | 你不该不去上课。 |
| | | | You should have gone to class. |
| 不 | 会 | 不 | 他不会不做作业。 |
| | | | It is impossible that he would not do the homework. |

## 🔲 PRACTICE

Try to come up with a situation where you can use the double negative structure. For example:

我得重感冒了，（所以不得不吃药，打针。）

明天有一个大考试，（今天我不敢不准备。）

## B. Using 没有…不… (Méi Yǒu...Bù...)

This is another double negative whereby "没有…不…" emphasizes that everyone is included. 没有 should be placed at the beginning of the sentence. See the examples below:

没有人不害怕。　　　　　Everyone is afraid.

没有人不喜欢吃中国饭。　Everyone likes to eat Chinese food.

## 🔲 PRACTICE

Try to come up with a situation where you can use the double negative structure "没有…不…." For example: 这个老师很厉害，（没有学生不怕他。）

## C. Using 非…不可… (Fēi...Bùkě...)

This adverbial structure indicates necessity or inevitability and is used together with a predicate verb. In this case, 不可 is placed at the end of the sentence to emphasize 非, which must be placed before the predicate verb.

要想早点儿恢复健康，你非按时吃药不可。

If you want to recover early, you must take your medicine on time.

你要想找工作，非得有你老师的推荐信不可。

If you want to find a job, you must have your teacher's letter of recommendation.

## 🔲 PRACTICE

Try to come up with a situation where you can use the double negative structure "非…不可."

## D. Using 不…不行 (Bù...Bùxíng)

The "不…不行" construction is used to indicate a necessity and means "to have to (do something)" or "must (do something)." Its usage is similar to that of "非…不可," but it is more colloquial.

你不吃药不行。                        You cannot *not* take the medicine. You must take it.

你的行李太大，不托运不行。        Your luggage is too big. You have to check it.

---

## 🔲 PRACTICE

Try to come up with a situation where you can use the double negative structure "不…不行."

# Textbook Exercises

---

## 🎧💻 TASK 1. 课文问答 (KÈWÉN WÈNDÁ) QUESTIONS AND ANSWERS

Check your comprehension of the text by answering the following questions.

1. 吴文德跟护士说李丽莉发高烧了，护士为什么说吴文德是在开玩笑？

2. 李丽莉怎么了？她哪儿不舒服？

3. 医生让李丽莉做了什么检查？

4. 李丽莉得了什么病？李丽莉要做什么治疗？要不要住院？

---

## 💻 TASK 2. 语法练习 (YǓ FǍ LIÀNXÍ) GRAMMATICAL STRUCTURE PRACTICE

### A. Sentence Completion

Use the 把 structure to complete the following sentences.

1. 楼上的房间里没有椅子，请你(搬) _____。

2. 墙上没有画，你能不能(挂) _____。

3. 这个病房太冷了，窗户还开着呢。请你(关) _____。

4. 这本小说是法文的，我看不懂，真希望有人能(翻译) _____。

5. 我没有听过那位文学家的故事，你可不可以(讲) _____？

6. 我朋友要乘火车去北京，我今天下午得(送) _____。

7. 我已经(交) _____ 老师了。你呢？

8.老师说我的作业写得太乱了。我不得不(再写) _____ 。

9.吴文德发烧了，请你(送退烧药) _____ 。

10.你得的是流感。你(带这些药) _____ ，在家每天按时吃。

## B. Use the 把 construction to rewrite the following sentences.

1. 他们叫我李先生。

2. 我给朋友尝了尝我做的点心。

3. 他说我是他最好的朋友。

4. 我的书在家里，我忘了带来。

5. 我用这块真丝做了一件衬衫。

6. 同学们选他当学生代表。

## C. Pick and Choose

In each of the following pairs there is a correct sentence and an incorrect one. Can you tell which one is correct and explain why the other one is incorrect?

1.

a) 请把一个病人带到急诊室来。

b) 别忘了把那个病人带去验血。

2.

a) 他生病了，医生叫他先去把血验一下儿。

b) 你发烧了，应该马上把药吃。

3.

a) 我把假条看不清楚，字太小了。

b) 请把假条的字写大一点，我看不清楚。

4.

a) 李丽莉告诉了我以后，我才把吴文德生病的事知道了。

b) 吴文德问了很多人才知道了李丽莉生病的事。

5.

a) 我把他生病的事儿听见了。

b) 我把这件事儿听清楚了。

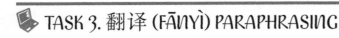

## TASK 3. 翻译 (FĀNYÌ) PARAPHRASING

Translate the following sentences into Chinese.

1. My roommate has a high fever. I have to take him to the emergency room, (Hint: 把 + Verb + Directional Complement) and then I'm going to the pharmacy to get medicine for him. (Hint: 把 + Verb + 了) Only after (I'm done with) that can I take you home. (Hint: 把 + Verb + Directional Complement)

2. I took my medicine this morning! (Hint: 把 + Verb + 了) Please don't treat this small illness as a big deal. (Hint: 把 + Verb 成) I will go back to the hospital for a follow-up after I finish taking the medicine the doctor gave me. (Hint: 把 + Verb + Resultative Complement)

3. I put the thermometer on the table. Can you help me take the patient's temperature? (Hint: 把 + Verb + 在, 把 + Verb + 一下儿)

4. A: Did you give my doctor's excuse to the teacher? (Hint: 把 with Direct Object and Indirect Object)
   B: I did. I also brought you my notes and your homework assignments. (Hint: 把 with Directional Complement)

5. You have a bad cough. You cannot avoid taking medicine. (Hint: 不能不) You shouldn't avoid having an injection, either. (Hint: 不该不) Otherwise, the doctor will have to hospitalize you. (Hint: 非···不可)

## TASK 4. 情景对话 (QÍNGJǏNG DUÌHUÀ) SITUATIONAL DIALOGUE

**Setting:**     A Chinese hospital
**Cast:**        A patient a visitor, and a nurse
**Situation:**   The friend of a hospitalized student comes for a visit while a nurse is also in the room. Construct a dialogue between the patient, the visitor, and the nurse. The visitor asks about (1) the patient's illness/condition, (2) the diagnosis and proposed treatments, and (3) directions that the patient should follow when taking medication.

# 37
# 过春节
# Happy Chinese New Year!

*In this lesson you will:*
- Learn the vocabulary for the Spring Festival.
- Discuss Chinese Spring Festival traditions.
- Compare and contrast the Western and Chinese New Year traditions.

中国什么节日都没有春节热闹。你如果有机会一定要去中国过一次春节、去听一听鞭炮的声音、看一看红灯笼、尝一尝饺子。我不说你也知道，过年的这种节日气氛，你一定要在中国才能知道什么是真正的过年。李丽莉和吴文德就很有福气。今年在中国过了一个春节，还学到了很多中国人过春节的风俗习惯。下面就看看李丽莉和吴文德在中国过第一个春节的小故事。

（李丽莉听到敲门声，把门打开一看，原来是吴文德。）

李丽莉：吴文德，哪阵风把你给吹来了[1]？

吴文德：春风啊。春节快到了，我从小到大还没有在一年之内庆祝过两个新年呢，真过瘾！

李丽莉：元旦那个新年可比春节差远了。春节对中国人来说，是个最大的节日。你没看见老师、学生都回家过年去了。

吴文德：怎么没看见，学校都空了。我昨天到街上去了一下儿，到处都很拥挤。大人、孩子好像谁都在忙。

李丽莉：很多人家在春节之前的好几个星期，就开始买年货、做吃的。家家户户的房子都打扫得干干净净，收拾得整整齐齐。我也跟着大家凑热闹。你看，我的灯笼都挂好了，春联也贴在门上了。对了，星期五是除夕，陈小云请我们去她家吃年夜饭。

吴文德：除夕是什么意思？什么是"年夜饭"？

李丽莉：春节前一天的晚上叫除夕。除夕的晚饭，就叫作"年夜饭"。那天晚上，全家人一起吃完年夜饭之后，很多人家都是一边包饺子，一边看春节联欢晚会。

吴文德：我这个人对玩儿非常感兴趣。我听说除夕之夜，很多人家都不睡觉。大家一边聊天，一边吃东西，一直要闹到天亮，是真的吗？

李丽莉：当然是真的啦。那叫守岁。

吴文德：原来守岁就是除夕晚上不睡觉啊。咱们买点儿鞭炮带到陈小云家去吧。

李丽莉：陈小云家那儿不一定让放鞭炮。我们给陈小云的弟弟一个红包吧。

吴文德：什么是"红包"？

李丽莉："红包"就是用红纸把钱包好，在孩子们给大人拜年的时候，作为礼物送给孩子。

吴文德：李丽莉，佩服，佩服。你现在懂的真多，快成一个中国通了。

（春节那天上午，李丽莉和吴文德从陈小云家出来。）

李丽莉：拜年，我以前在书上看到的意思是，春节的那天大家互相串门，互相说一些祝福的话，像"过年好"，"新年快乐"。可是给陈小云家打电话拜年的人比到她家来的人要多得多。

吴文德：你注意没注意到还有很多人用手机发短信来拜年。我要是有一个手机，我们也能用手机发短信给王老师拜年了。我们现在去王老师家拜年吧。

李丽莉：我们今天什么时候去王老师家拜年都可以，我想先回去换件红衣服。

吴文德：为什么？你的衣服哪件都好看，换不换都一样。

李丽莉：红色是中国人过节最喜欢的颜色。春节的时候，春联、灯笼、什么都是红色的。我想换件红衣服，给节日增加一点儿气氛。

吴文德：说到气氛，我突然想起来我今天下午还得去舞龙呢。这算是滥竽充数[2]吧！

李丽莉：你下午不会脚又疼了，走不动路了吧？

吴文德：你怎么总是哪壶不开提哪壶[3]呢？

## Notes

1. **哪阵风把你给吹来了？**    (Nǎ zhèn fēng bǎ nǐ gěi chuī lái le?)
   Literally, "Which gust of wind blew you here?" What brought you here?

2. **滥竽充数**   (làn yú chōng shù)
   This comes from a 成语故事 describing a person who does not play the flute but tries to pass himself off as a player in an ensemble. Nowadays, it is used to describe someone who is part of a group but does not have the qualifications. For more information, see Reading/Writing Task 3 in the Workbook.

3. **哪壶不开提哪壶。**    (Nǎ hú bù kāi tí nǎ hú.)
   Literally, "To pick up the one water pot in which the water is not boiling." The expression suggests picking on someone's weakness or shortcomings while ignoring his/her strength.

*Spring Festival "good luck" decorations.*

Xueying Wang

# 生词表 (Shēngcí Biǎo)
# Vocabulary

| Character | Pinyin | Part of Speech | English Definition |
|---|---|---|---|
| 1. 节日 | jiérì | *n.* | holidays |

你给我们介绍介绍中国的节日，怎么样？

| 2. 鞭炮 | biānpào | *n.* | firecrackers |

我们去放鞭炮吧。

| 3. 声音 | shēngyīn | *n.* | sound, voice |
|---|---|---|---|

你说话声（音）太大了。

| 声 | | *n.* | sound |
|---|---|---|---|

| 4. 灯笼 | dēnglong | *n.* | lantern |
|---|---|---|---|

很多家里都挂灯笼。

| 5. 过年 | guò nián | *v. obj.* | to celebrate a new year |
|---|---|---|---|

你明年准备在哪儿过年

| 6. 气氛 | qìfen | *n.* | atmosphere |
|---|---|---|---|

现在还不是新年，但是已经有节日的气氛了。

| 7. 风俗 | fēngsú | *n.* | customs |
|---|---|---|---|

这些都是那个地方的风俗。

| 8. 原来 | yuánlái | *adv.* | in the beginning, surprisingly (when the truth of a matter is revealed) |
|---|---|---|---|

我去开门一看，原来是我弟弟。

| | | *adj.* | original |
|---|---|---|---|

这件衣服原来的颜色是黑的。

| 9. 阵 | zhèn | *m.w.* | measure word for a period of intense activity, e.g., wind, rain, applause |
|---|---|---|---|

刚才刮了一阵风，又下了一阵雨。

| 10. 吹 | chuī | *v.* | to blow, to puff |
|---|---|---|---|

风把报纸吹走了。

| 11. …之内 | …zhī nèi | *phr.* | within… |
|---|---|---|---|

我们一定要在这几天之内好好地玩儿玩儿。

| 之 | zhī | *part.* | (classical Chinese) 的 |
|---|---|---|---|
| 内 | nèi | *n.* | in, inside |

| 12. 新年 | xīnnián | *n.* | New Year |
|---|---|---|---|

你新年准备去哪儿过？

| 13. 到处 | dàochù | *n.* | everywhere |
|---|---|---|---|

现在到处都在卖这种点心。

| 14. 拥挤 | yōngjǐ | *adj.* | crowded, jammed |
|---|---|---|---|

现在商店都这么拥挤。

| 挤 | | *v.* | to squeeze |
|---|---|---|---|

| 15. 家家户户 | jiājiāhùhù | *n.* | each and every family |
|---|---|---|---|

现在家家户户都在准备过新年。

16. 打扫　　　　dǎsǎo　　　*v.*　　　　to clean

你怎么还不打扫打扫你的房间？

扫　　　　　　　　　　*v.*　　　　to sweep

17. 干净　　　　gānjìng　　*adj.*　　　clean and neat

你说我的房间还不干净吗？

18. 贴　　　　　tiē　　　　*v.*　　　　to paste, to stick

这张你应该贴在门上。

19. 一边…一边　yībiān...yībiān　*adv.*　(lit.) at one side... at one side...; at the same time, simultaneously

我们一边吃，一边谈，好吗？

20. 包　　　　　bāo　　　　*n.*　　　　package

这个书包真漂亮。

　　　　　　　　　　　　*v.*　　　　to wrap

请把春联包好。

21. 饺子　　　　jiǎozi　　　*n.*　　　　dumplings

我不会包饺子。

22. 感兴趣　　　gǎn xìngqù　*v. obj.*　to be interested in...

你对这种电影感兴趣吗？

感　　　　　　　　　　　*v.*　　　　to feel, to sense

兴趣　　　　　　　　　　*n.*　　　　interest

23. 天亮　　　　tiān liàng　*n.*　　　　daybreak

我们聊天一直聊到了天亮。

天　　　　　　tiān　　　*n.*　　　　sky

亮　　　　　　liàng　　　*adj.*　　　bright, luminous, light

24. 放　　　　　fàng　　　*v.*　　　　release, set free, let go

他很喜欢放鞭炮。

25. 作为　　　　zuòwéi　　*v. comp.*　to act as, to take as, to use as

我作为一个中国人当然想回中国过年。

26. 佩服　　　　pèifu　　　*v.*　　　　to admire, to respect

我真佩服你。

27. 互相　　　　hùxiāng　　*adv.*　　　reciprocally, mutually

你们应该互相学习学习。

28. 祝福        zhù fú        *v. obj.*        to wish someone happiness

你去信的时候，应该说些祝福他的话。

福                                *n.*            blessing, happiness

29. 像          xiàng          *v.*            to resemble

他长得像他妈妈。

                                 *adv.*          to seem

外面像要下雨了。

30. 发短信      fā duǎnxìn     *v. obj.*       to send a text message via cellular phone

他怎么又给我发了个短信。

31. 增加        zēngjiā        *v.*            to augment, to increase, to add to

今天我要多做几个菜，增加一点儿节日气氛。

*Lauren Brown*

*Outdoor Spring Festival activities in Beijing.*

**Special Vocabulary for the Spring Festival**

1. 春节        chūnjié        *n.*            Spring Festival

2. 元旦        yuándàn        *n.*            January 1st

3. 春联        chūnlián       *n.*            Spring Festival couplet

4. 年货        niánhuò        *n.*            (lit.) new year's goods; special items prepared just for the new year celebration

5. 除夕        chúxī          *n.*            New Year's Eve

| 6. 年夜饭 | niányèfàn | *phr.* | dinner on the Lunar New Year's Eve |
| 7. 春节联欢晚会 | chūnjié liánhuān wǎnhuì | *phr.* | (lit.) Spring Festival Get-together Evening Party |
| 8. 守岁 | shǒu suì | *v. obj.* | to stay up all night on (Lunar) New Year's Eve |
| 9. 红包 | hóngbāo | *n.* | (lit.) red paper bag; here referring to a little red paper envelope with a gift of money inside, usually given to children |
| 10. 拜年 | bài nián | *v. obj.* | to pay respects (usually by bowing to someone) to wish the person a happy new year |
| 11. 舞龙 | wǔ lóng | *v. obj.* | to perform the dragon dance |

## 补充词汇 (Bǔchōng Cíhuì) Supplementary Vocabulary

| 1. 恭喜发财 | gōngxǐ fācái | *phr.* | Wishing you a prosperous New Year. |
| 2. 恭贺新禧 | gōnghè xīnxǐ | *phr.* | Happy New Year! |
| 3. 压岁钱 | yāsuìqián | *n.* | money given to children as a gift on New Year's Eve |
| 4. 放焰火 | fàng yànhuǒ | *v. obj.* | to set off fireworks |
| 5. 花灯 | huādēng | *n.* | decorative lantern |

## 口头用语 (Kǒutóu Yòngyǔ) Spoken Expressions

| 1. 过瘾 | guòyǐn | | to satisfy a craving |
| 2. 差远了 | chà yuǎn le | | far from it |
| 3. 凑 | còu | | to get closer to |
| 4. 中国通 | Zhōngguó tōng | | (lit.) thorough knowledge about China; usually used to describe a non-Chinese who has become very knowledgeable about Chinese culture |
| 5. 串门 | chuànmén | | to stop by, to stop in |
| 6. 这算是⋯ | zhè suàn shì | | this should be considered as... |

# 词汇注解 (Cíhuì Zhùjiě) Featured Vocabulary

## 1. 到处…都 (Dàochù…dōu)

到处 means "everywhere." It is frequently used with the adverb 都. For example: 街上到处都是人。

## 2. 好象 (Hǎoxiàng) vs. 像 (Xiàng)

| 好象 | *adv.* | it seems that… |
|---|---|---|
| 外面好象要下雨了。 | | It seems like it's going to rain. |
| 他们好象是学生。 | | They seem to be students. |

| 像 | *v.* | to resemble |
|---|---|---|
| 他长得像他妈妈。 | | He takes after his mother. |

| 像 | *adv.* | to seem (Here 像 is interchangeable with 好象.) |
|---|---|---|
| 外面像要下雨了。 | | It seems like it's going to rain. |

## 3. 家家户户 (Jiājiāhùhù)

In the phrase 家家户户, 家 and 户 are measure words. When both of these two words are repeated, they mean "each family" or "every family." For example: 家家户户 = 每家每户, every family and every household.

## 4. 全家人 (Quánjiārén), 大家 (Dàjiā), 家人 (Jiārén), 人家 (Rénjiā)

| | |
|---|---|
| 全家人 | the whole family |
| 大家 | everyone |
| 家人 | household, families |
| 人家 | other people |

## 5. 之 (Zhī)

之 is used in classical Chinese. It has the same meaning as 的. 之 is usually placed between the modifier and the noun, which is usually a monosyllabic noun.

| Modifier | 之 | Noun | |
|---|---|---|---|
| 除夕 | 之 | 夜 | New Year's Eve |
| 两个月 | 之 | 后 | two weeks after |
| 几个星期 | 之 | 前 | a few weeks ago |
| 一年 | 之 | 内 | within a year |

For example:

在美国买东西，一个月之内可以退换。
If you buy something in America, you can return it within a month.

这本书我几个星期之前就应该还给图书馆了。
I should have returned the book to the library a few weeks ago.

*Spring Festival couplets.*

Xueying Wang

 语法(Yǔfǎ)

# Grammar

## I. Unmarked Passive Sentences

When an action takes place, it usually involves a doer and a recipient. In a sentence with an active voice, the subject is the doer and the object is the recipient. For example:

| Doer | | Recipient |
|---|---|---|
| **Subject** | **Verb** | **Object (Somebody/Something)** |

我　　　　　包　　　　饺子。
I am making dumplings.

我　　　　　洗　　　　衣服。
I am washing my clothes.

When a recipient functions as a subject in a sentence, that sentence is in the passive voice. Some of the passive sentences have a passive voice marker, and others do not. In this lesson, you will learn an unmarked passive sentence where the object is placed at the beginning of the sentence, and the doer is left unmentioned.

| Recipient | |
|---|---|
| **Subject** | **Verb phrase** |

饺子　　　　包好了。
Dumplings have been made.

衣服　　　　洗完了。
Clothes have been washed.

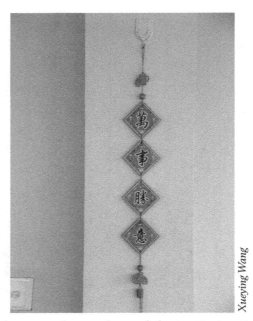

*This phrase is often exchanged during Spring Festival.*

This kind of sentence is called an unmarked passive sentence because it carries the sense of the passive voice without mentioning the doer. Unmarked passive is used when there is no need to mention the doer, or it is already implicit in the context. The requirements for this structure are identical to those in the 把 construction, where the "object" in the 把 construction becomes the recipient/topic in the unmarked passive sentence. The following are requirements for unmarked passive sentence:

Recipients: The recipient must be DEFINITE (a specific thing or person).

> CORRECT: 那个菜吃完了。

> xxx INCORRECT: 一个菜吃完了 xxx

Verbs: Only transitive action verbs can be used in this form. The verb predicate must contain one EXTRA ELEMENT such as a resultative/directional complement or the perfective 了. See the following examples for its usage:

## A. With Resultative/Directional Complement

| | Recipient | Action | Other elements |
|---|---|---|---|
| | **Subject** | **Verb** | **Resultative/Directional complement** |
| Positive: | 饺子 | 已经包 | 好了。 |

The dumplings have been made. (Resultative complement)

| | | | |
|---|---|---|---|
| | 桌子 | 搬 | 出去了。 |

The table is moved out. (Directional complement)

| | Recipient | Action | Other elements |
|---|---|---|---|
| Negative: | 饺子 | 还没有 | 包　好。 |

The dumplings have not been made yet.

| | | | |
|---|---|---|---|
| | 桌子 | 还没有搬 | 出去。 |

The table has not been moved out.

| Question: | 饺子 | 包 | 好了吗/没有？ |
|---|---|---|---|
| | Have the dumplings been made? | | |
| | 桌子 | 搬 | 出去了吗/没有？ |
| | Has the table been moved out? | | |

## Note

"没有" must be placed before the action verb to form the negative sentence. Do not use "不."

## 🔲 PRACTICE

Try using the above structure with the verb-object phrases 挂春联, 放鞭炮, 打扫房间, 准备年夜饭, and 寄信 to create a few unmarked passive sentences of your own.

## B. With Descriptive Complement

| | Recipient | Action | Other elements |
|---|---|---|---|
| | **Subject** | **Verb** | **Descriptive complement** |
| Positive: | 除夕 | 过 | 得很热闹。 |
| | New Year's Eve was very lively. | | |
| Negative: | 除夕 | 过 | 得不太好。 |
| | New Year's Eve was not that great. | | |
| Question: | 除夕 | 过 | 得怎么样？ |
| | How was your New Year's Eve? | | |

## Note

The negative form of this structure is "Verb + 得 + 不 + Adjective." For example:

    CORRECT: 除夕过得不热闹。

    xxx INCORRECT: 除夕没过得热闹。 xxx

## 🔲 PRACTICE

Try using the above structure with the verb-object phrases 写电子邮件, 开生日舞会, 举行运动会, 上数学课, and 包饺子 to create a few unmarked passive sentences of your own.

## C. With Perfective 了 (Le)

| | Recipient | Action | Other elements |
|---|---|---|---|
| | **Subject** | **Verb** | **Perfective 了** |
| Positive: | 药 | 吃 | 了。 |
| | The medicine has been taken. | | |

Negative:    药              还没有吃。
The medicine has not been taken yet.

Question:    药        吃              了吗？
Has the medicine been taken?

药        吃              了没有？
Has the medicine been taken or not?

## *Note*

Make sure that you don't add 了 in the negative form.
CORRECT: 药没吃。
xxx INCORRECT: 药没吃了。  xxx

---

## ⬛ PRACTICE

Try using this structure with the verb-object phrases 拜年, 买礼物, 换衣服, 开药方, and 打针 to create a few passive sentences of your own.

## II. Interrogative Pronouns for Non-Interrogative Usage

So far, you have learned how to use interrogative pronouns to form questions. You have learned the following words: 谁, 什么, 什么时候, 哪儿, 哪, 怎么, and 为什么. In this lesson you will learn how to use these interrogative pronouns (with the exception of 为什么) in declarative sentences to express all-inclusive usage in the positive sentence and all-exclusive usage in the negative sentences. These sentences always include a 都 or a 也, and it is usually placed before the verb. 都/也 reinforce the idea of all-inclusiveness or all-exclusiveness. 都 can be used in both positive and negative sentences and 也 is frequently used in some of the negative sentences. In this structure, interrogative pronouns can function as the subject, object,

*Celebrating Spring Festival with traditional dances in Beijing.*

attribute, or adverbial. When the interrogative word is used to emphasize the object, it should be placed before the verb. For more information, see the examples below:

## A. 谁 (Shéi/Shuí)

In this structure, 谁 is a term for person (everyone, anyone, or whoever).

| Subject |
| --- |

谁　　　　　都喜欢吃中国饭。

Everyone likes Chinese food.

| | Object |
| --- | --- |

我　　　　谁　　　　也不认识。

I do not know anyone.

| Attribute |
| --- |

谁的话　　　他　　　　都不听。

He's not listening to anyone.

## PRACTICE

Find a partner in class and take turns asking each other questions. For each question, provide a response using 谁 as a subject, object, or attribute. For example:

问：谁认识他？

答：他很有名，谁都认识他。

问：谁喜欢看这本书？

答：这本书没有意思，谁也不喜欢看。

问：他能回答谁的问题？

答：他很聪明，谁的问题他都能回答。

答：他很紧张，谁的问题他也没听懂。

## B. 什么 (Shénme)

In this structure, 什么 is a term for "anything" (whatever, any, etc.).

| | Attribute |
| --- | --- |

他　　　　什么　　　电影都看。

He will watch any movie.

| | Object |
| --- | --- |

我　　　　什么　　　也没吃过。

I have not eaten any kind of food.

你说　　　什么　　　我都不听。

No matter what you say, I will not listen.

## 🔲 PRACTICE

With a partner, carry out a series of short dialogues in which one person asks the questions and the other answers. When answering, make sure to use one of the structures given above. When you're done, switch roles and do it again. For example:

问：你买了什么？

答：东西太贵，我什么也没买。

问：你喜欢吃什么菜？

答：我什么菜都喜欢吃。

## C. 什么时候 (Shénme Shíhòu)

In this structure, 什么时候 is used to describe an ambiguous period of time (whenever).

| | Adverbial | |
|---|---|---|
| 你 | 什么时候 | 都可以给我打电话。 |

You can call me whenever you want.

| | | |
|---|---|---|
| 我 | 什么时候 | 去找你，你都不在家。 |

Whenever I look for you, you are never at home.

Note: Do not use 也 in this structure.

## 🔲 PRACTICE

Find a partner in class and take turns asking each other questions and then answering the questions using 什么时候. For example:

问：我什么时候可以去看你？

答：你什么时候都可以来。

问：他什么时候看电视？

答：我什么时候去找他，他都在看电视。

## D. 哪儿 (Nǎr)

In this structure, 哪儿 is a general term for place (wherever, everywhere, anywhere, etc.).

| | Subject | |
|---|---|---|
| 他的宿舍 | 哪儿都 | 干净。 |

His dorm is clean everywhere.

| | Object | |
|---|---|---|
| 放假的时候，他 | 哪儿也 | 没去。 |

He did not go anywhere during the break.

| Object of a preposition | | |
|---|---|---|
| 你 | 在哪儿看书 | 都可以。 |

You can read the books wherever you want.

---

## PRACTICE

Come up with three questions and then provide a response to each one using 哪. For example:

问：你去哪儿了？

答：我病了，哪儿也没去。

问：我在哪儿休息？

答：你在哪儿休息都行。

### E. 哪 (Nǎ) + Measure Word

"哪 + Measure Word" is a general word for choice (any, every, whichever, etc.).

| | Attribute | | | |
|---|---|---|---|---|
| | 哪 | Measure word | Noun | |
| 在 | 哪 | 个 | 房间 | 学习都方便。 |

It would be convenient to study in any room.

| | 哪 | 张 | 桌子 | 都是新的。 |
|---|---|---|---|---|

Every table is new.

---

## PRACTICE

Try asking a question and then provide both a positive and a negative response using the "哪 + Measure Word" structure. For example:

问：我应该穿哪件衬衫？

答：哪件都好看。

答：哪件我都不喜欢。

### F. 怎么 (Zěnme) + Verb

In this structure, 怎么 is a general word for "no matter how" or "by whatever means." The verb in this structure is usually repeated.

| Adverbial | | |
|---|---|---|
| 今天作业太多，我 | 怎么 | 做，也做不完。 |

There is too much homework. No matter how I tried, I couldn't finish it.

## ❀ PRACTICE

Ask a question and then provide a response using the "怎么 + Verb" structure. For example:

问：我怎么写这封信？

答：你怎么写都会写得很好。

问. 你信写得怎么样？

答：我怎么写也写不好。

# III. Using the Adverbial Conjunction 一边⋯一边⋯ (Yībiān...Yībiān...)

This adverbial phrase indicates two or more actions happening at the same time. This structure can only have one subject, never two. 一边 must be placed after the subject.

| Subject | 一边 | Verb Phrase， 一边 | Verb Phrase |
|---|---|---|---|
| 妈妈 | 一边 | 上大学，一边 | 工作，非常辛苦。 |

Mom attends college and works at the same time. She works very hard.

| | | | |
|---|---|---|---|
| 小李喜欢 | 一边 | 听音乐，一边 | 写作业。 |

Xiao Li likes to listen to music and do homework at the same time.

## *Note*

When the verbs connected by "一边⋯一边⋯" are single verbs without any object, 一 is frequently omitted. However, only certain verbs can be used in this structure. Here are some commonly used phrases:

边走边谈, 边听边写, 边读边想, 边唱边跳.

## ❀ PRACTICE

Try using the "一边⋯一边" structure to describe situations in a classroom, a post office, a bank, a train station, a night market, a hotel, a hospital, etc.

# IV. Using 原来 (Yuánlái)

原来 can be used as either an adjective or an adverb.

## A. As an Adjective

这条旧裙子原来的颜色是黑的。

This skirt was originally black.

我原来的意思是去吃中国饭。

My original idea was to go eat Chinese food.

## B. As an Adverb

As an adverb, it can be placed either before or after the subject.

### 1. *Originally*

In this structure, 原来 is frequently used with 现在.

| First clause (cause) | | | | Second clause (reason) | | |
|---|---|---|---|---|---|---|
| Subject | 原来 | Verb | Object | 现在 | Verb | Object |
| 他 | 原来 | 想当 | 医生， | 现在 | 又想当 | 老师。 |

Originally, he wanted to be a doctor. Now he wants to be a teacher.

### 2. *Discovering Something Hitherto Unknown*

| Subject | 原来 | Verb | Predicate |
|---|---|---|---|
| 拜年 | 原来 | 就是 | 春节的时候大家互相串门，互相祝福。 |

It turns out, a "New Year's visit" is when everyone goes to visit each other and exchange best wishes during the Spring Festival.

## *Note*

In this structure, 原来 is frequently used with 就是 or 是.

In the following structure, 原来 is frequently used with 怪不得.

| First clause (cause) | | | Second clause (reason) | | |
|---|---|---|---|---|---|
| Subject | Verb Object | 原来 | Subject | Verb | Object |
| 怪不得房间 | 那么冷， | 原来 | 窗户 | 开着呢。 | |

No wonder the room is so cold. The window is open!

---

## PRACTICE

Try to create some sentences of your own using 原来 as an adjective and as an adverb with two different meanings.

## V. Using the Preposition 对 (Duì)

In Lesson 18, you learned the preposition 对. In this lesson, you will learn two patterns that are frequently used with the preposition 对.

## A. 对⋯来说 (Duì...Lái Shuō)

This pattern means "speaking from the point of view of...." The noun that follows 对 should represent a person or an organization/institution. For example:

数学对我来说太容易了。

To me, math is very easy.

对我们宿舍来说，买一张桌子是一件大事。

Buying a table is a big deal for our dorm.

Note: "对⋯来说" can be placed before the subject or after the subject.

## B. 对⋯感兴趣 (Duì...Gǎn Xìngqù)

This pattern means "to be interested in someone or something." Thus, the noun that follows 对 can be a person or a thing. For example:

他对中国人的风俗习惯非常感兴趣。

He is very interested in Chinese customs and traditions.

张老师对我写的书很感兴趣。

Zhang Laoshi is very interested in my book.

## PRACTICE

Try using the two patterns above to ask a question and then provide an answer. For example:

问：你觉得拜年怎么样？

答：拜年对我来说是一个非常有意思的风俗习惯。

问：你对什么运动感兴趣？

答：我对打篮球很感兴趣。

# Textbook Exercises

## 🎧💻 TASK 1. 课文问答 (KÈWÉN WÈNDÁ) QUESTIONS AND ANSWERS

Check your comprehension of the text by answering the following questions.

1. 中国人在过春节前，都做些什么准备？
2. 中国人在除夕晚上都做些什么？
3. 中国人在春节都做些什么？
4. 李丽莉过春节的那天，穿什么颜色的衣服？为什么？

## 💻 TASK 2. 语法练习 (YǓ FǍ LIÀNXÍ) GRAMMATICAL STRUCTURE PRACTICE

### A. Sentence Construction

Use the unmarked passive voice to create your own sentences.

1. Situation:  春节快到了

   Objects:   年货, 春联, 灯笼, 家家户户的房子

2. Situation: 除夕的时候

   Objects: 饺子, 红包, 鞭炮, 年夜饭

3. Situation: 客人就要来了

   Objects: 饭菜, 饮料, 房间, 电视

4. Situation: 明天就要出发去旅行了

   Objects: 飞机票, 行李, 旅馆的房间, 朋友的地址和电话

## B. Sentence Completion

Read the following prompts and complete the sentences with the correct words or phrases.

1. 他两天没有来上课了，(谁) _____。

2. 这位作家写的小说都非常有意思，我(哪本) _____。

3. 我觉得这个问题太难了，(怎么) _____。

4. 屋子里的灯没开，真黑，我(什么) _____。

5. 这位老师对学生很关心，学生(什么时候) _____。

6. 箱子太小，我要带的东西太多，我(怎么) _____。

7. 今年放假，我除了吃饭睡觉以外，(哪儿) _____。

8. 我的车坏了，(怎么，什么地方) _____。

9. 我明天全天都没事儿，(什么时候，哪儿) _____。

10. 在中国(谁) _____ 自行车。

## C. Fill in the Blanks

Fill in the blanks by taking words from below and putting them into the appropriate places in the sentences. When you are done, translate the sentences into English.

怪不得　一边　现在　原来

1. 我 _____ 才明白 _____ 守岁就是在除夕的晚上大家不睡觉。

2. 他 _____ 什么中国的风俗都不知道，_____ 成了一个中国通了。

3. _____ 大家一晚上都不睡觉，_____ 今天是除夕。

4. 除夕之夜，全家人在一起 _____ 包饺子 _____ 聊天，一直闹到天亮。

##  TASK 3. 翻译 (FĀNYÌ) PARAPHRASING

Translate the following sentences into Chinese.

1. It is always very crowded whenever you go shopping in the shopping center during the Chinese New Year. (Hint: 什么时候…都…) No matter what New Year's goods you buy, you have to wait in line. (Hint: 什么…都…)

2. Everyone in my family wants to go pay New Year's visits. (Hint: 谁…都…) When I was paying New Year's visits, (Hint: 一边…一边…) I thought that if any adults and children could just express their New Year's wishes over the phone, (Hint: 谁…都…) the streets would not be so crowded with people everywhere. (Hint: 哪儿…都…)

3. In China, no celebration of any holiday is as tiring as the celebration of Spring Festival. (Hint: 什么… 也没有…) In the few weeks before the Spring Festival, my house has already been cleaned, (Hint: unmarked passive voice, reduplication of adjective) the spring couplets have been posted on my door, (Hint: unmarked passive voice) and the lanterns have already been hung up. (Hint: unmarked passive voice). But still, nobody in my family can stop working, (Hint: 谁…也…, 停 + 不 + Complement) and it seems that no matter how much we do the housework, we still can not finish (Hint: 好像, 怎么 + Verb …也 Verb 不 + Complement).

## 🖳 TASK 4. 情景对话 (QÍNGJǏNG DUÌHUÀ) SITUATIONAL DIALOGUE

**Setting:**       A Chinese home
**Cast:**          A foreign student and a member of a Chinese family
**Situation:**     A foreign student visits a Chinese family during the Chinese New Year. Construct a dialogue between the student and the Chinese family member. The conversation should proceed according to the relevant Chinese customs. Discuss Chinese New Year traditions. How is it different from the way the student celebrates the New Year? Remember to use the interrogative pronoun and unmarked passive structures.

# 38
# 打工
## Making Some Pocket Money

In this lesson you will:
- Discuss your summer plans.
- Learn how to look for summer jobs.
- Practice applying to summer jobs.

美国大部分的大学生都要打工。美国的暑假更是学生打工挣钱的好机会。但是在中国，大学生打工的不太多。大部分的家长虽然不是很有钱，但是他们不是很想让孩子出去打工。他们总是希望自己的孩子能把学习搞好，将来找一个好工作。中国的大学生也把学习和考试看得很重要。学习好的学生比较容易找到好工作。

（陈小云，李丽莉，吴文德三个人在吴文德的宿舍。）

陈小云：我听说美国很多人从高中起就开始打工挣零花钱。中国大部分的大学生还要靠父母给钱。

李丽莉：为什么？自己挣一点儿钱，开学的时候用，不好吗？

陈小云：中国的家长总是望子成龙，望女成凤[1]，希望孩子能多有一些时间学习，所以不是非常想让孩子出去打工。

吴文德：说起打工，李丽莉，暑假快到了。咱们找个临时工作，挣点儿钱，怎么样？

李丽莉：我知道暑期是挣钱的好机会。可是我不知道在中国怎么找工作？

陈小云：你们想做什么工作？

吴文德：我这个人从来不挑不拣，干什么都可以。

陈小云：其实，找工作不难。学校有一个布告栏，很多需要用人的单位都在那儿贴广告。要不你们到那儿去看看。报纸上、网上也有招聘广告。

李丽莉：学校暑期有没有什么工作呢？我很想在学校里搞一些翻译工作。

陈小云：在中国，学校暑假都关了，只有一些补习班，英文补习班，计算机补习班等。但是这些课都是由老师来教。如果你想做翻译工作，最好到出版社去问一问。

（陈小云走了以后，李丽莉对吴文德说：）

李丽莉：吴文德，咱们俩分一下儿工吧。到学校布告栏和报纸上看广告的事由我负责，上网查工作由你负责。晚上我们在你这儿碰头，商量一下儿找工作的事。

（晚上在吴文德的宿舍。）

李丽莉：吴文德，我在报纸上看到一个招聘广告。要找一个英文口语班老师，你喜欢跟人打交道，想不想去试一试。我把工作申请表格也复印下来了。

吴文德：我如果教英文，就会被学生叫作吴老师，也就是"没有"老师的意思[2]。真够有意思的。再说，我还可能被邀请到学生家去吃饭。这种工作可真够好的。

李丽莉：你在网上查到什么工作了吗？

吴文德：我刚查到一个翻译的工作。有家出版社要找一个翻译，帮着把中文小说翻译成英文。

李丽莉：我们赶快申请吧，好象找工作的人很多。布告栏上的招聘广告都快让人撕光了。我们要是申请晚了，工作叫别人占了，就太可惜了。

吴文德：唉，又要填表。我最不喜欢填表了。

李丽莉：你说喜欢当老师，但又不想填表。这不是跟叶公好龙[3]一样吗？

吴文德：我跟叶公好龙可不一样，我只是不喜欢填表。帮帮忙，好不好？

李丽莉：好是好，可是你这儿的空调坏了，我这个人一热，脑子就不好用了。

吴文德：这好办。给你扇扇子的事由我来做。咱们的表由你来填，好不好？

李丽莉：成交。

（一个小时以后，李丽莉填完了两份申请表格，高兴地对吴文德说：）

李丽莉：吴文德，表都填完了，一会儿咱们的个人简历打印出来，
　　　　就可以寄出去了。咦，我干了半天活，你怎么满头大汗的？

吴文德：李丽莉，我的扇子都被我扇坏了，我还没干活吗？

## Notes

1. 望子成龙，望女成凤。　　(Wàng zǐ chéng lóng, wàng nǚ chéng fèng.)
   (Lit.) "Parents expect their sons to grow into dragons, and their daughters phoenixes."

2. 吴老师，也就是"没有"老师的意思。　　(Wú lǎoshī, yě jiùshì "méiyǒu" lǎoshī de yìsi.)
   This is a pun. The surname 吴 and the word 无 ("have not") share the same sound and same tone. Therefore, "wú lǎoshī" could be either mean "没有老师" or "吴老师."

3. 叶公好龙　(Yè Gōng hào lóng)
   "The old man Ye likes dragons." This comes from a 成语故事. It is used to describe someone who loves his or her own fantastic ideas about a certain thing but cannot handle the reality. (See Task 3 in the Reading/Writing section of the Workbook for the full story.)

 生词表 (Shēngcí Biǎo)
# Vocabulary

| Character | Pinyin | Part of Speech | English Definition |
| --- | --- | --- | --- |
| 1. 打工 | dǎ gōng | *v. obj.* | to do odd jobs (usually temporary work paid by the hour) |
| 他现在还在饭馆打工吗？ | | | |
| 2. 大部分 | dàbùfen | *phr.* | majority |
| 大部分的学生都不工作。 | | | |
| 部分 | | *n.* | part, portion, fraction |
| 3. 挣钱 | zhèng qián | *v. obj.* | to make money |
| 我一定得找个工作，挣一点钱。 | | | |
| 挣 | | *v.* | to earn |
| 4. 家长 | jiāzhǎng | *n.* | (lit.) the head of the family; parents |
| 这个老师说他得跟这个学生的家长谈谈。 | | | |
| 5. 重要 | zhòngyào | *adj.* | important |
| 找一个好工作对我很重要。 | | | |

6. 开学      kāi xué     *v. obj.*     to begin school
你们夏天什么时候开学？

7. 临时      línshí     *adj.*     temporary
这个工作是临时的。

8. 暑期      shǔqī     *n.*     summer break
今年暑期你准备去哪儿？

9. 挑      tiāo     *v.*     to select
挑来挑去都一样。

10. 拣      jiǎn     *v.*     to pick
我在教室里拣到一本字典。

11. 其实      qíshí     *adv.*     as a matter of fact, in reality
他说他要去北京找工作，其实他去玩儿了。

12. 布告栏      bùgàolán     *n.*     bulletin board
你去看看布告栏上有没有你想找的工作。

13. 单位      dānwèi     *n.*     general term for an organization, institution, company, or workplace
很多单位都在那儿找人。

14. 广告      guǎnggào     *n.*     advertisement
你看见我们学校的广告了没有？

15. 招聘      zhāopìn     *v.*     to recruit (usually for a professional position)

我们学校想招聘一位汉语老师。

16. 翻译      fānyì     *v.*     to translate
请你给我翻译一下儿这几个字儿。

                            *n.*     translation
这几个字儿的翻译不好。

17. 补习班      bǔxíbān     *n.*     (lit.) supplementary study class; tutoring class, test prep classes
晚上他还要去上英文补习班。
    补习                             *v.*     (lit.) supplementary study

18. 计算机      jìsuànjī     *n.*     computers
我喜欢用计算机中文软件。

19. 由      yóu     *prep.*     from, by, via
这件事儿得由你自己来决定。

20. 出版社　　　　chūbǎnshè　　*n.*　　　　publisher

很多出版社都出这种书。

　　出版　　　　　　　　　　　　*v.*　　　　to publish

21. 分工　　　　　fēn gōng　　　*v. obj.*　　to divide the responsibilities, to divide the workload

我们现在分一下儿工吧。

　　分　　　　　　　　　　　　　*v.*　　　　to divide

22. 负责（任）　　fù zé(rèn)　　*v. obj.*　　to be responsible for, to be in charge of

这件事应该由你负责。

　　责任　　　　　　　　　　　　*v.*　　　　responsibility

23. 商量　　　　　shāngliang　　*v.*　　　　to discuss

这件事儿我们应该商量商量。

24. 口语　　　　　kǒuyǔ　　　　*n.*　　　　spoken language

他的中文口语非常好。

25. 复印　　　　　fùyìn　　　　　*v.*　　　　to photocopy, to duplicate

请你给我复印一下儿这两张照片。

　　复　　　　　　　　　　　　　*b.f.*　　　to duplicate, to repeat

　　印　　　　　　　　　　　　　*v.*　　　　to print

26. 邀请　　　　　yāoqǐng　　　　*v.*　　　　to invite

我们邀请老师去吃饭。

　　　　　　　　　　　　　　　　*n.*　　　　invitation

他收到我们的邀请了。

27. 撕　　　　　　sī　　　　　　　*v.*　　　　to tear

我把书撕坏了。

28. 光　　　　　　guāng　　　　　*adj.*　　empty, used up

他们把我的广告都撕光了。

29. 占　　　　　　zhàn　　　　　　*v.*　　　　to occupy

你先去给我占一个位子，好吗？

30. 空调　　　　　kōngtiáo　　　　*n.*　　　　air conditioner

你们那儿有没有空调？

31. 脑子　　　　　nǎozi　　　　　　*n.*　　　　brain

你这几天脑子怎么了，总是忘事儿？

| | | | |
|---|---|---|---|
| 32. 份 | fèn | *m.w.* | measure word for a portion or copy of something (such as application forms, newspapers, etc.) |
| 这份报你看了没有? | | | |
| 33. 打印 | dǎyìn | *v.* | (lit.) to type and print (e.g., on a type-writer, printer, etc.) |
| 这张表请你给我打印两份。 | | | |
| 34. 干活 | gàn huó | *v. obj.* | to do physical or manual work |
| 我得休息休息,不能总是干活吧。 | | | |
| 干 | | *v.* | to do (something) |
| 活 | | *n.* | work |
| 35. 满头大汗 | mǎntóu dàhàn | *phr.* | (lit.) the entire face soaked in sweat |
| 我跑步跑得满头大汗。 | | | |
| 汗 | hàn | *n.* | sweat |

## 补充词汇 (Bǔchōng Cíhuì) Supplementary Vocabulary

| | | | |
|---|---|---|---|
| 1. 零用钱 | língyòngqián | *phr.* | pocket money |
| 2. 春假 | chūnjià | *n.* | spring break |
| 3. 半工半读 | bàn gōng bàn dú | *phr.* | to work part-time and study part-time |
| 4. 应聘 | yìngpìn | *v.* | to accept a position |
| 5. 工资 | gōngzī | *n.* | wages, salary |
| 6. 薪水 | xīnshuǐ | *n.* | salary |

## 口头用语 (Kǒutóu Yòngyǔ) Spoken Expressions

| | | |
|---|---|---|
| 1. 说起 | shuōqǐ | speaking of... |
| 2. 搞好 | gǎohǎo | to do something well, to make some thing better |
| 3. 打交道 | dǎ jiāodao | to interact with |
| 4. 脑子就不好用了。 | Nǎozi jiù bù hǎo yòng le. | (Lit.) brain no longer good to use. In the text it means "when it is really hot, I cannot think anymore." |
| 5. 这好办。 | Zhè hǎo bàn. | This is easy to handle. |

| | | |
|---|---|---|
| 6. 成交 | chéngjiāo | to strike a deal, to reach an agreement |
| 7. 零花钱 | línghuāqián | pocket money |

## 词汇注解 (Cíhuì Zhùjiě) Featured Vocabulary

### 1. 打工 (Dǎ Gōng), 干活 (Gàn Huó), 工作 (Gōngzuò)

| | | |
|---|---|---|
| 打工 | *v. obj.* | to indicate hourly paid job or temporary job |
| 干活 | *v. obj.* | to do physical or manual work |
| 工作 | *v.* | to work |
| 工作 | *n.* | job |

### 2. 靠 (Kào)

| 靠 | ***prep.*** | **to lean on, to keep to, to stay near** |
|---|---|---|
| 靠窗户坐 | | to sit next to the window |
| 靠右走 | | to walk on the right side |

| 靠 | ***v.*** | **to rely on, to depend on** |
|---|---|---|
| 我靠自己，不靠我爸爸妈妈。 | | I depend on myself, not my parents. |

### 3. 等 (Děng)

| | | |
|---|---|---|
| 等 | *v.* | to wait |
| 等 | *nominal part.* | etc.  (等 can be followed by a noun, e.g., 等国，等人···) |
| 等等 | *repeated nominal part.* | etc.  (等等 cannot be followed by a noun.) |

## 语法 (Yǔfǎ)
# Grammar

## I. Passive Voice with Markers Using the Prepositions 被 (Bèi) / 让 (Ràng) / 叫 (Jiào)

In the last lesson, you learned how to make a passive sentence without a passive voice marker. In this lesson, you will learn to express the passive voice by using the prepositions 让, 叫, and 被, which are the passive voice markers. These markers function like the preposition "by" in English to introduce the doer of the action. These three passive voice markers have the same meaning, but 被 is more formal than 让 and 叫.

Although 让 and 叫 are used here in the passive voice, they can also be used as verbs in active voice sentences. Let's quickly review 让 and 叫 in the active voice.

*Outside the Shanghai Railway Station.*

## Review

# 让

a) to let somebody do something

这件事让他自己决定吧。    Let him make his own decision regarding this matter.

b) to allow somebody to do something

他妈妈不让他吸烟。    His mom does not allow him to smoke.

# 叫

a) somebody's name is...

她叫李丽莉。    Her name is Li Lili.

b) to shout, to yell, to call out to...

我大声地叫"小丽"。    I called out Xiaoli's name.

c) to ask somebody to do something

老师叫学生作练习。    The teacher asked the students to do exercises.

## A. Introduction

Now let's go back to 被, 让, and 叫 as passive voice markers. In the passive sentence, 被/叫 is sometimes used to describe something unfavorable or unfortunate.

| | Recipient | | Doer | | |
|---|---|---|---|---|---|
| | **Subject** | 被/让/叫 | **Someone** | **Verb** | **Other element** |
| Positive: | 那本小说 | 被/让/叫 | 别人(biéren) | 借 | 走了。 |

The novel has been checked out by someone else.

Here are a few requirements for the 被/让/叫 passive structure:

Verb: The verbs should be action verbs. They cannot stand alone and must be followed by another element, such as a complement or 了.

Recipient: The subjects should be specific recipients of an action known to the speakers. It can be a person as well as a thing that's acted upon.

Doer: In the sentence with 让/叫 introducing the passive voice, the doer must be mentioned. (The passive marker 被 is the exception in that it can be used with or without a doer.) If there is no specific doer, one can use a general noun such as 别人 or 人.

---

## PRACTICE

Use the 被/让/叫 passive structures along with the following phrases to ask questions, and then provide responses in both positive and negative forms.

Verbs:       吃完，搬开，骑坏，修好，刮走，买回来，洗干净，借走

Recipients:  衣服，报纸，饺子，行李，杂志，照相机，自行车，生日礼物

## B. Situations Where Only 被 Can Be Used

When doers are mentioned in passive sentences, 被/让/叫 are interchangeable. However, in the following situations, only 被 can be used.

### 1. Without a Doer

In passive sentences without agents, only "被" can be used, not 让 or 叫.

**Recipient**

| Subject | 被 | Verb | Other element |
|---------|----|------|---------------|
| 我要看的书 | 被 | 借 | 走了。 |

The book I want to read has been checked out.

*An employment center in Xi'an.*

## ✤ PRACTICE

Use the 被 passive structures (without a doer) along with the following verb phrases to ask questions, and then provide responses in both positive and negative format. Suggested verb phrases: to be returned, to be damaged, to be forgotten, to be invited, to be crossed out (in writing).

### 2. *With Certain Verb Complements*

When 作, 成, 到, and 去 are used as verb complements in the passive voice, only 被 can be used (NOT 让 or 叫). The common characteristic of the above examples is that verb complements can take objects. See the following examples.

a) Verb 作 (Verb + "As")

| Recipient | | (Doer) | | | |
|---|---|---|---|---|---|
| **Subject** | 被 | (Somebody) | **Verb** | 作 | |
| 我 | 会被 | 学生 | 叫 | 作 | 吴老师。 |

I will be called Wu Laoshi by students.

b) Verb 成 (Verb + "into" or "to Become")

| Recipient | | (Doer) | | | |
|---|---|---|---|---|---|
| **Subject** | 被 | (Somebody) | **Verb** | 成 | |
| 这本小说 | 还没被 | （她） | 翻译 | 成 | 英文。 |

This novel has not been translated into English yet.

c) Verb 去/到 Place

| Recipient | | (Doer) | | | |
|---|---|---|---|---|---|
| **Subject** | 被 | (Somebody) | **Verb** | 到 | Location |
| 我们 | 可能被 | （学生） | 邀请 | 到 | 他们家去吃饭。 |

We might be invited by students to their home for dinner.

| | | | | | |
|---|---|---|---|---|---|
| 他 | 被 | （学校） | 送 | 到 | 中国学中文去了。 |

He was sent to China by his school to study Chinese.

## ✤ PRACTICE

Use the 被 passive structures (with a doer) along with the following verb phrases to ask questions, and then provide responses in both positive and negative format. Suggested verb phrases for sentences: to be called as, to be treated as, to be listened to, to be invited to, and to be written as.

## II. Using the Preposition 由… (Yóu)

As a preposition, 由 points out who is responsible for an action or is in the role of doing something. This form is also a type of passive sentence. Only a limited number of verbs can be used with 由. The "由 + Noun" phrase makes up a preposition-object structure to function as an adverbial adjunct to the following verb. Unlike other forms of the passive voice, this structure does not need any additional elements.

|  | Subject |  | 由 | Noun | Verb phrase |
|---|---|---|---|---|---|
| Positive: | 看广告的事 |  | 由 | 我 | 负责。 |

To look at the advertisement is my responsibility.

| Negative: | 看广告的事 | 不(是) | 由 | 我 | 负责。 |
|---|---|---|---|---|---|

To look at the advertisement is not my responsibility.

| Question: | 看广告的事 |  | 由 | 谁 | 负责？ |
|---|---|---|---|---|---|

Who is responsible for looking at the advertisement?

|  | 看广告的事 | 是不是 | 由 | 你 | 负责？ |
|---|---|---|---|---|---|

Are you responsible for looking at the advertisement?

|  | 看广告的事 | 是 | 由 | 你 | 负责吗？ |
|---|---|---|---|---|---|

Are you responsible for looking at the advertisement?

## *Compare*

这本小说被他翻译成英文。    This novel was translated by him into English. (stating the fact)

这本小说由他翻译。    He is responsible for translating this novel into English. (stating responsibility)

*A job fair in Xi'an.*

## *Note*

The verb in the 由 structure is usually disyllabic. If a monosyllabic verb is used, just add 来 before the verb. For example: 这件事由我来做。

---

## PRACTICE

Find a partner in class and ask each other questions using the preposition 由. Provide a positive and negative response for each one. The following verbs might be helpful in creating your questions: 介绍, 决定, 翻译, 陪着, and 负责.

## III. Using 其实 (Qíshí)

其实 means "actually, in fact." As a conjunction, it implies that what was introduced earlier is not totally accurate. In this case, whatever follows 其实 can be taken as the real explanation, or as a supplementary part of it.

其实 can also be placed at the beginning of the sentence to state a fact. Sometimes it is followed by a clause, and sometimes it is not. For example:

其实找工作不难。

As a matter of fact, looking for a job is not difficult.

其实工作招聘广告很多地方都有。你去学校的布告栏看看，一定能找到一些。

In fact, lots of places post job advertisements. Go look at the school bulletin board, and you will surely find some.

其实 can also be used to introduce the second clause in a complex sentence. In this case, the first clause refers to what was previously believed, while the second clause states the actual fact. 其实 may be placed either before the verb or before the subject of the second clause.

| First clause | Second clause |
|---|---|
| 这次考试看起来很容易， | 其实回答起来很难。 |
| This exam looks easy, but in fact, it is very hard when it comes to answering the questions. | |
| 我以为他没去过中国， | 其实他已经去过好几次了。 |
| I didn't think he had ever been to China, but in reality he has been there several times already. | |

Note that 以为, meaning "to think (erroneously)," is sometimes used in the first clause to indicate a discrepancy between the two clauses.

---

## PRACTICE

Try using each of the patterns above to create a sentence of your own.

## IV. （自）从…（起）(Zìcóng...Qǐ)

In Lesson 35, you learned the phrase "自从…以后," which means "after a certain point." In this lesson you will learn "自从…起," which indicates a specific starting point and can be translated as "ever since…a certain time." 自 can sometimes be omitted. 自从 can only apply to the past. For the present, only 从 (not 自从) can be used. 从 can be used with past, present, and future. Also if there is an auxiliary verb, it is usually placed before 从. 就 can be placed before the verb for emphasis.

| Subject | （自）从 | Time | 起 | (Subject) | Verb | Object |
|---|---|---|---|---|---|---|
| 很多人 | 自从 | 高中 | 起， | | 就开始打工挣 | 零钱。 |

Many people start getting jobs and earning some pocket money from high school on (or "from the time they're in high school").

| | | | | | | |
|---|---|---|---|---|---|---|
| 我愿意 | 从 | 现在 | 起， | | 每天陪你去逛 | 商店。 |

From now on, I am willing to accompany you every day when you browse through the department stores.

## 🔳 PRACTICE

Find a partner in class and ask each other questions, using the structure above to discuss future plans or past experiences. For example:

Past experiences　问：你什么时候开始工作的？

答：我从去年起，就开始工作了。

Future plans　问：你什么时候可以教我用中文软件？

答：从明天起，我就教你。

# Textbook Exercises

## 🎧💻 TASK 1. 课文问答 (KÈWÉN WÈNDÁ) QUESTIONS AND ANSWERS

Check your comprehension of the text by responding to the following questions.

1. 中国的家长希望不希望自己的孩子暑假出去打工？为什么？

2. 中国学校暑期有没有学生可以做的暑期工作？为什么？

3. 李丽莉暑假想做什么暑期工作？她觉得吴文德应该做什么暑期工作？为什么？

4. 他们俩在申请暑期工作的时候，是一个人在干活，还是两个人都在干活？为什么？

# TASK 2. 语法练习 (YǓFǍ LIÀNXÍ) GRAMMATICAL STRUCTURE PRACTICE

## A. Sentence Construction

Use 让/叫/被/由 to change the following sentences into the passive voice.

1. 那个师傅把我的录音机修好了。

2. 那位作家把这本小说翻译成了英文。

3. 大家把他叫做中国通。

4. 我们请王先生来介绍中国风俗习惯。

5. 学生选陈小云当学生代表。

6. 他把我的行李拿到楼上，又把宿舍的门打开了。

7. 你负责上网看招聘广告、查工作。

8. 需要用人的单位把招聘广告贴在布告栏上。

## B. Word Insertion

Insert 把/让/叫/被/由 where applicable in the following sentences.

1. 妈妈已经 ＿＿＿＿＿＿ 做好了的饭菜摆在桌子上了。

   a) 把          b) 让          c) 由

2. 图书馆里我要看的新杂志都 ＿＿＿＿＿＿ 人借走了。

   a) 把          b) 叫          c) 由

3. 鞭炮都 ＿＿＿＿＿＿ 孩子们放完了。

   a) 把          b) 让          c) 由

4. 我的词典 ＿＿＿＿＿＿ 他的弟弟拿走了。

   a) 把          b) 被          c) 由

5. 那个作家的作品已经 ＿＿＿＿＿＿ 翻译成了几国语言。

   a) 让          b) 被          c) 由

6. 你病了，应该马上 ＿＿＿＿＿＿ 药吃下去。

   a) 把          b) 让          c) 被

7. 暑期补习班的课是 ＿＿＿＿＿＿ 谁来教的。

   a) 让          b) 被          c) 由

8. 这位有名的师傅 ＿＿＿＿＿＿＿＿ 请来教我们太极拳。

   a) 叫          b) 被          c) 由

## C. Sentence Completion

Read the following prompts and complete the sentences with the correct words or phrases.

1. 我以为中国大学生在暑假都打工，（其实）＿＿＿＿＿＿＿＿＿＿＿＿＿＿＿＿＿＿＿＿＿＿。

2. （以为）＿＿＿＿＿＿＿＿＿＿＿＿＿＿＿＿＿＿＿＿，其实他只想挣一点儿零花钱。

3. 其实找暑期工作不太难，＿＿＿＿＿＿＿＿＿＿＿＿＿＿＿＿＿＿＿＿＿＿＿＿＿＿。

4. 我自从开始学中文起，＿＿＿＿＿＿＿＿＿＿＿＿＿＿＿＿＿＿＿＿＿＿＿＿＿＿＿。

---

## 💻 TASK 3. 翻译 (FĀNYÌ) PARAPHRASING

Translate the following sentences into Chinese.

1. Since that novel was translated into English by Lin Li, she is frequently called a translation expert by her friends, (Hint: 自从, 被…Verb 成, 被…Verb 作) and this summer she has been invited by the publisher to do some translation work. (Hint: 被…Verb 到) As a matter of fact, Lin Li is now responsible for all of the translation work for the publisher. (Hint: 其实, 由)

2. A: It is not easy to find a temporary job this summer. Many ads posted on the school job bulletin boards have already been torn down. (Hint: 叫…Verb + Complement) Jobs posted on the Internet have already been taken. (Hint: 让… Verb + Complement) I hope you will be able to find a job next week.

   B: As a matter of fact, I was hired by the school to teach a math preparatory class. (Hint: 其实, 被… Verb 去) But the air conditioner in the classroom hasn't been repaired by Mr. Zhang (the repairman) yet, so there is no class this week. (Hint: 被…Verb 好) Starting next week, I will be officially teaching. (Hint: 从…起) I will be responsible for all of the elementary math classes. (Hint: 由)

---

## 💻 TASK 4. 情景对话 (QÍNGJǏNG DUÌHUÀ) SITUATIONAL DIALOGUE

**Setting:**    At a friend's house

**Cast:**    two students

**Situation:**    You and your friend are both looking for temporary jobs in the summer and you are discussing the options. What kinds of jobs are available for the summer? Do you like working in the summer, or do you prefer to work during the school year? Why or why not? Discuss the pros and cons of a summer job using the vocabulary and grammar from this lesson.

# 39
# 用手机
# Using Cell Phones

> *In this lesson you will:*
>
> ■ Learn how to open and maintain a cell phone account in China.
>
> ■ Discuss some common features on a cell phone.
>
> ■ Talk about the advantages and disadvantages of using calling cards and cell phones.

中国现在使用移动电话的人越来越多。移动电话也叫作手机。吴文德注意到校内、校外、还有大街上到处都是用手机的人。一天，他好奇地走进一家电信局的营业大厅，原来只是想随便了解一下儿手机的价格和怎么办手机开户，但是他从电信局出来的时候，他自己手里也拿了一个手机了。吴文德为什么不用他宿舍的免费电话，偏要花钱买手机呢？下面的小故事会给你一个很好的答案。

（一天下午，吴文德走进一家电信局的营业大厅。）

营业员：你是不是准备入网？

吴文德：入网？入网是什么意思？

营业员：入网就是办手机开户的意思。

吴文德：我还没决定呢。你们这儿手机多少钱一个？座机费多少钱？使用费多少？

营业员：那要看你买什么手机，买什么卡？

吴文德：买卡是什么意思？

营业员：光有手机，没有卡，顾客的手机还是不能用。只有买了卡，手机才能通。不同的卡，收不同的座机费和使用费。

吴文德：你们现在什么卡最便宜？

营业员：你是学生吧。我们现在正在促销校园卡，特别便宜。

吴文德：校园卡的座机费和使用费贵不贵？

营业员：不贵。校园卡没有免费分钟，所以座机费不高。每分钟的使用费，跟打公用电话差不多。不过，这种促销活动今天下班的时候就结束了。

吴文德：我今天来得真凑巧。校园卡非常有吸引力，但是手机多少钱呢？

营业员：我们现在有一种促销手机。只要你银行里有五千人民币，或五百美金，促销手机就不要钱。

吴文德：真的？我今天真有运气！你看，我的借记卡和我的定期存款单里正好有五百美金。我这儿还有银行的收据。麻烦你给我买一张校园卡吧。

营业员：好。请你填一下儿移动电话申请表……

（吃过晚饭以后，吴文德给李丽莉看他的刚买的手机。）

李丽莉：手机？你还挺会赶时髦的。

吴文德：我用手机是图方便。我这个人就是不喜欢呆在宿舍里。不在宿舍，除了我找别人不方便，别人找我也不方便。

李丽莉：你的手机真漂亮。都有什么功能？

吴文德：我这个手机除了有来电显示以外，也能发短信息，还能照相。

李丽莉：能打国际长途吗？

吴文德：能打我也不打。打国际长途太浪费钱了。

李丽莉：你平时挺大方的。怎么一下子变这么小气了？在中国用手机很贵吗？

吴文德：我以前认为很贵，后来才发现不是那么贵。我如果只打市内，每个月除了交一些座机费以外，我打多少电话，就交多少钱。

李丽莉：你办手机开户容易吗？

吴文德：很容易。我交了定金。然后再挑一个手机号码，手机就通了。你问了这么多的问题。是不是也想买一个手机？

李丽莉：没门儿。我可不想赶时髦。

吴文德：李丽莉，我的好朋友，我说了半天，怎么跟对牛弹琴[1]一样。我买手机不是赶时髦，是图方便。

李丽莉：你别生气好不好？我只不过是跟你开一个小玩笑罢了。

## Note

### 1. 对牛弹琴  (duì niú tán qín)

This set phrase comes from a classical 成语故事 and literally means "to play a musical instrument to a cow." It means that someone is wasting time talking to the wall. For more information behind this story, please read Task 2 in the Reading/Writing section.

*A store selling cell phones.*

 生词表 (Shēngcí Biǎo)

# Vocabulary

| Character | Pinyin | Part of Speech | English Definition |
|---|---|---|---|
| 1. 使用 | shǐyòng | *v.* | to use, to employ (a tool, a device, a gadget, a machine, etc.) |
| 我不会使用这种电话。 | | | |
| 2. 移动 | yídòng | *v.* | to move (the position of) |
| 你想不想办一个移动电话？ | | | |
| 移 | | *v.* | to move, to shift |
| 3. 电信局 | diànxìnjú | *n.* | telecommunications bureau |
| 我想去电信局问问。 | | | |
| 电信 | | *n.* | telecommunications |

4. 随便      suíbiàn      *adj.*      casual, informal

他说话很随便。

                                    *adv.*      casually, informally

请大家随便问问题。

5. 开户      kāi hù      *v. obj.*      to open an account

你知道怎么办银行开户手续吗？

6. 免费      miǎnfèi      *adj.*      to be exempt from payment, to be free of charge

这些服务都是免费的吗？

7. 答案      dá'àn      *n.*      answer, solution

你猜出这个问题的答案了没有？

8. 决定      juédìng      *v.*      to decide

今天晚上去哪儿，你们决定了没有？

                                    *n.*      decision

这是一个很好的决定。

9. 座机费      zuòjīfèi      *n.*      (lit.) the machine-anchoring fee; the monthly fee

他还没有付座机费。

10. 促销      cùxiāo      *v.*      to promote sales

这家商店正在搞促销，我们去那儿买吧。

    促                                       *v.*      to promote

    销                                       *b.f.*      sale

11. 校园      xiàoyuán      *n.*      campus

我们去校园走走，怎么样？

12. 特别      tèbié      *adj.*      special, peculiar

这种手机的样式很特别。

                                    *adv.*      especially, particularly

这种手机现在特别贵。

13. 公用      gōngyòng      *adj.*      (for) public use

这些都是公用电话。

14. 活动      huódòng      *n.*      activities

现在很多商店都有促销活动，你应该去看看。

                                    *v.*      to exercise

我们出去活动一下儿。

15. 下班          xià bān         *v. obj.*    to go/come off work
我下班以后一定去。

16. 结束          jiéshù          *v.*         to conclude, to finish
现在促销活动还没有结束吗？

17. 吸引力        xīyǐnlì         *n.*         power of attraction
那本书很有吸引力。
吸引                          *v.*         to attract
力                            *n.*         force, power, strength

18. 功能          gōngnéng        *n.*         function
这个手机的功能很多。

19. 运气          yùnqì           *n.*         good fortune, good luck
你们真有运气。

20. 赶            gǎn             *v.*         to catch up
我得去赶火车了。

21. 时髦          shímáo          *n.*         fashion
他总是喜欢赶时髦。
                             *adj.*       fashionable
他的衣服很时髦。

22. 除了…以外      chúle…yǐwài     *conj.*      in addition to…, apart from…
除了这个电话以外，你还有手机吗？

23. 别人          biéren          *n.*         other people, others
别人穿什么，他就要穿什么。

24. 来电显示      lái diàn xiǎnshì *phr.*      incoming message display
这些手机都有来电显示。
来电              lài diàn        *v. obj.*    to have an incoming message

25. 信息          xìnxī           *n.*         information, message, news
我的手机可以发短信息。

26. 国际          guójì           *n.*         international
他常常打国际长途。

27. 浪费          làngfèi         *v.*         to waste
你别浪费水了。
                             *adj.*       be extravagant
你太浪费了。

28. 平时          píngshí          *adv.*          in ordinary times, usually
他平时很爱学习。

29. 大方          dàfang           *adj.*          generous
他大方极了。

30. 小气          xiǎoqi           *adj.*          stingy, narrow-minded
你太小气了。

31. 后来          hòulái           *n.*           (in the) future, later on
我们先去了一家商店，后来又去了几家，都没有买到。

32. 发现          fāxiàn           *v.*           to discover
我们发现了一家商店卖这种手机。

                                  *n.*           discovery, finding

这是一个新发现。

33. 市内          shìnèi           *n.*           the area within a city
我可以用你的手机打一个市内电话吗？
市                               *n.*           city

34. 定金          dìngjīn          *n.*           down payment, deposit
你交定金了没有？

35. 生气          shēngqì          *v. obj.*      angry, mad
你现在太爱生气了。

## 补充词汇 (Bǔchōng Cíhuì) Supplementary Vocabulary

1. 费用          fèiyòng          *n.*           fee, expense
2. 电池          diànchí          *n.*           battery
3. 充电          chōng diàn       *v. obj.*      to charge a battery
4. 国内          guónèi           *adj.*         domestic
5. 通用          tōngyòng         *v.*           to use interchangeably
                                  *adj.*         interchangeable
6. 月租费         yuèzūfèi         *n.*           (lit.) the monthly rental fee

# 口头用语 (Kǒutóu Yòngyǔ) Spoken Expressions

1. 偏            piān                            deliberately, insistently (do something
                                                in one's own way), defiantly, to
                                                do something someone opposes

2. 入网          rùwǎng                          to open a cellular phone account

| 3. 那要看 | nà yào kàn | that depends on... |
|---|---|---|
| 4. 正好 | zhènghǎo | just right, at the exactly right time |
| 5. 捣什么鬼 | dǎo shénme guǐ | (lit.) to play what mischief; in the text it means "What mischief are you up to?" |
| 6. 图 | tú | (used as a verb) to aim at (a certain kind of benefit or profit); to take (something) as one's goal; to do (something) for the sake of something (as a noun, 图 means "picture" or "chart") |
| 7. 没门儿 | méi ménr | (idiom) (lit.) having no door; no way |
| 8. 罢了 | bàle | that's all, no more than that |

## 词汇注解 (Cíhuì Zhùjiě) Featured Vocabulary

### 1. 光 (Guāng)

| 光 | adv. | only | 你怎么光吃饭，不吃菜。 |
|---|---|---|---|
| 光 | adj. | empty | 我把饭都吃光了。 |

### 2. 呆 (Dāi)

| 呆 | adj. | to be in a daze | 发呆 (Lesson 14) |
|---|---|---|---|
| 呆 | v. | to stay | 呆在宿舍里 |

### 3. 后来 (Hòulái) vs. 以后 (Yǐhòu)

The differences in usage of 后来 and 以后 are:

**A. Structural Differences**

| Time word/phrase + 以后    after a certain amount of time or a point in time |
|---|

一个月以后，他才把我的书还给了我。    He returned my book after a month.

| Event + 以后    after an event |
|---|

开完会以后，我们再去看电影。    After the meeting, we will go to a movie.

后来 CANNOT be used after a time word/phrase or after an event.

**B. Time Differences**

| 以后    **adv.**    in the future (to describe an event or an action in the future) |
|---|

你以后应该常常去看他。
In the future, you should go and visit him often.

| 后来 | *adv.* | later on, afterwards (always used to describe a past event) |

我以前也是这么想的。后来进电信局一问，才发现手机没有那么贵。

I had the same thoughts before. Later on, I went to the telecommunications bureau. As soon as I asked the price, I discovered that a cellular phone is not that expensive anymore.

### C. Similarities

This is the only usage in which 以后 is interchangeable with 后来.

| 以后 | *adv.* | afterwards (to describe past events) |

我以后再也没有去看他了。    I did not go and visit him anymore.

| 后来 | *adv.* | afterwards (to describe past events) |

我后来再也没有去看他了。    I did not go and visit him anymore.

*China Mobile Shopping Center, where one can purchase cell phone services.*

 语法(Yǔfǎ)
## Grammar

## I. Using the Clause 除了⋯以外 (Chúle...Yǐwài) in a Complex Sentence

"除了⋯以外" means either "in addition to, aside from" or "with the exception of," depending on the meaning of the second clause. The meaning of the second clause is determined by adverbs such as 还, 也, 都, or 没有 in the structure. 以外 can be omitted if what is placed between 除了 and 以外 is very short. For example: 除了我 (以外) = 除了我. "除了⋯以外" itself introduces the first clause and it is always followed by a second clause. When the two clauses share one subject, that subject can be placed either before 还／也 in the second clause or before 除了 in the first clause. The meaning remains the same.

## A. Using the Adverbs 还 and 也 with 除了⋯以外

When "除了⋯以外" is used with 还 or 也 in the second clause, it means "in addition to" or "aside from." Although 还 and 也 have identical meanings and are interchangeable in some (but not all) structures, there are some differences in their usage.

### 1. When 还 and 也 are Interchangeable

还 and 也 are only interchangeable in the following two situations.

**In a Positive Sentence**

除了(有)中文书以外，他还/也有很多英文小说。
In addition to Chinese books, he also has a lot of English novels.

他除了在家学习以外，还/也在图书馆学习。
In addition to studying at home, he also studies in the library.

除了送他礼物以外，我还/也送别人礼物。
In addition to giving him a gift, I am also giving presents to others.

**When Used with the Question Word 吗**

除了(有)中文书以外，他还/也有日文书、英文书吗？
In addition to Chinese books, does he have English or Japanese books?

他除了在家学习以外，还/也在图书馆学习吗？
In addition to studying at home, does he also study at the library?

### 2. 除了⋯以外 Used with 还 Only

If the question word is NOT 吗 but another word such as 什么 or 哪儿, then only 还 can be used.

除了(有)中文书以外，他还有什么书？
In addition to Chinese books, what other books does he have?

他除了在家学习以外，还在哪儿学习？
In addition to studying at home, where else does he study?

### 3. 除了⋯以外 Used with 也 Only

Only 也 can be used in the following three situations.

**When There Are Two Different Time Phrases**

| First clause | Second clause (main sentence) |
| --- | --- |
| 他除了白天以外， | 晚上也在图书馆学习。 |
| 除了白天(在图书馆学习)以外， | 他晚上也在图书馆学习。 |

In addition to studying in the library during the day, he also studies there at night.

**When There Are Two Different Subjects**

When each of the two clauses in the "除了⋯以外" structure has two different subjects, you should always use 也, NOT 还. The first subject should always be placed after 除了, and the second subject should be placed at the beginning of the second clause.

*A China Telecom phone booth.*

| First clause | | | | Second clause (main sentence) | |
|---|---|---|---|---|---|
| 除了 | Subject1 | Verb phrase | 以外 | Subject2 | Verb phrase |
| 除了 | 我 | （送他礼物） | 以外， | 小云 | 也送他礼物了。 |

I wasn't the only one to give him a gift; Xiao Yun gave him one, too!

| | | | | | |
|---|---|---|---|---|---|
| 除了 | 学生 | （喜欢放假） | 以外， | 老师 | 也喜欢放假。 |

Students aren't the only ones who like vacations; teachers like them, too!

**When the Sentences Are in the Negative Format**

One subject:

| First clause | | | Second clause (main sentence) | |
|---|---|---|---|---|
| 除了 | Verb phrase | 以外 | Subject | Verb phrase |
| 除了 | 不喝酒 | 以外， | 他 | 也不吸烟。 |

In addition to not drinking, he also does not smoke.

Two subjects:

| First clause | | | | Second clause (main sentence) | |
|---|---|---|---|---|---|
| 除了 | Subject1 | Verb phrase | 以外 | Subject2 | Verb phrase |
| 除了 | 我 | 不去 | 以外， | 小云 | 也不去。 |

I am not going, and neither is Xiao Yun.

| | | | | | |
|---|---|---|---|---|---|
| 除了 | 吴文德 | 没有唱歌 | 以外， | 李丽莉 | 也没有唱。 |

In addition to Wu Wende, Li Lili doesn't sing either.

## ⚙ PRACTICE

Use the "除了…以外" structure to ask a question using one subject along with 也 and then another subject with 还. When you're done, try the same thing with two subjects. For example:

问：你除了（交座机费）以外，还（交什么费）？

答：我除了（交座机费）以外，也/还（交使用费）。

问1：除了你（交座机费）以外，别人也（交座机费）吗？

问2：除了（暑期）以外，（上课）的时候，你也（打工）吗？

问3：除了不（会跳舞）以外，他也不（唱歌）吗？

## B. Using the Adverbs 都 or 没有 with 除了…以外

When the "除了…以外"structure is used with 都 or 没有, it means "with the exception of" or "besides."

### 1. With One Subject

When there is only one subject, it can be placed either before 除了 or at the beginning of the second clause.

| First clause | | | | Second clause (main sentence) | |
| --- | --- | --- | --- | --- | --- |
| (Subject) | 除了 | Clause | 以外 | (Subject) 都/没有 | Verb phrase |
| 我 | 除了 | 星期天（有时间玩儿） | 以外， | 别的日子 | 都没有时间玩儿。 |

I usually don't have time to play, except on Sundays.

| | 除了 | （去过）中国以外， | | 他 | 没有去过别的国家。 |
| --- | --- | --- | --- | --- | --- |

He has not been to any other country besides China.

### 2. With Two Subjects

When there are two subjects, the first subject should be placed after 除了, and the second subject should be placed before 都/没有.

| First clause | | | Second clause (main sentence) | | |
| --- | --- | --- | --- | --- | --- |
| 除了 | Clause | 以外 | Subject | 都/没有 | Verb phrase |
| 除了 | 他走路去 | 以外， | 我们 | 都 | 坐公共汽车去。 |

We all take a bus except for him; he walks.

| 除了 | 他 | 以外， | 我们 | 都 | 是中国人。 |
| --- | --- | --- | --- | --- | --- |

We are all Chinese, except him.

| 除了 | 他（想去看电影） | 以外， | 没有人 | | 想去看电影。 |
| --- | --- | --- | --- | --- | --- |

No one wants to see a movie, except him.

## ❧ PRACTICE

Use the "除了…以外" to ask a question, first with one subject and then with two. Then try using the 都/没有 structure to create a response for each question. For example:

问1：昨天你除了（呆在宿舍）以外，还（去哪儿了）？

答：我除了（呆在宿舍）以外，我哪儿都没（有）去。

问2：除了（你）以外，还有人也（用手机）吗？

答：除了（我）以外，别人都（不用手机）。

# II. Using 只有…才… (Zhǐyǒu…Cái…)

The pair of adverbs "只有…才…" connects either two phrases or two clauses and indicates "only…then." 只有 provides a necessary condition for the result stated by the 才 phrase or clause. The "只有…才…" structure emphasizes that the action can only be done under the specific condition provided. 才 must be placed after the subject and it is often followed by an auxiliary verb such as 能, 可以, etc.

## A. With One Subject

When there is only one subject, it can be placed either before 只有 or before the adverb 才.

| First clause (condition) | | | Second phrase/clause (result) | | |
|---|---|---|---|---|---|
| **Subject** | 只有 | **Time** | **(Subject)** | 才 | **Verb phrase** |
| 他 | 只有 | 星期六 | | 才 | 可以看电影。 |

He can only watch movies on Saturday.

| First clause (condition) | | | Second phrase/clause (result) | | |
|---|---|---|---|---|---|
| **Subject** | 只有 | **Place** | **(Subject)** | 才 | **Verb-Objective** |
| | 只有 | 在图书馆 | 我 | 才 | 能读书。 |

I can only read in the library.

| First clause (condition) | | | Second phrase/clause (result) | | |
|---|---|---|---|---|---|
| **Subject** | 只有 | **Verb phrase** | **(Subject)** | 才 | **Verb phrase** |
| 我们 | 只有 | 到了冬天， | | 才 | 能看到雪。 |

We can see snow only in the winter.

| | 只有 | 去我们家， | 你 | 才 | 能吃到真正的中国饭。 |
|---|---|---|---|---|---|

Our home is the only place where you can eat authentic Chinese food.

*An IC card phone booth.*

## B. With Two Subjects

If there are two subjects, the first subject should be placed after 只有, and the second subject should be placed before 才.

| First clause (condition) | | | Second phrase/clause (result) | | |
|---|---|---|---|---|---|
| 只有 | Subject1 | Verb phrase | Subject2 | 才 | Verb phrase |
| 只有 | 他 | 来找我， | 我 | 才 | 去跳舞。 |

I will not go dancing unless he comes to get me.

| | | | | | |
|---|---|---|---|---|---|
| 只有 | 你 | 来帮我， | 我 | 才 | 能搬家。 |

I will only move if you help me.

## &#x25A6; PRACTICE

Try using the "只有…才" structure along with the following phrases as conditions to create some sentences of your own.

Suggested phrases for sentences with one subject: 星期天, 春节的时候, 免费, 认真学习, 记住生词.

Suggested phrases for sentences with two subjects: 告诉我密码, 修好我的车, 服务员拿来菜单, 爸爸给我寄钱来.

## III. The 只要…就 (Zhǐyào...Jiù) Structure

The pair of adverbs "只要…就" is the converse of the "只有…才" structure. "只有…才" strongly emphasizes that the action can take place only if the given condition is met. "只要…就" indicates that as long as a certain condition is met, the result or action will take place. To summarize, the condition stated in the "只有…才" structure states a necessary condition, whereas the condition stated in the "只要…就" is a sufficient condition.

## A. With One Subject

When there is only one subject, it can be placed either before 只要 or before the adverb 就.

| First clause (condition) | | | Second clause (result) | |
| --- | --- | --- | --- | --- |
| Subject | 只要 | Verb phrase | 就 | Verb phrase |
| 你 | 只要 | 拿一个号码 | 就 | 行了。 |

It will be okay as long as you get a number.

| | | | | |
| --- | --- | --- | --- | --- |
| 你 | 只要 | 去邮局， | 就 | 能买到杂志。 |

If you go to the post office, you can buy magazines.

## B. With Two Subjects

When there are two subjects, the first subject should be placed after 只要 and the second subject should be placed before 就.

| First clause (condition) | | | Second clause (result) | | |
| --- | --- | --- | --- | --- | --- |
| 只要 | Subject1 | Verb phrase | Subject2 | 就 | Verb phrase |
| 只要 | 你 | 给我的是支票， | 我 | 就 | 不能马上用。 |

If you give me a check, I cannot use it right away.

| | | | | | |
| --- | --- | --- | --- | --- | --- |
| 只要 | 你 | 请客， | 我 | 就 | 来。 |

As long as you are paying, I will come.

## C. Compare

只要你吃医生给你开的药，你的病就会好。

As long as you are taking the medicine the doctor gave you, your illness will be cured.

只有吃医生给你开的药，你的病才会好。

Only if you take the medicine the doctor gave you can your illness be cured.

(If you don't, you will not get well.)

---

## ⧉ PRACTICE

Try using the "只要…就" structure along with the suggested phrases as conditions to create a few sentences of your own. For each phrase, create two sentences, one with a single subject and the other with two subjects. Suggested phrases: 打开电视, 我有钱, 你帮我办手机开户, 你教我.

## IV. Non-Interrogative Usage of Interrogative Pronouns (Cont'd.)

In Lesson 37 you learned that interrogative pronouns can be used in declarative sentences to indicate all-inclusiveness in a positive sentence or to indicate all-exclusiveness in a negative sentence. In this lesson we will introduce another non-interrogative usage of interrogative pronouns that refers to unspecific things, people, and places, and indicates whatever, wherever, however, whenever, etc. The structure of this usage is "…QW…, …QW…" with the adverb 就 frequently placed in the second clause. For example:

*One subject:*

| First clause | Second clause |
| --- | --- |
| 学生要选什么课， | 就可以选什么课。 |

Students take whatever classes students want to take.

| | |
| --- | --- |
| 你想怎么做素菜， | 就怎么做。 |

Cook vegetables in whatever way you want.

| | |
| --- | --- |
| 你想跟谁去看电影， | 你就跟谁去看电影。 |

You go to a movie with whomever you want.

| | |
| --- | --- |
| 我打多少电话， | 就交多少钱。 |

I will pay for however many phone calls I make.

*Two subjects:*

| First clause | Second clause |
| --- | --- |
| 老师怎么教， | 学生就怎么说。 |

Students will speak the way their teacher teaches them.

| | |
| --- | --- |
| 你什么时候有时间， | 我们就什么时候去。 |

We will go whenever you have time.

## PRACTICE

Try using each of the questions words 谁, 什么, 那儿, 怎么, 多少, and 什么时候 to ask questions and then answer each question. For example:

问1：我今天跟谁一起去看电影？

答1：你想跟谁去，就跟谁去。

问2：我怎么说这个句子？

答2：老师怎么教你，你就怎么说吧。

# Textbook Exercises

## 🎧💻 TASK 1. 课文问答 (KÈWÉN WÈNDÁ) QUESTIONS AND ANSWERS

Check your comprehension of the text by responding to the following questions.

1. 吴文德说他为什么要买手机？李丽莉说吴文德为什么要买手机？你觉得呢？

2. 吴文德买的是什么卡？为什么？

3. 吴文德觉得在中国办手机开户容易吗？为什么？

4. 吴文德花了多少钱买的手机？为什么？

---

## 💻 TASK 2. 语法练习 (YǓFǍ LIÀNXÍ) GRAMMATICAL STRUCTURE PRACTICE

### A. Fill in the Blanks

Use 还/也/都/没有 where needed to fill in the blank spaces in the sentences below.

1. 你除了今天早上在百货商店买东西以外，你晚上 _____ 在百货商店买了东西了吗？

   a) 还          b) 也          c) 都          d) 没有

2. 在中国，除了北京，你 _____ 去过什么别的地方？

   a) 还          b) 也          c) 都          d) 没有

3. 除了放假或是有病的时候，这个学生每天 _____ 在图书馆学习。

   a) 还          b) 也          c) 都          d) 没有

4. 除了他一个人以外，_____ 别的人喜欢吃食堂的饭。

   a) 还          b) 也          c) 都          d) 没有

5. 这个地方除了冬天下雪，有时候春天 _____ 下雪。

   a) 还          b) 也          c) 都          d) 没有

### B. Sentence Completion

Read the following prompts and complete the sentences with the correct words or phrases.

1. 只要银行里有钱，你 _____ 。

2. 只有修好了这辆自行车，我 _____ 。

3. 他除了喜欢吃以外，还 _____ 。

4. 除了我以外，大家都 _____ 。

5. 除了吴文德以外，没有 _____ 。

6. 除了他以外，我 _____ 。

7. 哪家商店有促销活动或是免费的服务，我 _____ 。

8. 家里给他寄来多少钱，他 _____ 。

## C. *Sentence Construction*

Answer each question using as many conjunctions as possible. Make sure each of the conjunctions "因为…所以…," "不但…而且…," "只要…就…," "虽然…但是…," "要是…就…," and "只有…才…" is used at least once.

Questions

1. 他为什么喜欢用信用卡?
2. 医生为什么要他透视?
3. 他为什么那么激动?
4. 你为什么不喜欢去那家银行?
5. 他为什么没有拿到签证?
6. 你为什么用手机?

---

## 📖 TASK 3. 翻译 (FĀNYÌ) PARAPHRASING

Translate the following sentences into Chinese.

In addition to me, all my friends have cell phones. (Hint: 除了…以外 with 都) If I have money, I will buy a cell phone. (Hint: 只要…就…) Yesterday, I received a check from my family, so I opened a cell phone account. (Hint: 因为…所以…) This new cell phone is not very expensive, but it has a lot of useful functions. (Hint: 虽然…但是/可是…) In addition to displaying incoming messages, it can also send short messages. (Hint: 除了…以外 with 还) Every month, as long as I pay monthly fees, I can use the cell phone. (Hint: 只要…就…) In addition to free minutes, there is no charge for incoming calls. (Hint: 除了…以外 with 还) However, if I need to leave Beijing for a few days, I have to add additional services and pay a roaming fee. (Hint: 如果…就…) Only after that will I be able to use my cell phone. (Hint: 只有…才…) If I don't have a lot of money in my bank account, I just make fewer calls. (Hint: 要是…就…) In addition to fear of overdrawing my bank account, I am also afraid of exceeding my allowed minutes. (Hint: 除了…以外 with 也) Therefore, I go to the bank every month to check how much money I have left. Then, after that, I go to the cell phone company to pay my bill. How about you? (Hint: 先…然后再…)

---

## 📖 TASK 4. 情景对话 (QÍNGJǏNG DUÌHUÀ) SITUATIONAL DIALOGUE

**Setting:** A cell phone store

**Cast:** A sales clerk and a customer

**Situation:** The sales clerk is trying as hard as he/she can to sell you a cell phone and a card. He/she gives you the entire store's promotional information. Ask the clerk about the features offered, the cost of the phone, and what kinds of calling plans are available. You want to buy a cell phone, but only if it's a good deal. Do you come out of the store with a phone? Why or why not?

# 40

# 汉语水平考试
## Taking the HSK

*In this lesson you will:*
- Learn about the HSK.
- Learn how to prepare for the HSK.
- Make arrangements with your friends to study for an exam.

中国的汉语水平考试，简称 HSK，是一种标准化的考试，考试的主要对象是那些中文不是母语的外国人华侨等等。汉语水平考试一共有基础、初中等和高等三套试卷。基础考试有三部份：1) 听力理解；2) 语法；3) 阅读。初中等有四部份：1) 听力理解；2) 语法；3) 阅读；4) 综合填空。高等考试有六部份：1) 听力理解；2) 语法；3) 阅读；4) 综合表达；5) 写作；6) 口语。参加考试的学生不但可以得到中国政府发的汉语水平考试证书，而且还可以申请去中国大学学习的奖学金。李丽莉决定下个月参加汉语水平考试，但是吴文德参加不参加呢？下面请看李丽莉和吴文德的一段小对话。

（星期五吴文德一吃了晚饭就给李丽莉打电话。）

吴文德：李丽莉，今天晚上我们去看电影吧。

李丽莉：我现在要准备考试，连吃饭的时间都没有，哪儿有时间看电影？

吴文德：哎呀，你怎么连想都没想，就说不看呢？学校考试连我都不紧张，你有什么好紧张的。

李丽莉：要是学校考试，我根本就不会紧张。课前预习，课后复习，只要考试不粗心，就不会考糊。

吴文德：不是学校考试？那你考什么？你觉得学校考试考得还不够多，是吗？

李丽莉：不是，我想参加汉语水平考试，看看我能考几级。

吴文德：汉语水平考试一共有几级？

李丽莉：十一级。考完试以后还可以得到一个中国政府发的汉语水平证书。

吴文德：我也想知道我的汉语水平能达到几级？什么时候考试？

李丽莉：下个月第三个星期六。你也参加吧。我们一块儿复习，好吗？

吴文德：好吧。不过，还有一个多月呢，你急什么？

李丽莉：我可不是平时不烧香、临时抱佛脚[1]的那种人。我喜欢早早地复习好，考试的时候就不心慌了。

吴文德：李丽莉，我考试虽然都没有你成绩好，但是我考试从来不心慌，根本不在乎考试的分数。

李丽莉：说起来容易，做起来难。凡是参加过汉语水平考试的人都知道这种考试考的是综合知识，比学校的考试难多了。

吴文德：你越觉得难，考试就越难。我觉得咱们俩现在的汉语水平去参加考试应该没有问题。

李丽莉：我们越说，你的自信心就越高。看样子你是不想复习了，对不对？

吴文德：想啊。但是我们真的连星期五晚上都不能休息一下吗？要不，我们今天晚上早一点儿开始。复习完了，我们说不定还有时间看电影呢。

（星期五晚上，李丽莉和吴文德两个人在阅览室商量怎么准备汉语水平考试。）

吴文德：汉语水平考试都考些什么内容？

李丽莉：考试有听力理解，语法结构，阅读理解，和综合填空……。

吴文德：我们先复习听力吧。我有一个最好的复习听力的方法。这个方法不但能有很大的收获，而且能让我们感到放松。

李丽莉：别卖关子了。快说，你有什么好方法？

吴文德：看中文电影！我觉得看电影是练习听力的最好的方法。这也叫一举两得[2]。

李丽莉：我越叫你学习，你就越要看电影。我带了一些模拟考题，我们做题吧。

（过了一个半小时以后，李丽莉和吴文德开始互相检查他们做的练习题。）

李丽莉：吴文德，你是不是又想看电影了。你怎么连这么简单的字都
　　　　写成错别字了呢？

吴文德：你一定看错了。我填的空里，根本没有"错"字，也没
　　　　有"别"字。

## Notes

1. 平时不烧香，临时抱佛脚。　(Píngshí bù shāoxiāng, línshí bào Fójiǎo.)
   This idiomatic expression describes someone who never burns incense in front of the Buddha but would clasp to the Buddha's feet when emergency arises. In other words, it paints the picture of a procrastinator.

2. 一举两得　(yì jǔ liǎng dé)
   This set phrase comes from a 成语故事. Literally, it means "to obtain two things with one single act." It is similar to "kill two birds with one stone." For more information about the story behind this idiom, please read Task 3 in the Reading/Writing section.

# 生词表　(Shēngcí Biǎo)
# Vocabulary

| Character | Pinyin | Part of Speech | English Definition |
|---|---|---|---|
| 1. 简称 | jiǎnchēng | *n.* | (lit.) simply called; abbreviated name |
| 汉语水平考试的简称是什么？ | | | |
| | | *v.* | to be simply called |
| 汉语水平考试简称 HSK。 | | | |
| 2. 标准化 | biāozhǔnhuà | *phr.* | standardization |
| 这是一种标准化的考试。 | | | |
| 3. 主要 | zhǔyào | *adj.* | main, major |
| 我今天的主要任务是打扫房间。 | | | |
| 4. 母语 | mǔyǔ | *n.* | mother tongue |
| 我的母语是中文。 | | | |
| 5. 华侨 | huáqiáo | *n.* | overseas Chinese |
| 你是华侨吗？ | | | |

6. 基础　　　　jīchǔ　　　*n.*　　comprehension　basic
   他的汉语基础很好。

7. 高等　　　　gāoděng　　*n.*　　advanced level
   初等数学太容易，我想考高等数学。
   等　　　　　　　　　　*n.*　　level, category

8. 试卷　　　　shìjuàn　　*n.*　　examination paper; test paper
   请大家在十二点交试卷。
   卷　　　　　　　　　　*n.*　　(lit.) scroll; volume, file, folder

9. 听力　　　　tīnglì　　　*n.*　　listening ability
   我的汉字写得不太好，但是我听力还可以。

10. 理解　　　　lǐjiě　　　*n.*　　comprehension
    我们再看一遍阅读理解吧。
    　　　　　　　　　　　*v.*　　to comprehend, to understand
    这课语法我都理解了。

11. 阅读　　　　yuèdú　　　*n.*　　reading
    他的中文阅读水平很高。
    　　　　　　　　　　　*v.*　　to read
    我每天都要阅读中文报纸。

12. 综合　　　　zōnghé　　*adj.*　comprehensive, synthesized
    这是一种综合练习，很有用。
    　　　　　　　　　　　*v.*　　to synthesize, to bring together
    　　　　　　　　　　　　　　　(different parts, categories, etc.)
    我们把今天的学的东西综合一下儿。

13. 填空　　　　tiánkòng　　*v.*　to fill in the blanks
    请用我们学过的字填空。

14. 表达　　　　biǎodá　　　*v.*　to express
    你能不能用中文表达你的意思？

15. 写作　　　　xiězuò　　　*n.*　composition
    你能不能帮我练习练习中文写作？

16. 得到　　　　dédào　　　*v.*　to obtain
    这次中文考试第一名可以得到一本中文词典。

17. 政府　　　　zhèngfǔ　　*n.*　government
    现在他给中国政府工作。

18. 证书　　　　zhèngshū　　n.　　certificate
你得到汉语水平考试的证书了吗？

19. 奖学金　　　jiǎngxuéjīn　n.　　scholarship
他没有得到奖学金。

　　奖　　　　　　　　　　　n.　　prize, award

20. 段　　　　　duàn　　　　m.w.　section, paragraph
你懂不懂这段话的意思？

21. 对话　　　　duìhuà　　　n.　　dialogue
下面请听一段学生和老师的对话。

22. 连　　　　　lián　　　　　prep.　even
这段话连我们老师都听不懂。

23. 根本　　　　gēnběn　　　adj.　fundamental, basic
这是一个根本问题

　　　　　　　　　　　　　　adv.　(lit.) (from) the root; basically, totally
这种考试他根本不想参加。

24. 预习　　　　yùxí　　　　v.　　to preview
我们可以一起预习预习。

25. 粗心　　　　cūxīn　　　　adj.　careless
上次你太粗心了，这次你一定要细心一点儿。

26. 一块儿　　　yíkuàir　　　adv.　(lit.) in one block; together
我们一块儿去吧。

27. 在乎　　　　zàihu　　　　v.　　to care about, to attach importance to (something)
你去不去，我不在乎。

28. 分数　　　　fēnshù　　　n.　　scores
我考试的分数从来都不高。

29. 凡是　　　　fánshì　　　adv.　any, all, each and every
凡是你问的问题，我都能回答。

30. 知识　　　　zhīshi　　　n.　　knowledge
他的知识很丰富。

31. 内容　　　　nèiróng　　　n.　　content
内容太多了。

32. 结构        jiégòu      *n.*      structure, frame
这个房子的结构很像我们家。

33. 收获        shōuhuò      *n.*      results, harvest
我这次去中国收获很大。

34. 感到        gǎndào      *v. comp.*      to feel, to sense
他现在能去中国工作了。他感到非常高兴。

35. 模拟考题        mónǐ kǎotí      *phr.*      simulated test
他常常做中文汉语水平考试模拟考题。

    模拟                           *adj.*      simulated
    考题                           *n.*      test items

## 专有名词 (Zhuānyǒu Míngcí) Proper Nouns

汉语水平考试      Hànyǔ Shuǐpíng Kǎoshì (HSK)      Chinese Language Proficiency Test

## 补充词汇 (Bǔchōng Cíhuì) Supplementary Vocabulary

1. 高考      gāokǎo      *n.*      college entrance exam

2. 高级      gāojí      *n.*      advanced level

3. 及格      jí gé      *v. obj.*      (lit.) to reach the mark; to pass (an exam)

4. 通过      tōngguò      *v.*      to pass

5. 毕业      bì yè      *v. obj.*      to graduate
                                       *n.*      graduation

6. 磁带      cídài      *n.*      tape

7. 光盘      guāngpán      *n.*      laser disk, CD

## 口头用语 (Kǒutóu Yòngyǔ) Spoken Expressions

1. 有什么好紧张的。      Yǒu shénme hǎo jǐnzhāng de.      What is there to be nervous about?

2. 心慌      xīn huāng      to feel flustered in the heart, to panic

3. 看样子      kàn yàngzi      it looks like...

| 4. 卖关子 | mài guānzi | (lit.) "to sell on the crucial point," a trick of traditional storytellers in the market place; to keep the listeners in suspense |

# 词汇注解 (Cíhuì Zhùjiě) Featured Vocabulary

## 1. 到底 (Dàodǐ) vs. 根本 (Gēnběn)

| 到底 | *adv.* | Emphasizes the verb in the sentence. (It can be used in negative sentences or questions.) |

你到底参加不参加考试？    Are you going to take the exam or not?

你到底还是没参加考试。    You finally decided not to take the exam.

| 根本 | *adv.* | Emphasizes the verb in the sentence; usually modifies negative forms. (It can be followed by 就 without affecting the meaning.) |

老师说了半天，我根本不了解他的意思。
The teacher's been droning on and on, but I simply can't understand him.

我根本就没听说过这件事。
I've [simply] never heard of such a thing.

| 根本 | *adj.* | basic, fundamental |

学中文最根本的法子就是多听、多说、多写、多读。
The most fundamental ways of learning Chinese are by listening, speaking, reading, and writing more.

## 2. 感到 (Gǎndào) vs. 觉得 (Juéde)

| 觉得 | *v.* | to express someone's feelings |

吃完饭以后，他就觉得不舒服了。
After the dinner, he did not feel well.

| 觉得 | *v.* | to express someone's opinion |

李丽莉觉得考汉语水平考试非常有用。
Li Lili feels that taking the Chinese Proficiency Test is very useful.

| 感到 | *v.* | to express someone's feelings (more formal than 觉得) |

考完试以后，大家都感到很放松。
After the test, everyone feels relaxed.

## 3. 理解 (Lǐjiě) vs. 了解 (Liǎojiě) vs. 懂 (Dǒng)

| 理解 | *v.* | to understand with a thorough rational/intellectual understanding of something |
| 了解 | *v.* | to understand with a general understanding of something, usually from one's personal experience |
| 懂 | *v.* | to understand something on a simplistic level, such as understanding a sentence |

# 语法(Yǔfǎ)
# Grammar

## I. Using 连···都/也 (Lián...Dōu/Yě)

The meaning of 连 is similar to the word "even" in English. This structure is used to emphasize the subject, object, time, place, or verb in a sentence, and 连 is a preposition that marks the element being emphasized. In this structure, 连 must be coupled with the adverb 都 or 也. 都 can be used in both the positive and the negative forms, but 也 is more frequently used in the negative sentence.

### A. Emphasizing the Subject

When 连 is used to emphasize the subject, it should be placed before the subject.

**Placed before subject**

| 连 | Subject | 都/也 | Verb | Object |
|---|---|---|---|---|
| 连 | 我 | 都 | 认识 | 这个字。 |

Even I know this word.

| 连 | 我 | 也/都 | 不认识 | 这个字。 |
|---|---|---|---|---|

Even I don't recognize this character.

## PRACTICE

Try using the pattern above along with the nouns 孩子, 老板, 教授, 专家, and 研究生 as subjects to create sentences of your own.

### B. Emphasizing the Object

In this structure, the object is placed directly after 连 and before 也/都, instead of following the verb. Please note, however, that when you translate this kind of sentence into English, it looks like you are emphasizing the verb.

**Placed before object**

| Subject | 连 | Object | 也/都 | Verb |
|---|---|---|---|---|
| 他 | 连 | 我的朋友 | 都 | 认识。 |

He even knows my friends.

| 他 | 连 | 晚饭 | 也 | 没吃。 |
|---|---|---|---|---|

He did not even eat dinner.

| 他 | 连 | 一个朋友 | 也/都 | 没有。 |
|---|---|---|---|---|

He does not even have a single friend.

*Sign outside an HSK Testing Center.*

## ✙ PRACTICE

Try and see if you are able to use the 连 structure to emphasize the following nouns as objects: 电脑, 词典, 电话, 早饭, 价钱, 钥匙, 手机, 硬座, and 最贵的旅馆.

### C. Emphasizing a Particular Time

**Placed before time**

| Subject | 连 | Time | 也/都 | Other elements |
|---|---|---|---|---|
| 他 | 连 | 星期天 | 都 | 在图书馆学习。 |

Even on Sundays, he studies in the library.

| | | | | |
|---|---|---|---|---|
| 他 | 连 | 考试前 | 也/都 | 不学习。 |

Even right before the exam, he did not study.

## ✙ PRACTICE

Now use the 连 structure to emphasize the time phrases 除夕, 暑假, 比赛前, 生病时, and 逛夜市.

### D. Emphasizing the Place

**Placed before place**

| Subject | 连 | Place | 也/都 | Other elements |
|---|---|---|---|---|
| 他 | 连 | 在教室 | 都 | 吃东西。 |

He eats everywhere, even in the classroom.

| | | | | |
|---|---|---|---|---|
| 他 | 连 | 在图书馆 | 也/都 | 不看书。 |

He does not read, even in the library.

*Studying for exams at Xi'an Science and Technology University.*

## 🔲 PRACTICE

Try using the 连 structure to emphasize the following nouns representing places: 飞机场, 网上, 操场上, and 有空调的房间里.

### E. Emphasizing the Verb

In this pattern, 连 is an emphatic marker stressing that the action is the least one can do, even though the person does not do it. The verb that is emphasized in this pattern should be repeated in a negative form. 连 is frequently used with 都 or 也, which should be placed before 没/不. In addition, 连 is used in conjunction with 就, which appears in the second clause.

| First clause | | | | | Second clause | |
|---|---|---|---|---|---|---|
| **Subject** | 连 | **Verb** | **Adverb** | **Verb** | 就 | **Verb phrase** |
| 他 | 连 | 想 | 都没 | 想， | 就 | 说出来了。 |

He speaks out before he takes the time to think.

| | | | | | | |
|---|---|---|---|---|---|---|
| 他 | 连 | 吃 | 也没 | 吃， | 就 | 走了。 |

He left without eating anything.

| | | | | | | |
|---|---|---|---|---|---|---|
| 他 | 连 | 谢 | 都不 | 谢 | 就 | 拿走了。 |

He took it without saying "thank you."

## 🔲 PRACTICE

Try using the 连 structure to emphasize the verbs 商量, 等, 找, 问方向, and 试衣服.

## II. Using 凡是 (Fánshì)

凡是 means "all," including everyone and everything, without exception. 凡是 is often followed by a noun or nominal phrase, which functions as the subject or object. No matter whether 凡是 appears before a subject, an object, or a time word, it is always placed at the beginning of the sentence and is frequently used in conjunction with adverbs such as 都 or 总.

### A. 凡是 Before a Subject

凡是学生都怕考试。

All students fear taking tests.

凡是没有复习过的学生，考试的时候，都会心慌。

All students who haven't studied will have anxiety during the exam.

### B. 凡是 Before an Object

凡是中国的电影，我都一定会去看。

As long as it's a Chinese movie, I must go and see it.

### C. 凡是 Before a Time Phrase

凡是考试的时候，他总是心慌得要命。

Whenever it's test time, he feels extremely anxious.

## PRACTICE

Use "凡是…都/总" with 广告, 研究生, 单位, 运动员, and 银行 to create sentences of your own.

## III. Using the 越…越 (Yuè…Yuè) Structure

Review: In Lesson 26 you learned that the construction "越来越…，" which means "getting more and more…," is used as an adverb to modify adjectives and certain verbs. For example:

现在的考试是越来越多了。 (Followed by an adjective)

Now there are more and more tests.

我越来越喜欢喝中国茶了。 (Followed by a verb)

I like drinking Chinese tea more and more.

*A calligraphy demonstration outside the Summer Palace in Beijing.*

In this lesson, you will learn the "越···越" structure, which connects two directly related words, phrases, or clauses. It carries a similar meaning as "the more...the more..." In this structure, 越 must be placed after the subject and before the verb or adjective.

## A. With One Subject

**Main sentence**

| Subject | 越 | Verb/Adjective | 越 | Verb/Adjective |
|---|---|---|---|---|
| 我们 | 越 | 吃 | 越 | 爱吃。 |

The more we eat, the more we want to eat.

| Subject | 越 | Verb/Adjective | 越 | Verb/Adjective |
|---|---|---|---|---|
| 我 | 越 | 吃 | 越 | 饱，越饱越想睡。 |

The more I eat, the fuller I get. The fuller I get, the sleepier I get.

## B. With Two Subjects

| First clause | | | Second clause | | |
|---|---|---|---|---|---|
| Subject1 | 越 | Verb/Adjective, | Subject2 | 越 | Verb/Adjective |
| 节日 | 越 | 多， | 我们吃的机会也就 | 越 | 多。 |

The more holidays (we have), the more opportunities there are for us to eat.

---

## PRACTICE

Try using each of the two patterns above to create a sentence of your own. For example: 饺子, 我越吃越爱吃。

# IV. Grammar Summary

In this section, we will briefly summarize all the major grammar points you have learned in this volume.

## A. Actual and Potential Complements

A resultative complement follows an action verb to show the result of the action verb. Only limited verbs and adjectives can function as resultative complements. (Lesson 31) Certain verbs indicating direction can function as complements. The verb 来 (to come) or 去 (to go) are simple complements of direction, which follow the motion verb to indicate the direction of the action in relation to the speaker. This structure is "Motion Verb + Verb 来/去." (Lessons 32) The structure of compound complements of direction is "Action Verb + Motion Verb + Verb 来/去." (Lesson 33) The special compound directional complement, as its name indicates, is a compound directional complement, but it functions as a fixed phrase with special meanings. (Lesson 34)

The potential complement places 得 or 不 between the verb and the complement to indicate whether there is a possibility of achieving a result through an action. (Lesson 34)

## B. The Active 把 Construction and the Passive Voice Structure

Both the active voice (Lesson 36) and the passive voice of the 把 construction focus on what has happened to the object. The passive voice may be unmarked or may use the prepositions 被/让/叫 (Lesson 38). Both of these structures require their verbs to be transitive action verbs with other elements following the verb.

The major difference between the passive voice using prepositions 被/让/叫 and the unmarked passive voice is whether the agent is mentioned. The unmarked passive voice does not mention the agent (Lesson 37), while the 被/让/叫 passive voice does. Another kind of passive voice using 由 (Lesson 38) tells who is responsible for an action or is in the role of doing something.

## C. Structures That Indicate Special Focus

1. "既…也/又…" ("not only…but also…") indicates the simultaneous existence of two situations. (Lesson 32)

2. The "是…的" structure is used to place emphasis on a certain element related to a past action or event. While 是 is placed before the word group that is emphasized (indicating time, place, manner, purpose, etc.), 的 appears either at the end of the sentence or before the object. (Lesson 35)

3. Double negative words used in a sentence carry a strong positive meaning. So far you have learned 1) "不 + Auxiliary Verb + 不," 2) "没有…不," and 3) "非…不可." (Lesson 36)

4. Interrogative Pronouns such as 谁，什么，什么时候，哪儿，哪，and 怎么 can be used with 都/也 in declarative sentences to express all-inclusiveness or all-exclusiveness. (Lesson 37) These interrogative pronouns can also be used to refer to unspecific things, people, and places, indicating whatever, wherever, however, whenever, etc.

5. In the structure of "连…也都…," 连 (which means "even") is a preposition used to mark the subject, object, time, place, or verb being emphasized. (Lesson 40)

6. "凡是…都…" means "every, all" and it includes everyone without exception. (Lesson 40)

## D. Conjunctions

1. The adverbial phrase "一边…一边…" indicates two or more actions happening at the same time. (Lesson 37)

2. "除了…以外" with 都, 也, or 还 means "in addition to" or "with the exception of." (Lesson 39)

3. The "只有…才…" structure emphasizes that only under the condition provided by 只有 can the action be done. (Lesson 39)

4. The "只要…就…" structure indicates that as long as a certain condition is met, the action/event will take place. (Lesson 39)

5. The "越…越" structure connects two words, phrases or clauses to indicate "the more…the more." (Lesson 40)

6. "自从…以后" means "ever since a certain point (in the past). (Lesson 35)

7. "自从…起" indicates a starting point in time (in the past). (Lesson 38)

## E. Adjective and Adverbs

1. 原来 can be used as an adjective or an adverb. It carries the meaning of "originally" or "as it turns out" and indicates that the speaker discovered something that was not known to him/her before. (Lesson 37)

2. 其实 means "actually" or "in fact." It is used to indicate that what follows will reveal the truth, or at least provide some supplementary explanation. (Lesson 39)

 Textbook Exercises

## TASK 1. 课文问答 (KÈWÉN WÈNDÁ) QUESTIONS AND ANSWERS

Check your comprehension of the text by responding to the following questions.

1. 吴文德找李丽莉去看电影，李丽莉去不去？为什么？
2. 吴文德参加不参加 汉语水平考试？为什么？
3. 汉语水平考试都考些什么内容？吴文德想从哪儿开始复习？为什么？
4. 李丽莉说错别字的意思跟吴文德说的错别字的意思一样不一样？为什么？

## TASK 2. 语法练习 (YǓ FǍ LIÀNXÍ) GRAMMATICAL STRUCTURE PRACTICE

### A. Fill in the Blanks: Conjunctions

Look at the conjunctions below and choose the best one to fill in each blank.

1. 他 _____ 听音乐，_____ 做练习。

   a) 越…越…        b) 连…也…        c) 既…也…        d) 一边…一边…

2. 你中文电影看得 _____ 多，你的听力就提高得 _____ 快。

   a) 越…越…        b) 连…也…        c) 既…也…        d) 一边…一边…

3. 考试的时候，他 _____ 不心慌，_____ 不紧张。

   a) 越…越…        b) 连…也…        c) 既…也…        d) 一边…一边…

4. 他 _____ 汉语水平考试的综合填空 _____ 不觉得难。

   a) 越…越…        b) 连…也…        c) 既…也…        d) 一边…一边…

5. 你的方法我们 _____ 用 _____ 感到有收获。

    a) 越…越…       b) 连…也…       c) 既…也…       d) 一边…一边…

## B. *Fill in the Blanks: Adverbs*

Look at the adverbs below and choose the best one to fill in each blank.

1. 你连这么简单的字都不认识，你这种水平 _____ 就不可能参加汉语水平考试。

    a) 其实         b)原来         c) 到底         d) 根本

2. 连这么简单的填空题，你也填不对，你 _____ 复习了没有？

    a) 其实         b) 原来        c) 到底         d) 根本

3. 这些考题看起来很容易， _____ 做起来非常难。

    a) 其实         b) 原来        c) 到底         d) 根本

4. 怪不得你觉得这次考试很容易， _____ 你已经考过一次了。

    a) 其实         b) 原来        c) 到底         d) 根本

5. 你想得出想不出来一个 _____ 解决问题的方法？

    a) 其实         b) 原来        c) 到底         d) 根本

6. 你 _____ 准备怎么解决这个问题？

    a) 其实         b) 原来        c) 到底         d) 根本

## C. *Sentence Construction*

Rewrite the following sentences by using each of the emphatic structures given below.

1. 他喜欢一个东西，不问价钱，就买了。

    连：

    凡是：

2. 老师决定所有考试的时间和方法。

    是…的：

    凡是：

3. 我从网上找到一个合适的工作。

    是…的：

    连：

4. 只要平时多做汉语水平考试模拟考题，就能提高汉语水平考试的成绩。

谁：

凡是：

---

##  TASK 3. 翻译 (FĀNYÌ) PARAPHRASING

Translate the following sentences into Chinese.

1. For people whose mother tongue is not English, if they want to go to college or graduate school in America, they must take the TOEFL (托福, Tuōfú) exam. (Hint: 凡是…都)

2. A: My Chinese listening skills are very bad. I cannot even understand a single sentence; how could I understand a video tape? (Hint: 连…都…)

   B: Before you say that you will not be able to understand, why don't you even give it a try? (Hint: 连… 都…) The lower your self-confidence, the worse your listening skills will be. (Hint: 越…越…)

3. Before, the more I studied the grammatical structures, the more confused I became. (Hint: 越…越…) However, last time when I previewed the lesson with my roommate, I felt that I learned a lot (Hint: 收获). My roommate's level of Chinese is very high (Hint: 水平). Whether it is reading comprehension or comprehensive fill-in-the-blanks there is nothing he can't do! (Hint: 根本, 没有…不…) He can answer all the questions I ask him. (Hint: 凡是…都) Now the more I learn, the more I want to learn. (Hint: 越…越) I even feel that my self-confidence is getting higher and higher. (Hint: 连…也…, 越来越…) Now even on weekends I ask my roommate to go to the library and study with me. (Hint: 连…都…)

---

##  TASK 4. 情景对话 (QÍNGJǏNG DUÌHUÀ) SITUATIONAL DIALOGUE

| | |
|---|---|
| **Setting:** | A dorm room |
| **Cast:** | Two students |
| **Situation:** | You and a friend are discussing whether or not you want to take the HSK this year. Discuss the pros and cons. How long have you been studying Chinese, and do you feel like you will be ready for the exam? Are either of you planning to visit China this year? How much time will it take to study for the exam, and do you feel you will be prepared? Remember to use the vocabulary from this lesson, and have fun! |

# Appendix 1:
# List of Grammar Points

| Description | Lesson | Section |
|---|---|---|
| The Perfect Aspect 了 (Le) | 21 | I. |
| Summary of the Adverb 还 | 21 | II. |
| 多 and 少 as Adverbs | 21 | III. |
| Using the Preposition 为 | 21 | IV. |
| The Modal Particle 了 (Le) | 22 | I. |
| English Past Tense vs. Verb 了 | 22 | II. |
| Using Measure Words 次 (Cì) and 遍 (Biàn) | 22 | III. |
| Using the Preposition 离 (Lí) | 22 | IV. |
| The Impending Future Aspect | 23 | I. |
| The Perfect Aspect 了 with Repeated Verbs or 一下儿 | 23 | II. |
| Using the Adverb 又 (Yòu) | 23 | III. |
| Using 别/不要 (Bié/Bú Yào) | 23 | IV. |
| Time-duration Words | 24 | I. |
| Comparing 就 (Jiù) with 才 (Cái) | 24 | II. |
| Indicating Approximate Numbers | 24 | III. |
| Using 过 (Guò) to Talk about Past Experience | 25 | I. |
| Using 次/遍 (Cont'd.) | 25 | II. |
| The Time-duration Words (Cont'd.) | 25 | III. |
| A Brief Introduction to the "是…的" Structure | 25 | IV. |
| Modal Particle 了 (Cont'd.) | 26 | I. |
| Sentences without a Definite Subject | 26 | II. |
| Using "越来越…" (Yuè Lái Yuè…) | 26 | III. |
| Using "又…又…" (Yòu…Yòu…) | 26 | IV. |
| The Continuing Aspect Particle 着 (Zhe) | 27 | I. |

# Appendix 2:
# Traditional Character Texts

請吃飯
**Come Eat with Us!**

很多中國人搬了家以後，都會請自己的朋友來家裡吃飯。這叫慶祝"喬遷之喜[1]"。慶祝"喬遷之喜"也是一種中國文化。吳文德上個星期剛搬了家，林笛和李麗莉覺得這是一個大家能在一起說說話、吃吃飯、開開玩笑、放鬆放鬆的好機會！所以，一天下午林笛找了一個時間給吳文德打了一個電話。下面請看吳文德和他的室友高朋請林笛和李麗莉到家裡慶祝"喬遷之喜"的一個小故事。

（一天下午林笛在她的宿舍給吳文德打電話。）

林笛：喂，吳文德，那天面試你去了嗎？

吳文德：去了。一切順利。我下個星期去簽證。

林笛：太好了。我們應該慶祝慶祝。我請客。

吳文德：不敢當。不敢當。你幫我找了新住處，還幫我找了一位好室友。我得好好謝謝你。我來請客。

林笛：對啊。喬遷之喜，你應該請我和李麗莉吃飯。

吳文德：喬遷之喜是甚麼意思啊？

林笛：喬遷之喜就是慶祝搬新家。你搬了家，應該請我們大家去你那兒吃飯。

吳文德：好吧。這個星期六晚上，你們來我們的新家吃飯，怎麼樣？高朋做的飯你們一定喜歡吃。

林笛：太好了，李麗莉聽了一定非常高興，謝謝你們。

（星期六晚上，大家都在吳文德和高朋的餐廳裡。）

李麗莉：你們的餐廳真漂亮。

林笛：今天你們請我們吃甚麼好菜？這麼香！我都快餓死了。

吳文德：高師傅[2]今天做的都是他的拿手菜，有葷菜也有素菜。大家趁熱吃吧。

高朋：對，大家別客氣。這個魚你們嘗了沒有？

李麗莉：嘗了，真好吃。你也吃吧。我們自己來。

吳文德：高師傅做的雞肉也非常好吃，但是，這個菜用筷子吃太費勁了。

林笛：以後你去中國學習，每天都要用筷子。你應該多練習用筷子吃飯。

吳文德：但是我現在這麼瘦，再用筷子吃飯，半天吃一點兒，怎麼能長胖呢？

高朋：吳文德，別開玩笑了。快吃飯吧。

吳文德：遵命。但是我想少吃一點飯，多吃一點兒甜點。咱們現在上甜點，好嗎？

高朋：好。……甜點來了。大家慢慢吃。

……

李麗莉：我吃了這麼多甜點。我現在太飽了。

高朋：今天是喬遷之喜，應該多吃一點兒。你們渴不渴？想不想喝茶？

林笛：我有一點兒渴。你幫我倒一杯吧。

吳文德：來，我們今天慶祝喬遷之喜，一人喝一杯酒，怎麼樣？

李麗莉：好，我來祝酒。為你們的新家乾杯。

林笛：也為我們的友誼乾杯。

大家：乾杯！

## Lesson 22

辦簽證
### How Do I Get a Visa?

很多學中文的學生都希望能有一次去中國的機會。但是，去中國一定要辦簽證，你知道怎麼辦去中國的簽證嗎？你知道辦簽證要帶甚麼東西嗎？你知道怎麼填簽證申請表嗎？李麗莉的簽證辦得非常順利。可是，吳文德的簽證辦得不太順利，他去了好幾次中國大使館。你知道為甚麼嗎？下面請看吳文德去中國大使館辦簽證的小故事。

（剛上完了中文課，吳文德和李麗莉在教室聊天。）

吳文德：李麗莉，你去中國的簽證辦了嗎？

李麗莉：辦了。大使館離我家很近。我上個月就辦了簽證了。現在離我們去中國還有一個月。你的簽證辦了沒有？

吳文德：還沒有辦。我家離大使館太遠了。我得找個時間從學校去大使館。辦簽證都需要帶些甚麼東西？

李麗莉：學校的錄取通知書，美國護照，照片，還要帶美金。你得抓緊時間去辦簽證了。

吳文德：我知道。我這個星期就去辦簽證。辦簽證還要填表吧？

李麗莉：當然要填。你填表的時候一定要細心。字一定要寫得很清楚。寫得不清楚，大使館說不定會拒簽。

吳文德：你放心吧。我這個人辦事兒，不會有錯兒。

（在中國大使館）

吳文德：請問，這是中國大使館簽證處嗎？

工作人員：對。辦簽證請在那邊排隊。

……

吳文德：您好，麻煩您給我辦一個去中國的簽證。

工作人員：你辦甚麼簽證？旅遊簽證，學生簽證，還是工作簽證？

吳文德：學生簽證。這是中國學校的錄取通知書。這是我填的簽證申請表。

工作人員：請稍等。你的國籍怎麼沒有填？這是一個錯別字。請不要塗改。

吳文德：麻煩你再給我一張簽證申請表吧。我重填一遍。這次一定是天衣無縫[1]。

（幾分鐘以後……）

吳文德：表填好了，您看看，這次我填的表怎麼樣？

工作人員：不錯。但是你忘了簽名了。請在這兒簽名。……很好。您帶護照了嗎？

吳文德：帶了。咦……我的護照上哪兒去了？請稍等，我再找一下兒。……對不起，我可能忘了帶了。

工作人員：對不起，沒有護照不能辦簽證。你明天再來吧。

（下午在學校圖書館）

李麗莉：今天上午你怎麼沒上課，你去哪兒了？

吳文德：我吃了早飯，就去中國大使館了。

李麗莉：你辦好簽證了嗎？

吳文德：沒有。我忘帶護照了。我明天再去。反正辦簽證總是要去大使館兩次。一次申請簽證，一次取簽證。

李麗莉：你明天辦了簽證，就不再去取簽證了嗎[2]？

## Lesson 23

# 送人
## Seeing Someone Off

李麗莉和吳文德就要去北京了。林笛開車送他們去飛機場。到了飛機場以後，林笛去停車，李麗莉和吳文德去托運行李，取登機牌。吳文德給李麗莉要了一個靠走道的座位，給自己要了一個靠窗口的座位。他們辦完了登機手續以後，又去看了一下到港--離港的屏幕，飛機還是準時起飛。他們真的就要離開美國了。下面請看他們在飛機場辦手續的小故事。

（在去飛機場的路上）

林笛：快要到飛機場了，你們馬上就要離開美國了。

吳文德：是啊，我真高興。我們明天就要到北京了。

林笛：我難過極了。真不想讓你們走。

李麗莉：別難過了。我們也不想離開你。要不，你跟我們一起走吧。

林笛：別開玩笑了，我沒有簽證，想走也走不了[1]。前邊就是進站口了，你們去托運行李，取登機牌，我去停車。我們一會兒在那兒碰頭。

（在飛機場）

工作人員：您好，去哪兒？

　李麗莉：中國北京。這是我們的護照和機票。

工作人員：托運幾件行李？

　吳文德：四件。我們換飛機的時候，還要取行李嗎？

工作人員：不用，行李可以直接到北京。

　吳文德：麻煩你給我們一個靠窗口的座位，一個靠走道的座位。好嗎？

　李麗莉：我有的時候暈機，你能不能給我們兩個前邊的座位？

工作人員：我查查有沒有你們要的座位，請稍等……你們的座位是 A6 和 C6。這是你們的登機牌，
　　　　　請到 14 號登機口登機。祝你們旅途愉快。

（吳文德看了看時間跟李麗莉說）

　吳文德：李麗莉，時間還早，我還想再去買一杯咖啡。你在這兒等等，好不好？

　李麗莉：你怎麼又要喝咖啡。一會兒又要上廁所，多麻煩啊。你看，林笛來了。

　　林笛：你們的登機手續都辦好了嗎？行李都托運了嗎？

　吳文德：都辦了，行李也托運了。我們去候機室等飛機吧。那兒還有咖啡。

　　林笛：等一等，咱們再看一下到港--離港的屏幕，看看飛機是不是準時起飛。

　吳文德：剛才我看了一下兒，飛機還是準時起飛。

　　林笛：我們再看一下兒嘛。要是飛機晚點，我們還可以再說一會兒話。

……

　吳文德：前邊就到安全檢查口了，林笛你回學校吧。

　　林笛：好吧，李麗莉我給你買的那些暈機藥，你又忘了吃，是不是？上了飛機以後，別再忘了。
　　　　　祝你們一路平安，到了北京，就給我打電話。

　李麗莉：一定，謝謝。再見。

（在 14 號登機口）

　吳文德：飛機就要起飛了。我們去排隊準備登機吧。

　李麗莉：再見了，美國！我們要去北京了。

## Lesson 24

# 到達北京機場
## We Made It!

　　飛機從美國華盛頓特區到北京要飛十幾個小時。這是李麗莉和吳文德第一次去中國。他們非常激動，不吃飯也不睡覺，想用飛機上的時間練習中文。飛機快到北京的時候，乘務員給旅客發了入關卡和入境申報表。這些表格可以用中文填寫也可以用英文，但是他們都要用中文填寫。你知道他們填表填了多長時間嗎？

（在飛機上）

乘務員：請各位旅客注意。我們的乘務員馬上就要給大家發入關卡和入境申報表了，如果您填表有困難，我們的乘務員可以給您提供幫助。

……

吳文德：你填表了嗎？

李麗莉：我正在填，填了十幾分鐘，好多字不認識，還要查字典。你呢？

吳文德：我還沒填呢。不過，學了好幾年的中文了，這種表應該不太難，用七、八分鐘就應該能完成任務。

……

李麗莉：時間過得真快呀，我們填表填了一個多小時，才完成任務。吳文德，你怎麼不說話，你在想甚麼呢？

吳文德：我在想我怎麼這麼笨？填一張表還這麼吃力。你要是不幫我，我可能現在還在填表呢。

李麗莉：這是我們第一次填表，我們又填了好幾遍，當然要費時間了。飛機已經飛了十幾個小時了，每次乘務員送飯你都不吃。你現在餓不餓？

吳文德：有一點兒餓，但是我不想吃飛機上的飯，太難吃了。我們還有兩、三個小時就到北京了。我到了北京再好好吃飯。

……

吳文德：到北京了嗎？我睡了多長時間？

李麗莉：你真能睡[1]，睡了三個多小時了。

吳文德：飛機晚點了？

李麗莉：聽說晚了一個多小時，不過現在飛機已經開始下降了。

吳文德：飛機真的快要到北京機場了。我們準備下飛機吧。咦，我的行李在哪兒？

李麗莉：哎呀，你的行李在上邊的行李架子上。你別太激動了。

（下了飛機以後。）

吳文德：李麗莉，你看，那個人的牌子上有我們的名字，接我們的人在那兒。

李麗莉：你好，你是陳小雲吧？我是你的筆友李麗莉。

陳小雲：你好，李麗莉。我們通了那麼多次電話，寫了那麼多電子郵件，總算見面了。這位一定是吳文德吧。

吳文德：對。我是吳文德，謝謝你來機場接我們。

陳小雲：別客氣。我們頭回生，二回熟，三回成朋友[2]。你們路上辛苦了。

吳文德：路上還可以，挺順利。但是，我們飛了二十多個小時了，我還沒有吃飯，都快餓死了。

陳小雲：那我們取了行李，就去吃飯。我請客。

李麗莉：太好了，我們想在中國吃真正的中國飯想了二十多年了。

## Lesson 25

體檢
## Getting a Physical Examination

很多中國的大學都有自己的醫務所。學校的醫務所給學生體檢，還做簡單的治療。吳文德到學校已經快一個星期了。但是，他總是覺得不舒服，也沒精神。學校讓新生體檢。吳文德因為學習很忙，沒有時間去。但是，這幾天，他覺得他還是應該去學校的醫務所檢查一下兒。所以，他給陳小雲打了個電話，請她幫幫忙。

（吳文德在給陳小雲打電話。）

吳文德：喂，陳小雲，你去過學校的醫務所嗎？

陳小雲：去過一次，我去那兒做過體檢，但是，已經半年多沒去了。你有事嗎？

吳文德：我總是覺得沒精神，想去醫務所檢查一下兒。但是不知道醫務所在哪兒？

陳小雲：你人生地不熟的[1]，我帶你去吧。我明天早上十點下課。下了課五分鐘以後，我們在圖書館見面。我們從那兒去醫務所，好不好？

吳文德：太好了。謝謝。明天見。

（在學校醫務所）

陳小雲：這就是學校的醫務所。學校讓新生體檢，你做過體檢了嗎？

吳文德：還沒有。前幾天很忙，沒有時間。

陳小雲：先到左邊的窗口拿一張體檢表。填你的姓名、年齡、性別、國籍……

吳文德：這麼長的表格，這麼多問題，還要填地址、電話，你以前得過甚麼病……
　　　　我最不喜歡填表了。

陳小雲：快填吧。別叨叨了。填過表以後，坐在這兒等醫生叫你的名字。

……

醫生：吳文德，你好。你剛才量過身高，秤過體重了嗎？

吳文德：都做過了。這是我的體檢表。

醫生：你最近檢查過身體嗎？

吳文德：來中國以前，我檢查過一次，身體很健康。

醫生：你是甚麼時候離開美國的？

吳文德：我離開美國已經一個多星期了。

醫生：你哪兒不舒服？

吳文德：我這幾天頭疼，胃疼，不想吃飯，也沒有精神。我是不是感冒了？

醫生：來，我給你檢查一下兒。你不發燒，心臟，血壓也都很正常……我看你這是時差的問題。你剛來中國，還沒有習慣，你要多喝水，注意鍛鍊身體。過一、兩個星期就好了。不需要治療。

吳文德：謝謝。

……

陳小雲：怎麼樣？有甚麼病嗎？醫生給你開藥方了嗎？

吳文德：沒有，一切正常。醫生說是時差的問題，過幾天就好了。

陳小雲：現在天氣這麼熱，你應該注意身體，沒病應該預防，你吃過薑嗎？

吳文德：沒吃過，為甚麼要吃薑？

陳小雲：中國有句老話，"冬吃蘿蔔，夏吃薑，不勞醫生開藥方[2]"。

吳文德：你吃過薑嗎？

陳小雲：沒吃過，但是我喝過用薑沏的茶，想不想到我家去嘗一杯？

吳文德：我還是去鍛鍊鍛鍊身體吧。

## Lesson 26

# 談季節，談天氣
# Seasons and the Weather

李麗莉和吳文德剛到北京的時候，天氣又熱又悶。上個星期最熱的那一天，氣溫都達到了攝氏 40 多度。但是，最近幾天天氣開始涼快了一些了。李麗莉，吳文德和陳小雲覺得這麼好的天氣，大家應該找個時間去公園玩兒玩兒。陳小雲告訴李麗莉和吳文德她昨天晚上聽天氣預報說星期六是一個晴天，溫度不高也不低。可是，天氣預報準確不準確呢？下面請看他們那個星期六去公園玩兒的一個小故事。

（在學校圖書館外邊）

李麗莉：今天的天氣真好。真舒服。

吳文德：是啊。剛到北京的時候，天氣太熱了。

陳小雲：北京六月、七月、八月都熱。最熱的時候，氣溫能達到攝氏 40 多度。

李麗莉：北京是不是一年也有春、夏、秋、冬、四個季節？

陳小雲：對。但是春季和秋季短，夏季和冬季長。

吳文德：陳小雲，春、夏、秋、冬四季，你最喜歡哪個季節？

陳小雲：我最喜歡秋天。北京十月的秋天最好。

李麗莉：為甚麼？

陳小雲：那時候，天氣不冷也不熱。樹葉都紅了，又舒服又漂亮。

李麗莉：我覺得春天最好。天氣暖和了，花兒都開了，草也綠了……多漂亮啊！

陳小雲：不錯。但是北京的春天常常颳大風。

吳文德：北京的冬天怎麼樣？很冷嗎？

陳小雲：冬天很冷，最低氣溫能達到零下 20 度，常常下雪。

吳文德：現在應該是秋天了吧？天氣不那麼熱了。

陳小雲：八月六號就立秋了，但是有時候秋老虎非常厲害。八月二十一號是處暑，處暑以後天氣才開
　　　　始越來越涼快。

李麗莉：現在天氣這麼好，我們應該找個時間去公園玩兒玩兒。

陳小雲：行啊，天氣預報說今天晚上陰天，攝氏二十四度，有小雨。明天星期五多雲轉晴。星期六晴，
　　　　有小風。最高溫度二十六度。最低溫度二十四度。

吳文德：星期六天氣很舒服。我們去公園玩兒玩兒吧。

（星期六早上）

李麗莉：天氣預報會不會不準確呢？你們看天這麼陰，說不定會下雨。我們是不是應該拿一把傘？

陳小雲：不用拿傘。昨天天快黑的時候，半個天都是紅的。中國人常說：“早霞不出門，晚霞行
　　　　千里[1]。”你們放心吧，我的天氣預報不會錯。

吳文德：別吹牛了，我的天氣預報專家，你看現在開始颳風了，一會兒說不定真有雨呢。

陳小雲：你們別杞人憂天[2]了。今天是大晴天，我說沒有雨就沒雨。

（剛到公園一會兒，就開始下大雨了，李麗莉和吳文德撒腿就跑。）

陳小雲：你們別跑呀，前面也有雨。你們誰帶傘了？

## Lesson 27

# 去郵局
## Mail and the Post Office

　　中國的郵局服務項目很多，可以寄東西，可以打電話，可以買信封、郵票、明信片，還可以買雜誌、
報紙。在中國寄包裹要填包裹單，寄掛號信，要填掛號單。在美國寄信、寄包裹的時候信封的左上邊
寫著寄件人的地址，信封的中間寫著收件人的地址。在中國寄東西，左上邊應該寫收件人的地址，右
下邊寫寄件人的地址。吳文德覺得自己學了好幾年的中文了，寫中文地址應該沒有問題。但是他會不
會在包裹上寫中文地址呢？下面是吳文德寄包裹的一個小故事。

（在宿舍樓外面，李麗莉笑著問吳文德）

李麗莉：吳文德，你去哪兒？你手裡拿著甚麼？

吳文德：一個包裹。我去郵局給我家寄東西。

李麗莉：你知道地址怎麼寫嗎？

吳文德：學了這麼長時間的中文，寫地址還能不會？小菜一碟兒[1]。你放心吧。

（在郵局裡面）

吳文德：這個郵局開著這麼多窗口，每個窗口上都掛著一個牌子，我的眼睛都看花了。

營業員：每個窗口都有自己的服務項目。有的窗口可以寄包裹；有的窗口可以買郵票、信封。您是不
　　　　是要寄包裹？

吳文德：是啊。我應該去哪個窗口呢？

營業員：寄東西要填包裹單。您先坐著慢慢地填，然後去一號窗口。

吳文德：取包裹在哪個窗口？

營業員：(營業員指著一號窗口的牌子說)您看，一號窗口的牌子上面寫著"包裹"。寄包裹、取包裹都在那兒。

吳文德：謝謝。

(在一號窗口前)

吳文德：你好。我想給美國紐約寄一個包裹。這是我填的包裹單。

營業員：您帶證件了嗎？

吳文德：我有學生證，學生證也是證件吧？

營業員：對，我來秤一下包裹的重量。您要寄航空還是海運？

吳文德：哪種好？

營業員：寄航空快，兩個星期就到了。寄海運要兩、三個月，但是便宜。

吳文德：寄海運吧。你這兒也賣郵票和明信片嗎？

營業員：買郵票，買明信片都在三號窗口。您看三號窗口的牌子上寫著"航空信-掛號信-郵票"。左邊的櫃台裡放著十幾種明信片，您慢慢地選吧。

吳文德：謝謝！

(李麗莉在吳文德宿舍學習，有人在外面叫吳文德的名字。)

郵遞員：吳文德的包裹，請簽字。

吳文德：好，謝謝。咦，這個包裹怎麼這麼面熟。

李麗莉：哎呀，吳文德，你地址寫反了，這是你要寄紐約的包裹，怎麼寄到自己這兒了呢[2]？在中國寄東西，左上邊應該寫收件人的地址，右下邊寫寄件人的地址。

吳文德：我去寄包裹的那天早上你為甚麼不告訴我呢？

## Lesson 28

# 找路
# Knowing Where to Go

在中國，自己有車的人不多。出門常坐出租車有些貴。所以，很多人都坐公共汽車或地鐵。如果你在中國沒乘過公共汽車或坐過地鐵，有機會的時候，一定要去試試。吳文德在中國已經好幾個星期了。但是他沒有坐過公共汽車。有一天，吳文德要去購物中心給他媽媽買禮物，他覺得中國的公共汽車那麼多，坐公共汽車一定也很容易。所以，他讓李麗莉陪他一起坐公共汽車去。下面請看吳文德帶李麗莉坐公共汽車去購物中心的小故事。

(星期六早上吃過早飯以後，吳文德到李麗莉的宿舍來找李麗莉。)

吳文德：我媽媽的生日快到了，我得去購物中心買個禮物。上次我寄包裹鬧了一個大笑話。這次去購物中心不能再出醜了。你陪我去購物中心吧。

李麗莉：好吧。我和陳小雲上次坐出租車去，十分鐘就到了。坐地鐵可能也很方便。

吳文德：但是地鐵路線我還不熟悉，打的又太貴。我們坐公交去吧。

李麗莉：你坐過公交嗎？

吳文德：我沒坐過公交，但是我知道公交的路線。先在學校門口坐 22 路車，再換 9 路車就到了。咱們走吧。

（在學校門口）

李麗莉：來了好幾輛公共汽車，怎麼都不是 22 路？

吳文德：是啊，等了十幾分鐘了。我去問問。請問 22 路汽車甚麼時候來？

一位老師：22 路？22 路車站在學校的南門外。這是北門。你們出錯大門了。但是離這不遠的地方也有一個 22 路車站。你們從這兒往左邊拐，到第二個有紅綠燈的路口往右拐，再走十幾分鐘就能看見那個 22 路車站了。

吳文德：謝謝。（吳文德對李麗莉說）剛才是一個小小的失誤，咱們走錯大門了，現在應該不會再有錯了。

（在 22 路車上）

吳文德：怎麼樣，李麗莉，這次咱們坐對車了吧。你先往裡邊走。我去買票。

售票員：下一站就是終點站，請各位乘客拿好票，準備下車。

李麗莉：吳文德，售票員說大家都要下車了，我沒聽錯吧？

吳文德：她說甚麼我沒聽見，我去問一下兒。（對售票員說）請問，您剛才說甚麼？

售票員：下一站是終點站，請帶好自己的東西準備下車。

吳文德：就要到終點站了？請問我們去購物中心，在哪兒能換 9 路車呢？

售票員：你們坐錯方向了。你們應該坐往西開的 22 路車。這是往東開的，是開往北京醫院的 22 路車。

吳文德：那我們從這兒怎麼才能到 9 路車站呢？

售票員：你們在終點站下車，下車以後過馬路，換往西開的 22 路車。在北京圖書館站下車，下車以後往前走，過了十字路口就能看見 9 路車站了。

李麗莉：吳文德，你聽懂了嗎？

吳文德：這次我聽清楚了，你放心吧。

李麗莉：我們還是細心一點兒好。辦壞一件事太容易了。再出“南轅北轍[1]”這種事，購物中心就要關門了。

吳文德：你樂觀一點兒好不好？購物中心不是還沒關門嗎？

## Lesson 29

# 買禮物
# Choosing a Gift

在中國，一般百貨大樓裡每個櫃台都有賣東西的營業員，但是這些營業員不收錢，他們給顧客回答問題或者拿東西給顧客看。如果顧客要買東西，營業員馬上給顧客開一張發票。顧客拿著發票到收款台交錢。收款台的服務員收到錢以後，在發票上蓋紅章。顧客拿著蓋好紅章的發票，再到營業員那兒取東西。下面是李麗莉和吳文德去購物中心買東西的一個小故事。

（在購物中心）

李麗莉：如果我們沒坐錯車，我們早就到了。還好，購物中心還沒關門。時間不多了。我們快給你媽媽買禮物吧。

吳文德：我們今天沒白跑。你看這兒的東西真的比學校旁邊的百貨商店的東西多。三樓賣國畫，我們先去三樓看看吧。

李麗莉：好啊。那兒有電梯，坐電梯比走樓梯快。買完了禮物，我覺得我們應該騎自行車回學校。你給咱們買兩輛自行車吧。

吳文德：為甚麼？騎自行車沒有坐公共汽車快。

李麗莉：今天這個南轅北轍的故事你怎麼這麼快就忘了。我們如果再坐錯車，坐公交就可能真的要比騎自行車更慢呢。

吳文德：你現在一天比一天厲害，不停地揭我的短。吃一塹，長一智[1]。我們不會再走錯方向了，你放心吧。

……

（在三樓購物中心）

售貨員：請問，你們想買甚麼？

吳文德：我們想看看國畫。哪種國畫比較好？

售貨員：國畫有人物畫、山水畫和花鳥畫三種。我喜歡山水畫。您看這張山水畫畫得多漂亮啊。要不要買一張？

李麗莉：吳文德，國畫不好寄。我們去看看那邊的紗巾，好嗎？我聽說中國的真絲又有名，質量又好。

吳文德：國畫是沒有紗巾好寄，但是，給我媽媽送真絲紗巾是不是有點兒太輕了？

李麗莉：千里送鴻毛，禮輕情意重[2]嘛。我們去看看吧。

……

李麗莉：這麼多種紗巾，一條比一條漂亮。吳文德，你看那條更漂亮，上面還有國畫呢。

吳文德：那條紗巾比其它的都漂亮。質量也好，我媽媽一定會喜歡。請問，那條紗巾多少錢一條？

售貨員：一條一百六十五塊八毛錢。

吳文德：真不貴，比在美國買便宜。麻煩你給我拿一條。

售貨員：好。我給您開一張發票，請到前邊的收款台交錢，然後再來取貨。

（在收款台）

吳文德：我沒有零錢，這是二百塊。

收款員：找您三十四塊兩毛。這是您的發票，請收好，你買的東西如果有問題，可以憑收據來退換。

吳文德：謝謝。再見！

## Lesson 30

# 逛夜市
# Browsing at the Night Market

中國夜市非常熱鬧。每天晚上天快黑的時候，小販就在夜市的街道兩邊擺起了小攤子，開始賣東西。夜市的東西比商店的便宜，顧客還可以討價還價。但是在夜市裡買的東西不能保證質量，買了以後一般不能退換。討價還價的最好方法是用本地話。如果你是外地人，小販就會想辦法跟你多要錢。下面請看李麗莉和吳文德逛夜市的故事。

（在李麗莉的房間。）

吳文德：李麗莉，我們今天晚上去逛逛夜市吧，練一練討價還價的本領。

李麗莉：我看咱們別去了。夜市的小販跟商店的營業員不一樣，他們太油了。我們不會講價錢，去了一定會吃虧。

吳文德：我們只去看看熱鬧，不買東西，怎麼會吃虧呢？咱們走吧。早一點兒去夜市，人會少一些。

（吳文德和李麗莉到夜市的時候，小販們已經在忙著賣東西了。）

小販：先生，今天我的東西大降價，打八折。我這兒有毛衣，有西服；要不，您買一件襯衫吧。您看這件襯衫多好啊，百分之百真絲的。比您身上穿的那件帥多了。

吳文德：我們不買東西，只是看一看。

小販：你們不會說本地話，一定是外地人吧？

李麗莉：我們是美國人。

小販：可是你們說的中國話跟美國人說的不一樣。你們的中文說得真棒！

李麗莉：哪裡，哪裡。你過獎了。

小販：美國人最喜歡買我的牛仔褲。我這兒長的、短的、肥的、瘦的都有。您要不要買一條？穿多大公分的？您要是再晚來半小時，就沒有了。

李麗莉：謝謝。牛仔褲我不想買。這種夾克多少錢一件？都有甚麼顏色的？

小販：三百五十塊一件。我這兒有藍的、有黑的、也有深紅色的。質量很好，是全棉的。您試試吧。如果您買兩件，三百塊一件。每件便宜五十塊。

吳文德：李麗莉，小心上當受騙[1]。這兒的東西可都是金玉其外，敗絮其中[2]。

……

小販：小姐，您不胖，不瘦，長得苗條，上次來的一個姑娘穿這種夾克就沒有您穿著好看。這兩件夾克就跟給您訂做的一樣，長短、肥瘦正合適。您穿這兩件，就跟電影明星一樣。

李麗莉：這件黑色夾克跟那件藍色夾克有甚麼不一樣？

小販：一樣。您穿這件黑色的跟穿那件藍色的一樣好看。

李麗莉：可是，這兩件不一樣長。這件黑色的比藍色的長一點兒。

小販：差不多，只長三釐米。要不，您再少給十塊錢吧，我今天要賠本兒了。

李麗莉：這兩件夾克我都想買。但是，藍色的三百塊，黑色的兩百九十塊。一共五百九十塊。太貴了！能不能便宜一點兒？五百五十塊，你賣不賣？

小販：不能再便宜了。我真的沒賺上幾個錢。

吳文德：李麗莉，你講價錢沒有小販講得那麼油，小心吃虧。你看，這件夾克上邊的顏色比下邊的要深得多。算了吧。別買了。

小販：那是一種新樣式。好吧。您交五百五十塊。唉，我這次賠本賠大了。

李麗莉：好。這是六百塊。麻煩你給我找五十塊。

## Lesson 31

## 去銀行
## Opening a Bank Account

在中國，每家銀行的利息都是一樣的，外匯的兌換率也是一樣的。中國的銀行有大有小，大的銀行有叫號機，顧客不用站在視窗前邊排隊。進了銀行以後，先拿一個號碼，然後坐在椅子上等叫號機在螢幕上顯示自己的號碼。等輪到你的時候，叫號機會告訴你去幾號視窗。小的銀行因為沒有叫號機，所以顧客得站在櫃檯前排隊，一般也沒有外匯服務項目。外國學生在中國開銀行帳戶的時候，不用拿號，可直接去外匯視窗。下面請看吳文德和李麗莉去銀行存錢、取錢的小故事。

（一輛計程車在銀行門口停住了。李麗莉和吳文德下了車，就進了銀行。）

吳文德：這個銀行這麼大，開著這麼多視窗，我應該去哪個視窗呢？

李麗莉：存美金去外匯視窗。我先去問一下兒在哪兒能辦外卡取現，一會兒見。

（在銀行的一個辦公室裡。）

李麗莉：你好。我聽說在你們這個銀行我可以用美國的信用卡取一些人民幣，對嗎？

營業員：對。這種手續叫外卡取現。今天美金和人民幣的兌換率是 1 比 8.4[1]。您想取多少？

李麗莉：我取兩百五十塊。謝謝。

（外匯視窗）

吳文德：你好。麻煩你給我開一個銀行帳戶。

營業員：您要存多少錢？想存定期，還是活期？

吳文德：我想存五百美金。你給我開一個活期的帳戶吧。

營業員：這麼多美金都存活期，不值得。活期利息很低。

吳文德：定期利息高嗎？

營業員：定期利息雖然也不高。但是比活期高一些。

吳文德：好極了。麻煩你幫我把這張兩百美元的旅行支票存在活期帳戶裡，把這張三百美元的私人支票存在定期帳戶裡，好不好？

營業員：旅行支票是銀行支票。我可以馬上給您存。但是私人支票要等錢到銀行後，才能給您開定期存款單。

吳文德：那我要等多長時間？

營業員：要等二到四個星期。等錢到了銀行，我們會給您打電話。這是您的活期帳號的存摺。您以後
每次存錢、取錢都會記錄在這個存摺上。

吳文德：太好了！有了存摺，我就能記住我銀行裡還有多少錢了。

營業員：有了銀行帳戶，您現在可以申請辦借記卡或者信用卡了。

吳文德：借記卡和信用卡哪種好？

營業員：都好。但是借記卡容易辦，可是不能超支。信用卡可以超支。但是辦信用卡不但自己在銀行
要有帳戶，而且還要有人擔保才能辦。

吳文德：這麼麻煩！你給我辦一張借記卡吧。我這個人總是丟三落四的[2]。我要是把現金丟了，那就
太可惜了。

……

李麗莉：看你那個高興的樣子，你的銀行帳戶一定辦好了。

吳文德：我不但銀行帳戶辦好了，而且還辦了一個借記卡。我以後任何時候都能從門口外邊的自助機
裡取錢、存錢、查帳號。方便不方便？

李麗莉：方便！你現在有卡了，就不應該一毛不拔[3]了吧？現在越來越多的商店都可以刷卡了，很多
飯館也收借記卡。我們現在去吃飯，你請客怎麼樣？

## Lesson 32

# 訂火車票
# Taking the Train

在中國，很多人出去旅遊的時候，都喜歡乘火車，因為火車比飛機便宜。乘火車可以選硬座、軟座、
硬臥和軟臥。硬座最便宜，軟臥最貴最舒服。火車票可以直接在火車站的售票處買，也可以在火車站
代售點買。有些地方還可以上網，或打電話預訂。李麗莉和吳文德想乘火車到西安去玩玩兒。他們會
不會買火車票？買的是哪種火車票？下面請看他們買火車票的故事。

（李麗莉在宿舍看書，外邊有人敲門。）

李麗莉：進來。

吳文德：來北京這麼長時間，還沒到外地玩兒過。現在要放長假了，我們出去到外地逛一逛，見見世面，
好不好？我們再不出去，就快成井底之蛙[1]了。

李麗莉：好是好，可是我們去哪兒玩呢？

吳文德：我一直想到西安去看看，那兒有著名的兵馬俑。我聽說那些兵和馬都跟真人真馬一樣。你想
不想去看看？

李麗莉：想是想，可是誰帶我們去呢？陳小雲還沒有從上海回來呢。

吳文德：不要緊。你聽說過塞翁失馬[2]的故事嗎？陳小雲不在，我們自己坐火車去，既學了本領，
又見了世面。這不是壞事變成好事嗎？

李麗莉：那我們得趕快訂火車票，我聽說火車票很難買。既不能上網預訂，也不能打電話預訂。

吳文德：那是老皇曆了，現在火車票比以前好買多了。你就等著我的好消息吧。

（第二天早上，吳文德在火車站售票處）

吳文德：我想買兩張下個晚上從北京去西安的火車票。都有幾點的火車？

售票員：列車時刻表在牆上掛著呢。晚上從北京出發去西安的是 K81 次特快，晚上 7:50 分出發，第二天早上 9:30 分到。

吳文德：這趟車時間很方便，請你給我買兩張來回票。

售票員：您要買甚麼票？硬座、軟座還是臥鋪？硬臥、軟臥？

吳文德：硬座、軟座不能睡覺，短途還可以，長途太累，軟臥又太貴了。麻煩您給我兩張硬臥吧。

售票員：對不起，沒有下鋪了。上鋪、中鋪行不行？

吳文德：可以。謝謝。

（吳文德從火車站回來以後就給李麗莉打電話。）

吳文德：我給咱們買了兩張下個星期四去西安的硬臥票。你想過來取票，還是讓我給你送去。

李麗莉：我正忙著呢，你給我送來好嗎？

吳文德：好吧。下鋪沒有了，我買了一張上鋪，一張中鋪。你想要哪張？

李麗莉：上鋪上來下去很不方便。你給我一張中鋪吧。

吳文德：好，一會兒見。

（在李麗莉的宿舍。）

吳文德：我明天給咱們定一個旅遊計畫。我當導遊，帶你去參觀西安的名勝古跡。照一些漂漂亮亮的風景照片，給你家寄去，你家裡的人一定會很羨慕你。

李麗莉：你也沒去過西安，怎麼當導遊呢？

吳文德：我買了一本西安旅遊指南，還有一張大大的西安地圖。我當導遊沒問題。

李麗莉：吳文德，你當導遊，要是我能在西安火車站照幾張相給我爸爸媽媽寄去，我就滿足了。

吳文德：哎，你這個人太悲觀了。

## Lesson 33

## 風味小吃
## A Taste of China

小吃店跟飯館不太一樣。小吃店一般比飯館便宜。小吃店吃的東西一般是一種地方風味的。有些小一點兒的小吃店，沒有菜單。小吃的名字和價格都寫在牌子上。有的小吃店沒有服務員。點菜要到櫃檯去點。西安的回民小吃很有名。所以，李麗莉和吳文德到了西安以後，第一件事就是去嘗嘗西安的回民小吃。下面請看他們在小吃店吃小吃的故事。

（從火車站出來）

李麗莉：坐了一晚上的火車，我現在又累又餓，我們先去吃一點兒東西吧。

吳文德：好啊，西安的羊肉泡饃很有名，離這兒不遠有一家回民小吃店。我帶你去嘗嘗吧。

（李麗莉和吳文德從火車站對面那條馬路穿過去，走過兩條街，十幾分鐘後，就走進了一家回民小吃店。一個服務員走了過來。）

服務員：幾位？

李麗莉：兩位。

服務員：樓下已經滿了，請跟我來，我帶你們上樓去。樓上還有好幾張桌子。

吳文德：這家小吃店的小吃一定不錯，你看，顧客很多，差不多都沒有空位了。

……

吳文德：我一走進來就覺得餓了，快坐下來點菜吧。

李麗莉：勞駕，你們有菜單嗎？

服務員：沒有。牆上掛著價格表。我們店有二十多種風味小吃，有甜的、有鹹的、有酸的、有辣的、有熱的、也有冷的……你們先看看再點吧，一定有適合你們口味的。

（幾分鐘以後，服務員又走了過來。）

服務員：你們想來一點兒甚麼？

吳文德：我們是第一次來這兒。你給我們推薦幾個菜吧。

服務員：我們這兒羊肉泡饃非常有名，味道純正，要不要嘗嘗？

吳文德：我餓極了，給我兩碗吧。對不起，我口淡，請不要放太多鹽。

服務員：好。小姐，您想吃一點兒甚麼？

李麗莉：我想吃一點兒素的。

服務員：我們這是回民小吃。吃得東西都是素的。我們這兒的油餅都是用素油炸的，香噴噴的。豆漿也是剛剛煮好的，熱騰騰的。保證讓你吃得樂呵呵的。想不想嘗一嘗？

李麗莉：好，我聽你的。給我兩個油餅，一碗豆漿，豆漿請不要加糖，我不喜歡吃甜的。

服務員：請稍等幾分鐘，我很快就給你們送過來。

吳文德：怪不得這家小吃店生意這麼好，你看這兒的服務員服務得多周到。我們應該多給一些小費來感謝他。

李麗莉：在中國吃飯，一般都不用給小費。

……

服務員：來了，二位點的小吃都到齊了，要是不夠可以再點。

吳文德：真香。我一聞到香味，就更餓了。我一會兒可能還得再要一碗。

……

李麗莉：吳文德，你第一碗幾分鐘就吃完了，怎麼第二碗吃了這麼長時間還在吃？你是不是眼大肚子小[1]，吃不完了？

吳文德：誰說吃不完？我吃得完。這飯實在是好吃。你耐心地等一會兒。讓我慢慢吃。

李麗莉：飽了就別再使勁吃了。肚子撐破了不值得[2]。要不，咱們把剩下的打包，帶回旅館去，晚上再吃。咱們走吧。

吳文德：我太撐了！現在已經站不起來了，怎麼能走得到旅館去呢？等一會兒再走，好不好？

## Lesson 34

## 住旅館
## Staying in a Hotel

去中國旅遊，訂旅館可以上網預訂也可以打電話預訂，如果你不知道旅館的電話號碼，可以打 114 查電話號碼。在中國住旅館一定要有證件。只有好一些的旅館才允許招待外國人。能招待外國人的旅館裡，一般每個房間裡都有純淨水，因為中國的自來水不能喝。現在很多的旅館還有給顧客訂飛機票和火車票的服務項目。下面是李麗莉和吳文德在西安住旅館的小故事。

（從小吃店出來）

吳文德：這家小吃店真不錯，我下火車的時候還擔心我們找不到這個小吃店呢。

李麗莉：你這個導遊當得夠水平。這家小吃店的位址你記下來了嗎？我們在離開西安以前，你再帶我過來一次，好不好？

吳文德：沒問題。我保證讓你吃個夠。我們現在打的去旅館吧。

李麗莉：打的？我聽說有些計程車司機可會"宰"人了，開著計程車在街上繞圈子。你要是問司機，他會告訴你這條路開不進去，那條路走不出來。

吳文德：這種事現在越來越少。就是真的"宰"了我們，也沒事。他的計程表旁邊有行車執照，抄下來他的執照號碼，有事可以告他。

（吳文德在馬路邊上揮了揮手，開過來了一輛計程車。）

（在旅客登記處）

吳文德：你好，我叫吳文德，她叫李麗莉。我們預訂了兩個單人間。

服務員：請稍等，我查一下……找到了。你們打算住幾個晚上？

吳文德：兩個晚上，星期天上午退房。

服務員：一個人一個晚上 120 塊。一共 480 塊。每個房間還要交 100 塊錢押金。

吳文德：交押金？為甚麼？

服務員：我看出來了，你們從來沒有在中國住過旅館。

吳文德：是啊。這是我們第一次住旅館，麻煩你給我們解釋一下。

服務員：在中國住旅館一般都要交押金。在您退房間的那天，如果您沒打長途電話，也沒有損壞東西，押金會全部退還給您。這是您房間的鑰匙，有問題請給我們前檯打電話。

（李麗莉在自己的房間給吳文德打電話。）

李麗莉：吳文德，我的房間有一些飲料，你過來我們一起喝吧。

吳文德：那些飲料你可千萬不要喝。貴得要死。在我們退房的時候，服務員就會上來檢查，少一件東西就要交一件東西的錢。每件東西的價格都貴得嚇人。

李麗莉：幸虧我還沒有喝。我還給你泡了一杯香噴噴的茶。你要不要我給你送過去？

吳文德：來不及了。還有 40 分鐘，旅遊車就要出發了。半個小時以後咱們在一樓大廳見面的時候，你給我帶下來，好不好？

李麗莉：好吧。一會兒見。

（李麗莉和吳文德在大廳裡等旅遊車。）

李麗莉：導遊先生，你走來走去的，在想甚麼呢？是不是在想明天我們應該去哪兒參觀？

吳文德：看起來你挺瞭解我。我想來想去，總算想出來了一個好主意。我們明天去嘗嘗西安著名的餃子宴，怎麼樣？

李麗莉：我早就想跟你說吃餃子宴的事了。但是，你是導遊，我不敢班門弄斧[1]。

---

## Lesson 35

# 鍛煉身體
# Keep Fit!

在中國，很多大學每年都要開一次運動會，學生想參加比賽，就可以報名參加，比賽成績好的運動員，又可以代表自己的學校參加省裡的大學生運動會。學校運動會一般要開兩、三天，學校那幾天也不上課了。不參加比賽的學生也都去為自己的朋友加油。大學生運動會很熱鬧。李麗莉自從到中國以後就很注意鍛煉身體，這次學校的運動會，她也參加了比賽。

（在學校的操場）

吳文德：陳小雲，今天李麗莉也要參加比賽。她自從來中國以後，就天天跑步鍛煉身體。

陳小雲：我知道，這次運動會，她參加了短跑和長跑比賽。吳文德，你參加比賽了沒有？

吳文德：沒有參加。我喜歡游泳，打籃球。但是大學生運動會沒有這些項目。不過，我參加了太極拳表演。

陳小雲：你是甚麼時候開始學打太極拳的？

吳文德：我是兩個月以前開始學的。太極拳課有初級班也有中級班，我一個月修一門太極拳課。

陳小雲：你真不簡單，都修到中級班了。我以前也學過太極拳，學了幾天就沒有耐心了。你是跟誰學的？

吳文德：我是跟王老師學的。想不想讓我給你表演一下？

陳小雲：免了，免了。你是中級班的學生，一定打得很像一回事兒。

吳文德：你參加比賽了嗎？

陳小雲：我這個人跑不動，參加不了比賽。我今天是來給李麗莉加油的。我還想給她照幾張照片。

吳文德：這麼遠，你能照得上嗎？

陳小雲：照得上。李麗莉能贏就好了。

吳文德：你放心。她輸不了。你看運動會開始了。

陳小雲：李麗莉跑在最前邊。就要到終點了。加油！加油！李麗莉加油！

……

陳小雲：李麗莉太棒了！得了個第一名，還打破了學校記錄。

吳文德：運動會真帶勁兒。你看觀眾比運動員還激動呢。所有的觀眾都站起來了，過了這麼長時間還在鼓掌。陳小雲，你給李麗莉照相了嗎？

陳小雲：沒照上。剛才我一著急，就打不開鏡頭了。

廣播員：現在太極拳表演就要開始了，請太極班的同學到操場東邊集合，準備排隊入場。

陳小雲：吳文德，這回該你露一手了。快去吧。

吳文德：唉呦，你看多不湊巧，我剛要走，左腳就扭了。疼得我實在站不起來了。

陳小雲：你怎麼這麼不小心，該參加表演了，腳突然又扭了。讓我給你看看。

吳文德：你看我的右腳腫得多厲害。我走不了路了。不能去表演了。

陳小雲：吳文德，你到底是哪個腳扭了？怎麼自相矛盾[1]！一會兒是左腳疼，一會兒是右腳腫的？

吳文德：不瞞你說，我是有點兒怯場了。我雖然很喜歡打太極拳，但是總是學不會。學了前邊忘後邊，現在一緊張，就都忘了。

陳小雲：你別太緊張了。你要是打太極拳打得不好，怎麼能從初級班升到中級班呢？你應該有一些自信心。

吳文德：哎，我上的兩個班都是初級班。

## Lesson 36

# 我生病了
# I Don't Feel Well...

　　在中國看病跟在美國看病不太一樣，中國的醫生一般都在醫院的門診部給病人看病。病人看病不需要預約時間，早上到醫院的掛號處掛號，拿一個號碼。等輪到自己的號碼的時候，病人才能看病。看完病，交錢取藥也在醫院的藥房裡。一天晚上李麗莉覺得全身發冷，身上沒勁兒。她用從美國帶來的體溫表給自己量了一下兒體溫，才知道自己發高燒了。第二天早上李麗莉還是病得很厲害，吳文德不得不把李麗莉帶到醫院去看病。

（李麗莉和吳文德來到了內科門診的服務台。）

吳文德：我的朋友發高燒了，體溫 104 度。請醫生先給她看看吧。

　護士：你開甚麼玩笑，100 度水都開了。請你們先去掛號處掛號。

吳文德：我沒開玩笑，她真的是 104 度。你看，這是我用的那個體溫表。

　護士：噢，我把你說的華氏當成攝氏了。華氏的 104 度也就是攝氏的 40 度。你馬上去掛號處給她掛急診。

吳文德：掛號處在哪兒？

　護士：出了這個門診大樓，往右一拐就有一座樓，一進門就是掛號處。

（在急診室，醫生正在給李麗莉看病。）

醫生李麗莉，你在發高燒，你還覺得哪兒不舒服？

李麗莉：我頭疼得厲害，嗓子疼，胸也疼，還咳嗽。

醫　生：你把嘴張開一下兒，讓我先檢查一下兒你的嗓子，嗓子有點紅腫。我聽一聽你的肺和心臟，都很正常。可是你應該先到二樓 205 室去透視，再到 208 室把血驗一驗。

……

醫　生：李麗莉，你得了重感冒。先叫護士給你打一下兒針，再去藥房取藥。退燒的藥一天吃三次，每次一片，飯後半小時吃。止咳糖漿早晚各一次，空腹吃，每次一勺。

李麗莉：我還以為我得了流感或非典了呢。感冒不傳染。我可以回家了嗎？

醫　生：可以，我給你開了五天的藥，要是吃了藥，打了針，高燒還不退，你就不能不住院治療了。

吳文德：李麗莉，你在這兒等我一下兒，我先去藥房把藥取了，再送你回宿舍。

（第二天，李麗莉正躺著休息。她看見吳文德走進來就坐了起來。）

吳文德：李麗莉，怎麼這麼客氣，不把我當作朋友了，趕快躺下。藥吃了沒有？

李麗莉：醫生的話我可不敢不聽。我不但把藥吃完了，而且把今天的針也打了，現在覺得好多了。你幫我把醫生開的假條交給老師了嗎？

吳文德：我一忙就把這事兒忘了，實在對不起，我一會兒就把你的假條送到老師的辦公室去。你的咳嗽好像好一些了。頭還疼嗎？

李麗莉：我的頭已經不疼了。你別把我這一點兒小病當成大病，好不好？

吳文德：昨天我沒把體溫的事說清楚，鬧了一個小笑話。中國用攝氏，不用華氏。我說你體溫 104 度。把護士嚇了一大跳。她以為你燒到攝氏 104 度了。

李麗莉：發燒發到攝氏 104 度，沒有人不害怕。吃一塹，長一智。下次再生病咱們就能把體溫的事說得清楚一點兒了。

吳文德：你可別亂說，生病可不是開玩笑的事。多虧那個醫生挺棒的，對症下藥[1]，一下子就把你的病治好了。不過，你要想早點兒恢復健康，你就非按時吃藥不可。不吃藥不行。

李麗莉：聽見了，吳醫生。我也希望自己早點兒恢復健康。對了，我還要麻煩你把陳小雲的筆記還給她，你可別忘了。

吳文德：你放心吧。我現在就去。再見。

## Lesson 37

過春節
### Happy Chinese New Year!

中國甚麼節日都沒有春節熱鬧。你如果有機會一定要去中國過一次春節、去聽一聽鞭炮的聲音、看一看紅燈籠、嘗一嘗餃子。我不說你也知道，過年的這種節日氣氛，你一定要在中國才能知道甚麼是真正的過年。李麗莉和吳文德就很有福氣。今年在中國過了一個春節，還學到了很多中國人過春節的風俗習慣。下面就看看李麗莉和吳文德在中國過第一個春節的小故事。

（李麗莉聽到敲門聲，把門打開一看，原來是吳文德。）

李麗莉：吳文德，哪陣風把你給吹來了[1]？

吳文德：春風啊。春節快到了，我從小到大還沒有在一年之內慶祝過兩個新年呢，真過癮！

李麗莉：元旦那個新年可比春節差遠了。春節對中國人來說，是個最大的節日。你沒看見老師、學生都回家過年去了。

吳文德：怎麼沒看見，學校都空了。我昨天到街上去了一下兒，到處都很擁擠。大人、孩子好像誰都在忙。

李麗莉：很多人家在春節之前的好幾個星期，就開始買年貨、做吃的。家家戶戶的房子都打掃得乾乾淨淨，收拾得整整齊齊。我也跟著大家湊熱鬧。你看，我的燈籠都掛好了，春聯也貼在門上了。對了，星期五是除夕，陳小雲請我們去她家吃年夜飯。

吳文德：除夕是甚麼意思？甚麼是"年夜飯"？

李麗莉：春節前一天的晚上叫除夕。除夕的晚飯，就叫作"年夜飯"。那天晚上，全家人一起吃完年夜飯之後，很多人家都是一邊包餃子，一邊看春節聯歡晚會。

吳文德：我這個人對玩兒非常感興趣。我聽說除夕之夜，很多人家都不睡覺。大家一邊聊天，一邊吃東西，一直要鬧到天亮，是真的嗎？

李麗莉：當然是真的啦。那叫守歲。

吳文德：原來守歲就是除夕晚上不睡覺啊。咱們買點兒鞭炮帶到陳小雲家去吧。

李麗莉：陳小雲家那兒不一定讓放鞭炮。我們給陳小雲的弟弟一個紅包吧。

吳文德：甚麼是"紅包"？

李麗莉："紅包"就是用紅紙把錢包好，在孩子們給大人拜年的時候，作為禮物送給孩子。

吳文德：李麗莉，佩服，佩服。你現在懂的真多，快成一個中國通了。

（春節那天上午，李麗莉和吳文德從陳小雲家出來。）

李麗莉：拜年，我以前在書上看到的意思是，春節的那天大家互相串門，互相說一些祝福的話，像"過年好"，"新年快樂"。可是給陳小雲家打電話拜年的人比到她家來的人要多得多。

吳文德：你注意沒注意到還有很多人用手機發短信來拜年。我要是有一個手機，我們也能用手機發短信給王老師拜年了。我們現在去王老師家拜年吧。

李麗莉：我們今天甚麼時候去王老師家拜年都可以，我想先回去換件紅衣服。

吳文德：為甚麼？你的衣服哪件都好看，換不換都一樣。

李麗莉：紅色是中國人過節最喜歡的顏色。春節的時候，春聯、燈籠、甚麼都是紅色的。我想換件紅衣服，給節日增加一點兒氣氛。

吳文德：說到氣氛，我突然想起來我今天下午還得去舞龍呢。這算是濫竽充數[2]吧！

李麗莉：你下午不會腳又疼了，走不動路了吧？

吳文德：你怎麼總是哪壺不開提哪壺[3]呢？

## Lesson 38

打工
### Making Some Pocket Money

美國大部分的大學生都要打工。美國的暑假更是學生打工掙錢的好機會。但是在中國，大學生打工的不太多。大部分的家長雖然不是很有錢，但是他們不是很想讓孩子出去打工。他們總是希望自己的孩子能把學習搞好，將來找一個好工作。中國的大學生也把學習和考試看得很重要。學習好的學生比較容易找到好工作。

（陳小雲，李麗莉，吳文德三個人在吳文德的宿舍。）

陳小雲：我聽說美國很多人從高中起就開始打工掙零花錢。中國大部分的大學生還要靠父母給錢。

李麗莉：為甚麼？自己掙一點兒錢，開學的時候用，不好嗎？

陳小雲：中國的家長總是望子成龍，望女成鳳[1]，希望孩子能多有一些時間學習，所以不是非常想讓孩子出去打工。

吳文德：說起打工，李麗莉，暑假快到了。咱們找個臨時工作，掙點兒錢，怎麼樣？

李麗莉：我知道暑期是掙錢的好機會。可是我不知道在中國怎麼找工作？

陳小雲：你們想做甚麼工作？

吳文德：我這個人從來不挑不揀，幹甚麼都可以。

陳小雲：其實，找工作不難。學校有一個佈告欄，很多需要用人的單位都在那兒貼廣告。要不你們到那兒去看看。報紙上、網上也有招聘廣告。

李麗莉：學校暑期有沒有甚麼工作呢？我很想在學校裡搞一些翻譯工作。

陳小雲：在中國，學校暑假都關了，只有一些補習班，英文補習班，計算機補習班等。但是這些課都是由老師來教。如果你想做翻譯工作，最好到出版社去問一問。

（陳小雲走了以後，李麗莉對吳文德說：）

李麗莉：吳文德，咱們倆分一下兒工吧。到學校佈告欄和報紙上看廣告的事由我負責，上網查工作由你負責。晚上我們在你這兒碰頭，商量一下兒找工作的事。

（晚上在吳文德的宿舍。）

李麗莉：吳文德，我在報紙上看到一個招聘廣告。要找一個英文口語班老師，你喜歡跟人打交道，想不想去試一試。我把工作申請表格也複印下來了。

吳文德：我如果教英文，就會被學生叫作吳老師，也就是"沒有"老師的意思[2]。真夠有意思的。再說，我還可能被邀請到學生家去吃飯。這種工作可真夠好的。

李麗莉：你在網上查到甚麼工作了嗎？

吳文德：我剛查到一個翻譯的工作。有家出版社要找一個翻譯，幫著把中文小說翻譯成英文。

李麗莉：我們趕快申請吧，好像找工作的人很多。佈告欄上的招聘廣告都快讓人撕光了。我們要是申請晚了，工作叫別人占了，就太可惜了。

吳文德：唉，又要填表。我最不喜歡填表了。

李麗莉：你說喜歡當老師，但又不想填表。這不是跟葉公好龍[3]一樣嗎？

吳文德：我跟葉公好龍可不一樣，我只是不喜歡填表。幫幫忙，好不好？

李麗莉：好是好，可是你這兒的空調壞了，我這個人一熱，腦子就不好用了。

吳文德：這好辦。給你扇扇子的事由我來做。咱們的表由你來填，好不好？

李麗莉：成交。

（一個小時以後，李麗莉填完了兩份申請表格，高興地對吳文德說：）

李麗莉：吳文德，表都填完了，一會兒咱們的個人簡歷列印出來，就可以寄出去了。咦，我幹了半
天活，你怎麼滿頭大汗的？

吳文德：李麗莉，我的扇子都被我扇壞了，我還沒幹活嗎？

## Lesson 39

用手機
### Using Cell Phones

中國現在使用移動電話的人越來越多。移動電話也叫作手機。吳文德注意到校內、校外、還有大街上
到處都是用手機的人。一天，他好奇地走進一家電信局的營業大廳，原來只是想隨便瞭解一下兒手機
的價格和怎麼辦手機開戶，但是他從電信局出來的時候，他自己手裡也拿了一個手機了。吳文德為甚
麼不用他宿舍的免費電話，偏要花錢買手機呢？下面的小故事會給你一個很好的答案。

（一天下午，吳文德走進一家電信局的營業大廳。）

營業員：你是不是準備入網？

吳文德：入網？入網是甚麼意思？

營業員：入網就是辦手機開戶的意思。

吳文德：我還沒決定呢。你們這兒手機多少錢一個？座機費多少錢？使用費多少？

營業員：那要看你買甚麼手機，買甚麼卡？

吳文德：買卡是甚麼意思？

營業員：光有手機，沒有卡，顧客的手機還是不能用。只有買了卡，手機才能通。不同的卡，收不同
的座機費和使用費。

吳文德：你們現在甚麼卡最便宜？

營業員：你是學生吧。我們現在正在促銷校園卡，特別便宜。

吳文德：校園卡的座機費和使用費貴不貴？

營業員：不貴。校園卡沒有免費分鐘，所以座機費不高。每分鐘的使用費，跟打公用電話差不多。
不過，這種促銷活動今天下班的時候就結束了。

吳文德：我今天來得真湊巧。校園卡非常有吸引力，但是手機多少錢呢？

營業員：我們現在有一種促銷手機。只要你銀行裡有五千人民幣，或五百美金，促銷手機就不要錢。

吳文德：真的？我今天真有運氣！你看，我的借記卡和我的定期存款單裡正好有五百美金。我這兒還有銀行的收據。麻煩你給我買一張校園卡吧。

營業員：好。請你填一下兒移動電話申請表⋯⋯

（吃過晚飯以後，吳文德給李麗莉看他的剛買的手機。）

李麗莉：手機？你還挺會趕時髦的。

吳文德：我用手機是圖方便。我這個人就是不喜歡待在宿舍裡。不在宿舍，除了我找別人不方便，別人找我也不方便。

李麗莉：你的手機真漂亮。都有甚麼功能？

吳文德：我這個手機除了有來電顯示以外，也能發短資訊，還能照相。

李麗莉：能打國際長途嗎？

吳文德：能打我也不打。打國際長途太浪費錢了。

李麗莉：你平時挺大方的。怎麼一下子變這麼小氣了？在中國用手機很貴嗎？

吳文德：我以前認為很貴，後來才發現不是那麼貴。我如果只打市內，每個月除了交一些座機費以外，我打多少電話，就交多少錢。

李麗莉：你辦手機開戶容易嗎？

吳文德：很容易。我交了訂金。然後再挑一個手機號碼，手機就通了。你問了這麼多的問題。是不是也想買一個手機？

李麗莉：沒門兒。我可不想趕時髦。

吳文德：李麗莉，我的好朋友，我說了半天，怎麼跟對牛彈琴[1]一樣。我買手機不是趕時髦，是圖方便。

李麗莉：你別生氣好不好？我只不過是跟你開一個小玩笑罷了。

# Lesson 40

## 漢語水平考試
## Taking the HSK

中國的漢語水平考試，簡稱 HSK，是一種標準化的考試，考試的主要對象是那些中文不是母語的外國人、華僑、等等。漢語水平考試一共有基礎、初中等和高等三套試卷。基礎考試有三部份：1)聽力理解；2)語法；3)閱讀。初中等有四部份：1)聽力理解；2)語法；3)閱讀；4)綜合填空。高等考試有六部份：1)聽力理解；2)語法；3)閱讀；4)綜合表達；5)寫作；6)口語。參加考試的學生不但可以得到中國政府發的漢語水平考試證書，而且還可以申請去中國大學學習的獎學金。李麗莉決定下個月參加漢語水平考試，但是吳文德參加不參加呢？下面請看李麗莉和吳文德的一段小對話。

（星期五吳文德一吃了晚飯就給李麗莉打電話。）

吳文德：李麗莉，今天晚上我們去看電影吧。

李麗莉：我現在要準備考試，連吃飯的時間都沒有，哪兒有時間看電影？

吳文德：哎呀，你怎麼連想都沒想，就說不看呢？學校考試連我都不緊張，你有甚麼好緊張的。

李麗莉：要是學校考試，我根本就不會緊張。課前預習，課後復習，只要考試不粗心，就不會考糊。

吳文德：不是學校考試？那你考甚麼？你覺得學校考試考得還不夠多，是嗎？

李麗莉：不是，我想參加漢語水平考試，看看我能考幾級。

吳文德：漢語水平考試一共有幾級？

李麗莉：十一級。考完試以後還可以得到一個中國政府發的漢語水平證書。

吳文德：我也想知道我的漢語水平能達到幾級？甚麼時候考試？

李麗莉：下個月第三個星期六。你也參加吧。我們一塊兒復習，好嗎？

吳文德：好吧。不過，還有一個多月呢，你急甚麼？

李麗莉：我可不是平時不燒香、臨時抱佛腳1的那種人。我喜歡早早地復習好，考試的時候就不心慌了。

吳文德：李麗莉，我考試雖然都沒有你成績好，但是我考試從來不心慌，根本不在乎考試的分數。

李麗莉：說起來容易，做起來難。凡是參加過漢語水平考試的人都知道這種考試考的是綜合知識，比學校的考試難多了。

吳文德：你越覺得難，考試就越難。我覺得咱們倆現在的漢語水平去參加考試應該沒有問題。

李麗莉：我們越說，你的自信心就越高。看樣子你是不想復習了，對不對？

吳文德：想啊。但是我們真的連星期五晚上都不能休息一下嗎？要不，我們今天晚上早一點兒開始。復習完了，我們說不定還有時間看電影呢。

（星期五晚上，李麗莉和吳文德兩個人在閱覽室商量怎麼準備漢語水平考試。）

吳文德：漢語水平考試都考些甚麼內容？

李麗莉：考試有聽力理解，語法結構，閱讀理解，和綜合填空……。

吳文德：我們先復習聽力吧。我有一個最好的復習聽力的方法。這個方法不但能有很大的收穫，而且能讓我們感到放鬆。

李麗莉：別賣關子了。快說，你有甚麼好方法？

吳文德：看中文電影！我覺得看電影是練習聽力的最好的方法。這也叫一舉兩得2。

李麗莉：我越叫你學習，你就越要看電影。我帶了一些模擬考題，我們做題吧。

（過了一個半小時以後，李麗莉和吳文德開始互相檢查他們做的練習題。）

李麗莉：吳文德，你是不是又想看電影了。你怎麼連這麼簡單的字都寫成錯別字了呢？

吳文德：你一定看錯了。我填的空裡，根本沒有"錯"字，也沒有"別"字。

# Chinese-English Vocabulary Glossary, Arranged Alphabetically by Pinyin

This vocabulary glossary includes all regular vocabulary, spoken expressions, and supplementary vocabulary. An "s" after a lesson number means that the word comes from a supplementary vocabulary list. For proper nouns, see the Glossary of Proper Nouns.

| Simplified | Traditional | Pinyin | Part of Speech | English | Lesson |
|---|---|---|---|---|---|
| 安全 | 安全 | ānquán | adj., n. | secure, safe; security | 23 |
| 安全检查口 | 安全檢查口 | ānquán jiǎnchá kǒu | n. phr. | security inspection gate | 23 |
| 按时 | 按時 | ànshí | adv. | on time; to be on time, to go by schedule | 23s, 36 |
| 奥运会 | 奧運會 | Àoyùnhuì | n. | the Olympic Games | 35s |
| 罢了 | 罷了 | bàle | s.e. | that's all, no more than that | 39 |
| 白跑 | 白跑 | bái pǎo | s.e. | to make a trip in vain | 29 |
| 百分之百 | 百分之百 | bǎifēn zhī bǎi | phr. | 100 percent; (lit.) one hundred out of one hundred divisions | 30 |
| 百货 | 百貨 | bǎihuò | n. | general merchandise; (lit.) a hundred goods | 29 |
| 百货大楼 | 百貨大樓 | bǎihuò dàlóu | n. | department store | 29 |
| 摆(起) | 擺(起) | bǎi(qǐ) | v. (comp.) | to set (up) | 30 |
| 拜年 | 拜年 | bài nián | v. obj. | to pay respects (usually by bowing to someone); to wish the person a happy new year | 37 |
| 班机 | 班機 | bānjī | n. | scheduled flight | 23s |
| 半个天 | 半個天 | bàn ge tiān | s.e. | half the sky | 26 |
| 半工半读 | 半工半讀 | bàn gōng bàn dú | phr. | to work part-time and study part-time | 38s |

| Simplified | Traditional | Pinyin | Part of Speech | English | Lesson |
|---|---|---|---|---|---|
| 办事儿 | 辦事兒 | bànshìr | s.e. | to run an errand, to perform a task | 22 |
| 半天 | 半天 | bàntiān | s.e. | (lit.) half a day, a long while | 21 |
| 包 | 包 | bāo | n., v. | package; to wrap | 37 |
| 包裹 | 包裹 | bāoguǒ | n. | parcel, package | 27 |
| 包裹单 | 包裹單 | bāoguǒdān | n. | form for mailing a parcel | 27 |
| 饱 | 飽 | bǎo | adj. | (of stomach) full, filled up | 21 |
| 保证 | 保證 | bǎozhèng | v. | to guarantee | 30 |
| 报 | 報 | bào | v. | to report | 35 |
| 报名 | 報名 | bào míng | v. obj. | to register, to sign up | 35 |
| 杯 | 杯 | bēi | m.w. | cup, glass | 21 |
| 悲观 | 悲觀 | bēiguān | adj. | pessimistic | 28s, 32 |
| 北 | 北 | běi | n. | north | 28 |
| 本地话 | 本地話 | běndì huà | n. | local dialect | 30 |
| 本领 | 本領 | běnlǐng | n. | ability, skills | 30 |
| 比 | 比 | bǐ | prep. | compared with, compared to | 29 |
| 比较 | 比較 | bǐjiào | adv., v. | comparatively, relatively; to compare | 29 |
| 比赛 | 比賽 | bǐsài | n., v. | competition; to compete | 35 |
| 毕业 | 畢業 | bì yè | n., v. obj. | graduation; to graduate | 40s |
| 鞭炮 | 鞭炮 | biānpào | n. | firecrackers | 37 |
| 变 | 變 | biàn | v. | to change | 32 |
| 遍 | 遍 | biàn | m.w. | measure word for actions | 22 |
| 变成 | 變成 | biàn chéng | v. comp. | to change into, to turn into | 32 |
| 标准房间 | 標準房間 | biāozhǔn fángjiān | n. | standard room | 34s |
| 标准化 | 標準化 | biāozhǔnhuà | phr. | standardization | 40 |

| Simplified | Traditional | Pinyin | Part of Speech | English | Lesson |
|---|---|---|---|---|---|
| 表达 | 表達 | biǎodá | v. | to express | 40 |
| 表演 | 表演 | biǎoyǎn | n., v. | performance; to perform | 35 |
| 别人 | 別人 | biéren | n. | other people, others | 39 |
| 宾馆 | 賓館 | bīnguǎn | n. | guesthouse, hotel | 34s |
| 冰雹 | 冰雹 | bīngbáo | n. | hail | 26s |
| 病 | 病 | bìng | n., v. | sickness, disease, illness; to get sick, to have a disease | 25 |
| 补习 | 補習 | bǔxí | v. | (lit.) supplementary study | 38 |
| 补习班 | 補習班 | bǔxíbān | n. | (lit.) supplementary study class; tutoring class, test prep classes | 38 |
| 不但…而且… | 不但…而且… | bùdàn…érqiě… | conj. | not only…but also… | 31 |
| 不过 | 不過 | bùguò | conj. | however, but | 24 |
| 不瞒你说 | 不瞞你說 | bù mán nǐ shuō | s.e. | to tell you the truth | 35 |
| 不要紧 | 不要緊 | bù yàojǐn | s.e. | It does not matter. | 32 |
| 布告栏 | 佈告欄 | bùgàolán | n. | bulletin board | 38 |
| 步 | 步 | bù | n. | step | 35 |
| 部 | 部 | bù | n. | unit, department, ministry | 36 |
| 部分 | 部分 | bùfèn | n. | part, portion, fraction | 38 |
| 才 | 才 | cái | adv. | only, only when | 24 |
| 裁判员 | 裁判員 | cáipànyuán | n. | referee, umpire | 35s |
| 菜 | 菜 | cài | n. | vegetables, dish | 21 |
| 菜单 | 菜單 | càidān | n. | menu | 33 |
| 参观 | 參觀 | cānguān | v. | to visit | 34 |
| 餐 | 餐 | cān | b.f. | meal | 21 |
| 餐厅 | 餐廳 | cāntīng | n. | dining hall, dining room | 21 |
| 操场 | 操場 | cāochǎng | n. | sports ground | 35 |
| 草 | 草 | cǎo | n. | grass, herbs | 26 |

| Simplified | Traditional | Pinyin | Part of Speech | English | Lesson |
|---|---|---|---|---|---|
| 差不多 | 差不多 | chàbuduō | phr. | almost there; (lit.) missing by not very much | 33 |
| 差远了 | 差遠了 | chà yuǎn le | s.e. | far from it | 37 |
| 尝 | 嘗 | cháng | v. | to taste (food) | 21 |
| 场 | 場 | chǎng | n. | an area designated for a specific use; place, stage | 23, 35 |
| 抄 | 抄 | chāo | v. | to copy, to write down | 34 |
| 超 | 超 | chāo | v. | to surpass, to exceed | 31 |
| 超支 | 超支 | chāo zhī | v. obj. | to overdraw one's bank account | 31 |
| 炒 | 炒 | chǎo | v. | to stir-fry | 33s |
| 炒饭 | 炒飯 | chǎofàn | n., v. obj. | fried rice; to fry rice | 21s |
| 车厢 | 車廂 | chēxiāng | n. | compartment of a train | 32s |
| 车站 | 車站 | chēzhàn | n. | station, stop (for buses, trains) | 28 |
| 趁 | 趁 | chèn | v. | to take advantage of, to avail oneself of | 21 |
| 称 | 秤 | chēng | v. | to weigh | 25 |
| 撑 | 撑 | chēng | v. | to prop up | 33 |
| 成绩 | 成績 | chéngjī | n. | achievement, score, results | 35, 40s |
| 成交 | 成交 | chéngjiāo | s.e. | to strike a deal, to reach an agreement | 38 |
| 乘 | 乘 | chéng | v. | to ride, to take (a bus, train, taxi, or boat) | 28 |
| 乘客 | 乘客 | chéngkè | n. | passengers | 28 |
| 乘务员 | 乘務員 | chéngwùyuán | n. | flight attendant | 24 |
| 吃个够 | 吃個夠 | chī gè gòu | s.e. | to eat as much as you want, to eat until you are full | 34 |
| 吃亏 | 吃虧 | chī kuī | v. obj. | suffer a loss | 30 |

| Simplified | Traditional | Pinyin | Part of Speech | English | Lesson |
|---|---|---|---|---|---|
| 吃力 | 吃力 | chīlì | s.e. | difficult; (lit.) to eat energy, to be energy-consuming (used to describe something that is very difficult to do physically or mentally) | 24 |
| 充电 | 充電 | chōng diàn | v. obj. | to charge a battery | 39s |
| 重 | 重 | chóng | adv. | again | 22 |
| 初 | 初 | chū | b.f. | elementary | 35 |
| 出版 | 出版 | chūbǎn | v. | to publish | 38 |
| 出版社 | 出版社 | chūbǎnshè | n. | publisher | 38 |
| 出丑 | 出醜 | chū chǒu | s.e. | to make a fool of oneself; (lit.) to let out one's foolishness | 28 |
| 出发 | 出發 | chūfā | v. | to set out, to start out | 32 |
| 初级 | 初級 | chūjí | n. | elementary level | 35 |
| 出境 | 出境 | chū jìng | v. | to leave a country | 24s |
| 出门 | 出門 | chū mén | v. obj. | to go out, to leave home | 28 |
| 出那种事 | 出那種事 | chū nà zhǒng shì | s.e. | for that kind of thing to happen; (lit.) to make that kind of thing come out | 28 |
| 出去 | 出去 | chū qù | v. comp. | to go out | 32 |
| 出租 | 出租 | chūzū | n., v. | rental; to rent (out) | 28 |
| 出租车 | 出租車 | chūzū chē | n. | taxi | 28 |
| 除了…以外 | 除了…以外 | chúle...yǐwài | conj. | in addition to..., apart from... | 39 |
| 除夕 | 除夕 | chúxī | n. | New Year's Eve | 37 |
| 处 | 處 | chù | b.f., n. | office (of...), a division in an institution; place, office | 22, 36 |
| 传染 | 傳染 | chuánrǎn | v. | to be contagious | 36 |
| 串门 | 串門 | chuànmén | s.e. | to stop by, to stop in | 37 |

| Simplified | Traditional | Pinyin | Part of Speech | English | Lesson |
|---|---|---|---|---|---|
| 窗口 | 窗口 | chuāngkǒu | n. | window, wicket | 23 |
| 吹 | 吹 | chuī | v. | to blow, to puff | 37 |
| 吹牛 | 吹牛 | chuī niú | v. obj. | to brag, to boast | 26 |
| 春假 | 春假 | chūnjià | n. | spring break | 38s |
| 春节 | 春節 | chūnjié | n. | Spring Festival | 37 |
| 春节联欢晚会 | 春節聯歡晚會 | chūnjié liánhuān wǎnhuì | phr. | (lit.) Spring Festival Get-together Evening Party | 37 |
| 春联 | 春聯 | chūnlián | n. | Spring Festival couplet | 37 |
| 春夏秋冬 | 春夏秋冬 | chūn xià qiū dōng | phr. | the four seasons; (lit.) spring, summer, fall, and winter | 26 |
| 纯净 | 純淨 | chúnjìng | adj. | pure | 34 |
| 纯净水 | 純淨水 | chúnjìng shuǐ | n. | purified or filtered water; (lit.) pure clean water | 34 |
| 纯正 | 純正 | chúnzhèng | adj. | pure, authentic | 33 |
| 磁带 | 磁帶 | cídài | n. | tape | 40s |
| 次 | 次 | cì | m.w. | measure word for actions | 22 |
| 从来(不/没) | 從來(不/沒) | cónglái(bù/méi) | adv. | never | 34 |
| 凑 | 湊 | còu | s.e. | to get closer to | 37 |
| 凑巧 | 湊巧 | còuqiǎo | adv. | by coincidence | 35 |
| 粗心 | 粗心 | cūxīn | adj. | careless | 22s, 40 |
| 促 | 促 | cù | v. | to promote | 39 |
| 促销 | 促銷 | cùxiāo | v. | to promote sales | 39 |
| 存款单 | 存款單 | cúnkuǎndān | n. | deposit slip | 31 |
| 存钱 | 存錢 | cún qián | v. obj. | to deposit money | 31 |
| 存折 | 存摺 | cúnzhé | n. | bank book | 31 |
| 错别字 | 錯別字 | cuòbiézì | n. | incorrectly written characters | 22 |
| 搭乘 | 搭乘 | dāchéng | v. | (formal) to ride (in public transportation) | 23s |

| Simplified | Traditional | Pinyin | Part of Speech | English | Lesson |
|---|---|---|---|---|---|
| 达到 | 達到 | dádào | v. | to reach, to achieve (a certain degree, level, etc.) | 26 |
| 答案 | 答案 | dá'àn | n. | answer, solution | 39 |
| 打包 | 打包 | dǎ bāo | s.e. | to wrap/pack a doggy bag | 33 |
| 打的 | 打的 | dǎ dī | s.e. | to take a taxi (a very colloquial expression) | 28 |
| 打工 | 打工 | dǎ gōng | v. obj. | to do odd jobs (usually temporary work paid by the hour) | 38 |
| 打交道 | 打交道 | dǎ jiāodao | s.e. | to interact with | 38 |
| 打篮球 | 打籃球 | dǎ lánqiú | v. obj. | to play basketball | 35 |
| 打破 | 打破 | dǎpò | v. | to break, to smash | 35 |
| 打破记录 | 打破記錄 | dǎpò jìlù | v. obj. | to break a record | 35 |
| 打扫 | 打掃 | dǎsǎo | v. | to clean | 37 |
| 打算 | 打算 | dǎsuàn | n., v. | plan; to plan | 34 |
| 打网球 | 打網球 | dǎ wǎngqiú | v. obj. | to play tennis | 35s |
| 打印 | 打印 | dǎyìn | v. | (lit.) to type and print (e.g. on a typewriter, printer, etc.) | 38 |
| 打折 | 打折 | dǎ zhé | v. obj. | to sell at a discount, to take off a percentage (of the original price); (lit.) to make a break in the price | 30 |
| 打针 | 打針 | dǎzhēn | v. obj. | to give or receive an injection | 36 |
| 大部份 | 大部份 | dàbùfen | phr. | majority | 38 |
| 大方 | 大方 | dàfang | adj. | generous | 39 |
| 大楼 | 大樓 | dàlóu | n. | a big multistoried building | 29 |
| 大拍卖 | 大拍賣 | dà pāimài | phr. | clearance sale, auction sale | 30s |

| Simplified | Traditional | Pinyin | Part of Speech | English | Lesson |
|---|---|---|---|---|---|
| 大晴天 | 大晴天 | dà qíngtiān | s.e. | very clear day; (lit.) a big clear sky | 26 |
| 大使 | 大使 | dàshǐ | n. | ambassador | 22 |
| 大使馆 | 大使館 | dàshǐguǎn | n. | embassy | 22 |
| 大厅 | 大廳 | dàtīng | n. | lobby | 34 |
| 代售 | 代售 | dàishòu | v. phr. | to sell on behalf of..., to sell as a substitute | 32 |
| 代售点 | 代售點 | dàishòudiǎn | n. | a place commissioned to sell something (e.g., train tickets) | 32 |
| 带劲儿 | 帶勁兒 | dài jìnr | s.e. | energetic, energizing; (lit.) bring energy | 35 |
| 贷款 | 貸款 | dài kuǎn | v. obj. | to get a loan | 31s |
| 单 | 單 | dān | n., b.f. | list, sheet; single, a sheet | 27, 34 |
| 单人间 | 單人間 | dānrénjiān | n. | single room | 34 |
| 单位 | 單位 | dānwèi | n. | general term for an organization, institution, company, or workplace | 38 |
| 担心 | 擔心 | dān xīn | v. obj. | to be anxious, to worry; (lit.) to lift up one's heart | 34 |
| 担保 | 擔保 | dānbǎo | v. | to guarantee, to vouch for | 31 |
| 淡 | 淡 | dàn | adj. | (of flavor) mild, not strong | 33 |
| 叨叨 | 叨叨 | dāodao | s.e. | to nag | 25 |
| 导游 | 導遊 | dǎoyóu | n. | tour guide | 32 |
| 搞什么鬼 | 搞什麼鬼 | dǎo shénme guǐ | s.e. | (lit.) to play what mischief; in the text it means "What mischief are you up to?" | 39 |
| 到处 | 到處 | dàochù | n. | everywhere | 37 |
| 到达 | 到達 | dàodá | v. | to arrive (usually referring to formal or long-distance travel) | 24 |

| Simplified | Traditional | Pinyin | Part of Speech | English | Lesson |
|---|---|---|---|---|---|
| 到港 | 到港 | dào gǎng | v. obj | to arrive at a port or an airport | 23 |
| 到期 | 到期 | dào qī | v. obj. | be due, (arrive at the) due date | 22s |
| 到齐 | 到齊 | dàoqí | v. comp. | to arrive in completion | 33 |
| 倒 | 倒 | dào | v. | to invert, to turn upside down, to pour | 21 |
| 道 | 道 | dào | n. | path | 23 |
| 地 | 地 | de | part. | attached to an adjective to make an adverbial expression | 27 |
| 得 | 得 | dé | v. | to earn, to obtain, to achieve | 35 |
| 得到 | 得到 | dédào | v. | to obtain | 40 |
| 得(第一)名 | 得(第一)名 | dé (dìyī) míng | v. obj. | to earn (first) place | 35 |
| 灯 | 燈 | dēng | n. | light | 28 |
| 灯笼 | 燈籠 | dēnglong | n. | lantern | 37 |
| 登 | 登 | dēng | v. | to climb, to get on, to board | 23 |
| 登记 | 登記 | dēngjì | v. | to enter a record | 34 |
| 登记处 | 登記處 | dēngjìchù | n. | registration desk, front desk; (lit.) record-entering place | 34 |
| 登机牌 | 登機牌 | dēngjī pái | n. | boarding pass | 23 |
| 等 | 等 | děng | n. | level, category | 40 |
| 低 | 低 | dī | adj. | low, down | 26 |
| 第 | 第 | dì | pref. | used before a number to change it into an ordinal number | 24 |
| 递 | 遞 | dì | v. | to hand over, to pass on (sth.), to deliver | 27 |
| 地铁 | 地鐵 | dìtiě | n. | subway, metro | 28 |
| 地图 | 地圖 | dìtú | n. | map | 32 |

| Simplified | Traditional | Pinyin | Part of Speech | English | Lesson |
|---|---|---|---|---|---|
| 点 | 點 | diǎn | n., v. | a place; to order (dishes) | 32, 33 |
| 点菜 | 點菜 | diǎn cài | v. obj. | to order dishes | 33 |
| 电车 | 電車 | diànchē | n. | trolley | 28s |
| 电池 | 電池 | diànchí | n. | battery | 39s |
| 电梯 | 電梯 | diàntī | n. | elevator; (lit.) electric stairs | 29 |
| 电信 | 電信 | diànxìn | n. | telecommunications | 39 |
| 电信局 | 電信局 | diànxìnjú | n. | telecommunications bureau | 39 |
| 定 | 定 | dìng | v. | to decide, to determine | 32 |
| 定金 | 定金 | dìngjīn | n. | down payment, deposit | 39 |
| 定期 | 定期 | dìngqī | attr. | (lit.) a fixed period | 31 |
| 丢 | 丢 | diū | v. | to lose, to discard, to put aside | 31 |
| 东 | 東 | dōng | n. | east | 28 |
| 东/南/西/北 | 東/南/西/北 | dōng/nán/xī/běi | n. | the four directions | 28 |
| 冻 | 凍 | dòng | v. | to freeze | 26s |
| 都看花了 | 都看花了 | dōu kàn huā le | s.e. | There are so many things and you don't know where to look. | 27 |
| 豆浆 | 豆漿 | dòujiāng | n. | soy milk | 33 |
| 度 | 度 | dù | m.w. | degree | 26 |
| 短 | 短 | duǎn | adj. | short | 26 |
| 段 | 段 | duàn | m.w. | section, paragraph | 40 |
| 队 | 隊 | duì | n. | line, team | 22 |
| 对话 | 對話 | duìhuà | n. | dialogue | 40 |
| 兑换率 | 兌換率 | duìhuàn lǜ | n. | exchange rate | 29s, 31 |
| 多亏 | 多虧 | duōkuī | adv. | thanks to (someone/something for...) | 36 |
| 多云 | 多雲 | duō yún | phr. | cloudy; (lit.) a lot of clouds | 26 |

| Simplified | Traditional | Pinyin | Part of Speech | English | Lesson |
|---|---|---|---|---|---|
| 多云偶雨 | 多雲偶雨 | duō yún ǒu yǔ | phr. | cloudy with occasional showers | 26s |
| 多云转晴 | 多雲轉晴 | duō yún zhuǎn qíng | phr. | cloudy turning clear | 26 |
| 饿 | 餓 | è | adj. | to be hungry (in contrast to full, 饱), to starve (especially animals) | 21 |
| 而且 | 而且 | érqiě | conj. | moreover, furthermore, on top of | 31 |
| 耳鼻喉科 | 耳鼻喉科 | ěrbíhóukē | n. | Otolaryngology Department | 36s |
| 耳机 | 耳機 | ěrjī | n. | headphones | 24s |
| 发短信 | 發短信 | fā duǎnxìn | v. obj. | to send a text message via cellular phone | 37 |
| 发票 | 發票 | fāpiào | n. | receipt, bill, invoice | 29 |
| 发烧 | 發燒 | fāshāo | v. obj. | to develop a fever | 25 |
| 发现 | 發現 | fāxiàn | n., v. | discovery, finding; to discover | 39 |
| 发炎 | 發炎 | fā yán | v. obj. | to become inflamed | 36s |
| 翻译 | 翻譯 | fānyì | v., n. | to translate; translation | 38 |
| 凡是 | 凡是 | fánshì | adv. | any, all, each and every | 40 |
| 反 | 反 | fǎn | adj. | the opposite (side), the reverse (side) | 22, 27 |
| 反正 | 反正 | fǎnzhèng | adv. | anyway, no matter what, in any case | 22 |
| 方向 | 方向 | fāngxiàng | n. | direction, orientation | 28 |
| 防 | 防 | fáng | v. | to guard against, to take precautions against | 25 |
| 放 | 放 | fàng | v. | to release, to set free, to let go, to send off/away, to leave (sth. at a certain place) | 22, 27, 37 |

| Simplified | Traditional | Pinyin | Part of Speech | English | Lesson |
|---|---|---|---|---|---|
| 放假 | 放假 | fàng jià | v. obj. | (for institutions) to give a vacation, (for individuals) to have a vacation | 32 |
| 放射科 | 放射科 | fàngshèkē | n. | Radiology Department | 36s |
| 放心 | 放心 | fàng xīn | v. obj. | to rest at ease; (lit.) to release worry | 22 |
| 放焰火 | 放焰火 | fàng yànhuǒ | v. obj. | to set off fireworks | 37s |
| 飞 | 飛 | fēi | v. | to fly | 23 |
| 飞机 | 飛機 | fēijī | n. | airplane | 23 |
| 飞机场 | 飛機場 | fēijī chǎng | n. | airport | 23 |
| 飞行员 | 飛行員 | fēixíngyuán | n. | pilot | 24s |
| 非…不可 | 非…不可 | fēi...bùkě | conj. | must; it is not permissible unless | 36 |
| 肥 | 肥 | féi | adj. | (of food) fatty; (of human beings or animals) fat; (of clothing) loose | 21s, 30 |
| 肺 | 肺 | fèi | n. | lungs | 36 |
| 费劲 | 費勁 | fèijìng | s.e. | requiring great effort (physical or mental) | 21 |
| 费用 | 費用 | fèiyòng | n. | fee, expense | 39s |
| 分 | 分 | fēn | v. | to divide | 38 |
| 分工 | 分工 | fēn gōng | v. obj. | to divide the responsibilities, to divide the workload | 38 |
| 分数 | 分數 | fēnshù | n. | scores | 40 |
| 份 | 份 | fèn | m.w. | measure word for a portion or copy of something (such as application forms, newspapers, etc.) | 38 |
| 风 | 風 | fēng | n. | (of weather) wind | 26 |

| Simplified | Traditional | Pinyin | Part of Speech | English | Lesson |
|---|---|---|---|---|---|
| 风景 | 風景 | fēngjǐng | n. | scenery | 32 |
| 风俗 | 風俗 | fēngsú | n. | customs | 37 |
| 风味 | 風味 | fēngwèi | n. | flavor or style of food | 33 |
| 封 | 封 | fēng | m.w. | measure word for letters | 27 |
| 服务 | 服務 | fúwù | n., v. | service; to serve | 27 |
| 服务项目 | 服務項目 | fúwù xiàngmù | n.phr. | services offered; (lit.) service items | 27 |
| 福 | 福 | fú | n. | blessing, happiness | 37 |
| 妇科 | 婦科 | fùkē | n. | Gynecology Department | 36s |
| 负责 | 負責 | fùzé | v. | to be responsible for, to be in charge of | 38 |
| 复 | 複 | fù | b.f. | to duplicate, to repeat | 38 |
| 复印 | 複印 | fùyìn | v. | to photocopy, to duplicate | 38 |
| 腹 | 腹 | fù | n. | stomach | 36 |
| 改 | 改 | gǎi | v. | to make corrections, to revise, to edit | 22 |
| 盖 | 蓋 | gài | v. | to cover, to put a lid on | 29 |
| 盖章 | 蓋章 | gài zhāng | v. obj. | to stamp a seal (usually as a sign of approval by an authority figure) | 29 |
| 干 | 乾 | gān | adj., v. | dry; to dry, to empty (a wine glass) | 21 |
| 干杯 | 乾杯 | gān bēi | v. obj. | to make a toast; (lit.) to dry up the cup | 21 |
| 干净 | 乾淨 | gānjìng | adj. | clean and neat | 37 |
| 赶 | 趕 | gǎn | v. | to catch up | 39 |
| 赶快 | 趕快 | gǎnkuài | adv. | quickly | 32 |
| 感 | 感 | gǎn | v. | to feel, to sense | 37 |
| 感到 | 感到 | gǎndào | v. comp. | to feel, to sense | 40 |
| 感冒 | 感冒 | gǎnmào | n., v. | cold; to catch a cold | 25 |

| Simplified | Traditional | Pinyin | Part of Speech | English | Lesson |
|---|---|---|---|---|---|
| 感兴趣 | 感興趣 | gǎn xìngqù | v. obj. | to be interested in... | 37 |
| 干 | 幹 | gàn | v. | to do (something) | 38 |
| 干活 | 幹活 | gàn huó | v. obj. | to do physical or manual work | 38 |
| 港 | 港 | gǎng | n. | port, harbor | 23 |
| 高 | 高 | gāo | n., adj. | high; height | 25 |
| 高等 | 高等 | gāoděng | n. | advanced level | 40 |
| 高级 | 高級 | gāojí | n. | advanced level | 40s |
| 高考 | 高考 | gāokǎo | n. | college entrance exam | 40s |
| 搞好 | 搞好 | gǎohǎo | s.e. | to do something well, to make something better | 38 |
| 告 | 告 | gào | v. | to tell on (somebody), to accuse | 34 |
| 各 | 各 | gè | adj. | each, every | 24, 36 |
| 根本 | 根本 | gēnběn | adj., adv. | fundamental, basic; (lit.) (from) the root, basically, totally | 40 |
| 更 | 更 | gèng | adv. | even more | 29 |
| 工资 | 工資 | gōngzī | n. | wages | 38s |
| 工作单位 | 工作單位 | gōngzuò dānwèi | n. phr. | workplace | 22s |
| 公 | 公 | gōng | adj. | public | 26 |
| 公分 | 公分 | gōngfēn | m.w. | centimeter | 30 |
| 公共 | 公共 | gōnggòng | adj. | public, communal | 28 |
| 公共汽车 | 公共汽車 | gōnggòng qìchē | n. | public bus | 28 |
| 公交 | 公交 | gōng jiāo | s.e. | colloquial expression for 公共汽车 | 28 |
| 公用 | 公用 | gōngyòng | adj. | (for) public use | 39 |
| 公园 | 公園 | gōngyuán | n. | public park | 26 |
| 功能 | 功能 | gōngnéng | n. | function | 39 |
| 恭贺新禧 | 恭賀新禧 | gōnghè xīnxǐ | phr. | Happy New Year! | 37s |

| Simplified | Traditional | Pinyin | Part of Speech | English | Lesson |
|---|---|---|---|---|---|
| 恭喜发财 | 恭喜發財 | gōngxǐ fācái | phr. | Wishing you a prosperous New Year. | 37s |
| 够 | 夠 | gòu | adj., v. | enough, adequate, sufficient; to reach, to attain | 34 |
| 购物 | 購物 | gòuwù | v. obj. | to purchase things, to go shopping | 28 |
| 购物中心 | 購物中心 | gòuwù zhōngxīn | n. | shopping center, mall | 28 |
| 鼓 | 鼓 | gǔ | n., v. | drum; to beat | 35 |
| 鼓掌 | 鼓掌 | gǔ zhǎng | v. obj. | to applaud | 35 |
| 顾客 | 顧客 | gùkè | n. | customer | 29 |
| 刮 | 颳 | guā | v. | to scrape, to shave, to spread | 26 |
| 刮风 | 颳風 | guā fēng | v. obj. | to be windy; (lit.) to blow wind | 26 |
| 挂 | 掛 | guà | v. | to hang (something on a wall, etc.) | 27 |
| 挂号 | 掛號 | guàhào | v. obj. | (lit.) to register a number (for something); to register, to sign in | 27, 36 |
| 挂号处 | 掛號處 | guàhàochù | n. phr. | hospital registration office | 36 |
| 挂号信 | 掛號信 | guàhàoxìn | n. | registered mail | 27 |
| 拐 | 拐 | guǎi | v. | to make a turn, to change direction | 28 |
| 拐弯 | 拐彎 | guǎi wān | v. obj. | to make a turn, to turn a corner | 28s |
| 怪不得 | 怪不得 | guàibude | phr. | no wonder | 33 |
| 关 | 關 | guān | n., v. | pass, customs station; to close a door/gate, (of a business) to be closed | 24, 28 |

| Simplified | Traditional | Pinyin | Part of Speech | English | Lesson |
|---|---|---|---|---|---|
| 观众 | 觀眾 | guānzhòng | n. | spectator | 35 |
| 光 | 光 | guāng | adj. | empty, used up | 38 |
| 光盘 | 光盤 | guāngpán | n. | laser disk, CD | 40s |
| 广播 | 廣播 | guǎngbō | n., v. | a broadcast; to broadcast | 35 |
| 广播员 | 廣播員 | guǎngbōyuán | n. | radio announcer | 35 |
| 广告 | 廣告 | guǎnggào | n. | advertisement | 38 |
| 逛 | 逛 | guàng | v. | to take a stroll in (a store, market, etc.) | 30 |
| 贵 | 貴 | guì | adj. | expensive | 28 |
| 柜台 | 櫃檯 | guìtái | n. | counter | 27 |
| 国籍 | 國籍 | guójí | n. | nationality, international | 22, 39 |
| 国内 | 國內 | guónèi | adj. | domestic | 39s |
| 过年 | 過年 | guò nián | v. obj. | to celebrate a new year | 37 |
| 过期 | 過期 | guò qī | v. obj. | to be overdue, to pass the due date | 22s |
| 过瘾 | 過癮 | guòyǐn | s.e. | to satisfy a craving | 37 |
| 海 | 海 | hǎi | n. | sea | 27 |
| 海关 | 海關 | hǎiguān | n. | customs (at a national border) | 24s |
| 海运 | 海運 | hǎiyùn | n. | sea transportation | 27 |
| 汗 | 汗 | hàn | n. | sweat | 38 |
| 航 | 航 | háng | n. | navigation | 27 |
| 航空 | 航空 | hángkōng | adv., n. | to travel by air; aviation, air transportation, airmail | 23s, 27 |
| 豪华间 | 豪華間 | háohuájiān | n. | deluxe room | 34s |
| 好像 | 好像 | hǎoxiàng | adv. | it seems that ... | 36 |
| 合适 | 合適 | héshì | adj. | suitable | 30 |
| 红包 | 紅包 | hóngbāo | n. | (lit.) red paper bag; here referring to a little red paper envelope with money in it given as a gift, usually to children | 37 |

| Simplified | Traditional | Pinyin | Part of Speech | English | Lesson |
|---|---|---|---|---|---|
| 红绿灯 | 紅綠燈 | hónglǜdēng | n. | traffic light; (lit.) red-green light | 28 |
| 红肿 | 紅腫 | hóngzhǒng | adj. | red and swollen | 36 |
| 喉咙 | 喉嚨 | hóulóng | n. | throat | 36s |
| 后来 | 後來 | hòulái | n. | (in the) future, later on | 39 |
| 候 | 候 | hòu | v. | (formal) to wait, to await | 23 |
| 候车室 | 候車室 | hòuchēshì | n. | waiting room | 32s |
| 候机室 | 候機室 | hòujīshì | n. | airport waiting room | 23 |
| 候诊室 | 候診室 | hòuzhěnshì | n. | hospital waiting room | 36s |
| 胡椒 | 胡椒 | hújiāo | n. | pepper | 33s |
| 互相 | 互相 | hùxiāng | adv. | reciprocally, mutually | 37 |
| 护照 | 護照 | hùzhào | n. | passport | 22 |
| 花灯 | 花燈 | huādēng | n. | decorative lantern | 37s |
| 花鸟画 | 花鳥畫 | huāniǎo huà | n. | flower-and-bird painting | 29 |
| 华侨 | 華僑 | huáqiáo | n. | overseas Chinese | 40 |
| 华氏 | 華氏 | huáshì | n. | Fahrenheit | 26s |
| 画 | 畫 | huà | n., v. | painting, drawing; to paint, to draw | 29 |
| 坏 | 壞 | huài | adj. | broken, bad, evil | 28 |
| 还清 | 還清 | huán qīng | v. comp. | to pay off (debt) | 31s |
| 换 | 換 | huàn | v. | to exchange | 23, 29 |
| 挥 | 揮 | huī | v. | to wave | 34 |
| 挥(手) | 揮(手) | huī (shǒu) | v. obj. | to wave (hand) | 34 |
| 恢复 | 恢復 | huīfù | v. | to recover, rehabilitate | 36 |
| 回答 | 回答 | huídá | v. | to answer | 29 |
| 荤 | 葷 | hūn | adj., n. | (of food) containing meat, fish, or poultry; meat, fish, or poultry | 21 |
| 荤菜 | 葷菜 | hūncài | n. | meat dish | 21 |
| 活 | 活 | huó | n. | work | 38 |
| 活动 | 活動 | huódòng | n., v. | activities; to exercise | 39 |

| Simplified | Traditional | Pinyin | Part of Speech | English | Lesson |
|---|---|---|---|---|---|
| 活期 | 活期 | huóqī | attr. | (lit.) a non-fixed period | 31 |
| 火车 | 火車 | huǒchē | n. | train | 28s, 32 |
| 火车头 | 火車頭 | huǒchētóu | n. | locomotive | 32s |
| 或者 | 或者 | huòzhě | conj. | or (used in a statement) | 29 |
| 机 | 機 | jī | n. | machine, machinery | 23 |
| 机票 | 機票 | jīpiào | n. | (abbreviation of 飞机票) plane ticket | 23 |
| 鸡 | 雞 | jī | n. | chicken | 21 |
| 基础 | 基礎 | jīchǔ | n. | basic | 40 |
| 激动 | 激動 | jīdòng | adj. | excited | 24 |
| 及格 | 及格 | jí gé | v. obj. | (lit.) to reach mark; to pass (an exam) | 40s |
| 级 | 級 | jí | n. | grade, level, rank | 35 |
| 急诊 | 急診 | jízhěn | n. | emergency treatment | 36 |
| 急诊室 | 急診室 | jízhěnshì | n. | emergency room | 25s |
| 集合 | 集合 | jíhé | v. | to assemble | 35 |
| 计程表 | 計程表 | jìchéngbiǎo | n. | taxi meter; (lit.) distance-calculating meter | 34 |
| 计程车 | 計程車 | jìchéngchē | n. | taxi (Taiwan usage) | 34s |
| 计划 | 計畫 | jìhuá | n., v. | plan; to plan | 32 |
| 计算机 | 計算機 | jìsuànjī | n. | computers | 38 |
| 记录 | 記錄 | jìlù | n., v. | record; to record | 31, 35 |
| 纪念邮票 | 紀念郵票 | jìniàn yóupiào | n. | commemorative stamp | 27s |
| 季 | 季 | jì | n. | season (of a year), agricultural season | 26 |
| 季节 | 季節 | jìjié | n. | season (of a year) | 26 |
| 寄 | 寄 | jì | v. | to send by mail | 27 |
| 寄件人 | 寄件人 | jìjiànrén | n. | the sender (of a letter, parcel, etc.) | 27 |
| 寄平信 | 寄平信 | jì píngxìn | v. obj. | to send by ordinary mail | 27s |
| 寄信人 | 寄信人 | jìxìnrén | n. | sender (of a letter) | 27s |

| Simplified | Traditional | Pinyin | Part of Speech | English | Lesson |
|---|---|---|---|---|---|
| 既…也/又 | 既…也/又 | jì... yě/yòu | conj. | not only...but also | 32 |
| 加 | 加 | jiā | v. | to add | 33, 35 |
| 加油 | 加油 | jiā yóu | v. obj. | to cheer (someone) on; (lit.) to add oil | 35 |
| 家 | 家 | jiā | suff. | suffix used to indicate an expert or specialist in a certain field | 26 |
| 家家户户 | 家家戶戶 | jiājiāhùhù | n. | each and every family | 37 |
| 家长 | 家長 | jiāzhǎng | n. | (lit.) the head of the family; parents | 38 |
| 夹克 | 夾克 | jiákè | n. | jacket | 30 |
| 价格 | 價格 | jiàgé | n. | price | 30s, 33 |
| 价廉物美 | 價廉物美 | jià lián wù měi | phr. | high-quality products at bargain prices | 30s |
| 价钱 | 價錢 | jiàqian | n. | price | 30 |
| 架(子) | 架(子) | jià(zi) | n. | shelf, rack | 24 |
| 驾车执照 | 駕車執照 | jiàchē zhízhào | n. | driver's license | 34s |
| 假 | 假 | jià | b.f. | vacation | 32 |
| 假条 | 假條 | jiàtiáo | n. | a written excuse for being absent | 36 |
| 拣 | 揀 | jiǎn | v. | to pick | 38 |
| 简称 | 簡稱 | jiǎnchēng | n., v. | (lit.) simply called, abbreviated name; to be simply called | 40 |
| 检查 | 檢查 | jiǎnchá | n., v. | inspection; to inspect, to check | 23 |
| 见世面 | 見世面 | jiàn shìmiàn | s.e. | to see the world | 32 |
| 件 | 件 | jiàn | n. | item, piece | 27 |
| 健康 | 健康 | jiànkāng | adj., n. | healthy; health | 25 |
| 讲价钱 | 講價錢 | jiǎng jiàqian | v. obj. | to bargain a price | 30 |
| 奖 | 獎 | jiǎng | n. | prize, award | 40 |
| 奖学金 | 獎學金 | jiǎngxuéjīn | n. | scholarship | 40 |

| Simplified | Traditional | Pinyin | Part of Speech | English | Lesson |
|---|---|---|---|---|---|
| 降价 | 降價 | jiàng jià | v. obj. | to discount or lower the price | 30 |
| 降落 | 降落 | jiàngluò | v. | (of an airplane) to descend, to land | 23s, 24s |
| 酱油 | 醬油 | jiàngyóu | n. | soy sauce | 33s |
| 交通 | 交通 | jiāotōng | n. | traffic | 32s |
| 饺子 | 餃子 | jiǎozi | n. | dumplings | 21s, 37 |
| 饺子宴 | 餃子宴 | jiǎoziyàn | prop. n. | dumpling banquet | 34 |
| 脚 | 腳 | jiǎo | n. | foot, ankle | 35 |
| 叫号机 | 叫號機 | jiàohàojī | n. | (lit.) number-calling machine | 31 |
| 接 | 接 | jiē | v. | to connect, to join | 23 |
| 接人 | 接人 | jiē rén | v. obj. | to pick up someone (from somewhere, e.g., airport, bus station) | 24 |
| 揭我的短 | 揭我的短 | jiē wǒ de duǎn | s.e. | to expose my weaknesses (揭短 is to reveal someone's shortcomings.) | 29 |
| 街道 | 街道 | jiēdào | n. | street | 30 |
| 节 | 節 | jié | n. | festival, holiday | 26 |
| 节日 | 節日 | jiérì | n. | holidays | 37 |
| 结构 | 結構 | jiégòu | n. | structure, frame | 40 |
| 结束 | 結束 | jiéshù | v. | to conclude, to finish | 39 |
| 解释 | 解釋 | jiěshì | n., v. | explanation, interpretation; to explain | 34 |
| 借记卡 | 借記卡 | jièjìkǎ | n. | debit card | 31 |
| 巾 | 巾 | jīn | n. | kerchief, scarf, turban | 29 |
| 金 | 金 | jīn | n. | gold, money | 22, 31 |
| 近 | 近 | jìn | adj. | close, near | 22 |
| 进站口 | 進站口 | jìnzhànkǒu | n. | arrival gate, entrance (where a plane, train, etc. comes in) | 23 |

| Simplified | Traditional | Pinyin | Part of Speech | English | Lesson |
|---|---|---|---|---|---|
| 精神 | 精神 | jīngshen | n. | energy, vigor, spirit | 25 |
| 景点 | 景點 | jǐngdiǎn | n. | scenic spot | 32s |
| 境 | 境 | jìng | n. | boundary, border, frontier | 24 |
| 镜头 | 鏡頭 | jìngtóu | n. | lens | 35 |
| 酒店 | 酒店 | jiǔdiàn | n. | restaurant or hotel | 34s |
| 救生衣 | 救生衣 | jiùshēngyī | n. | life jacket | 24s |
| 局 | 局 | jú | n. | office, bureau | 27 |
| 拒 | 拒 | jù | b.f. | to refuse, to reject, to resist | 22 |
| 拒签 | 拒簽 | jù qiān | v. obj. | to refuse to issue a visa | 22 |
| 卷 | 卷 | juàn | n. | (lit.) scroll; volume, file, folder | 40 |
| 决定 | 決定 | juédìng | n., v. | decision; to decide | 39 |
| 卡 | 卡 | kǎ | n. | card | 24 |
| 开刀 | 開刀 | kāi dāo | v. obj. | (of a patient) to be operated on, (of a doctor) to operate | 36s |
| 开发票 | 開發票 | kāi fāpiào | v. obj. | to write out a receipt | 29 |
| 开户 | 開戶 | kāi hù | v. obj. | to open an account | 39 |
| 开户头 | 開戶頭 | kāi hùtóu | v. obj. | to open an account | 31s |
| 开学 | 開學 | kāi xué | v. obj. | to begin school | 38 |
| 开药方 | 開藥方 | kāi yàofāng | v. obj. | to write out a prescription | 25 |
| 看你那个高兴的样子。 | 看你那個高興的樣子。 | Kàn nǐ nà ge gāoxìng de yàngzi. | s.e. | Look how happy you are. | 31 |
| 看样子 | 看樣子 | kàn yàngzi | s.e. | it looks like... | 40 |
| 考题 | 考題 | kǎotí | n. | test items | 40 |
| 烤鸭 | 烤鴨 | kǎoyā | n. | roast duck | 21s |
| 靠 | 靠 | kào | prep., v. | next to; to lean against, to rely on, to depend on | 23 |

| Simplified | Traditional | Pinyin | Part of Speech | English | Lesson |
|---|---|---|---|---|---|
| 咳嗽 | 咳嗽 | késòu | v. obj. | to cough | 36 |
| 可能 | 可能 | kěnéng | adv. | maybe, probably, possibly | 28 |
| 可惜 | 可惜 | kěxī | adj., conj. | (it's) a pity, too bad, a shame; it is a pity that… | 31 |
| 渴 | 渴 | kě | adj. | thirsty | 21 |
| 空 | 空 | kōng | n. | air | 27 |
| 空调 | 空調 | kōngtiáo | n. | air conditioning | 38 |
| 空位 | 空位 | kòngwèi | n. | empty seat | 33 |
| 口 | 口 | kǒu | n. | (formal) mouth, opening, gate | 23, 33 |
| 口淡 | 口淡 | kǒu dàn | phr. | (lit.) mouth preferring mild flavors | 33 |
| 口味 | 口味 | kǒuwèi | n. | taste | 33 |
| 口语 | 口語 | kǒuyǔ | n. | spoken language | 38 |
| 块 | 塊 | kuài | m.w. | unit of Chinese currency (its amount is the same as 元, but it is more colloquial than 元); (lit.) a piece or a lump | 29 |
| 快递 | 快遞 | kuàidì | n. | (lit.) quick delivery, express mail | 27s |
| 筷子 | 筷子 | kuàizi | n. | chopsticks | 21 |
| 款 | 款 | kuǎn | b.f. | fund, sum of money | 31 |
| 拉肚子 | 拉肚子 | lā dùzi | v. obj. | to have diarrhea | 36s |
| 辣 | 辣 | là | adj. | hot and spicy | 33 |
| 来不及 | 來不及 | lái bu jí | v. comp. | to not have enough time | 34 |
| 来电 | 來電 | lái diàn | v. obj. | to have an incoming message | 39 |
| 来电显示 | 來電顯示 | lái diàn xiǎnshì | phr. | incoming message display | 39 |
| 来回票 | 來回票 | láihuípiào | n. | round-trip ticket | 32 |
| 篮球 | 籃球 | lánqiú | n. | basketball | 35 |

| Simplified | Traditional | Pinyin | Part of Speech | English | Lesson |
|---|---|---|---|---|---|
| 浪费 | 浪費 | làngfèi | adj., v. | to be extravagant; to waste | 39 |
| 劳驾 | 勞駕 | láojià | s.e. | excuse me, may I trouble you | 28s, 33 |
| 老皇历 | 老皇曆 | lǎo huánglì | s.e. | very old; (lit.) very old imperial calendar | 32 |
| 乐观 | 樂觀 | lèguān | adj. | (having) a joyful outlook, optimistic | 28 |
| 乐呵呵 | 樂呵呵 | lè hēhē | phr. | smiling happily | 33 |
| 冷 | 冷 | lěng | adj. | cold, chilly, freezing | 26 |
| 冷盘 | 冷盤 | lěngpán | n. | cold dishes | 33s |
| 厘米 | 釐米 | límǐ | m.w. | centimeter | 30 |
| 离 | 離 | lí | prep. | measuring from (one place or time to another, used to describe distance between places or times) | 22 |
| 离港 | 離港 | lí gǎng | v. obj | to depart from a port or an airport | 23 |
| 离开 | 離開 | líkāi | v. comp. | to leave (a place or a person) | 23 |
| 理解 | 理解 | lǐjiě | n., v. | comprehension; to comprehend, to understand | 40 |
| 力 | 力 | lì | n. | force, power, strength | 39 |
| 利率 | 利率 | lìlǜ | n. | interest rate | 31s |
| 利息 | 利息 | lìxī | n. | (of a monetary account) interest | 31 |
| 连 | 連 | lián | prep. | even | 40 |
| 凉 | 涼 | liáng | adj. | cool, cold | 26 |
| 凉快 | 涼快 | liángkuai | adj. | pleasantly cool | 26 |
| 量 | 量 | liáng | v. | to measure | 25 |
| 亮 | 亮 | liàng | adj. | bright, luminous, light | 37 |

| Simplified | Traditional | Pinyin | Part of Speech | English | Lesson |
|---|---|---|---|---|---|
| 辆 | 輛 | liàng | m.w. | measure word for vehicles | 28 |
| 量 | 量 | liàng | n. | amount | 29 |
| 疗 | 療 | liáo | b.f. | to heal, to cure | 25 |
| 临时 | 臨時 | línshí | adj. | temporary | 38 |
| 零 | 零 | líng | num. | zero | 29 |
| 零花钱 | 零花錢 | línghuāqián | s.e. | pocket money | 38 |
| 零钱 | 零錢 | língqián | n. | small change, pocket money | 29 |
| 零下 | 零下 | língxià | n. | below zero | 26 |
| 零用钱 | 零用錢 | língyòngqián | phr. | pocket money | 38s |
| 领事馆 | 領事館 | lǐngshìguǎn | n. | consulate | 22s |
| 流感 | 流感 | liúgǎn | n. | flu | 25s, 36 |
| 楼梯 | 樓梯 | lóutī | n. | stairs in a multistoried building | 29 |
| 旅馆 | 旅館 | lǚguǎn | n. | hotel | 34 |
| 旅客 | 旅客 | lǚkè | n. | passenger | 24 |
| 旅行 | 旅行 | lǚxíng | n., v. | travel; to travel | 31 |
| 旅行社 | 旅行社 | lǚxíngshè | n. | travel agency | 34s |
| 旅游 | 旅遊 | lǚyóu | n., v. | travel, tourism; to travel | 22 |
| 旅游车 | 旅遊車 | lǚyóuchē | n. | tour bus | 32s |
| 录取 | 錄取 | lùqǔ | v. | to admit, to be accepted | 22 |
| 录取通知书 | 錄取通知書 | lùqǔ tōngzhī shū | phr. | letter of admission from a school | 22 |
| 路口 | 路口 | lùkǒu | n. | street intersection | 28 |
| 路上 | 路上 | lù shang | n. phr. | on the road | 24 |
| 路线 | 路线 | lùxiàn | n. | route, itinerary | 28 |
| 绿 | 綠 | lù | adj. | green | 26 |
| 乱说 | 亂說 | luànshuō | s.e. | to speak irresponsibly, to talk nonsense | 36 |
| 轮到 | 輪到 | lún dào | v. comp. | to be someone's turn | 31 |

| Simplified | Traditional | Pinyin | Part of Speech | English | Lesson |
|---|---|---|---|---|---|
| 麻油 | 麻油 | máyóu | n. | sesame oil | 33s |
| 马路 | 馬路 | mǎlù | n. | street, avenue | 28 |
| 卖 | 賣 | mài | v. | to sell | 27 |
| 卖关子 | 賣關子 | mài guānzi | s.e | (lit.) "to sell on the crucial point," a trick of traditional storytellers in the marketplace; to keep the listeners in suspense | 40 |
| 满 | 滿 | mǎn | adj. | full, filled | 33 |
| 满头大汗 | 滿頭大汗 | mǎntóu dàhàn | phr. | (lit.) the entire face soaked in sweat | 38 |
| 满足 | 滿足 | mǎnzú | adj., v. | content, satisfied; to satisfy | 32 |
| 毛 | 毛 | máo | m.w. | one-tenth of a yuan | 29 |
| 毛衣 | 毛衣 | máoyī | n. | sweater (usually knit of wool or wool-like yarn) | 30 |
| 没门儿 | 沒門兒 | méiménr | s.e. | (idiom) (lit.) having no door; no way | 39 |
| 没事(儿)/有事 | 沒事(兒)/有事 | méishì/yǒushì | s.e. | In colloquial Chinese, 没事 is frequently used to say "no problem" while 有事 means either "there is something to do," or "there is a problem..." | 34 |
| 美金 | 美金 | měijīn | n. | U.S. money, American dollar | 22 |
| 美式足球 | 美式足球 | měishì zúqiú | n. | American football | 35s |
| 美元 | 美元 | Měiyuán | n. | U.S. dollar | 29s |
| 闷 | 悶 | mēn | adj. | (of weather) stuffy, (of a room) lacking ventilation | 26 |
| 门 | 門 | mén | m.w. | measure word for courses | 35 |
| 门诊 | 門診 | ménzhěn | phr. | treatment of patients | 36 |

| Simplified | Traditional | Pinyin | Part of Speech | English | Lesson |
|---|---|---|---|---|---|
| 门诊部 | 門診部 | ménzhěnbù | n. phr. | outpatient center | 36 |
| 棉 | 棉 | mián | n. | cotton, (100%) cotton | 30 |
| 免费 | 免費 | miǎnfèi | adj. | to be exempt from payment, to be free of charge | 39 |
| 免了 | 免了 | miǎn le | s.e. | That's OK, you don't have to do it. | 35 |
| 免税 | 免稅 | miǎnshuì | adj. | duty-free | 24s |
| 面熟 | 面熟 | miànshú | s.e. | (usually of a person) to look familiar | 27 |
| 面条 | 麵條 | miàntiáo | n. | noodles | 21s, 33s |
| 米饭 | 米飯 | mǐfàn | n. | cooked rice | 21s |
| 苗条 | 苗條 | miáotiao | adj. | (usually of a woman's figure) slender | 30 |
| 名胜古迹 | 名勝古跡 | míngshèng gǔjì | phr. | famous ancient sites (for tourists) | 32 |
| 明星 | 明星 | míngxīng | n. | (movie, pop, etc.) star | 30 |
| 明信片 | 明信片 | míngxìnpiàn | n. | postcard | 27 |
| 模拟 | 模擬 | mónǐ | adj. | simulated | 40 |
| 模拟考题 | 模擬考題 | mónǐ kǎotí | phr. | simulated test | 40 |
| 母语 | 母語 | mǔyǔ | n. | mother tongue | 40 |
| 幕 | 幕 | mù | n. | curtain | 23 |
| 拿 | 拿 | ná | v. | to hold (in hand), to grasp | 26 |
| 拿手 | 拿手 | náshǒu | adj. | especially good (at something) | 21 |
| 拿手菜 | 拿手菜 | náshǒucài | phr. | the cook's specialty dish | 21 |
| 那要看 | 那要看 | nà yào kàn | s.e. | that depends on... | 39 |
| 南 | 南 | nán | n. | south | 28 |
| 难过 | 難過 | nánguò | adj. | sad | 23 |
| 脑子 | 腦子 | nǎozi | n. | brain | 38 |

| Simplified | Traditional | Pinyin | Part of Speech | English | Lesson |
|---|---|---|---|---|---|
| 脑子就<br>不好用了。 | 腦子就<br>不好用了。 | Nǎozi jiù bù<br>hǎo yòng le. | s.e. | (lit.) brain is no longer<br>good to use | 38 |
| 闹 | 鬧 | nào | adj., v. | noisy; to make noise, to<br>make a lively scene | 30 |
| 内 | 內 | nèi | n. | in, inside | 37 |
| 内宾 | 內賓 | nèibīn | n. | Chinese guest | 34s |
| 内科 | 內科 | nèikē | n. | internal medicine | 36 |
| 内容 | 內容 | nèiróng | n. | content | 40 |
| 你过奖了。 | 你過獎了。 | Nǐ guòjiǎng le. | s.e. | You flatter me. (Lit.)<br>You overly praise me. | 30 |
| 你怎么了？ | 你怎麼了？ | Nǐ zěnme le? | s.e. | What's wrong with you? | 24 |
| 年货 | 年貨 | niánhuò | n. | (lit.) new year's goods;<br>special items prepared<br>just for the new year<br>celebration | 37 |
| 年龄 | 年齡 | niánlíng | n. | age | 25 |
| 年夜饭 | 年夜飯 | niányèfàn | phr. | dinner on the Lunar<br>New Year's Eve | 37 |
| 牛仔 | 牛仔 | niúzǎi | n. | cowboy | 30 |
| 牛仔裤 | 牛仔褲 | niúzǎikù | n. | jeans; (lit.) cowboy pants | 30 |
| 扭 | 扭 | niǔ | v. | to twist, sprain | 35 |
| 暖和 | 暖和 | nuǎnhuo | àdj. | pleasantly warm,<br>nice and warm | 26 |
| 欧元 | 歐元 | Oūyuán | n. | Euro | 29s |
| 爬山 | 爬山 | pá shān | v. obj. | to climb a mountain | 35s |
| 排 | 排 | pái | v. | to arrange, to put<br>in order, to line up | 22 |
| 排队 | 排隊 | pái duì | v. obj. | to stand in line,<br>to line up | 22 |
| 牌（子） | 牌（子） | pái | n. | piece of board,<br>plate, card, sign, tablet | 23, 24 |

| Simplified | Traditional | Pinyin | Part of Speech | English | Lesson |
|---|---|---|---|---|---|
| 胖 | 胖 | pàng | adj. | (of people or animals) plump, fat | 21 |
| 跑 | 跑 | pǎo | v. | to run | 35 |
| 跑步 | 跑步 | pǎo bù | v. obj. | to run, to jog | 35 |
| 陪 | 陪 | péi | v. | to accompany, to keep (somebody) company | 28 |
| 赔本 | 賠本 | péi běn | v. obj. | to lose money on a sale, to make less money than what you invested | 30 |
| 佩服 | 佩服 | pèifu | v. | to admire, to respect | 37 |
| 碰头 | 碰頭 | pèngtóu | s.e. | (lit.) to touch heads; to meet informally | 23 |
| 批准 | 批准 | pīzhǔn | v. | to approve | 22s |
| 偏 | 偏 | piān | s.e. | deliberately, insistently (do something in one's own way), defiantly, to do something someone opposes | 39 |
| 便宜 | 便宜 | piányì | adj. | inexpensive, cheap | 27 |
| 片 | 片 | piàn | m.w., n. | piece, tablet; slice, piece | 22, 36 |
| 票 | 票 | piào | n. | ticket | 32 |
| 平了记录 | 平了記錄 | píng le jìlù | v. obj. | to tie a record | 35s |
| 平时 | 平時 | píngshí | adv. | in ordinary times, usually | 39 |
| 凭 | 憑 | píng | v. | to depend on, to rely on | 29 |
| 屏 | 屏 | píng | n. | screen, shield | 23 |
| 屏幕 | 屏幕 | píngmù | n. | screen (of a television, computer, etc.) | 23 |
| 破 | 破 | pò | adj. | broken, damaged | 33 |
| 铺 | 鋪 | pù | n. | bed | 32 |
| 沏 | 沏 | qī | v. | to steep, to infuse (tea) | 25 |
| 其实 | 其實 | qíshí | adv. | as a matter of fact, in reality | 38 |
| 其它 | 其它 | qítā | adj. | other, the rest | 29 |

| Simplified | Traditional | Pinyin | Part of Speech | English | Lesson |
|---|---|---|---|---|---|
| 骑 | 騎 | qí | v. | to ride astride (e.g., a horse, a bike) | 29 |
| 起飞 | 起飛 | qǐfēi | v. | (of an airplane) to take off | 23 |
| 气 | 氣 | qì | n. | air, atmosphere, climate | 25 |
| 气氛 | 氣氛 | qìfēn | n. | atmosphere | 37 |
| 气候 | 氣候 | qìhòu | n. | climate | 26s |
| 气温 | 氣溫 | qìwēn | n. | (of weather) temperature | 26 |
| 汽车 | 汽車 | qìchē | n. | automobile, vehicle | 28 |
| 千万 | 千萬 | qiānwàn | adv. | making sure (usually followed by a warning); (lit.) ten million | 34 |
| 签名 | 簽名 | qiān míng | v. obj. | to sign one's name | 22 |
| 签证 | 簽證 | qiānzhèng | n., v. obj. | visa; to apply for a visa | 21 |
| 签字 | 簽字 | qiān zì | n., v. obj. | signature; to sign (one's name) | 22s, 27 |
| 前台 | 前臺 | qiántái | n. | front desk | 34 |
| 钱 | 錢 | qián | n. | money, cash | 29 |
| 欠债 | 欠債 | qiàn zhài | v. obj. | to owe money | 31s |
| 墙 | 牆 | qiáng | n. | wall | 32 |
| 敲 | 敲 | qiāo | v. | to knock | 32 |
| 怯场 | 怯場 | qièchǎng | v. obj. | to have stage fright | 35 |
| 青菜 | 青菜 | qīngcài | n. | green vegetables | 21s |
| 轻 | 輕 | qīng | adj. | light (weight) | 29 |
| 清楚 | 清楚 | qīngchǔ | adj. | clear and distinct | 22 |
| 晴 | 晴 | qíng | adj., n. | (of weather) clear, fine; clear weather, fine weather | 26 |
| 晴天 | 晴天 | qíngtiān | n. | clear weather | 26 |

| Simplified | Traditional | Pinyin | Part of Speech | English | Lesson |
|---|---|---|---|---|---|
| 秋老虎 | 秋老虎 | qiū lǎohǔ | s.e. | (lit.) the autumn tiger, an idiomatic expression for the very hot days in the early fall | 26 |
| 取 | 取 | qǔ | v. | to pick up (sth. from sw.), to get (sth.) back (from sw.) | 22 |
| 取货 | 取貨 | qǔ huò | v. obj. | to pick up merchandise | 29 |
| 取钱 | 取錢 | qǔ qián | v. obj. | to withdraw money | 31 |
| 全 | 全 | quán | adj., adv. | entire; the whole, entirely | 36 |
| 全部 | 全部 | quánbù | adv. | all, in total | 34 |
| 然后 | 然後 | ránhòu | conj. | afterwards, thereupon | 27 |
| 绕路 | 繞路 | rào lù | v. obj. | to circle around | 34s |
| 绕圈子 | 繞圈子 | rào quānzi | s.e. | (lit.) to move in a circle; to take a detour | 34 |
| 热 | 熱 | rè | adj. | hot | 21, 25 |
| 热闹 | 熱鬧 | rènao | adj., n. | bustling with excitement, lively; (lit.) warm and loud; a lively scene | 30 |
| 热腾腾 | 熱騰騰 | rètēngtēng | phr. | (lit.) so steaming hot that vapor can still be seen (rising from the object) | 33 |
| 人民币 | 人民幣 | Rénmínbì | n. | Chinese currency; (lit.) People's currency | 29s, 31 |
| 人物画 | 人物畫 | rénwù huà | n. | portrait painting | 29 |
| 人员 | 人員 | rényuán | n. | personnel, staff members | 22 |
| 任何 | 任何 | rènhé | adj. | any | 31 |
| 任务 | 任務 | rènwu | n. | task, assignment | 24 |
| 日元 | 日元 | Rìyuán | n. | Japanese yen | 29s |
| 肉 | 肉 | ròu | n. | (of animals) meat, flesh | 21 |
| 如果 | 如果 | rúguǒ | conj. | if, in case | 24 |

| Simplified | Traditional | Pinyin | Part of Speech | English | Lesson |
|---|---|---|---|---|---|
| 入 | 入 | rù | v. | (formal) to enter | 24, 35 |
| 入场 | 入場 | rù chǎng | v. obj. | to enter a stadium or a field of play | 35 |
| 入关卡 | 入關卡 | rùguān kǎ | n. | customs entry card | 24 |
| 入境 | 入境 | rù jìng | v. obj. | to enter a country | 24 |
| 入境日期 | 入境日期 | rùjìng rìqī | n. phr. | entry date | 22s |
| 入网 | 入網 | rùwǎng | s.e. | to open a cellular phone account | 39 |
| 软 | 軟 | ruǎn | adj. | soft | 32 |
| 撒腿就跑 | 撒腿就跑 | sā tuǐ jiù pǎo | s.e. | to start running immediately; (lit.) let go of one's legs and run | 26 |
| 伞 | 傘 | sǎn | n. | umbrella | 26 |
| 扫 | 掃 | sǎo | v. | to sweep | 37 |
| 嗓子 | 嗓子 | sǎngzi | n. | throat | 36 |
| 杀价 | 殺價 | shā jià | v. obj. | to slash the price | 30s |
| 纱 | 紗 | shā | n. | gauze, gauze-like material | 29 |
| 纱巾 | 紗巾 | shājīn | n. | scarf made of silk or silk-like fabric | 29 |
| 山水画 | 山水畫 | shānshuǐ huà | n. | landscape painting | 29 |
| 商量 | 商量 | shāngliáng | v. | to discuss | 38 |
| 上 | 上 | shàng | v. | to board / to get on (a vehicle, boat, or airplane) | 23s |
| 上(菜/甜点) | 上(菜/甜點) | shàng (cài/diǎnxin) | s.e. | (lit.) to bring up (the food to be served) | 21 |
| 上飞机 | 上飛機 | shàng fēijī | v. obj. | to get on an airplane, to board an airplane | 23s |
| 上哪儿去了? | 上哪兒去了? | Shàng nǎr qù le? | s.e. | (lit.) Where has it/something gone? | 22 |
| 上网 | 上網 | shàng wǎng | v. obj. | to go online | 32 |
| 勺 | 勺 | sháo | m.w., n. | spoonful; spoon | 36 |

| Simplified | Traditional | Pinyin | Part of Speech | English | Lesson |
|---|---|---|---|---|---|
| 申报 | 申報 | shēnbào | v. | to report (to an authority) | 24 |
| 申报表 | 申報表 | shēnbào biǎo | n. | customs declaration form | 24 |
| 身高 | 身高 | shēngāo | n. | (lit.) the body height (of a person) | 25 |
| 升 | 升 | shēng | v. | to rise | 35 |
| 生气 | 生氣 | shēngqì | adj. | angry, mad | 39 |
| 声 | 聲 | shēng | n. | sound | 37 |
| 声音 | 聲音 | shēngyīn | n. | sound, voice | 37 |
| 省 | 省 | shěng | n. | province | 35 |
| 剩下 | 剩下 | shèngxia | v. comp. | left over | 33 |
| 失 | 失 | shī | n. | loss | 28 |
| 失误 | 失誤 | shīwù | n. | fault (in ball games), error, mistake | 28 |
| 师傅 | 師傅 | shīfu | n. | skilled worker, master (often used as a form of polite address) | 21 |
| 湿 | 濕 | shī | adj. | wet | 26s |
| 十字 | 十字 | shízì | n. | the character 十 | 28 |
| 十字(路口) | 十字(路口) | shízì (lùkǒu) | n. | crossroads (lit.) an intersection that is shaped like the Chinese character 十 | 28 |
| 时差 | 時差 | shíchā | n. | jet lag | 25 |
| 时刻 | 時刻 | shíkè | n. | time | 32 |
| 时刻表 | 時刻表 | shíkèbiǎo | n. | (of buses, trains, planes) timetable, schedule | 32 |
| 时髦 | 時髦 | shímáo | adj., n. | fashionable; fashion | 39 |
| 实在 | 實在 | shízài | adv. | truly, indeed | 33 |
| 食物中毒 | 食物中毒 | shíwù zhòngdú | n. | food poisoning | 25s |
| 食欲 | 食慾 | shíyù | n. | appetite; (lit.) food desire | 25s |

| Simplified | Traditional | Pinyin | Part of Speech | English | Lesson |
|---|---|---|---|---|---|
| 使劲 | 使劲 | shǐ jìng | s.e. | to make an effort, to exert oneself | 33 |
| 使用 | 使用 | shǐyòng | v. | to use, to employ (a tool, a device, a gadget, etc.) | 39 |
| 市 | 市 | shì | n. | city | 39 |
| 市内 | 市內 | shìnèi | n. | the area within a city | 39 |
| 适合 | 適合 | shìhé | v. | to fit, to be suitable | 33 |
| 试卷 | 試卷 | shìjuàn | n. | examination paper; test paper | 40 |
| 收获 | 收穫 | shōuhuò | n. | results, harvest | 40 |
| 收件人 | 收件人 | shōujiànrén | n. | the recipient (of a letter, parcel, etc.) | 27 |
| 收据 | 收據 | shōujù | n. | receipt | 29 |
| 收款 | 收款 | shōukuǎn | v. obj. | to receive/collect money | 29 |
| 收款台 | 收款臺 | shōukuǎntái | n. | cashier's counter | 29 |
| (收)钱 | (收)錢 | (shōu) qián | v. obj. | to collect money | 29 |
| 收信人 | 收信人 | shōuxìnrén | n. | addressee, recipient (of a letter) | 27s |
| 手续 | 手續 | shǒuxù | n. | procedure | 23 |
| 守岁 | 守歲 | shǒu suì | v. obj. | to stay up all night on (Lunar) New Year's Eve | 37 |
| 售 | 售 | shòu | v. | to sell | 28, 32 |
| 售票处 | 售票處 | shòupiàochù | n. | ticket office | 32 |
| 售票员 | 售票員 | shòupiàoyuán | n. | ticket seller | 28 |
| 瘦 | 瘦 | shòu | adj. | thin | 21 |
| 书 | 書 | shū | b.f., n. | (classical Chinese) letter, correspondence; book | 22 |
| 舒服 | 舒服 | shūfu | adj. | comfortable | 25 |
| 输 | 輸 | shū | v. | to lose | 35 |
| 熟悉 | 熟悉 | shúxī | adj. | familiar | 28 |
| 暑期 | 暑期 | shǔqī | n. | summer break | 38 |

| Simplified | Traditional | Pinyin | Part of Speech | English | Lesson |
|---|---|---|---|---|---|
| 树 | 樹 | shù | n. | trees | 26 |
| 树叶 | 樹葉 | shùyè | n. | tree leaves, foliage | 26 |
| 刷 | 刷 | shuā | v. obj. | (lit.) to swipe | 31 |
| 刷卡 | 刷卡 | shuā kǎ | v. obj. | (lit.) to swipe a card; to accept a credit or debit card | 31 |
| 霜 | 霜 | shuāng | n. | frost | 26s |
| 水平 | 水平 | shuǐpíng | n. | standard; (lit.) water level | 34 |
| 说不定 | 說不定 | shuō bu dìng | s.e. | maybe, perhaps | 22 |
| 说起 | 說起 | shuōqǐ | s.e. | speaking of... | 38 |
| 丝 | 絲 | sī | n. | silk | 29 |
| 司机 | 司機 | sījī | n. | chauffeur, (professional) driver; driver | 28s, 34 |
| 私人 | 私人 | sīrén | adj. | personal, private | 31 |
| 撕 | 撕 | sī | v. | to tear | 38 |
| 四菜一汤 | 四菜一湯 | sì cài yī tāng | phr. | four dishes and a soup | 33s |
| 送(人) | 送(人) | sòng (rén) | v. (obj.) | to see someone off | 23 |
| 送行 | 送行 | sòng xíng | v. phr. | to see someone off | 23s |
| 素 | 素 | sù | adj., n. | simple, plain; vegetarian food | 21 |
| 素菜 | 素菜 | sùcài | n. | vegetarian dish, vegetables | 21 |
| 酸 | 酸 | suān | adj. | sour | 33 |
| 算了 | 算了 | suàn le | s.e. | forget it, drop it, let it go | 30 |
| 虽然…但是… | 雖然…但是… | suīrán...dànshì... | conj. | although...but/still/yet... | 31 |
| 随便 | 隨便 | suíbiàn | adj., adv. | casual, informal; casually, informally | 39 |
| 损坏 | 損壞 | sǔnhuài | v. comp. | to damage, to break | 34 |
| 所 | 所 | suǒ | suff. | institute, office | 25 |
| 所有 | 所有 | suǒyǒu | adj. | all | 35 |
| 太极拳 | 太極拳 | tàijíquán | prop. n. | traditional Chinese shadow boxing | 35 |

| Simplified | Traditional | Pinyin | Part of Speech | English | Lesson |
|---|---|---|---|---|---|
| 台 | 臺 | tái | n. | table, desk, platform | 27 |
| 台币 | 台幣 | Táibì | n. | Taiwanese currency | 29s |
| 太油了 | 太油了 | tài yóu le | s.e. | (derogatory) too slick, too much of a smooth-talker | 30 |
| 摊子 | 攤子 | tānzi | n. | street vendor booth | 30 |
| 躺 | 躺 | tǎng | v. | to lie down | 36 |
| 趟 | 趟 | tàng | m.w. | (of trips) the number of times, (of trains, buses, planes, etc.) number, code, flight, etc. | 32 |
| 讨价还价 | 討價還價 | tǎojià huánjià | v. phr. | to negotiate a price, to bargain; (lit.) to make a (price) offer and to counter a (price) offer | 30 |
| 套房 | 套房 | tàofáng | n. | suite | 34s |
| 特别 | 特別 | tèbié | adv., adj. | especially, particularly; special, peculiar | 39 |
| 疼 | 疼 | téng | n., v. | ache, pain; to hurt | 25 |
| 梯 | 梯 | tī | b.f. | stair, ladder | 29 |
| 踢足球 | 踢足球 | tī zúqiú | v. obj. | to play soccer | 35s |
| 提供 | 提供 | tígōng | v. | (formal) to provide | 24 |
| 体操 | 體操 | tǐcāo | n. | gymnastics | 35s |
| 体检 | 體檢 | tǐjiǎn | n. | physical examination | 25 |
| 体温 | 體溫 | tǐwēn | n. | body temperature | 36 |
| 体温表 | 體溫表 | tǐwēnbiǎo | n. | clinical thermometer | 36 |
| 体育馆 | 體育館 | tǐyùguǎn | n. | gym | 35s |
| 体重 | 體重 | tǐzhòng | n. | body weight | 25 |
| 天 | 天 | tiān | n. | sky, heaven | 25, 37 |
| 天亮 | 天亮 | tiān liàng | n. | daybreak | 37 |
| 天气 | 天氣 | tiānqì | n. | weather | 25 |
| 甜 | 甜 | tián | adj. | sweet | 33 |

| Simplified | Traditional | Pinyin | Part of Speech | English | Lesson |
|---|---|---|---|---|---|
| 甜点 | 甜點 | tiándiǎn | n. | dessert, sweets | 21 |
| 甜酸苦辣 | 甜酸苦辣 | tián suān kǔ là | phr. | (lit.) sweet, sour, bitter, and spicy, a phrase used to describe the many varieties of food flavors | 21s |
| 填空 | 填空 | tiánkòng | v. | to fill in the blanks | 40 |
| 挑 | 挑 | tiāo | v. | to select | 38 |
| 调料 | 調料 | tiáoliào | n. | seasoning | 33s |
| 贴 | 貼 | tiē | v. | to paste, to stick | 37 |
| 铁轨 | 鐵軌 | tiěguǐ | n. | rail | 32s |
| 铁路 | 鐵路 | tiělù | n. | railroad | 32s |
| 听力 | 聽力 | tīnglì | n. | listening ability | 40 |
| 挺棒 | 挺棒 | tǐng bàng | s.e. | pretty good | 36 |
| 通 | 通 | tōng | v. | to go through, to make/let (sth.) go through | 24 |
| 通过 | 通過 | tōngguò | v. | to pass | 40s |
| 通用 | 通用 | tōngyòng | adj., v. | interchangeable; to use interchangeably | 39s |
| 通知 | 通知 | tōngzhī | n., v. | announcement; to announce | 22 |
| 头 | 頭 | tóu | n. | head | 25, 38 |
| 头疼 | 頭疼 | tóuténg | n. phr. | headache | 25 |
| 透视 | 透視 | tòushì | n., v. | X Ray; to have an X Ray | 25s, 36 |
| 突然 | 突然 | tūrán | adv. | suddenly | 35 |
| 图 | 圖 | tú | s.e. | (used as a verb) to aim at (a certain kind of benefit or profit), to take (something) as one's goal, to do (something) for the sake of something (as a noun, 图 means "picture", "chart") | 39 |
| 涂 | 塗 | tú | v. | to erase, to cross out | 22 |

| Simplified | Traditional | Pinyin | Part of Speech | English | Lesson |
|---|---|---|---|---|---|
| 涂改 | 塗改 | túgǎi | v. | to erase and change | 22 |
| 退 | 退 | tuì | v. | to go backwards, to reverse, to return | 29, 34 |
| 退房 | 退房 | tuì fáng | v. obj. | to check out (of a hotel) | 34 |
| 退还 | 退還 | tuìhuán | v. | to return (something to its original owner), to give back; to return and/or exchange something bought | 29, 34 |
| 退烧 | 退燒 | tuì shāo | v. obj. | to alleviate a fever | 36 |
| 托运 | 托運 | tuōyùn | v. | to check in (luggage) | 23 |
| 外宾 | 外賓 | wàibīn | n. | foreign guest | 34s |
| 外地人 | 外地人 | wàidì rén | n. | person from another region | 30 |
| 外国 | 外國 | wàiguó | n. | foreign country | 22 |
| 外汇 | 外匯 | wàihuì | n. | foreign currency | 31 |
| 外卡取现 | 外卡取現 | wài kǎ qǔ xiàn | s.e. | to withdraw cash from a foreign credit card | 31 |
| 外科 | 外科 | wàikē | n. | Surgery Department | 36s |
| 完成 | 完成 | wánchéng | v. | to complete, to finish | 24 |
| 晚点 | 晚點 | wǎndiǎn | v. | to arrive later than expected or scheduled | 23 |
| 碗 | 碗 | wǎn | m.w., n. | bowl | 33 |
| 往 | 往 | wǎng/wàng | prep., v. | toward; to go toward | 28 |
| 忘 | 忘 | wàng | v. | to forget | 22 |
| 为 | 為 | wèi | prep. | for, for the sake of | 21 |
| 胃 | 胃 | wèi | n. | stomach | 25 |
| 味道 | 味道 | wèidào | n. | flavor of a dish/food | 33 |
| 温 | 溫 | wēn | adj., n. | warm, lukewarm; warmth, temperature | 26 |
| 闻 | 聞 | wén | v. | to smell, to listen | 33 |

| Simplified | Traditional | Pinyin | Part of Speech | English | Lesson |
|---|---|---|---|---|---|
| 我看… | 我看… | wǒkàn... | s.e. | I think... (to express someone's opinion) | 25 |
| 我听你的 | 我聽你的 | wǒ tīng nǐ de | s.e. | I will listen to you. | 33 |
| 我这个人 | 我這個人 | wǒ zhè ge rén | s.e. | I myself; (lit.) I, this person | 31 |
| 卧铺 | 臥鋪 | wòpù | n. | sleeping berth (in a train) | 32 |
| 舞龙 | 舞龍 | wǔ lóng | v. obj. | to perform the dragon dance | 37 |
| 误 | 誤 | wù | n. | error, mistake | 28 |
| 雾 | 霧 | wù | n. | fog | 26s |
| 西 | 西 | xī | n. | west | 28 |
| 吸引 | 吸引 | xīyǐn | v. | to attract | 39 |
| 吸引力 | 吸引力 | xīyǐnlì | n. | power of attraction | 39 |
| 希望 | 希望 | xīwàng | n., v. | hope, wish; to hope, to wish for | 22, 36 |
| 习惯 | 習慣 | xíguàn | n., v. | habit, custom; to be accustomed to, to be used to | 25, 37 |
| 细 | 細 | xì | adj. | fine, thin (of texture) | 22 |
| 细心 | 細心 | xìxīn | adj. | careful, attentive | 22 |
| 下 | 下 | xià | v. | to drop, to fall (of rain, snow); to get off a vehicle, boat, or airplane, to disembark | 23s, 26 |
| 下班 | 下班 | xià bān | v. obj. | to go/come off work | 39 |
| 下飞机 | 下飛機 | xià fēijī | v. obj. | to get off an airplane | 23s |
| 下降 | 下降 | xiàjiàng | v. | to descend, to decline | 24 |
| 吓(人) | 嚇(人) | xià (rén) | v. | to scare (someone) | 34 |
| 下雪 | 下雪 | xià xuě | v. obj. | to snow | 26 |
| 吓一跳 | 嚇一跳 | xià yí tiào | s.e. | (lit.) to "jump from fright" or "to make someone jump from fright" | 36 |

| Simplified | Traditional | Pinyin | Part of Speech | English | Lesson |
|---|---|---|---|---|---|
| 下雨 | 下雨 | xià yǔ | v. obj. | to rain | 26 |
| 先 | 先 | xiān | adv. | first, before | 27 |
| 先···然后 | 先···然後 | xiān...ránhòu | conj. | first...then | 27 |
| 咸 | 鹹 | xián | adj. | salty | 33 |
| 显示 | 顯示 | xiǎnshì | v. | (usually on a screen) to display | 31 |
| 线 | 線 | xiàn | n. | line, thread | 28 |
| 现金 | 現金 | xiànjīn | n. | cash | 31 |
| 羡慕 | 羨慕 | xiànmù | v. | to envy, to admire | 32 |
| 香 | 香 | xiāng | adj. | (of food) delicious, flavorful, fragrant | 21 |
| 香喷喷 | 香噴噴 | xiāngpēnpēn | phr. | (of food) so delicious smelling that it hits one in the face | 33 |
| 项目 | 項目 | xiàngmù | n. | item, project | 27 |
| 像 | 像 | xiàng | v. | to resemble | 37 |
| 像 | 像 | xiàng | adv. | to seem | 37 |
| 像一回事儿 | 像一回事兒 | xiàng yīhuí shìr | s.e. | to look like "something," to be quite good | 35 |
| 消息 | 消息 | xiāoxi | n. | information | 32 |
| 销 | 銷 | xiāo | b.f. | sale | 39 |
| 小菜 | 小菜 | xiǎocài | n. | appetizer | 33s |
| 小吃 | 小吃 | xiǎochī | n. | local specialties (food/dishes) | 33 |
| 小吃店 | 小吃店 | xiǎochīdiàn | n. | a bistro-style restaurant that serves local specialties | 33 |
| 小儿科 | 小兒科 | xiáo'ér kē | n. | Pediatrics Department | 36s |
| 小贩（子） | 小販（子） | xiǎofàn(zi) | n. | street vendor | 30 |
| 小费 | 小費 | xiǎofèi | n. | tip | 33 |
| 小气 | 小氣 | xiǎoqi | adj. | stingy, narrow-minded | 39 |
| 小时 | 小時 | xiǎoshí | n. | hour (period of time) | 24 |

| Simplified | Traditional | Pinyin | Part of Speech | English | Lesson |
|---|---|---|---|---|---|
| 小心 | 小心 | xiǎoxīn | adj. | careful, cautious, wary | 30 |
| 校园 | 校園 | xiàoyuán | n. | campus | 39 |
| 写作 | 寫作 | xiězuò | n. | composition | 40 |
| 心电图 | 心電圖 | xīndiàntú | n. | EKG | 25s |
| 心慌 | 心慌 | xīn huāng | s.e | to feel flustered in the heart, to panic | 40 |
| 心脏 | 心臟 | xīnzàng | n. | the heart | 25 |
| 辛苦 | 辛苦 | xīnkǔ | adj. | toilsome, laborious, hard-working, painstaking (often used in polite expressions) | 24 |
| 新年 | 新年 | xīnnián | n. | New Year | 37 |
| 新生 | 新生 | xīnshēng | n. | freshman | 25 |
| 薪水 | 薪水 | xīnshuǐ | n. | salary | 38s |
| 信封 | 信封 | xìnfēng | n. | envelope | 27 |
| 信息 | 信息 | xìnxī | n. | information, message, news | 39 |
| 信用 | 信用 | xìnyòng | n. | credibility, trust worthiness | 31 |
| 信用卡 | 信用卡 | xìnyòngkǎ | n. | credit card | 31 |
| 信纸 | 信紙 | xìnzhǐ | n. | letter paper, stationery | 27s |
| 行车 | 行車 | xíng chē | v. obj. | to drive a vehicle | 34 |
| 行车执照 | 行車執照 | xíng chē zhízhào | n. phr. | license for operating a vehicle | 34 |
| 行李 | 行李 | xíngli | n. | baggage, luggage | 23 |
| 性别 | 性別 | xìngbié | n. | gender | 25 |
| 幸亏 | 幸虧 | xìngkuī | adv. | luckily | 34 |
| 兴趣 | 興趣 | xìngqù | n. | interest | 37 |
| 胸 | 胸 | xiōng | n. | chest | 36 |
| 修改 | 修改 | xiūgǎi | v. | to edit, to make corrections | 22s |

| Simplified | Traditional | Pinyin | Part of Speech | English | Lesson |
|---|---|---|---|---|---|
| 选 | 選 | xuǎn | v. | to choose, to select, to elect | 27 |
| 雪 | 雪 | xuě | n. | snow | 26 |
| 血 | 血 | xuè | n. | blood | 25, 36 |
| 血压 | 血壓 | xuèyā | n. | blood pressure | 25 |
| 询问 | 詢問 | xúnwèn | n., v. | inquiry; (formal) to inquire | 22s |
| 压 | 壓 | yā | n., v. | pressure; to hold down, to press | 25 |
| 压岁钱 | 壓歲錢 | yāsuìqián | n. | money given to children as a gift on New Year's Eve | 37s |
| 押金 | 押金 | yājīn | n. | deposit | 34 |
| 盐 | 鹽 | yán | n. | salt | 33 |
| 眼睛 | 眼睛 | yǎnjing | n. | (human) eyes | 27 |
| 验 | 驗 | yàn | v. | to examine, to check | 36 |
| 验尿 | 驗尿 | yàn niào | v. obj. | urine test | 25s |
| 验血 | 驗血 | yàn xiě | v. obj. | to do a blood test | 25s, 36 |
| 羊肉泡馍 | 羊肉泡饃 | yángròu pàomó | n. | bread soaked in mutton soup | 33 |
| 邀请 | 邀請 | yāoqǐng | n., v. | invitation; to invite | 38 |
| 药 | 藥 | yào | n. | medicine | 23 |
| 药方 | 藥方 | yàofāng | n. | prescription | 25 |
| 药房 | 藥房 | yàofáng | n. | drugstore, pharmacy | 25s, 36 |
| 要不 | 要不 | yàobù | s.e. | otherwise | 23 |
| 要是 | 要是 | yàoshi | conj. | if, in case | 23 |
| 要死 | 要死 | yàosǐ | s.e. | (lit.) to be on the verge of death; this phrase carries the similar meaning of "极了" | 34 |
| 钥匙 | 鑰匙 | yàoshi | n. | key | 34 |
| 叶 | 葉 | yè | n. | (of plants) leaves | 26 |

| Simplified | Traditional | Pinyin | Part of Speech | English | Lesson |
|---|---|---|---|---|---|
| 夜市 | 夜市 | yèshì | n. | night market | 30 |
| 一般 | 一般 | yībān | adj., adv. | ordinary, common; generally speaking | 29 |
| 一边…一边 | 一邊…一邊 | yībiān…yībiān | adv. | (lit.) at one side…at one side…, at the same time, simultaneously | 37 |
| 一共 | 一共 | yīgòng | adv. | totally, altogether | 30 |
| 一块儿 | 一塊兒 | yīkuàir | adv. | (lit.) in one block; together | 40 |
| 一切 | 一切 | yīqiè | n. | the whole thing, the entire matter | 21 |
| 一下子 | 一下子 | yīxiàzi | s.e. | a short duration or a single occurrence | 36 |
| 一样 | 一樣 | yīyàng | adj., adv. | identical; (lit.) of one shape; similarly, in the same way | 30 |
| 一直 | 一直 | yīzhí | adv. | all the way through, all along | 32 |
| 医务 | 醫務 | yīwù | n. | medical service | 25 |
| 医务所 | 醫務所 | yīwùsuǒ | n. | clinic | 25 |
| 医院 | 醫院 | yīyuàn | n. | hospital | 25s, 28 |
| 移 | 移 | yí | v. | to move, to shift | 39 |
| 移动 | 移動 | yídòng | v. | to move (the position of) | 39 |
| 已经 | 已經 | yǐjing | adv. | already | 24 |
| 阴 | 陰 | yīn | adj. | cloudy, overcast | 26 |
| 阴天 | 陰天 | yīntiān | n. | overcast sky, cloudy day | 26 |
| 银行 | 銀行 | yínháng | n. | bank | 31 |
| 饮料 | 飲料 | yǐnliào | n. | soft drinks | 34 |
| 印 | 印 | yìn | v. | to print | 38 |
| 英镑 | 英鎊 | Yīngbàng | n. | English pound | 29s |
| 营业 | 營業 | yíngyè | n., v. obj. | business; (of a business or shop) to be open, to do business | 27 |

| Simplified | Traditional | Pinyin | Part of Speech | English | Lesson |
|---|---|---|---|---|---|
| 营业员 | 營業員 | yíngyèyuán | n. | shop assistant | 27 |
| 赢 | 赢 | yíng | v. | to win | 35 |
| 应聘 | 應聘 | yìngpìn | v. | to accept a position | 38s |
| 硬 | 硬 | yìng | adj. | stiff, inflexible, hard | 32 |
| 拥挤 | 擁擠 | yōngjǐ | adj. | crowded, jammed | 37 |
| 优惠 | 優惠 | yōuhuì | adj., n. | preferential, favorable; preferential treatment | 30s |
| 由 | 由 | yóu | prep. | from, by, via | 38 |
| 油 | 油 | yóu | n. | oil | 35 |
| 油饼 | 油餅 | yóubǐng | n. | deep-fried cake | 33 |
| 邮递员 | 郵遞員 | yóudìyuán | n. | mail-delivery worker, postal worker, letter carrier | 27 |
| 邮局 | 郵局 | yóujú | n. | post office | 27 |
| 邮票 | 郵票 | yóupiào | n. | stamps | 27 |
| 邮政编码 | 郵政編碼 | yóuzhèng biānmǎ | phr. | zip code | 27s |
| 游泳 | 游泳 | yóuyǒng | v. obj. | to swim | 35 |
| 友谊 | 友誼 | yǒuyì | n. | friendship | 21 |
| 有错儿 | 有錯兒 | yǒu cuòr | s.e. | to have/make mistakes | 22 |
| 有名 | 有名 | yǒumíng | adj. | well-known, famous | 29 |
| 有什么好紧张的。 | 有什麼好緊張的。 | Yǒu shénme hǎo jǐnzhāng de. | s.e | (informal) "There is no need to be nervous." | 40 |
| 又 | 又 | yòu | adv. | again (used when talking about formerly recurring events) | 23 |
| 鱼 | 魚 | yú | n. | fish | 21 |
| 雨 | 雨 | yǔ | n. | rain | 26 |
| 预 | 預 | yù | adv., b.f. | beforehand, in advance | 25, 40 |
| 预报 | 預報 | yùbào | n. | forecast | 26 |
| 预订 | 預訂 | yùdìng | v. | to place an order, book ahead | 32 |

| Simplified | Traditional | Pinyin | Part of Speech | English | Lesson |
|---|---|---|---|---|---|
| 预防 | 預防 | yùfáng | n., v. | prevention; to take preventive measures | 25 |
| 预习 | 預習 | yùxí | v. | to preview | 40 |
| 元旦 | 元旦 | yuándàn | n. | January 1st | 37 |
| 园 | 園 | yuán | n. | park | 26 |
| 原来 | 原來 | yuánlái | adj., adv. | original; in the beginning, surprisingly (when the truth of a matter is revealed) | 37 |
| 远 | 遠 | yuǎn | adj. | distant, far away | 22 |
| 院 | 院 | yuàn | n. | courtyard, yard, institute, academy | 28 |
| 月租费 | 月租費 | yuèzūfèi | n. | (lit.) the monthly rental fee | 39s |
| 阅读 | 閱讀 | yuèdú | n., v. | reading; to read | 40 |
| 越来越 | 越來越 | yuè lái yuè | adv. | more and more | 26 |
| 晕 | 暈 | yūn | adj. | dizzy | 23 |
| 允许 | 允許 | yǔnxǔ | v. | to permit, to allow | 34 |
| 运 | 運 | yùn | n. | motion, transportation | 27 |
| 运动 | 運動 | yùndòng | n., v. | sports; to exercise | 35 |
| 运动会 | 運動會 | yùndònghuì | n. | sports meet | 35 |
| 运动员 | 運動員 | yùndòngyuán | n. | athlete | 35 |
| 运气 | 運氣 | yùnqì | n. | good fortune, good luck | 39 |
| 晕 | 暈 | yùn | v. | to feel dizzy, to faint | 23 |
| 晕机 | 暈機 | yùnjī | n. | motion sickness | 23 |
| 宰人 | 宰人 | zǎirén | s.e. | By itself, 宰 usually means "to slaughter, to butcher." In the colloquial language, 宰人 means "to rip someone off." | 34 |
| 在乎 | 在乎 | zàihu | v. | to care about, to attach importance to (something) | 40 |

| Simplified | Traditional | Pinyin | Part of Speech | English | Lesson |
|---|---|---|---|---|---|
| 脏 | 臟 | zàng | n. | internal organs | 25 |
| 增加 | 增加 | zēngjiā | v. | to augment, to increase, to add to | 37 |
| 炸 | 炸 | zhá | v. | to deep-fry | 33 |
| 占 | 占 | zhàn | v. | to occupy | 38 |
| 站 | 站 | zhàn | n., v. | station, stop (for a bus, train, airplane); to stand | 23, 31 |
| 张开 | 張開 | zhāngkāi | v. comp. | to open up | 36 |
| 长 | 長 | zhǎng | v. | to grow | 21 |
| 掌 | 掌 | zhǎng | n. | palm | 35 |
| 帐户 | 帳戶 | zhànghù | n. | account | 31 |
| 招待 | 招待 | zhāodài | v. | to act like a host, to entertain (guests, customers, etc.) | 34 |
| 招聘 | 招聘 | zhāopìn | v. | to recruit (usually for a professional position) | 38 |
| 照 | 照 | zhào | v. | to reflect, to take a photo | 22 |
| 照片 | 照片 | zhàopiàn | n. | photo | 22 |
| 照相 | 照相 | zhào xiàng | v. obj. | to take a photo | 35 |
| 着 | 著 | zhe | part. | a grammatical component indicating the status of an action | 27 |
| 折扣 | 折扣 | zhékòu | n. | discount | 30s |
| 这好办。 | 這好辦。 | Zhè hǎo bàn. | s.e. | This is easy to handle. | 38 |
| 这就 | 這就 | zhè jiù | s.e. | (lit.) as early as this very moment, right away, right now | 36 |
| 这算是… | 這算是… | zhè suàn shì | s.e. | this should be considered as... | 37 |
| 真正 | 真正 | zhēnzhèng | adj. | authentic | 24 |

| Simplified | Traditional | Pinyin | Part of Speech | English | Lesson |
|---|---|---|---|---|---|
| 阵 | 陣 | zhèn | m.w. | measure word for a period of intense activity, e.g. wind, rain, applause | 37 |
| 蒸 | 蒸 | zhēng | v. | to steam | 33s |
| 正 | 正 | zhèng | adj. | the right (side) | 22 |
| 正餐 | 正餐 | zhèngcān | n. | entrée | 33s |
| 正常 | 正常 | zhèngcháng | adj. | normal | 25 |
| 正好 | 正好 | zhènghǎo | s.e. | just right, at the exactly right time | 39 |
| 证件 | 證件 | zhèngjiàn | n. | certificate, ID | 27 |
| 证书 | 證書 | zhèngshū | n. | certificate | 40 |
| 政府 | 政府 | zhèngfǔ | n. | government | 40 |
| 挣 | 掙 | zhèng | v. | to earn | 38 |
| 挣钱 | 掙錢 | zhèng qián | v. obj. | to make money | 38 |
| 之 | 之 | zhī | part. | (classical Chinese) 的 | 37 |
| …之内 | …之內 | zhī nèi | phr. | within… | 37 |
| 支票 | 支票 | zhīpiào | n. | check | 31 |
| 知识 | 知識 | zhīshi | n. | knowledge | 40 |
| 执照 | 執照 | zhízhào | n. | license | 34 |
| 直 | 直 | zhí | adj. | straight, direct | 23 |
| 直接 | 直接 | zhíjiē | adv. | directly | 23 |
| 值得 | 值得 | zhídé | v. | to deserve, to be worth | 31 |
| 指 | 指 | zhǐ | v. | to point (with a finger) to/at | 27 |
| 指南 | 指南 | zhǐnán | n. | guidebook, guide | 32 |
| 治 | 治 | zhì | v. | to regulate, to put in order | 25 |
| 止咳糖浆 | 止咳糖漿 | zhǐké tángjiāng | n. | cough syrup | 36 |
| 治疗 | 治療 | zhìliáo | n., v. | medical treatment; to treat (a disease), to cure | 25 |

| Simplified | Traditional | Pinyin | Part of Speech | English | Lesson |
|---|---|---|---|---|---|
| 质 | 質 | zhì | n. | original nature, character, quality | 29 |
| 质量 | 質量 | zhìliàng | n. | quality | 29 |
| 中国通 | 中國通 | Zhōngguó tōng | s.e. | (lit.) thorough knowledge about China, usually used for a non-Chinese who has become very knowledgeable about Chinese culture | 37 |
| 中级 | 中級 | zhōngjí | n. | intermediate level | 35 |
| 中心 | 中心 | zhōngxīn | n. | center | 28 |
| 终 | 終 | zhōng | n. | end (as opposed to beginning) | 28 |
| 终点 | 終點 | zhōngdiǎn | n. | terminal point | 28 |
| 重 | 重 | zhòng | adj. | heavy | 25 |
| 重量 | 重量 | zhòngliàng | n. | weight | 27 |
| 重要 | 重要 | zhòngyào | adj. | important | 38 |
| 周到 | 周到 | zhōudào | adj. | complete, all-encompassing | 33 |
| 主要 | 主要 | zhǔyào | adj. | main, major | 40 |
| 煮 | 煮 | zhǔ | v. | to boil | 33 |
| 助威 | 助威 | zhù wēi | v. obj. | to cheer someone on | 35s |
| 住院 | 住院 | zhù yuàn | v. obj. | to be hospitalized | 36 |
| 注意 | 注意 | zhùyì | v. | to pay attention to | 24 |
| 祝福 | 祝福 | zhùfú | n., v. obj. | to wish someone happiness | 37 |
| 祝酒 | 祝酒 | zhù jiǔ | v. obj. | to make a toast | 21 |
| 著名 | 著名 | zhùmíng | adj. | famous | 32 |
| 专 | 專 | zhuān | adj. | focusing (on a certain field), specializing (in sth.) | 26 |
| 专家 | 專家 | zhuānjiā | n. | expert, specialist | 26 |

| Simplified | Traditional | Pinyin | Part of Speech | English | Lesson |
|---|---|---|---|---|---|
| 转 | 轉 | zhuǎn | v. | to shift, change direction | 26 |
| 转车 | 轉車 | zhuǎn chē | v. obj. | to transfer (vehicles) | 28s |
| 转弯 | 轉彎 | zhuǎn wān | v. obj. | to make a turn | 28s |
| 赚 | 賺 | zhuàn | v. | to make money, to earn (a profit from), (derogatory) to rip off | 30 |
| 准确 | 準確 | zhǔnquè | adj. | accurate, precise, to the point | 26 |
| 准时 | 準時 | zhǔnshí | adj., adv. | on time, punctual; in accordance with the schedule | 23 |
| 自从…就 | 自從…就 | zìcóng...jiù | conj. | (ever) since | 35 |
| 自来水 | 自來水 | zìláishuǐ | n. | tap water | 34 |
| 自信心 | 自信心 | zìxìnxīn | n. | self-confidence | 35 |
| 自行车 | 自行車 | zìxíngchē | n. | bike | 29 |
| 自助机 | 自助機 | zìzhùjī | n. | ATM machine | 31 |
| 综合 | 綜合 | zōnghé | adj., v. | comprehensive, synthesized; to synthesize, to bring together | 40 |
| 总算 | 總算 | zǒngsuàn | adv. | at long last, finally | 24 |
| 走道 | 走道 | zǒudào | n. | (in a theater, airplane, etc.) walkway, aisle | 23 |
| 最 | 最 | zuì | pref. | (a superlative prefix used before adjectives) the most | 25 |
| 遵命 | 遵命 | zūnmìng | s.e. | Yes, Sir. (lit.) respect/ follow (your) orders | 21 |
| 坐 | 坐 | zuò | v. | to ride, to go by, to take (public transportation, i.e. airplane, bus, train, etc.) | 23s |
| 坐飞机 | 坐飛機 | zuò fēijī | v. obj. | to travel by airplane | 23s |

| Simplified | Traditional | Pinyin | Part of Speech | English | Lesson |
|---|---|---|---|---|---|
| 座机费 | 座機費 | zuòjīfèi | n. | (lit.) the machine-anchoring fee; the monthly fee | 39 |
| 座位 | 座位 | zuòwèi | n. | seat | 23 |
| 作为 | 作為 | zuòwéi | v. comp. | to act as, to take as, to use as | 37 |

# Glossary of Proper Nouns

| Simplified | Traditional | Pinyin | Definition | Lesson |
|---|---|---|---|---|
| 华盛顿特区 | 華盛頓特區 | Huáshèngdùn Tèqū | Washington, D.C. | 24 |
| 摄氏 | 攝氏 | Shèshì | Celsius | 26 |
| 处暑 | 處暑 | Chùshǔ | the end of the summer; (lit.) "cessation of heat," the fourteenth period of the twenty-four divisions of the traditional Chinese calendar, occurring in late August | 26 |
| 立秋 | 立秋 | Lìqiū | the beginning of autumn; (lit.) establishing autumn, the thirteenth of the twenty-four seasonal divisions of the traditional Chinese calendar, usually occurring in early August. | 26 |
| 纽约 | 紐約 | Niǔyuē | New York | 27 |
| 西安 | 西安 | Xī'ān | a city in China | 32 |
| 兵马俑 | 兵馬俑 | Bīngmǎyǒng | Terracotta Soldiers | 32 |
| K81 次特快 | K81 次特快 | K81 cì tèkuài | Super-express Train K81 (次 is a measure word.) | 32 |
| 回民 | 回民 | Huímín | A Muslim ethnic group in China | 33 |
| 奥运会 | | Àoyùnhuì | the Olympic Games | 35 |
| 华氏 | 華氏 | Huáshì | Fahrenheit | 36 |
| 非典 | 非典 | Fēidiǎn | SARS | 36 |
| 汉语水平考试 | 漢語水平考試 | Hànyǔ Shuǐpíng Kǎoshì (HSK) | Chinese Language Proficiency Test | 40 |